Praise for *Jews and Gentiles in the Early Jesus Movement*

"An important work...Sensitive and deeply researched...In the deepest sense, a profound theological work."
— Professor Clark M. Williamson, Christian Theological Seminary, Indiana; author of *Way of Blessing, Way of Life: A Christian Theology*

"An original and plausible claim that goes beyond most of modern scholarship...a solid contribution to the study of anti-Judaism in early Christianity."
— Professor Joseph B. Tyson, Religious Studies, Southern Methodist University; author of *Marcion and Luke-Acts: A Defining Struggle*

"In methodical and precise fashion Bibliowicz takes the reader through the relevant ancient Christian texts bearing on the question at hand. In so doing, he proposes an intriguing, compelling thesis. The book should prove to be a major voice in the ongoing debate."
— Brooks Schramm, Professor of Biblical Studies, Lutheran Theological Seminary

"Impressive work...With this impassioned study available to us, it will no longer be possible for us to ignore the unintended ways the unthinkable came to be and still say 'we did not know.'"
— Professor Didier Pollefeyt, Faculty of Theology and Religious Studies, Katholieke Universiteit Leuven Belgium; coauthor of *Anti-Judaism and the Fourth Gospel* and *Paul and Judaism*

"May this book find a wide readership among people devoted to the cause of the healing of memories between Jews and Christians."
— Professor Peter C. Phan, Chair of Catholic Social Thought, Georgetown University; President of the Catholic Theological Society of America

"A significant contribution to our understanding of the Christian-Jewish relationship in the first centuries of the Common Era."
— Professor John T. Pawlikowski, Director, Catholic-Jewish Studies Program, Catholic Theological Union, Chicago; author of *The Challenge of the Holocaust for Christian Theology*

"Well-researched and thorough. Intelligent and thoughtful...accessible, the argumentation compelling."
— Professor M. Murray, Bishop's University, Canada; author of *Playing a Jewish Game: Gentile Christian Judaizing in the First and Second Centuries C.E.*

"Mr. Bibliowicz's book will challenge all readers to reexamine their foundational religious narratives as to how they regard 'the other.' And this exercise may be as painful as it is necessary."
— Rev. Michael McGarry, C. S. P. President, The Paulist Fathers; author of *Christology after Auschwitz*

JEWS AND GENTILES IN THE EARLY JESUS MOVEMENT

AN UNINTENDED JOURNEY

ABEL MORDECHAI BIBLIOWICZ

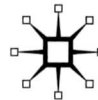

First published in 2013 by
PALGRAVE MACMILLAN®
in the United States—a division of St. Martin's Press LLC,
175 Fifth Avenue, New York, NY 10010.

Where this book is distributed in the UK, Europe and the rest of the world,
this is by Palgrave Macmillan, a division of Macmillan Publishers Limited,
registered in England, company number 785998, of Houndmills,
Basingstoke, Hampshire RG21 6XS.

Palgrave Macmillan is the global academic imprint of the above companies
and has companies and representatives throughout the world.

Palgrave® and Macmillan® are registered trademarks in the United States,
the United Kingdom, Europe and other countries.

ISBN: 978–1–137–28109–8

Library of Congress Cataloging-in-Publication Data

Bibliowicz, Abel Mordechai.
    Jews and Gentiles in the early Jesus movement : an unintended
journey / by Abel Mordechai Bibliowicz.
        pages cm
    ISBN 978–1–137–28109–8 (hardcover : alk. paper)
    1. Bible. N.T.—Criticism, interpretation, etc. 2. Judaism (Christian
theology)—Biblical teaching. 3. Church history—Primitive and early
church, ca. 30-600. 4. Christianity and other religions—Judaism.
5. Judaism—Relations—Christianity. 6. Judaism—History—
Post-exilic period, 586 B.C.-210 A.D. I. Title.
BS2545.J44B53 2013
261.2'609015—dc23   2012040885

A catalogue record of the book is available from the British Library.

Design by Newgen Imaging Systems (P) Ltd., Chennai, India.

First edition: April 2013

10 9 8 7 6 5 4 3 2 1

To Ronnie

Gideon, Yonatan, and Michal

Pablo, Samia, and Shiri

Contents

List of Tables		ix
Foreword Norman A. Beck		xi
Foreword Clark M. Williamson		xiii
Personal Introduction		xv
Preview		xix
The Protagonists		xxiii
Timeline		xxv
Acknowledgments		xxvii
1	The Anti-Jewish Strand in the New Testament	1
2	The Anti-Jewish Strand—The First Years	11
3	The Anti-Judaic Strand in Paul	21
4	The Anti-Judaic Strand in Mark: The Need to Explain	39
5	The Anti-Judaic Strand in Matthew: The Saga of the Jewish Followers of Jesus	49
6	The Anti-Judaic Strand in Luke/Acts: Yearning for Respectability	59
7	The Anti-Judaic Strand in John: Estrangement	67
8	The Anti-Judaic Strand in Revelation: Judaism within	87
9	The Anti-Jewish Strand—The Embryonic Stage Summary	93
10	Supersession	103

11	The Anti-Jewish Strand in Hebrews	115
12	The Anti-Jewish Strand in Barnabas	139
13	The Second-Century Protagonists	151
14	The Anti-Jewish Strand in Ignatius	167
15	The Anti-Jewish Strand in Justin: The Dialogue with Trypho the Jew	173
16	The Anti-Jewish Strand in Melito	179
17	The Anti-Jewish Strand in Chrysostom	185
18	Recapitulation	193
	Appendix I: Paul in Modern Scholarship	225
	Notes	231
	Bibliography	265
	Thematic Index	283

Tables

1.1	Anti-Jewish Bias in Mark	4
1.2	Anti-Jewish Bias in Matthew's Use of Q Material	5
1.3	Matthew's Increased Anti-Jewish Bias in Material Originating in Mark	5
1.4	Anti-Jewish Bias in Matthew and in His Use of Unidentified Sources	6
1.5	Luke's Increased Anti-Jewish Bias in Material Originating in Mark	6
1.6	Anti-Jewish Bias in Luke's Use of Q Material	7
1.7	Anti-Jewish Bias in Luke's Own Material and in His Use of Unidentified Sources	7
1.8	Anti-Jewish Bias in Acts	8
1.9	Anti-Jewish Bias in John and the Johannine Epistles	9
1.10	Anti-Jewish Bias in Paul	9
1.11	Anti-Jewish Bias in Revelation	10
1.12	Anti-Jewish Bias in Hebrews	10
1.13	Anti-Jewish Bias in 1 Peter	10
3.1	Views on the Revised Paul	33
13.1	The Emergence of a Compromise Creed	155

Foreword

Research by Jewish and Christian scholars during the past few decades indicates clearly that during the first centuries of the Common Era there were "Judaisms" and there were "Christianities." Neither group was monolithic at that time, just as neither group is monolithic today and never has been. The development of religion and of religious systems and the lifestyles of people within them is complex. Most of this development and the relevant information about these religious lifestyles are not recorded for people centuries later to peruse.

Bibliowicz has studied meticulously the literature that is accessible to us from among the writings of followers of Jesus of Nazareth during the early centuries of the development and practices of these "Christianities." He goes beyond other scholars in his interpretation of the evidence, tracing and documenting distinctions and tensions between the Jewish background descendants of disciples of Jesus and non-Jewish background converts to belief in Jesus that can be seen already within the canonical Newer Testament texts. His analysis of the evidence is that this conflict between groups of those who expressed their belief in Jesus was still embryonic within the Newer Testament texts, but developed rapidly during the early decades of the second century and continued well into the fifth.

Bibliowicz considers that the rejection of Judaism by most Gentile believers in Jesus and the rejection by the descendants of Jesus's disciples and first followers of the many forms of Gentile belief in Jesus that surfaced following the missions to the Gentiles are the triggers of a protracted and bitter struggle about identity, legitimacy, and authority that burst into the open during the early decades of the second century, and continued well into the fifth. Misunderstood by later believers and misrepresented by the later guardians of orthodoxy, the tensions and the trauma produced by this crisis are the fountainhead of the anti-Jewish strand that permeates the canonical and the authoritative lore.

Bibliowicz concludes that the denigration of Torah observance and of "the Jews" within the Four Gospels and in the writings of followers of Jesus during the first centuries of the common era reflect the efforts to degrade not the people who were Jews and remained Jews, but followers of Jesus who were of Jewish background.

Norman A. Beck- is Poehlmann Professor of Theology and Classical Languages at Texas Lutheran University. He is the author of *Mature Christianity in the 21st Century: The Recognition and Repudiation of the Anti-Jewish Polemic of the New Testament* (also published in Germany as *Muendiges Christentum im 21. Jahrhundert by the Institut Kirche und Judentum*), *The New Testament: A New Translation and Redaction, Lectionary Scripture Notes Cycle A, Lectionary Scripture Notes Cycle B, Lectionary Scripture Notes Cycle C, Anti-Roman Cryptograms in the New Testament: Hidden Transcripts of Hope and Liberation, Blessed to be a Blessing to Each Other: Jews and Muslims as Children of Abraham in the Middle East*, and a movie script "Jesus, the Man." He is a Minnie Stevens Piper Foundation Professor, active in Jewish-Christian-Islamic dialogue, the Jesus of history and early church development research, and the current political and religious situation in the Middle East.

NORMAN A. BECK

Foreword

Bibliowicz has written a sensitive and deeply researched description of the long history of Christian anti-Judaism. This is a story that needs to be told and retold because Christians, who most need to hear and learn it, are by and large totally unaware of it. This is not a "learned ignorance," that is, the kind of ignorance that is good because we know that we do not know, and can therefore be appropriately humble in our claims. Instead, it is an ignorance of which Christians are ignorant. What that means is that the ancient and long-standing teaching and practice of contempt for Jews and Judaism can continue to fly under the radar, undetected, poisoning the intentions and consequences of Christian action without our even knowing that it is doing so. It is the ideologies we hold but of which we are unaware that have effective control of us.

Bibliowicz's work will bring this ideology into the full light of day and enable Christians to begin to liberate themselves from it. In the deepest sense, this is a profound theological work, one that seeks to liberate us from our inherited ideology of displacing Jews in God's covenant and being superior to them in all things religious. His subtitle, "An Unintended Journey," a recurring motif in his work, has the benefit of enabling Christians to come to see that although several New Testament writings have been appealed to in the history of Christian anti-Judaism for support, no such thing was ever intended by those writers. Instead, what happened was that earlier conflicts between different kinds of Jesus followers, representing a wide variety of both Jewish and Gentile followers, were later taken up by an entirely Gentile set of Jesus followers as conflict with Jews and Judaism, with tragic consequences. And, to make matters worse, this resulting and growing ideology of anti-Judaism was elaborated and put into practice in shaping the social, political, and economic fabric of Christendom and the lives of Jews within Christendom.

This is an important book. For all the work done by all kinds of Christian scholars and theologians, the grassroots reality is that typical, decent, warm-hearted Christian pastors can still give voice to unintended anti-Judaism and it still goes unnoticed by laypeople who have, after all, heard it all their lives.

Clark M. Williamson is Indiana Professor of Christian Thought, Emeritus, at Christian Theological Seminary. A systematic theologian, he concentrates on rethinking Christian theology after the Holocaust. His books include: *Preaching the Old Testament without Supersessionism: A Lectionary Commentary*, with Ronald J. Allen (forthcoming), *Preaching the Letters without Denigrating the Law: A Lectionary Commentary*, with Ronald J. Allen, *Preaching the Gospels without Blaming the Jews: A Lectionary Commentary*, with Ronald J. Allen, *Way of Blessing, Way of Life: A Christian Theology, Adventures of the Spirit: A Guide to Worship from the Perspective of Process Theology*, with Ronald J. Allen, *A Guest in the House of Israel: Post-Holocaust Church Theology, The Church and the Jewish People* (editor), *A Mutual Witness: Toward Critical Solidarity Between Jews and Christians* (editor), *Interpreting Difficult Texts: Anti-Judaism and Christian Preaching*, with Ronald J. Allen, *When Jews and Christians Meet: A Guide for Christian Preaching and Teaching*, and *Has God Rejected His People? Anti-Judaism in the Christian Church*. Williamson is a member of the Christian Scholars Group on Judaism, the American Academy of Religion, the Association of Disciples for Theological Discussion, and the American Theological Society. He is a member of the committee on the Church and the Holocaust of the United States Holocaust Memorial Museum and of the Christian Scholars Group on Judaism. In 1990 he was noted by the Disciples Theological Digest as a "distinguished Disciples Scholar."

CLARK M. WILLIAMSON

Personal Introduction

Circa 80–100 CE: So when Pilate saw that he was gaining nothing, but rather that a riot was beginning, he took water and washed his hands before the crowd, saying, "I am innocent of this man's blood; see to it yourselves." And all the people answered, "His blood be on us and on our children!" (Matt. 27:24–25).[1]

For Jews of my generation, the Holocaust is the acknowledged, or repressed, watershed event of our lives, an ever-present shadow. Most of my immediate family was spared. My great uncle Mordechai and all his family, my eldest cousin Ciwia, and my aunt Bronia were among the victims. My aunt Helena was a Holocaust survivor.

The need to understand Christian attitudes toward Judaism has been with me for many years. After searching in various directions, I stopped at the gates of Christian scripture. Without any foreknowledge or expectations, I started reading the New Testament. The anti-Jewish bias of the texts surprised me. I did not return to the New Testament for many years.

Some 20 years ago, I started rereading the New Testament. I also began studying, on my own, The New Testament, Christian history, and Christian theology. Throughout these years I have been deeply touched and influenced by the encounter with Christian scholars and theologians. I have benefited from their guidance and counsel, which was given with open hearts and open minds. During these years of study I have learned that the New Testament is a complex corpus that includes unique theological statements, extraordinary spiritual insights, edifying stories and parables, and different and differing perspectives on the ministry of Jesus. In the New Testament I also encountered confusing and conflicting messages about the attitudes of early Gentile believers in Jesus toward Judaism and toward the Jewish people. I have also learned that pro-Jewish and anti-Jewish strands have cohabited in the traditions of believers in Jesus from the earliest years and have wrestled since for their minds, hearts, and souls.

For individual believers, Christianity is a religion of faith, love, grace, salvation, and redemption. The vast majority of today's believers in Jesus have no anti-Jewish or anti-Semitic inclinations. Most are unaware of the deep and pervasive presence of the anti-Jewish strand in their theology, culture, and lore. "Most Christians are unaware of the role that Christians have played in the oppression of the Jewish people."[2] Furthermore, many of today's believers consider Jews to be God's chosen people and have but the warmest attitudes toward them. For most, whose life in Christ is one of loving kindness and mercy, awakening to the anti-Jewish bent that permeates the canonical and authoritative lore is a troubling and disconcerting experience.[3] The presence of an anti-Jewish bias in the religious tradition that gave the world the inspiring and sublime writings of Perpetua of Carthage, Francis of Assisi, Hildegard of Bingen, Bonaventure, Meister Eckhardt, Catherine de Siena, Thomas a' Kempis, John of the Cross, Teresa de Avila, and Teilhard de Chardin is disconcerting. The abyss between the wholesomeness and the authenticity of individual belief and sixteen hundred years of anti-Jewish teachings is hard to reconcile.

For Jews, studying the canonical and the authoritative Christian literature is a gut-wrenching and unsettling encounter with a strange universe in which we, and our religious traditions, are denigrated, vilified, and ridiculed in a myriad of ways.

When revisiting the New Testament and the authoritative texts, we need to be aware of the cultural, religious, and emotional filters through which we approach the text.[4] To transpose oneself to the time and place of the New Testament writers, and to capture the circumstances and the issues that the scribes, the editors, and the compilers of the texts were trying to address, one needs to divest sixteen hundred years of traditional interpretations and dogmas. In order to read the canonical texts as a first-century inhabitant of the Roman Empire would, we also need to divest deeply held beliefs, values, and sensibilities. These preconditions are necessary to capture the events as they unfolded, without the formidable impact of centuries of retroactive editing and dogmatic indoctrination. Moreover, the destruction of the textual traditions of differing believers in Jesus, the complexities of the texts, the intricacy of the circumstances, the fog of history, active obstruction by the guardians of orthodoxy and the emotional and cultural shields that protect religious dogma conspire to make this quest difficult.

The enormous corpus of New Testament scholarship is not fully surveyed here. Theological, Christological, and creedal elements are only marginally addressed. Many derivative topics are addressed and discussed only as they impact the subject at hand. Furthermore, my presentation of these complex topics is not exhaustive; they are explored only to the extent needed to develop the main themes of the monograph. Readers not acquainted with the vastness of New Testament scholarship should be aware that most issues touched upon here have been interpreted and understood in different and differing ways by qualified scholars and theologians, which I am not. Furthermore, this work is not a religious statement, nor is it a statement about religion. The sensitive and emotionally charged nature of the subject at hand may cause some readers to shut-off to the presentation and to precategorize this book, or portions of it, in unintended ways. Some may find the journey emotionally difficult. The reader should continuously keep in his or her mind that this is not a critique of the faith and beliefs of believers in Jesus, nor is it about their vast, rich, and empowering religious heritage. The focus of this work is limited to the emergence and the evolution of anti-Jewish attitudes among early Gentile believers in Jesus.

I invite Christian readers to attempt to read this book from a Jewish perspective, to explore the New Testament and the authoritative texts anew. I present my work with great trepidation, with an apprehension born out of the tension between my affinity with religious belief and my quest to decipher the anti-Jewish strand. This affinity permeates and informs my life-long interest in the religions experience and its mystical manifestations. The task of rereading the New Testament in a new light requires substantial effort. The evidence and the clues that sustain my conclusions emerge gradually and slowly throughout the monograph. I hope that readers will find this rendition of my journey edifying. Despite many unanswered questions the ongoing quest has been rewarding, the conclusions surprising.

I was summoned to this task by dark and painful memories deeply etched in the Jewish consciousness, and by ever-present storms that cloud the Jewish horizon. In this quest I have been nurtured by the deep and powerful wells of the Jewish collective past. Throughout this journey I found myself surprised again and again by intense emotions, triggered by this experience, and reflected in an emotional under-pitch that I do not identify in my rational self. Twenty years after the beginning of this journey, the texts can still overwhelm me. The images of their unintended consequences still haunt me. Paradoxically, as I read and reread the canonical and authoritative texts, I detected a gradual change in their impact on me: to my surprise, the more I immersed myself in the material, the more I became desensitized to the anti-Jewish content. It seems that with time, one becomes accustomed to heavy dosages of rhetoric; it becomes an almost nonexistent background noise. It would appear that overexposure to verbal violence leads to numbness to it.

Any attempt at channeling the chaos, the diversity, and the uncertainty of the first centuries of belief in Jesus into a structured narrative will fail to fully encompass the underlying complexity. Furthermore, the enigmas, the dissonances, and the inconsistencies that we encounter in the texts before us require a harmonizing narrative that must go beyond the evidence. Therefore, it was necessary to sketch on this canvass a picture that cannot be fully substantiated. However, and significantly, none of the traditional or modern models does exhaust the textual evidence either. Nonetheless, many discrepancies and difficulties, many mystifying puzzles and previously dis-connected phenomena, yield new meanings and interpretations when ana-lyzed in light of the suggested socio-theological trajectory. Whether the proposed alternative, which is an expansion of the work of many scholars and theologians, is deemed to better fit the evidence and better reflect the evolution of belief in Jesus is a judgment that readers will cast.

Preview

Paul introduced monotheism, scriptural religion, and teleology[1] to the Roman world. He also pioneered the rich and fruitful universe of personal belief. He was the first theologian to acquaint Western minds with the emotional and intellectual universe that moderns call individual consciousness and belief. Paul's emphasis on belief was revolutionary. The notion that what each and every individual believed was the arena where the drama of salvation unfolded must have been exhilarating in a society where individual freedom, regardless of class, was very limited. The idea that individual belief not only mattered but was "the" essence of human existence, and the only measure for salvation, must have been an empowering insight. We can only imagine the excitement that this encounter must have caused among spiritual seekers in the Roman world. However, tensions arose as Gentile converts to Paul's form of belief in Jesus encountered the descendants of Jesus's disciples and first followers in the public arena. Most of the descendents fo the founding fathers seem to have conditioned fellowship on Torah observance and may have considered Gentile forms of belief in Jesus insufficient and lacking.

The canonical tradition seems to shadow the embryonic stages of a Gentile challenge to the authority and to the legitimacy of the descendants of Jesus's disciples and first followers as the exclusive guardians and interpreters of Jesus's legacy.

During the last decades of the first century we encounter Gentile believers whose contention vis-à-vis the descendants of Jesus's disciples and first followers seems to have been as follows:

> They claim to be the rightful guardians of Jesus legacy, but they are not. Their ancestors misunderstood Jesus' ministry. They misunderstood him, denied him, abandoned, and betrayed him in his hour of need. They exalt Jesus but misunderstand the true meaning of his ministry. To them, he is a human. To us he is the divine savior. They claim that our belief is inadequate and lacking, and that we must keep all their traditions, but we are the ones that seek martyrdom for his sake. Jesus came to bring salvation to all, not only to the Jews. Their Torah and their customs have no value anymore. Their scriptures tell us that the Jews forfeited the covenant and God's favor. They are no longer God's chosen. We believe in Jesus as the fulfillment of

God's promises to all. Don't let anyone cast any doubt on your legitimacy as followers of Jesus. Their ancestors did not understand their sacred lore and they did not understand the true meaning of Jesus' legacy either. We are the true and rightful inheritors of Jesus' legacy. We are the new people of God, God's chosen, the New Israel.

The response of the descendants of Jesus's disciples and first followers and their Gentile sympathizers seems to have been:

In order to be rightful followers of Jesus you need to embrace his ministry and his faith. To be a true follower of Jesus you must live like him and worship like him. Jesus and his closest associates were Jews. You follow Paul who was not a disciple and did not know Jesus. The Jerusalem leaders did not embrace Paul's views. We don't accept Paul's claims that Jesus revealed to him what he did not reveal to his disciples.

Pauline communities experiencing anxiety and doubt caused by this crisis, needed reassurance and guidance. They needed a legitimating foundational discourse, a dissonance-reducing narrative. In the New Testament we can identify attempts by Pauline leaders to reassure the rank and file that they were rightful followers of Jesus despite their rejection of the beliefs and religious traditions espoused by Jesus and by those chosen by him to be the custodians of his legacy. Facing an uphill struggle against the founding faction, and standing on a still-evolving theology, Pauline leaders and intellectuals seem to have gravitated toward a strategy built on the belittling of the disciples and on the denigration of their beliefs and traditions. They also opted for the subversion and the appropriation of elements, themes, and motifs quarried from their adversaries' traditions and texts. In the anti-Jewish-establishment traditions of the Jewish followers of Jesus and other Judean sectarians, they found a "ready to deploy" arsenal that could be used to demote the establishment of the Jesus movement. The lore of the founding faction turned out to be a trove of anti-Jewish-establishment stones that Gentile believers could use to denigrate the Jewish faction. By decontextualizing the Hebrew Scriptures and the Jewish traditions of prophetic exhortation and self-criticism, and by appropriating the founders' identity and anti-Jewish-establishment lore, Pauline leaders and intellectuals eventually crafted a strategy that was ultimately successful in de-Judaizing belief in Jesus.

Until the twentieth century, the anti-Jewish bent of the lore of early Gentile believers in Jesus was understood, by the vast majority of scholars and believers, to be the consequence of the Jewish rejection of Jesus, the Jewish responsibility for Jesus's death, and the Jewish loss of God's favor. By and large, Judaism was seen as a legalistic and morally inferior tradition that had forfeited its place as YHWH's chosen. During the second half of the twentieth century, aided by the fortuitous findings at Qumran and Nag

Hammadi, new paradigms emerged as New Testament scholarship yielded new insights and perspectives.

At the dawn of the twenty-first century, mainstream scholarship and the majority of believers have turned away from the traditional views on Jews and Judaism. The view that a proselytizing struggle between turn of the era Judaism and early Christianity may have been the main generator of anti-Jewish attitudes among early Gentile believers in Jesus seems to be espoused by many. Scholars that embrace this model often describe anti-Judaism as the consequence of excessive militancy by the more aggressive and vigorous proselytizer; the result of hyper-competitiveness gone awry. A variant of this "competitive model" sees the attraction of some turn-of-the-era Gentiles to Judaism as a generator of anti-Jewish sentiment among early Gentile believers. Under this construct, attraction to Judaism infuriated Gentile leaders and intellectuals and fueled the anti-Jewish fervor that is embryonic in the canonical lore and permeates the authoritative texts thereafter.

This study suggests that the anti-Jewish strand embedded in the lore is the consequence of a debate about Judaism within the Jesus movement that, through a complex trajectory of loss of context, misinterpretation, and misrepresentation, came to be perceived by later believers as reflective of a conflict between Judaism and Christianity. It is suggested that by the last decades of the first century, followers of Jesus with varying degrees of Jewish, Pagan, and Gnostic affinities, affiliations, and inclinations were drawn into a theological whirlwind and became the protagonists in a protracted multilateral religious conflict within the Jesus movement. Judaism, Gnosticism, and Paganism were not participants in this struggle; they were the subjects of contention. Thus, contrary to traditional and modern interpretations, the New Testament texts do not reflect a struggle between "Christians" and "Jews." Nor do they reflect a conflict between "Judaism" and "Christianity." Rather, they reflect a conflict about what belief in Jesus should be—among followers of Jesus with varying degrees of Jewish, Pagan, and Gnostic affinities, affiliations, and inclinations.

The Protagonists

The terms commonly used to identify the protagonists in the early evolution of belief in Jesus reflect the lingering influence of orthodoxy over the discourse. Scholars have wrestled over a precise, and neutral, terminology to describe the participants. The terms suggested here are my best effort to meet that goal.

I have chosen to name the two factions that claimed Paul's heritage Pauline-Marcionite and Pauline-Lukan. This choice reflects the fact, often neglected, that both strands were legitimate inheritors of Paul's legacy. The assertion that Pauline-Lukan believers were "Pauline" or "Christians" whereas Pauline-Marcionites were "Marcionite" or "heretic" has no inherent validity and perpetuates an anachronistic bias that maintains the discourse in bondage to a posterior hegemony.

For the most part, when the canonical and authoritative texts condemn Judaism, Paganism, or Gnosticism they do not reflect an active confrontation with these religious communities. Rather, they reflect internal debates within the Jesus movement. Whether believers in Jesus should adopt Jewish, Pagan, or Gnostic beliefs and customs was the subject of these disputes. Therefore, and for the most part, the anti-Jewish, anti-Pagan, and anti-Gnostic biases of the canonical and authoritative texts should be understood to reflect debates within the Jesus movement—not struggles with other religious communities.

Throughout this journey we will encounter various strands that will evolve into proto-factions and then into factions:

The Jewish followers of Jesus—Jesus's disciples and first followers were Jesus's chosen successors; the original guardians and interpreters of his legacy. Their beliefs, customs, and traditions were grounded in first-century Judaism. These messianic Jews seem to have venerated Jesus as an exalted human. Most rejected the many Gentile forms of belief in Jesus that emerged following the success of the Pauline and Gnostic missions to the Gentiles.[1] Alternative identifiers: Jewish faction, founding fathers, descendants of the Jewish founders, founding faction, Jerusalem faction.

Pauline-Marcionite believers in Jesus—called for the rejection of the beliefs and traditions of the descendants of Jesus's disciples and first followers.

Marcion's Jesus was a new and unprecedented figure that revealed a previously unknown deity of love and mercy.[2] He viewed the God of the "Old Testament" as an inferior deity, lacking in wisdom and justice. Marcionites considered themselves to be the true interpreters of Paul's legacy. Marcion made the earliest and most radical attempt to sever the link between Gentile believers in Jesus and the founding faction. Contrary to the orthodox complex and ambivalent reject-but-appropriate approach to the beliefs and traditions of the founding fathers, Marcion advocated a complete and radical rejection of any affiliation with their legacy[3] and strived for a thorough de-Judaizing of belief in Jesus.

The Pauline-Lukan faction—claimed to supersede the descendants of Jesus's disciples and first followers as the "God's chosen" and as the guardians of Jesus's legacy. They struggled to define and articulate a theological compromise. Often identified by scholars as Christian, Paulines, or proto-orthodox, they came to dominate belief in Jesus.[4] Pauline-Lukan believers saw themselves as the true interpreters of Paul's legacy.[5] Ignatius may be considered the third pillar of this faction. Ignatius adds emphasis on unity and hierarchy to Paul's and Luke's foundations. Paul and Ignatius emphasized belief in Jesus's death and resurrection (not his life and ministry)[6] and strove for a complex midway positioning of appropriation and supersession[7]—a cluster of themes associated with the faction I identify throughout as Pauline-Lukan. The full lineage of the strand would include Mark, Luke/Acts, Hebrews, Ignatius, Justin, Polycarp, Tertullian, Irenaeus, and Eusebius (despite significant theological variance within the group). I use the terms "Lukan," "Pauline-Lukan," and "proto-orthodox" for this faction.

Gnostic believers in Jesus[8]—Gnosticism, a controversial term, is a later designation for a variety of syncretic spiritual trends that flourished during the first centuries of the Common Era (Hermetica, Valentians, Mandaeans, Manichaeans). The usefulness and the relevance of the term have been criticized. However, an alternative term has not emerged.[9] In many Gnostic systems, the world is the creation of a lesser and evil God (the Jewish God). Despair and pessimism are pronounced and permanent. The world is evil and there is no hope for change. Salvation from this world is through secret knowledge taught by a divine savior (Jesus) and understood only by few, the elect. Various Gnostic schools evolved from the "Gnostic Fathers" Ptolomey, Cerinthus, and Valentius.

Gentile sympathizers with the Jewish faction—Gentiles attracted to the descendants of Jesus's disciples and first followers. Some converted to Judaism. Most seem to have embraced some of the beliefs and traditions of the founding fathers of the movement. Commitment, affinity, and affiliation with the Jewish faction varied greatly. These "Gentile Judaizers" drew some of the most vitriolic fire from Gentile leaders and literati who were incensed by their attraction to the beliefs and traditions of the founding fathers.

Timeline

BCE 1900–1700	The Patriarchs (Abraham, Isaac, and Jacob)
BCE 1200–1000	The Judges
BCE 1000–922	Davidic monarchy ("J" writer of Pentateuch)
BCE 850–720	Elijah, Jezebel, and Ahab, Amos, Hosea
BCE 850–720	Assyrian conquest of Northern Kingdom (Israel)
BCE 718–688	Hezekiah
BCE 700	First Isaiah
BCE 640–609	Josiah (Deuteronomic reform)
BCE 625–595	Jeremiah
BCE 597	First deportation (Babylon)
BCE 587	Nebuchadnezzar conquers Jerusalem
BCE 587–538	Ezekiel and Second Isaiah
BCE 465–424	Ezra and Nehemiah
BCE 63	Romans conquer Palestine
BCE 40–4	King Herod
BCE 4?	Jesus's birth
CE 26–36	Pilate in Judea
CE 30?	Jesus's crucifixion
CE 42?	Paul's mission begins
CE 37–41	Emperor Caligula
CE 54–68	Emperor Nero
CE 50–60	Paul's Epistles (New Testament)
CE 65–70	Gospel of Mark (New Testament)
CE 70	Destruction of the Jerusalem Temple
CE 69–79	Emperor Vespasian
CE 80–90?	Matthew, Luke/Acts (New Testament)
CE 81–96	Emperor Domitian
CE 95–105?	John, The Book of Revelation (New Testament)
CE 80–135	The Epistle of Barnabas
CE 95?	1 Clement of Rome (Church Fathers)
CE 70–100	The Didache (Church Fathers)
CE 80–117	Ignatius of Antioch (Church Fathers)
CE 98–117	Emperor Trajan
CE 100–160	Justin the Martyr
CE 100–170	Marcion

TIMELINE

CE 110–130?	Gospels of Peter and Thomas (Gnostic gospel)
CE 110–140?	The Shepherd of Hermes (Church Fathers)
CE 120–140?	Papias (Church Fathers)
CE 120–156	Polycarp of Smyrna
CE 130–200	Irenaeus (The first "New Testament" canon)
CE 132–135	Second Jewish revolt (Bar Kochba)—Jerusalem destroyed
CE 160–251	Tertullian and Origen of Alexandria
CE 190?	Melito of Sardis
CE 260–340	Eusebius
CE 300–375	Athanasius
CE 303–312	The "Great Persecution"
CE 306–337	Emperor Constantine
CE 325	Council of Nicea
CE 379–395	Theodosius Emperor (the Empire is Christianized)
CE 347–407	Chrysostom

Note: The chart is arranged according to the approximate period of the individual's ministry or preeminence, or according to the approximate date of text authorship. Most of these dates are the subject of ongoing, and inconclusive, debates.

Acknowledgments

Scholars and lifelong students of the Jewish-Christian saga that read, commented, and criticized drafts of this monograph: Reverend Dr. Phillip W. Tolliday, and Professors D. Fiensy and W. B. Tatum who supported and encouraged, despite a rather crude first draft. Professor N. Beck whose wise guidance helped me navigate difficult waters and whose encouragement and empathy made this journey a unique experience. Professor C. Williamson whose support and kind words are deeply appreciated. Professors A. R. Culpepper, D. P. Efroymson, Burton L. Mack, and M. Murray who reviewed drafts of the monograph and contributed insightful commentary and prepublication reviews. Professors D. Allison, P. Cunningham, J. Pawlikowski, J. T. Townsend, and J. Tyson who made helpful suggestions and observations.

Special acknowledgment and gratitude is due to the 14 scholars that submitted prepublication endorsements.

Zali Gurevitch, whose warm and early encouragement played an important role in my persevering. Friends that read the early drafts and contributed comments and much appreciated encouragement: Hanna Bibliowicz, Jeremy Evnine, Robert Hoffman, Emanuel Jolish, Henry Kadoch, and Henya Shanun-Klein, the guardian angel of this monograph. Finally, Ronnie, our children (Gideon, Yonatan, and Michal), and their spouses (Shiri, Samia, and Pablo) who were supportive throughout, read, and made valuable observations.

The views presented in this book are the sole responsibility of the author. The readers' support was a gracious gift, not an endorsement of the writer's views or conclusions.

Cover images: Fifth century mosaic in the interior of the basilica of Santa Sabina (Rome) on the Aventine over the entrance to the nave. One figure (smiling and welcoming) represents the Ecclesia ex Gentibus (Church of the Gentiles—The Gentile followers of Jesus), the other figure (stern and unwelcoming) represents the Ecclesia ex circumcisione (Church of the Circumcised—The Jewish followers of Jesus). Courtesy of Holly Hayes, Art History Images (www.art-history-images.com).

Chapter 1

The Anti-Jewish Strand in the New Testament

The anti-Jewish strand that we encounter in the New Testament has two manifestations:

1. Segments that contain language that disparages Jews, Judaism, or Jewish beliefs and traditions. The segments in this chapter include some of the best-known instances of anti-Jewish bias in the New Testament. The charts that follow are my summary of 233 segments identified by N. Beck as reflective of anti-Jewish textual bias[1]; 44 segments are redundancies that originate in the Synoptic phenomenon. They do, however, contribute independently to the anti-Jewish impact of the texts.
2. Themes, motifs, and theological constructs that disparage Jews, Judaism, or Jewish beliefs and traditions. These will be introduced in the chapters ahead.

The anti-Jewish strand is a complex and multi-layered phenomenon that has six main sources:[2]

1. Polemic by the Jewish followers of Jesus against the Judean establishment.
2. Polemic by Gentile believers against the Jewish establishment of the Jesus movement, its beliefs, and traditions.
3. Appropriation Theology—The claim that Pauline-Lukan believers in Jesus replaced the Jewish followers of Jesus as the New Israel, as God's chosen.

4. Supersession Theology—The view that the Pauline-Lukan interpretation of Jesus's legacy replaced and annulled the beliefs and traditions of Jesus's disciples and first followers.
5. Decontextualization and subversion of the Judean tradition of self-criticism and prophetic anti-establishment censure.
6. Loss of context, fusion, confusion, and misinterpretation of these rhetorical layers resulting in their projection onto Judaism.

Throughout the texts we will survey, these sources will surface, and resurface, in a variety of configurations. Intertwined, layered, appropriated, projected, retrojected, subverted, or de-contextualized they will challenge our ability to understand and discuss the emergence and the evolution of the anti-Jewish strand. This layered trajectory created the puzzling collage of anti-Jewish polemic that we encounter in the New Testament texts. Disputes among Jews about Jesus (was Jesus the messiah or not), disputes among differing followers of Jesus (was Jesus human, divine, or both), and disputes about what theological worldview should be adopted (Jewish, Pauline, or Gnostic) lay fused and intertwined in the authoritative texts.

Here are some of the better known examples of the anti-Jewish strand in the New Testament:

You brood of vipers! Who warned you to flee from the wrath to come? Bear fruit that befits repentance, and do not presume to say to yourselves, "We have Abraham as our father"; for I tell you, God is able from these stones to raise up children to Abraham. Even now the axe is laid to the root of the trees; every tree therefore that does not bear good fruit is cut down and thrown into the fire. (Matt. 3:7–10)

Woe to you, scribes and Pharisees, hypocrites! for you are like whitewashed tombs, which outwardly appear beautiful, but within are full of dead people's bones and all uncleanness. So you also outwardly appear righteous to people, but within you are full of hypocrisy and iniquity. Woe to you, scribes and Pharisees, hypocrites! for you build the tombs of the prophets and adorn the monuments of the righteous, saying, "If we had lived in the days of our fathers, we would not have taken part with them in shedding the blood of the prophets." Thus you witness against yourselves, that you are sons of those who murdered the prophets. Fill up, then, the measure of your fathers. You serpents, you brood of vipers, how are you to escape being sentenced to hell? (Matt. 23:27–33)

Therefore I send you prophets and wise men and scribes, some of whom you will kill and crucify, and some of whom you will scourge in your synagogues and persecute from town to town, that upon you may come all the righteous blood shed on earth, from the blood of the innocent Abel to the blood of Zechariah the son of Barachiah, whom you murdered between the sanctuary and the altar. Truly, I say to you, all this will come upon this generation. (Matt. 23:34–36)

O Jerusalem, Jerusalem, killing the prophets and stoning those who are sent to you! How often would I have gathered your children together as a hen gathers her brood under her wings, and you would not! Behold, your house is forsaken and desolate. (Matt. 23:37–38)

Jesus said to them [i.e., the "Jews"], "If God were your Father, you would love me, for I proceeded and came forth from God; I came not of my own accord, but he sent me. Why do you not understand what I say? It is due to the fact you cannot bear to hear my word. You are of your father the devil, and your will is to do your father's desires. He was a murderer from the beginning, and has nothing to do with the truth, due to the fact there is no truth in him... He who is of God hears the words of God; the reason why you do not hear them is that you are not of God." (John 8:42–47)

You stiff-necked people, uncircumcised in heart and ears, you always resist the Holy Spirit. As your fathers did, so do you. Which of the prophets did not your fathers persecute? And they killed those who announced beforehand the coming of the Righteous One, whom you have now betrayed and murdered, you who received the law as delivered by angels and did not keep it. (Acts 7:51–53)

And Paul and Barnabas spoke out boldly, saying, "It was necessary that the word of God should be spoken first to you. Since you thrust it from you, and judge yourselves unworthy of eternal life, behold, we turn to the Gentiles"... and when the Gentiles heard this, they were glad. (Acts 13:46–48)

And when [the Jews] opposed and reviled [Paul], he shook out his garments and said to them, "Your blood be upon your heads! I am innocent. From now on I will go to the Gentiles." (Acts 18:6)

So, as [the Jews] disagreed among themselves, they departed, after Paul had made one statement: "The Holy Spirit was right in saying to your fathers through Isaiah the prophet: 'Go to this people, and say, You shall indeed hear but never understand...' Let it be known to you then that this salvation of God has been sent to the Gentiles; they will listen." (Acts 28:25–29)

For you, brethren, became imitators of the churches of God in Christ Jesus which are in Judea; for you suffered the same things from your own countrymen as they did from the Jews, who killed both the Lord Jesus and the prophets, and drove us out, and displease God and oppose all men by hindering us from speaking to the Gentiles that they may be saved—so as always to fill up the measure of their sins. But God's wrath has come upon them at last! (1 Thess. 2:14–16)

I know your tribulation and your poverty (but you are rich) and the slander of those who say that they are Jews and are not, but are a synagogue of Satan. (Rev. 2:9)

Behold, I will make those of the synagogue of Satan who say that they are Jews and are not, but lie—behold, I will make them come and bow down before your feet, and learn that I have loved you. (Rev. 3:9)[3]

Table 1.1   Anti-Jewish Bias in Mark

Mark	2:1–12
Mark	2:13–17
Mark	2:18–20
Mark	2:23.28
Mark	3:1–6
Mark	3:20–30
Mark	5:21–43
Mark	6:1–6a
Mark	7:1–23
Mark	8:11–12
Mark	8:15
Mark	9:14c
Mark	10:1–12
Mark	10:17–31
Mark	8:31
Mark	9:31
Mark	10:33–34
Mark	11:12–25
Mark	11:27–33
Mark	12:1–12
Mark	12:13–17
Mark	12:18–27
Mark	12:28–34
Mark	12:35–37a
Mark	12:37b–40
Mark	14:2
Mark	14:10–11
Mark	14:43
Mark	14:53–55
Mark	14:64
Mark	15:43
Mark	15:3, 10, 11
Mark	15:8, 11, 15
Mark	15:38
Mark	15:39
Mark	15:29
Mark	15:31, 38, 39

The Q document or Q (German Quelle, "source") is believed to be, by most scholars, the oldest "text" of the tradition and is usually dated about 50 CE.[4] Q is mostly a collection of Jesus's sayings. Q's existence has been inferred. No actual Q document, in full or in part, has survived. It seems to have been used by the authors of Matthew and Luke.

Table 1.2 Anti-Jewish Bias in Matthew's Use of Q Material

Matthew	3:7b–10	Luke	3:7b–9
Matthew	5:11–12	Luke	6:22–23
Matthew	8:10	Luke	7:9; 13:28–29
Matthew	11:16–19	Luke	7:31–35
Matthew	11:20–24	Luke	10:12–15
Matthew	12:27–28, 30	Luke	11:19–20, 23
Matthew	12:41	Luke	11:32
Matthew	12:42	Luke	11:31
Matthew	23:37–39	Luke	13:34–35
Matthew	11:12–13	Luke	16:16–17
Matthew	5:18, 11:12–13	Luke	16:16–17
Matthew	15:14b	Luke	6:39
Matthew	11:20–24	Luke	10:12–15
Matthew	12:42	Luke	11:31
Matthew	23:37–39	Luke	13:34–35
Matthew	19:28d	Luke	22:30b

Table 1.3 Matthew's Increased Anti-Jewish Bias in Material Originating in Mark

Matthew	7:29b	Mark	1:22c
Matthew	8:16–17	Mark	1:32–34
Matthew	9:4	Mark	2:8
Matthew	12:1–8	Mark	2:23–28
Matthew	12:9–14	Mark	3:1–6
Matthew	10:1–16	Mark	6:7; 3:13–19a; 6:8–11
Matthew	16:53–58	Mark	6:1–6a
Matthew	15:1–11, 15–20	Mark	7:1–23
Matthew	16:5–12	Mark	8:14–21
Matthew	21:33–46	Mark	12:1–12
Matthew	22:15–22	Mark	12:13–17
Matthew	22:34–40	Mark	12:28–34
Matthew	22:41–46	Mark	12:35–37a
Matthew	23:1–12(14)	Mark	12:37b–40
Matthew	24:1–51; 10:17–22a; 25:13–15	Mark	13:1–37
Matthew	26:1–5	Mark	14:1–2
Matthew	27:1–2	Mark	15:1
Matthew	27:11–23, 26	Mark	15:2–15
Matthew	27:33–42, 44–56	Mark	15:22–41

Table 1.4 Anti-Jewish Bias in Matthew and in His Use of Unidentified Sources

Matthew	1:1–17
Matthew	1:18–25
Matthew	3:1–6, 11–12
Matthew	3:13–17
Matthew	5:20–22, 27–28, 31–32a, 33–39, 43–44a
Matthew	6:1–8, 16–18
Matthew	10:23
Matthew	12:17–21
Matthew	12:34a
Matthew	12:45c
Matthew	15:12–14a
Matthew	16:17–19; 18:18
Matthew	21:31b–32
Matthew	22:1–10
Matthew	23:12, 15–33
Matthew	23:34–36
Matthew	27:24–25
Matthew	27:43
Matthew	27:62–66; 28:4, 11–15

Table 1.5 Luke's Increased Anti-Jewish Bias in Material Originating in Mark

Luke	4:14–30	Mark	1:14–15; 6:1–6a
Luke	5:17–26	Mark	2:1–12
Luke	5:27–32	Mark	2:13–17
Luke	5:33–35	Mark	2:18–20
Luke	6:6–11	Mark	3:1–6
Luke	11:14–23	Mark	3:22–30
Luke	8:40–56	Mark	5:21–43
Luke	11:37–41	Mark	7:1–23
Luke	12:1	Mark	8:15
Luke	16:18	Mark	10:1–12
Luke	9:22; 9:44; 18:31b–33	Mark	8:31; 9:31; 10:33–34
Luke	13:6–9; 19:45–48; 21:37–38	Mark	11:12–25
Luke	20:1–8	Mark	11:27
Luke	20:9–19	Mark	12:1–12
Luke	20:20–26	Mark	12:13
Luke	20:27–40	Mark	12:18–27
Luke	10:25–28	Mark	12:28–34
Luke	21:5–36; 12:11–12; 12:40; 17:23; 19:12–13	Mark	13:1–37

continued

Table 1.5 Continued

Luke	22:1–2	Mark	14:1–2
Luke	7:36–50	Mark	14:3–9
Luke	22:3–6	Mark	14:10–11
Luke	22:47–53	Mark	14:43
Luke	22:54a, 63–65	Mark	14:53, 55–65
Luke	23:2–5, 13–25	Mark	15:2–15
Luke	23:33–49	Mark	15:22

Table 1.6 Anti-Jewish Bias in Luke's Use of Q Material

Luke	3:7b–9	Matthew	3:b–10
Luke	6:22–23	Matthew	5:11–12
Luke	6:26		
Luke	7:9	Matthew	8:10
Luke	7:31–35	Matthew	11:16–19
Luke	10:12–15	Matthew	11:20–24
Luke	12:54–56	Matthew	16:2–3
Luke	13:34–35	Matthew	23:37–39
Luke	16:16–17	Matthew	11:12–13; 5:18

Table 1.7 Anti-Jewish Bias in Luke's Own Material and in His Use of Unidentified Sources

Luke	1:5–23
Luke	1:26–38
Luke	1:39–45, 56
Luke	1:68–79
Luke	2:8–15
Luke	2:34–35
Luke	2:38
Luke	2:46–47
Luke	7:29–30
Luke	10:29–37
Luke	10:38–40
Luke	11:27–28
Luke	11:42–48, 52
Luke	11:49–51
Luke	11:53–54
Luke	13:10–17
Luke	13:31–33
Luke	14:1–6
Luke	14:7–24
Luke	14:1–32

continued

Table 1.7 Continued

Luke	16:14–15
Luke	16:19–31
Luke	17:11–19
Luke	17:20–21
Luke	17:25
Luke	18:9–14
Luke	19:3–40
Luke	19:41–44
Luke	23:6–12
Luke	23:27–31
Luke	23:50b–51a
Luke	24:6–8
Luke	24:20

Table 1.8 Anti-Jewish Bias in Acts

Acts	2:1–47
Acts	3:1–26
Acts	4:1–31
Acts	5:17–42
Acts	6:8–8:3
Acts	9:1–31
Acts	10:1–11 12:1–24
Acts	13:6–12
Acts	13:14–52
Acts	14:1–7
Acts	14:19–20
Acts	15:1–35
Acts	17:1–9
Acts	17:10–14
Acts	17:16–17
Acts	18:4–6
Acts	18:12–17
Acts	18:19–21
Acts	18:28
Acts	19:8–10
Acts	19:11–20
Acts	19:33–34
Acts	20:1–3
Acts	20:17–38
Acts	21:11
Acts	21:27–36
Acts	22:30–23:10
Acts	23:12–35
Acts	24:1–27

continued

Table 1.8 Continued

Acts	25:1–12
Acts	25:13–22
Acts	25:23–26:32
Acts	28:17–28

Table 1.9 Anti-Jewish Bias in John and the Johannine Epistles

John	1:1–18
John	1:19–34
John	1:35–51
John	2:1–11
John	2:13–22
John	3:1–21
John	3:25
John	4:1–3
John	4:4–42
John	5:1–47
John	6:1–71
John	7:1–52
John	7:53–8:11
John	8:12–59
John	9:1–41
John	10:1–21
John	10:22–39
John	11:1–54
John	12:9–11, 17–19
John	12:42–43
John	13:33
John	15:18–25
John	15:18–25
John	16:2
John	18:1–12
John	18:13–23
John	15:28–19:16

Table 1.10 Anti-Jewish Bias in Paul

Romans	3:20
Romans	9:31
Romans	11:28
2 Corinthians	3:14f
Galatians	3:10
Galatians	3:11
Galatians	6:15

Table 1.11   Anti-Jewish Bias in Revelation

Revelation	2:9
Revelation	3:9

Table 1.12   Anti-Jewish Bias in Hebrews

Hebrews	7:5–12
Hebrews	7:18, 28
Hebrews	8:1–13
Hebrews	10:1

Table 1.13   Anti-Jewish Bias in 1 Peter

1 Peter	2:4–5, 7–8
1 Peter	2:9–10

Chapter 2

The Anti-Jewish Strand—
The First Years

Introduction

The legacies of paradigmatic founders anchor the great religious traditions of the world. Most of the great religious leaders (Moses, Buddha, Confucius, Mohammad, and Paul) enjoyed long ministries. A lifetime of leadership and teaching enabled them to develop and articulate a comprehensive world-view and to inculcate in their followers a solid understanding of their legacy. Long ministries also helped them develop, clarify, and cement their legacy among their followers. Upon their death, their followers had a path to follow and they could rally around an authoritative doctrinal legacy.

According to the Synoptic Gospels, Jesus's ministry lasted somewhere between 18 and 36 months.[1] This extraordinarily short ministry may account for the fact that his followers seem to have been unprepared for his death. Jesus's death plunged his disciples and followers into a crisis that may have contributed to the theological and doctrinal chaos that followed. Instead of embracing a clear legacy, Jesus's followers had to figure out what his legacy should be. The absence of a substantial formative period and a large influx of converts from Paganism seem to have contributed to the emergence of a variety of incompatible Gentile forms of belief in Jesus.[2]

In Judaism, with the probable exception of Qumran, messianic movements have unraveled upon the leader's death. Thus, continuation of the Jesus movement required the articulation of a vision of Jesus's life and ministry that would support continuity. Lacking an authoritative pattern to follow, some may have left the movement. Others searched the Jewish sacred scriptures for an explanation. Paul's Epistles seem to have been authored a decade or two later and are the earliest integral texts in the New

Testament. Other attempts to understand the meaning of Jesus's life and death produced Q, James, proto-Matthew, and proto-John. This would be the earliest, and Jewish, layer of the New Testament. Later texts, the canonical Gospels, the Epistle to the Hebrews, Revelation, Barnabas, the Gnostic Gospels of Mary, Thomas, and Phillip, the Gospel of the Truth, the Apocryphon of John, and the Dialogue of the Savior, showcase the diversity of the early Gentile strands.

Attempting to decipher the pre-Synoptic period is an excursion fraught by low visibility and unstable ground. Any attempt to gaze at the two–three decades following Jesus's death must be highly qualified. Of special interest to our quest is whether the anti-Judaic[3] bent of the canonical texts has pre-Synoptic precursors. Whether these attitudes were held by the descendents of Jesus's disciples and first followers or flourished mostly among non-Jews is crucial to our attempts to understand the emergence of anti-Judaic attitudes among early Gentile believers. The pre-Synoptic phase of the Passion narratives is also the arena where we may find important clues for the emergence of the "Jewish responsibility" libel.[4] If the Passion narratives originate in one of the proto-Gospel traditions, the anti-Jewish strand can be assigned to a unique and conjectural situation (one community, one faction, one set of circumstances). On the other hand, if the canonical Passion narratives emanate from a wide spectrum of pre-Gospel traditions or from a single but widespread tradition, the anti-Jewish strand would have emerged out of a wider foundation. If the former is upheld, we have one tradition that has overtaken others. If the latter is upheld, it may indicate that there was a tradition of anti-Jewish resentment regarding Jesus's death that was widely espoused.

There is substantial evidence that turn-of-the-era religious quarrels were intense and vitriolic. Debate was vicious. "Bashing the competition" was the norm. Misrepresenting the opposition was commonplace. Thus, as we travel backward in time we need to tune our sensibilities to fit the confrontational tone that characterized religious clashes during the first centuries of the era. Furthermore, we need emphasize that, for the most part, religious texts were deployed to indoctrinate—not to inform. They were authored to shape the beliefs and attitudes of the believers, rather than to provide an accurate historical account. Moreover, as we try to understand the spirit of the age, we must separate our analysis of the author's original intent from its subordination-appropriation to service later agendas.

Anti-Jewish-establishment Rhetoric

In most religious traditions, pro-establishment theologies are generally associated with the fortunate, the successful, the socially connected, and the powerful. These theologies tend to promote the belief that one's fortune is a reflection of God's favor and of the truthfulness of one's belief. Establishment theologies tend to adhere to tradition and to "things as they are." These are theologies of the content and tend to tilt toward serene, sublime, and harmonious themes and imagery. Anti-establishment theologies, on the other hand, tend to surface among sectarians and among the marginalized, the poor, the vanquished, and the suffering. Belief in the coming end of times, dualism, retribution, vindication, and God's eventual just judgment, are commonly attested features of anti-establishment theologies. These are theologies of the discontent and tend to tilt toward intense emotions and extreme imagery. Throughout the New Testament we seem to encounter the footprints of both pro-establishment and anti-establishment theological inclinations, with a preponderance of the later.

We will encounter in the New Testament texts traces of three types of anti-establishment rhetoric-polemic:

1. Judean self-criticism and Prophetic anti-Jewish-establishment censure, as found among the Jewish prophets and in the Hebrew Scriptures.
2. Rhetoric by the Jewish followers of Jesus against the Judean establishment.
3. Rhetoric by Gentile believers in Jesus against the Jewish establishment of the Jesus movement.

According to the texts available to us, sometime during the second half of the first century some Gentile believers in Jesus started to think, perceive, and express themselves in apparent emulation of Jewish sectarians. How this migration of lore and self-perception did take place is one of the great enigmas that accompany the emergence of Gentile forms of belief in Jesus. This question will take center stage in our inquiry and will be bountiful in insights on the emergence of anti-Jewish attitudes among early Gentile believers in Jesus.

The New Testament and Qumran

The Qumranites[5], similar to other Judean sectarians, saw themselves as the only rightful holders of the covenant with YHWH.[6] The members of the community understood themselves to be "the true Israel," living apart from the rest of Israel, which is seen as wicked and sinful.[7] The Qumran sect scourges those outside the sect as "the congregation of traitors" (CD 1.12). The antagonists in the Thanksgiving Hymns are: "an assembly of deceit, and a horde of Satan" (2.2.2). In the War Rule: they are "the company of the sons of darkness, the army of Satan" (CD 1.1). The Pharisees (the arch-villains of Matthew) may be among Qumran's adversaries too: "Those who seek smooth things" and the "deceivers" are identified by some scholars as Pharisees. Segment 4QMMT appears to confirm that Pharisees were among the Qumran's opponents. These Jewish sectarians also believed in a coming judgment. Qumran is a community of repentance and of renewed commitment to Torah observance. Qumran sees the world in stark contrasts of "good and evil," "light and darkness"; it is strict and militant. One's status as a true Israelite, as one of the righteous, and the receipt of God's blessings require the observance of the divine law. The "separate assembly and house" (1QS 8:4–10) and attacks on those who reject them (e.g., 1QS 2:4–10) could be seen as anticipating the polemic in the Gospel of Matthew.[8]

The Qumran community is the clearest example of a "sect" (in the modern sense of the word) within first-century Judaism. Its distinctiveness has become more apparent as the more sectarian of the Dead Sea Scrolls (from Cave 4) have been published, showcasing strong predestinarian, dualistic, and mystical themes and motifs. The community evidently regarded itself as an alternative to the Jerusalem Temple (hence its withdrawal to the wilderness), determined membership by reference to its own understanding and interpretation of Scripture, and applied strict rules for novitiate and continuing membership (1QS 5–9). Most like the earliest Jesus movement in its sense of divine grace (1QS 11; 1QH) and eschatological fulfillment and anticipation (IQpHab, IQSa, 1QM), it was distinct from the former in a strict application of purity rules and discipline.[9] Qumran, I Enoch and Jubilees provide us additional windows into the worldview of Jewish sectarian communities. I Enoch scourges fellow Jews and presents the world in sharp binary contrasts: "sinners/irreverent" on one side, "righteous/pious" on the other (1.1, 7–9; 5.6–7). I Enoch seems to have contributed to the substantial apocalyptic literature that we encounter in the late Second Temple period and had a definitive impact on messianic imagery among Jews (the son of man, a primordial being, who would preside over a final Judgment and would usher in the resurrection of the faithful) and later on among early believers in Jesus.

Dualism is another possible link between the early Jesus movement and the Judean sectarian milieu. "Two Ways" is the designation given by scholars to a worldview that surfaced during the two centuries prior to the turn of the era and that, for the first time in Jewish history, saw this world as the battleground between the forces of good and evil. The Two Ways theology resonates with the Gnostic understanding of this world as dominated by evil and suffering; the creation of an evil God. The resentful, righteous, and militant posturing of Judean sectarians is oftentimes intertwined with the Two Ways material. The juxtaposition of "good—evil," "us—them," "sons of light—sons of darkness," which we encounter among some Gentile

believers in Jesus, may have originated in the sectarian-separatist posture
of the descendants of the Jewish founders and in the Two Ways mindset
developed by Judean sectarians, most notably at Qumran.[10]

Dead Sea Scrolls research has yielded insights that we may harness to
our quest to identify the cultural and religious traditions and templates
that the New Testament authors may have used to fashion their accounts of
Jesus's ministry. Knohl[11] argues the intriguing possibility that Jesus knew
himself to be the Messiah, and expected to be rejected, killed, and resurrected—based on the antecedent of the messiah from Qumran. Moreover,
in the Self-Glorification Hymn we see a combination of divine or angelic
status and of suffering not previously known outside the Jesus story. The
author describes himself in the image of the suffering servant in Isaiah 53,
an imagery that was emulated-incorporated-appropriated by early Gentile
believers in Jesus.

Overall, I see strong similarities, parallels, and resonances between the
texts found in Qumran and the earliest strata of the New Testament, pointing to a significant connection whose observable elements will surface
throughout our inquiry. This understanding of the affinities between some
New Testament texts and the Judean sectarian milieu diverges somewhat
from the consensus among scholars. The current consensus seems to be
moving away from dependence and tends to tone down the importance of
continuity. A minority of New Testament scholars see significant affinity
between Paul's theology and the Qumran Dead Sea Scrolls, and little affinity between Jesus and his disciples, and Qumran.[12] According to D. Flusser
(a minority view) there existed a stratum of thought that was influenced
by sectarian ideas, and John the Evangelist, Paul, and the authors of some
NT Epistles based themselves on the theological achievements of this
stratum.[13]

The similarities, parallels, and resonances between the texts found in
Qumran and the earliest strata of the New Testament:

1. The Pesher exegetical method (Typology)[14] was unique to Qumran
   and was emulated-appropriated by Pauline-Lukan believers. The
   main Pesher texts in Qumran are of the prophetic books Habakkuk,
   Hosea, Isaiah, Micah, Nahum, and the book of Psalms, which are
   also popular typological texts in the New Testament.[15]

2. In the Qumran library, the most attested and most important biblical
   books are Deuteronomy, Isaiah, and Psalms. These are also central in
   the New Testament.

3. Both Qumran and some early believers in Jesus followed a charismatic leader and considered themselves communities of the "chosen," guided by divine revelation, existing between the powers of
   good and evil.

4. Both communities lived in anticipation of an eminent end of times and a final judgment. The pitch is militant and resentful, as we would expect from separatist and self-righteous groups.

5. The arguments, attitudes, language, and imagery deployed by the Pauline-Lukan faction against the establishment of the Jesus movement seem to emulate the arguments, attitudes, language, and imagery that Jewish sectarians, most notably Qumran, deployed against the Jewish establishment.

6. With the exception of the Qumran community, there was no antecedent for the survival of a messianic sect after the death of its leader.[16] Following Jesus's death, the Qumran community (having survived the death of The Teacher of Righteousness) may have offered a template to follow.

7. The Qumran Messiah was believed to have resurrected after three days and his second coming was anticipated. Jesus's suffering, death, and resurrection after three days suggest that his followers may have used the pre-existing template of this messianic predecessor, the suffering servant of the Dead Sea Scrolls.[17]

8. Qumran, contrary to mainstream Judaism, believed in continued revelation beyond the biblical prophets, a theological stance present in the New Testament.

9. Both communities had a sense of divine grace (1QS 11; 1QH) and eschatological fulfillment and anticipation (IQpHab, IQSa, 1QM). An end-of-times and earth-shattering battle is described in the War Scroll, in the Rule of the Congregation IQSa, and in Revelation.[18]

10. The "new covenant," of great significance to Qumran (CD 6:19; 8:21; 20:12; IQpHab 2:3f.), is also a central theme in the New Testament (cf. Rom. 7:1–6; Gal. 3:23–25; Heb. 8:1–15, 8:6–13, 10). However, Qumran reads Jeremiah 31:31–34 as emphasizing renewal, the NT as emphasizing replacement.[19]

11. The covenant, as a result of the intervention of an extraordinary individual,[20] is the possession of the community and not those outside it, who have forfeited their right to it through their sins.

12. Dualism and the Two Ways imagery[21] are present in Qumran's Community Rule (I QS 3.13–4.16) and in the New Testament (mostly Paul and John).[22] Qumran's world is divided into good and evil. "Sons of light" imagery occurs in The War Scroll in Qumran, and in John 12:38 and 1 Thessalonians 5:5.

13. In Qumran's Self-Glorification Hymn the author describes himself in the image of the suffering servant in Isaiah 53, an imagery that was later emulated-incorporated-appropriated by early Gentile believers in Jesus.

14. Both Qumran and early believers in Jesus distanced themselves from the official Jewish sacrificial system and considered the priesthood unqualified and sacrilegious.

15. Celibacy, disapproved of in Judaism, was practiced by some Essenes and was idealized by early Paulines. Polygamy and divorce, approved by first-century Judaism, were forbidden by both communities.

16. Similar to some early communities of believers in Jesus, Qumran led a communal lifestyle with communal meals and no personal possessions.

17. Ritual immersion for the removal of ritual impurity was normative for first-century Jews, but Qumran and the New Testament present something new: immersion as an initiation rite (baptism).

18. The most probable influence on Hebrews' priesthood of Melchizedek seems to be IQMelchizedek discovered at Qumran Cave 11,[23] although Attridge instructs us of other instances of Melchizedek speculation (Philo, the fragmentary Nag Hammadi tractate Melchizedek [NHC 9, 1], 2 Enoch, and 3 Enoch).[24]

19. John the Baptist and Jesus ministered within walking distance from Qumran,[25] at a time when the community seems to have been active, pointing to a plausible connection.

However, despite substantial evidence for a link between Qumran and the early Jesus movement, we should be cautious about its interpretation. The availability of large numbers of Qumran texts, compared to other sectarian communities, may cause us to overemphasize this connection. Rather, we should contemplate the possibility that this nexus may be indicative of a connection between the early, and pre-Gentile, Jesus movement with the general Judean sectarian milieu (Qumran being a specific example of this broader phenomenon). It seems to be the case that the Qumran sect and the pre-Gentile Jesus movement were contemporaneous sectarian Jewish streams, accounting for the similarities we have encountered.

It is important to emphasize that the chances that early Pauline believers in Jesus, mostly recent converts from Paganism, developed ex-nihilo a typological (Pesher) exegesis of a religious tradition alien to them—are close to nil. Consequently, the use of typology is one of the strongest indications that some Gentile believers emulated-appropriated a number of Qumran peculiarities. The emulation of this exegetical idiosyncrasy by early Gentile believers in Jesus is one of many hints that Judean sectarian lore, views, and traditions migrated to a Gentile setting (most probably) through the agency of Jesus's disciples and first followers or their descendants.

In summary, the parallels between the Judean sectarian milieu and the New Testament are too numerous and too substantial to be set aside, and point to a significant and important connection. Although none of the similarities and parallels would be (by itself) conclusive proof of a nexus, their cumulative impact should tilt the balance toward the view that Pauline believers in Jesus inherited-appropriated many Qumran-like idiosyncrasies. Since we do not have any indication of direct contact between Gentile believers in Jesus and Qumran, we must assume that Jesus's disciples and first followers (who were Jewish sectarians with, plausibly, significant affinities and similarities with Qumran) are the most likely agents of this migration of lore and self-perception to non-Jews.

What Is at Stake

Many scholars active in the twenty-first century have embraced the diversity of the early Jesus movement. The argument as to whether the Jesus movement was significantly uniform, or substantially diverse, still rages—but the balance is tilting toward the latter. The common ground was Jesus's ministry, but beyond that anchor, the view that the emerging factions were diverse to the point of incompatibility is gaining support. For the pre-Synoptic period, the three–four decades prior to Mark, scholars have identified communities with differing theological anchors: Torah observance (the descendants of the founding faction), Jesus's death and resurrection (Pauline believers in Jesus),[26] Jesus's sayings and teachings (the Jewish followers of Jesus, Q, and some Gnostic communities[27]), and esoteric and sacred knowledge (Gnostic believers in Jesus).

Theories about pre-Gospel passion narrative traditions[28] are crucial for our search for they can illuminate the origins of the anti-Jewish strand we encounter in the canonical passion narratives. For our purposes, the relevant questions at the pre-Synoptic level can be phrased in several ways: Were anti-Jewish feelings central to all pre-Synoptic communities? Are the anti-Judaic arguments, themes, and imagery that permeate the canonical passion narratives factional or are they widely attested throughout the pre-Synoptic lore and texts? Was the "Jewish responsibility" motif present in all the pre-Synoptic groups? If widely held, did it have the same meaning, centrality, and intensity for all believers? Was the focus on Jesus's death a characteristically Pauline-Lukan theme or was it widely accepted and authoritative? Is there a connection between focus on Jesus's death and anti-Judaic attitudes?

Some scholars have classified early Gentile believers in Jesus according to their affiliation to either of two broad and somewhat mutually exclusive Jesus traditions:

- The "life tradition" is an academic identifier given to traditions about Jesus's life and ministry. This tradition included Jesus's teachings and sayings and had a strong anti-establishment bent that would alienate the Roman elites. The life tradition is reflected in the gospel according to Thomas, Q, the opponents of Paul in 1 Corinthian 1–4, in Gnostic texts, and in some of the opponents of the Johannines. It also surfaces in the Gospel of Matthew.

- The "Cross tradition" is an academic identifier given to the tradition focused on Jesus's death and resurrection. This tradition, embraced by the Pauline factions, deemphasized the subversive and anti-establishment message of Jesus's ministry and emphasized Jesus's death and an otherworldly creed. The Cross tradition deemphasized "Jesus the social critic"[29] and emphasized "Jesus the divine being" and thus opened the door for the successful introduction of the new faith to the Roman elites. This tradition dominates most of the New Testament texts.

Whether the anti-Judaic bent of the canonical passion narratives is mostly an intensification or decontextualization of the anti-Jewish-establishment sentiment of the Jewish followers of Jesus or mostly the creation of non-Jewish believers, is significant to our journey. More significant, however, is the growing recognition that anti-Jewish themes were central for some, but were not universally authoritative for all early Gentile believers in Jesus. The work of Crossan, Flusser, Koester, and others on the pre-Gospel stages of the passion narratives (although still a minority view) points to a sectarian origin. The work of these scholars supports the view that the canonical passion narratives emerged as part of a legacy that was not an intrinsic and constitutive theme for all believers in Jesus.

The question is, in a nutshell, whether the Passion narratives we encounter in the canonical Gospels originate in one of multiple and differing pre-Synoptic strands (Flusser, Crossan, Koester) or in a wider pre-existing tradition (Brown). Whether the canonical Passion Narratives represent independent attestations or not has shadowed the battle over variants of the "Jewish responsibility for Jesus' death." If Mark and John are independent, and stand on a widely embraced pre-Synoptic tradition, it supports those hanging on to some variant of the claim. If Mark and John are dependent, and stand on one of multiple pre-Synoptic traditions, it points to a factional origin.

Summary

Turn-of-the-era Jewish theological battles were occasionally vitriolic but they were also mostly harmless. Although the pitch could be intense, there were few instances of violence between Jewish sectarians and the Jewish mainstream. In line with other Jewish sectarians, the Jewish followers of Jesus may have considered themselves to be the "New Israel," a community living against apostate and sinful Israel. Characteristically, those outside the community were seen as bound for damnation and outside God's favor. The anti-Jewish-establishment rhetoric that the Jewish followers of Jesus may have deployed against fellow Jews, a characteristic motif among Jewish sectarians, is not extant outside the Christian authoritative texts.

The Qumran community and the communities that produced other Judean sectarian texts may have been precursors or templates for the Jewish followers of Jesus and may provide "the missing link" and help us re-place the early Jesus movement in continuation to turn-of-the-era sectarian Judaism. Acknowledgment of the similarities between Gentile anti-Jewish language and the anti-Jewish-establishment rhetoric of turn-of-the-era Jewish sectarian movements is an important shift in our understanding of the attitudes of Gentile believers in Jesus toward Judaism. Probable parallels between the lore of the early Jesus movement and the lore of Jewish sectarians provide us a new perspective on the early anti-Judaic polemic we encounter in the New Testament. Many themes, motifs, traits, and imagery traditionally seen as radically new and opposing Judaism may have originated in the Jewish sectarian milieu.

As we start our journey, we will overhear the descendants of Jesus's disciples and first followers denigrating fellow Jews. As our train stops at the midway stations scattered along our route, we will eavesdrop on debates, mostly among Gentile believers. We will hear them vilify "the Jews" (their Jewish opponents within the Jesus movement) with ever-increasing viciousness. At the later stations of our voyage we will hear non-Jews denigrating all Jews. The question before us will be: How and why did Gentile believers in Jesus come to address Jews and Judaism emulating the vocabulary, imagery, and intensity that Jewish sectarians used against the Jewish establishment?

Chapter 3

The Anti-Judaic Strand in Paul

Introduction

Paul is one of the most studied and researched individuals in the Western tradition. Paul is the foremost theologian of the New Testament and he is, without doubt, the New Testament's anchor. Paul is also a charismatic, enigmatic, and frustrated religious visionary that was unable to reach, in his lifetime, the recognition and the legitimacy he yearned for. The Pauline letters that are accepted as authentic by most scholars (Romans, 1 and 2 Corinthians, Galatians, Philippians, 1 Thessalonians, and Philemon) are the earliest integral New Testament documents available to us. Great efforts have been made by theologians and by academics to interpret and to harmonize Paul's theological statements. These efforts have produced a bewildering maze of arguments and counter-arguments. Incursions into this minefield are demanding and rewarding. The superstore of Paul interpretation offers a wide array of brands. Each creedal, theological, and denominational predisposition has its team of favorite scholars.[1]

I will not attempt to present a comprehensive study of Paul's theology, personality, thought, or deeds. My interest centers on the controversial, polemical, and rhetorical Paul—the apparent originator of the anti-Jewish strand, according to traditional scholarship. Whether this role is in substantial harmony or dissonance with Paul's intent is one of the puzzles that will confront us.

Paul and Judaism

A couple generations after Paul's death, his followers appear to have split into two main strands: Marcionite and Lukan. Paul's legacy, as it regards

Jews and Judaism, was interpreted by both groups to signal ambivalence and antagonism.[2] Throughout the ages Judaism has viewed Paul as a renegade that betrayed his people and caused great suffering. Paul's relationship with, and attitudes toward, Judaism are complex matters that are the subject of intense debate and study. Paul's statements about Jews and about Judaism are, to many readers and scholars, erratic, contradictory, confusing, and inconsistent. According to Gager[3] any reader of Paul has to address two separate sets of statements that are in full contradiction:

1. *The anti-Israel and anti-Law set*: Gal. 3:10, 11; 6:15; Rom. 3:20; 9:31; 2 Cor. 3:14f.
   i. For all who rely on works of the law are under a curse. (Gal. 3:10)
   ii. [N]o man is justified before God by the law. (Gal. 3:11)
   iii. For neither circumcision counts for anything, nor uncircumcision, but a new creation. (Gal. 6:15)
   iv. For no human being will be justified in his [God's] sight by works of the law, since through the law comes knowledge of sin. (Rom. 3:20)
   v. Israel who pursued the righteousness which is based on law did not succeed in fulfilling that law. (Rom. 9:31)
   vi. But their minds were hardened; for to this day, when they read the old covenant, that same veil remains unlifted, because only through Christ is it taken away. Yes, to this day whenever Moses is read a veil lies over their minds. (2 Cor. 3:14–15)
2. *The pro-Israel and pro-Law set*: Rom. 3:1, 31; 7:7, 12; 9:4; 11:1, 26; Gal. 3:21.
   i. Then what advantage has the Jew? Or what is the value of circumcision? Much in every way. (Rom. 3:1–2)
   ii. Do we then overthrow the law by this faith? By no means! On the contrary, we uphold the law. (Rom. 3:31)
      i. What then shall we say? That the law is sin? By no means! (Rom. 7:7)
   iii. So the law is holy, and the commandment is holy and just and good. (Rom. 7:12)
   iv. They are Israelites, and to them belong the sonship, the glory, the covenants, the giving of the law, the worship, and the promises; to them belong the patriarchs, and of their race, according to the flesh, is the Christ. (Rom. 9:4–5)
   v. I ask, then, has God rejected his people? By no means! (Rom. 11:1)
   vi. [A]nd so all Israel will be saved. (Rom. 11:26)
   vii. Is the law then against the promises of God? Certainly not. (Gal. 3:21)

Although throughout the centuries theologians and thinkers have wrestled with the apparent inconsistency and incompatibility of these statements, for eighteen hundred years Paul's letters were read to the faithful as supportive and suggestive of anti-Judaism and provided a theological foundation for it. Unfortunately, Paul did not write an explicit and comprehensive theological summary. His Epistles were not written in expectation of their becoming sacred scripture. Paul's letters were crafted to address issues at hand; they were not intended to form a coherent theological whole. The closest we have to a theological summary may be the Epistle to the Romans. Thus, whether we reach the conclusion that Paul was anti-Judaic (as the traditionalists would have it) or not-anti-Judaic (as the revisionists would have it) will color our understanding of his theology. Whereas traditional scholarship has emphasized Acts as a guide to deciphering Paul, revisionist-liberal modern scholarship attempts to understand Paul through his own writings and rejects other texts as biased and tendentious.

The historical setting of Paul's Epistles is crucial. Sanders points out that the Epistle to the Romans, 1 and 2 Corinthians and Galatians were all written within a very short period of time. 1 Thessalonians seems to be from several years earlier, and Philippians is somewhat difficult to date. Sanders, reflecting mainstream scholarship, concludes that since most discussions of Paul inevitably focus on the letters first mentioned, it must be recalled that they represent Paul at a crucial moment in his history—with difficulties in his previously evangelized churches breaking out just as he was hoping to complete the collection for Jerusalem and press on to the west—and these circumstances forced him into a critical examination of his gospel and the restatement of it vis-à-vis seriously competing views.[4]

Students of Paul also have to address the tensions and the discrepancies between the two main early sources of information about his ministry: the Acts/Luke rendition and Paul's Epistles. One's conclusions on the complex questions that surround Paul's legacy will depend, to a large extent, on one's assessment of the reliability of the sources available to us. Scholars also differ on Acts' agenda. Was Acts written to present an historical account, as implied? Or was it crafted to portray followers of Jesus as loyal to Rome, to mitigate Rome's persecution, to exonerate Rome from responsibility for Jesus's death, to oppose Marcion or to legitimate Paul by presenting him as respectful of authority and hierarchy?[5] To assess Paul's contribution to the anti-Jewish sentiment among early Gentile believers in Jesus, we need to address the following questions:

1. What were Paul's teachings regarding Jews and Judaism?
2. Were Paul's teachings regarding Jews and Judaism consistent or erratic?
3. Did Paul attempt to lure Jews away from Judaism?

The Theological Paul

Many traditionalists (Bousset, Harnack, Holtzmann, Morgan, Reitzenstein, and others) supported an understanding of Paul as grounded in the syncretistic religious milieu of the first century. Accordingly, Judaism, Gnosticism, Platonism, and the Mystery Religions were seen as contributing to the new religion. However, at the dawn of the twenty-first century, an increasing number of scholars see Judaism as the dominant component of Paul's background and thinking. Great interest and excitement has been generated by affinities between the theological imagery of Paul and of the Dead Sea Scrolls. Although traditional scholarship has seen a fundamental antithesis between Paul and Judaism, there is a growing emphasis on continuity (Davis, Sanders, Gager, Gaston, and many others). W. D. Davis pioneered the shift of emphasis from anti-thetical to consonant and derivative. Davies emphasized Paul's close relation to Rabbinic Judaism and concluded that we cannot too strongly insist that for Paul the acceptance of the Gospel was not the rejection of Judaism nor the discovery of a new religion wholly antithetical to it (as his polemics might lead us to assume). Rather, according to Davies, Paul advocates the recognition of the advent of the true and final form of Judaism, in other words, the advent of the Messianic age of Jewish expectations.[6] During the last decades of the twentieth century new inroads have been made in the attempt to carve out a "revised" Paul, free from the anti-Jewish interpretations of his immediate and later followers. My understanding of the theological anchors visible in Paul's Epistles is as follows.

Judaism—Judaism contributed monotheism (one omniscient, omnipresent, and omnipotent God), a teleological view of history (history unfolds toward a destination and reveals God's purposes) and a scriptural religion (scripture as a vehicle for safeguarding, transmitting, and legitimating religion, tradition, and political power). Dead Sea Scrolls research has yielded an increasing recognition of the debt of the Kerygma[7] to Jewish sectarian theology. We have posited earlier that Judean sectarians, as exemplified by the Qumran community, may have had a strong influence on Pauline tenets and may have contributed elements that were attributed by earlier research to non-Jewish sources. Dead Sea Scrolls research has contributed to the growing understanding that Paul's dualism may have originated from Jewish sectarian lore. Thus, Paul's vision of the world as a battleground between dualistic forces (good and evil, soul and flesh, sin and righteousness, light and darkness) may have originated in Jewish sectarian-eschatological-dualistic theologies to the inclusion of the Two Ways tradition.[8]

Gnosticism—Gnosticism is a modern designation for a variety of spiritual trends that flourished during the first centuries of the Common Era (Hermetica, Valentians, Mandaeans, and Manichaeans). According to

Gnosticism, salvation comes from secret knowledge received and understood only by the few, the elect. The divine spark within is to be freed, and a redeemer/savior will provide escape from suffering (Gal. 4:3; Eph, 3:10, 12; Col. 2:8).[9] Gnostics believed that both their origin and their destiny lay in a supreme deity. This supreme God dwells in a heavenly place removed from the evil world, which is seen as the creation of a rebellious angel or demiurge. A divine messenger will come and awaken humans and relieve them from the bonds of ignorance by bringing true knowledge. The demiurge seeks to hold humans in ignorance of their true identity, in sleepiness and intoxication.[10] Harnack and others since see some features of Paul's theology as deriving from Gnosticism.[11]

Mystery Religions—the cults of Mithra, Isis, Osiris, Attis, Dyonisus, Adonis, Demeter, and others are known as "mystery religions." This is a modern designation for a variety of ancient Greek, Persian, and Egyptian cults that competed for Roman interest and patronage. Little is known about these religious groups given that their members held their rituals and beliefs in secret. The Mystery Religions have been a preferred source for the sacrifice of the savior as a vehicle for atonement and salvation, for the negative view of the flesh and of sex, and for a pervasive and overwhelming sense of sinfulness and deprivation. (Sandon, the official god of Paul's birthplace, is a suffering and resurrecting savior God). As the Jewish grounding of Paul has been increasingly acknowledged, the emphasis on this source seems to have weakened.[12]

Paul's theological synthesis is unique and powerful—so much so that it would not be recognized by Jesus.[13] Paul's integration of Jewish and non-Jewish influences is a personal synthesis reinforced by a claim to revelation (Gal. 1:11–17; 2 Cor. 12:1–6; 1 Cor. 9:1; 15:8). His extraordinary theological synthesis seems to reflect his personal cultural background, and may be substantially dependent on Qumran theology.[14] Although Paul's synthesis could be seen as emerging out of his personal experiences and exposures, it is nonetheless a remarkable accomplishment. Paul's emphasis on salvation by faith alone was a daring attempt to introduce the ethical core of Judaism to Gentiles, without those idiosyncrasies that were most alien to Gentile converts: Torah observance, circumcision, and dietary Law.[15]

The Controversial Paul

Paul was a charismatic religious visionary deeply convinced of the centrality of Jesus's death and resurrection as the pivotal event of human history. This belief overrode all else. Paul's sense of mission and uniqueness centered in his claim to superior standing over the disciples and was based on his experience of direct revelation from Jesus (Gal. 1:11–12). Unfortunately,

Paul left us only sketchy descriptions of the revelation he experienced and of his meetings in Jerusalem. On these crucial events we are almost wholly dependent on the author of Acts. Although sympathetic to Paul, Acts seems to deny him the status he yearned for. Paul's claims to higher status on the basis of revelation are addressed by omission. According to Acts, when confronted by the Jewish followers of Jesus in the Jerusalem meetings, Paul submits to the authority of the Pillars. In Acts, when confronted by James, Paul is submissive and subservient and does not claim authority of any type. In Acts, James is the undisputed leader and Paul submits to his authority.[16]

Paul is also a surprisingly candid and self-professed master of theological gymnastics. He displays an approach to proselytizing that is unparalleled in religious recruiting. In his own astonishing self-description:

> To the Jews I became as a Jew, in order to win Jews; to those under the law I became as one under the law—though not being myself under the law—that I might win those under the law. To those outside the law I became as one outside the law—not being without law toward God but under the law of Christ—that I might win those outside the law. To the weak I became weak, that I might win the weak. I have become all things to all men, that I might by all means save some. (1 Cor. 9: 20–22)[17]

Paul, the center of gravity of the New Testament is difficult to pin down.[18] Attempts to salvage a consistent Paul have intensified in recent decades. Some assign the inconsistencies and contradictions in Paul to his contingent target audiences; others point to his rhetorical technique (Lloyd Gaston, John Gager, Stanley Stowers, Neil Elliott, and George Kennedy).[19] Most academic studies attempt to bypass the "controversial Paul" by assigning one text (mostly Galatians or Romans) as the pivotal and defining text. This approach understates the contradictions that surface when all the Pauline texts are compared.

Paul and the Jewish Followers of Jesus

Paul's relationship with the "founding fathers" was difficult, complex, and turbulent.[20] The New Testament texts and later orthodoxy attempt to convey recognition of Paul and of his mission (and by inference of his theology) by James and the disciples—while understating the ambivalence and opposition he seems to have faced.[21] Furthermore, Paul claims pre-eminence over the founding fathers on the basis of revelation, a stance that must have infuriated them—if aware of it:[22]

> For I would have you know, brethren, that the gospel which was preached by me is not man's gospel. For I did not receive it from man, nor was I taught

it, but it came through a revelation of Jesus Christ. (Gal 1:11–12)...was pleased to reveal his Son to me, in order that I might preach him among the Gentiles, I did not confer with flesh and blood. (Gal. 1:16).

Furthermore, James's blessing of Paul's mission to the gentiles (Acts 15) is short and leaves many questions unanswered. Although Acts and the Epistle of James are clear on James's wish for the Jewish followers of Jesus to remain Jews and to obey the Torah, scripture does not clarify James's vision on how the missions to the Jews and to the Gentiles were to relate to each other. According to the Acts rendition of the second meeting (Acts 21) James expected Paul to limit his activities to Gentiles. Chances are that we will never know what James's intentions were. James's blessing of Paul's mission to the Gentiles may have inadvertently created a two-tier movement and may have sown the seeds of future frictions between the factions. According to Acts, during the period between the first and second meetings with James, Paul breached James's blessing by promoting attitudes toward the Torah and toward Judaism that would be unacceptable to followers of Jesus of Jewish origin. Paul's anti-Law hyperbole, even if used only while addressing Gentile audiences, was detrimental to the status of the Torah and would be anathema to the Pillars. Paul's claim that the Law (the Torah) was to be considered replaced by belief in Jesus's death and resurrection (Gal. 3:10, 11; 6:15; Rom. 3:20; 9:31) would be an affront to the "founding fathers." Whether Paul's style can be explained and justified on the grounds that his audiences were Gentile, as some modern scholars contend, is part of an inconclusive debate. Tensions between Paul and the Jewish leaders of the Jesus movement escalated due to the fact that he had not kept his side of the deal; Paul was accused of luring Jews away from Judaism (Rom. 7:1–5; Gal. 4:21–29; 1 Cor. 9:20–22; Acts 21:21) and Acts corroborates that point.[23] According to Hare, "It was not Paul's proclamation of Jesus that aroused the deepest animosity against him in Jerusalem, but the report, perhaps largely untrue but not entirely without basis, that he was teaching Jews in the Diaspora 'to forsake Moses, telling them not to circumcise their children or observe the customs' (Acts 21:21)."[24]

The tensions between Paul and the disciples were eventually blurred by a variety of means, to the inclusion of terminology. The Apostolic succession and the Jerusalem Church are examples of later terminology deployed to cover up the Jewish grounding of the early Jesus movement and the theologically embarrassing later demotion of the descendants of the disciples and first followers. For two millennia, these terms did veil the Jewish founding fathers and did perpetuate the Eusebian transformation of the Gentile drive to de-Judaize belief in Jesus into a quasi-consensual transfer of leadership and authority. Moreover, the authoritative lore does not educate us as to the extent of James's awareness of Paul's ambivalent proclamations on Torah observance and Judaism. I speculate that James, an upholder of the Law, would have had no room for Paul's ambivalence toward Torah observance, even while addressing Gentile audiences. Corroboration of James's position about Torah observance and works may have been preserved in the Epistle that bears his name:

> For whoever keeps the whole law but fails in one point has become guilty of all of it... What does it profit, my brethren, if a man says he has faith but has not works? Can his faith save him?... So faith by itself, if it has no works, is dead... But some one will say, "You have faith and I have works." Show me your faith apart from your works, and I by my works will show you my faith. (James 2:10–18)

We can summarize the position of James, as reflected in Acts and James, as follows:

1. James blessed Paul's mission to the Gentiles.
2. Gentiles don't need to keep the Torah.[25]
3. The Torah was not abrogated, superseded, or changed in any way.[26]

Paul's position would have become untenable: he needed James's blessing to vest his mission to the Gentiles with respectability and with legitimacy, but he was transgressing his directives. It took years before gossip became rumor, and rumor became suspicion. Eventually, Paul had to answer the accusations leveled against him that he was luring Jews away from Judaism; of targeting Jewish communities and of breaching the boundaries of James's blessing. The Acts rendition of the second summons to Jerusalem is a masterful attempt to present an embarrassing situation in the best possible light. Paul was undermining the status of the founding faction as the authoritative leaders of the movement—while evangelizing under the respectability bestowed upon him by James's blessing. Paul, claimant to independent and superior status before Christ, was confronted about his theological acrobatics. Although the author of Acts places Paul center stage, he did not want Paul as the founder of Christianity. For the author of Luke/Acts and for his audience, the maverick Paul was problematic. The author of Luke/Acts fashioned a legitimating narrative that emanates from Jesus and his disciples, not from Paul. The Acts rendition of this episode is laconic: the charges are presented and James orders to conduct a ceremonial ritual that would demonstrate Paul's Judaism. He was to undergo a public ceremony designed to demonstrate his unequivocal adherence to the Torah. The announcement is made without giving Paul an opportunity to respond and without Paul asking for one. Acts makes every effort to cast Paul as a Torah-observant Jew[27] and subordinates Paul to James, inheritor of Jesus's leadership. According to Acts, James tried (by the device of the ceremony), to no avail, to save him from the mob. The ceremony (Acts 21) was not sufficient; Jews were incensed by Paul's actions. Paul was arrested to protect him from people that were out to kill him.

Moreover, the highly emotional pitch of Paul's anti-Law diatribes is suspect. If James blessed the mission to the Gentiles and ruled that Gentiles need not keep the Law, why would Paul make The Law and Jewish customs a central rhetorical theme? It seems to me that by associating followers of Jesus of Jewish origin with the "inflexible," "sinful," and "enslaving" Law, Paul was attempting to diminish the influence that the founding fathers had among his followers. Indeed, a significant number of today's scholars do embrace the view that Paul's targets and opponents are not Jews but anti-Pauline apostles within the Jesus-movement.[28] We can only guess why the guidelines set by James were breached. We have indications that they may have collapsed at both ends: whereas "some from James" may have caused a split in the Antiochene community by demanding that Gentiles keep the Torah (Gal. 2:11–14), Paul may have lured Jews away from Judaism (1 Cor. 9:20– 22 and Acts 21:18– 26). It would appear that, if historical, James's blessing of the mission to the Gentiles was unclear and/or dysfunctional. It seems that James's directive disintegrated upon impact with reality on the ground.[29]

Paul, Faith, and the Law

Paul's use of the imaginary juxtaposition faith/Law is peculiar and requires looking into. Contrary to traditional Gentile presentations, the Torah/Law does not replace or negate faith; it reinforces it. The Torah edifies the individual and promotes good and compassionate behavior.[30] Paul's dramatic juxtaposition of faith and the Law, of belief and works, and of spirit and flesh is heavily influenced by Gnostic and Jewish sectarian dualism. It carries the Gnostic seal of infatuation with sin and a negative attitude toward the body (flesh) as the incarcerator of the spirit. Paul emphasized a series of dualistic pairs that have been central in apologetics since, and are a distortion of first-century Judaism. Paul's presentation states:

Jewish belief	Torah/Law	Sinful	Flesh	Works	Darkness	Superseded
Pauline belief	Faith/Belief	Saved	Spirit	Belief	Light	Supersedes

These polemical tools are the surgeon's scissors that will sever the Gentile followers of Paul from the founding faction. These illusory juxtapositions were successful with audiences that had no prior knowledge of what the Torah, or Judaism, actually were. With time, the Gentile followers of Paul became infused with high doses of anti-Law rhetoric and the

Law became a major emotional "red flag," a central "wedge issue" in the drive to de-Judaize belief in Jesus.

Significantly, Paul's rejection of the Law seems to have contributed to misbehavior among some of his converts. The extent of the confusion engendered by Paul's anti-Law rhetoric is highlighted by indications of an ethical void among some believers that inferred that rejection of the Law implied rejection of moral behavior. It would appear that Paul's anti-Law polemic created an ethical vacuum that engendered confusion, anarchy (Rom. 16:17–19; 1 Cor. 1:10–13; 15:23–24; Gal. 1:6–9; Phil. 3:1–2), sin, and transgression (Rom. 3:8; 6:1; 6:15; 7:7; 13:10–14; 1 Cor. 5:1–5; 2 Cor. 2:17; 1 Thess. 4:3–10). This result was unforeseen and unintended by Paul who often calls upon his congregations to behave ethically, and to restrain deviant behavior.

Paul in Modern Scholarship

Traditional orthodoxy reads Paul as anti-Jewish. Traditional scholars emphasized Paul's confrontation with Judaism and have attempted, by all means possible, to present a consistent Paul. Traditional interpretations of Paul's writings are on the defensive following path breaking works by scholars such as K. Stendahl, W. D. Davies, E. P. Sanders, P. Gaston, and J. Gager who stand on earlier calls against orthodox readings in this matter by G. F. Moore, James Parkes, and T. Herford (see appendix I for a survey of modern scholarship on the "revised" Paul). This paradigmatic[31] shift in scholarship has gained momentum in the last three–four decades. This shift has two main pivots:[32]

1. The discovery by Christian scholars of real first-century Judaism.
2. The attempts to understand Paul outside the orthodox hegemony (a "revised" Paul).

Gager best summarized traditional views about Paul as follows:

1. Paul underwent a typical conversion from one religion to another, in this case from Judaism to Christianity.
2. As a result of this conversion, he preached against the Jewish Law, against Judaism, and against Israel. The content of this negative teaching was that the Law, the old covenant with Israel, was no longer the path to salvation, for Jews or for Gentiles. Indeed God had never intended it to be. God had rejected the Jews/Israel as the chosen people.
3. The radical antithesis between Judaism and Christianity is represented as a decisive transition from religious particularism to religious universalism.

4. Most traditional interpreters maintain that Paul's attacks against the Law are founded on a sound understanding of ancient Judaism.
5. Paul transcended Judaism. There remains a deep ambivalence as to whether Paul the convert can in any way be understood against the background of ancient Judaism.

Gager articulates Paul's unintended origination of the anti-Jewish strand and his centuries-long status as the fountainhead of anti-Judaism as follows:

> This rejection-replacement view of Judaism quickly became the dominant stance within Christian circles in the early centuries; it underlies the message and structure of the New Testament as a whole. And it is within this structure that Paul stands as the central figure. For the New Testament and certainly for those who created it, Paul was the theologian of Christian anti-Judaism.[33]

Pivotal turning points in scholarship emerge gradually.[34] Most originate in changes in focus and emphasis. Krister Stendahl stands at such an historical juncture. A shift of emphasis by Stendahl (1964) and E. P. Sander's obliteration of the view of Judaism as work-righteousness (1977) were paradigmatic shifts in New Testament scholarship that are still shaking the foundations of the traditional Christian understanding of Judaism. Stendahl, a leading Lutheran theologian, articulated his revolutionary views on Paul:

> [A] doctrine of justification by faith was hammered out by Paul for the very specific and limited purpose of defending the rights of Gentile converts to be full and genuine heirs to the promises of God to Israel. Their rights were based solely on faith in Jesus Christ. This was Paul's very special stance, and he defended it zealously against any compromise that required circumcision or the keeping of kosher food laws by Gentile Christians. As the apostle to the gentiles he defended this view as part and parcel of the special assignment and revelation that he had received directly from God. In none of his writings does he give us information about what he thought to be proper in these matters for Jewish-Christians.[35]

In other words, Stendahl changed the focus of Paul scholarship by giving to Paul's letters a conjectural status. The "revised and new Paul" may be labeled "non-anti-Judaic."[36] According to Stendhal, we should not read Paul's letters as general theological statements addressed to Jews and Gentiles. Stendahl reads Paul's letters as directed toward, and applying to, his Gentile audience exclusively. Consequently, Paul's anti-Law and anti-Judaic statements are to be read within the context of his fierce battle against those among the Jewish founders and their Gentile sympathizers who opposed a separate dispensation for the Gentiles. These opponents insisted on a stronger affinity to, and affiliation with, Judaism.[37] Thus, according to Stendahl, Paul's statements are irrelevant to Jews, or to the relationship between Judaism and the Law.

In summary form, Stendahl's understanding of Paul may be summarized as follows:

1. The focus is "Paul the apostle to the Gentiles." Failure to retain this focus can only lead to distortions, misconstructions, and blocked access to Paul's original thought.
2. In particular, it was Augustine's discoveryof Paul's introspective conscience, along with Luther's focus on justification by faith, that led readers to impose (to read back) meanings that were absolutely the opposite of what Paul said.
3. Modern translations of the Bible regularly reflect this Augustinian and Lutheran Paul.
4. In Galatians, Paul is defending his Gospel against Judaizers within the Jesus movement, not against Jews outside.
5. Romans Chapters 9–11 represent the culmination of his thinking, not an incidental appendix.
6. If Paul argues against anything in Romans, it is against the first signs of anti-Judaism among Jesus worshipers, not against Judaism.[38]
7. We should not speak of Paul's conversion as if it implied a transfer out of Judaism; he had no concept of "Christianity as we know it" or of his Gospel as a new religion.
8. Paul remained a Jew throughout his life; we should always read him within the context of traditional Jewish thought, not against it.
9. Paul does not speak of Jews and of Judaism in terms of the customary stereotypes put forward by many scholars.

Fifty years after Stendahl's proposal for a revisedPaul, a significant number of scholars have elaborated and nuanced Stendahl's views. New voices have taken center stage. Prominent New Testament scholars are working toward a new understanding of Paul's ministry and of his relationship to Judaism. For the most part, Luther's Paul is now seen as embarrassing and as irrelevant to the true nature of first-century Judaism.[39] However, each scholar reads Paul somewhat differently. Positioning is highly nuanced. My understanding of the views of the proponents of a "revised" Paul may be summarized as shown in table 3.1.

For Sanders, all religions, including Judaism, have to be understood from within their own context and through their texts. Therefore, Judaism cannot be understood or defined by reading Paul. Sanders also repudiated the view that first-century Judaism was legalistic and he opposed interpretations of Paul as anti-Jewish. Nonetheless, he sees Paul as understating and deemphasizing Judaism: The Law is good, even doing the Law is good, but salvation is only by Christ; therefore the entire system represented by the Law is worthless for

Table 3.1 Views on the Revised Paul

Summary of Positions	Traditional	Gager	Gaston	W. D. Davies	Stendahl	E. P. Sanders
Paul repudiated some interpretations of the Torah/Law	Yes	No	No	No	No	No
According to Paul, Jews forfeited God's choice	Yes	No	No	No	No	No
According to Paul, Jews forfeited salvation by rejecting Jesus	Yes	No	No	No	No	No
According to Paul, Jews need to believe in Jesus to achieve salvation	Yes	No	No	Yes	No	Yes
According to Paul, Gentiles don't have to keep the Torah/Law	Yes	Yes	Yes	Yes	Yes	Yes

salvation…Paul in fact explicitly denies that the Jewish covenant can be effective for salvation, thus consciously denying the basis of Judaism.'[40] The "new" Paul is nothing short of a revolution, not only in Paul scholarship, but also in New Testament studies—and inevitably in the Christian self-understanding. Since Paul is the theological anchor of the New Testament, reconstructing Paul leads to the inevitable reconstructing of the tradition. However, the anti-Judaic/anti-Law Paul is still deeply ingrained in the lore and in the minds and hearts of believers. Many have made one or more steps toward the "revised" Paul, but have difficulties in divorcing themselves from the traditional paradigm altogether. In addition, whether Paul was obscure but consistent or clear but erratic remains a contentious topic.[41]

The Acts Rendition

The Jewish national-ethnic boundaries had been breached. A Jewish sect faced unprecedented circumstances: it had to define its relationship to non-Jews claiming belief in a Jewish messiah, while rejecting Jewish beliefs and traditions. We may never know whether Acts' rendition of James's blessing of Paul's mission to the Gentiles is to be read as historical or as a legitimating myth. The Act accounts are cryptic and focused on vesting Paul's ministry with the approval of James. We do not know whether Paul and the "Pillars" debated his understanding of Jesus's legacy, his rejection of Judaism as it pertains to Gentiles, the possible emergence of two parallel but incompatible communities, or his claim to higher standing based on direct revelation from Jesus—a claim he seems to have made while addressing Gentiles. Paul's journeys to Jerusalem indicate that James's blessing was quintessential to Paul. It remains unclear whether James granted non-Jews equal standing in the covenant, or just reiterated the Noachide Laws. However, we must assume that Paul traveled twice to Jerusalem in search of something more than a reiteration of the Noachide Laws. The Acts version of the events, two dispensations—one to the Jews and one to the Gentiles—could be a posterior Pauline expansion of James's reiteration of the Noachide Laws. Paul's later statements and the tensions between Jews and Gentiles in the Jesus movement would appear to signal that Paul may have heard more than James said.[42]

Paul, unlike Buddha, Plato, and Mohammed, did not write or transmit to his followers a comprehensive and systematic articulation of his views—triggering the emergence of radically divergent interpretations of his legacy. In the absence of a methodical and comprehensive presentation of his mature theology, believers have created a cacophony of Pauline voices. Paul, the elusive first-century religious visionary, who wanted to mold himself to fit all audiences, got a fitting legacy: every denomination and faction has its Pauline scholars of preference. Every predisposition has its affiliated branch of Paul scholarship.

It seems that the understanding reached in the first Jerusalem council, if historical, whereby there would be two separate missions, one to the Jews and one to the Gentiles, proved to be unworkable. Paul and/or some among the Jewish followers of Jesus reached the conclusion that the compromise had to be discarded.

Summary

According to the supporters of the "new" Paul, the traditional "anti-Jewish" and "anti-Law" Paul is (mostly) based on a distortion of his message and intent, and on the misreading of his letters as a systematic theological statement. Unfortunately, the revised Paul is difficult to articulate and defend for it requires divergence from long-ingrained and more inherently intuitive readings of the texts. Centuries of traditional readings of Paul make the revised versions counterintuitive, too contrary to the literal Paul that people encounter when reading the New Testament.[43]

Great exegetical effort has been invested in order to explain Paul and to make him more appealing to modern sensibilities. It is unclear what impact this shift will have on non-academic readers of the texts. So far, access and exposure to the revised Paul has been limited. For the most part, the anti-Jewish impact of the texts on the literal reader remains unchanged. Attempts have been made to re-translate and re-edit the New Testament in a more Jewish-neutral way. Only the test of time will show whether these attempts will be fruitful.[44]

Ironically, Paul's rejection of The Law" was revisited by his followers a few generations later. During the second and third centuries, the Gentile followers of Paul split into those supporting a complete break with the beliefs and traditions of the founding fathers (Pauline Marcionites and most Gnostics) and those advocating appropriation-supersession of some of their core tenets (Pauline-Lukan). Both camps understood Paul's legacy as anti-Jewish. However, the Lukan faction will call for the incorporation of elements, themes, and tenets of the identity and lore of the founding faction into the compromise creed that they will advocate.

My Paul

Paul not only introduced monotheism,[45] scriptural religion, and teleology[46] to the Roman world, he also pioneered the rich and fruitful universe of personal belief. He was the first to acquaint "Western" minds with the emotional and intellectual universe that moderns call "individual consciousness and belief." This contribution has not received proper credit due to our intuitive classification of beliefs and values within the realm of religion and to our (modern) familiarity with "individual belief." However, for first-century Romans, belief (i.e., the beliefs of individuals) was to a large extent an unknown and unappreciated dimension of the human cognitive and religious experience. Individual belief was of no concern to the Roman authorities, religious or secular. The focus of Roman life, culture, and religion was on actions and deeds—not on the beliefs of individuals. Religion was largely cultic. To most Romans, religion was a ceremonial act of allegiance with few requirements, guidelines, or restrictions. Beliefs and values, so central to moderns, were part of philosophy, not of religion.

St. Augustine is considered by many to be the first existentialist of the Western tradition for his early exploration of inner consciousness. However, after studying Paul, I consider him to be the true precursor of the Western exploration of individual introspection.[47] Moreover, by gravitating to the Gentile world, Paul became one of the great transcultural figures. Paul's emphasis on individual belief must have been novel and empowering. By distilling the Jewish message to its essence and by choosing belief as the delivery vehicle, Paul designed one of the most effective campaigns in the history of ideological-theological transcultural marketing.[48] "Sola Fide" (by belief alone), Paul's theological battle cry, turned out to be the perfect channel, the perfect vehicle for the penetration of the Roman cultural and psychological defenses for it "delivered" the essence of Judaism to the "target market." Belief, as understood by moderns, was a non-existent, and consequently unprotected, dimension in Roman religious thought. By concentrating on belief, Paul fashioned an intellectual and religious Trojan horse that targeted an open flank in the Roman armor that did penetrate the Roman cultural and emotional defenses, without triggering the defense mechanisms that protect sacred tenets.

Furthermore, Paul's emphasis on belief must have been revolutionary. The notion that the beliefs of each and every individual were the arena where the drama of salvation unfolded must have been exhilarating in a society where individual freedom, regardless of class, was very limited. The idea that individual belief not only mattered but was "the" essence of human existence, and the only measure for salvation, must have been an empowering insight. For the first time in Western history what each individual believed mattered. We can only imagine the great impact that this encounter must have caused in the Roman mind. Paul understood that Judaism's customs and traditions were a stumbling block on the path to bringing righteousness to the Pagan masses.[49] Judaism was too alien, demanding, and idiosyncratic for most. "Selling" Judaism to the Romans would have required a multi-dimensional overhaul of Roman society and was doomed to fail. Similar to the Muslim, Hindu, and Parsee religions, first-century Judaism was a comprehensive system of prescriptions and regulations that governed the totality of individual and community life.[50] Although (mostly) respectful of Judaism and intrigued by it, most Romans would not embrace it. Since Paul was expecting an imminent second coming (Rom. 8:18) it seems that his ministry was not aimed at the creation of a new religion. Nonetheless, in retrospect, we can see that Paul's ministry was the beginning of a new religion with a strong anti-Jewish bent. Both may have been unintended outcomes.

My reading emphasizes Paul's confrontation with fellow Jewish followers of Jesus and their Gentile sympathizers. What incenses Paul is the opposition of the founding fathers to his de-Judaized interpretation of Jesus's legacy, and their rejection of his claims to pre-eminence based on direct revelation (Gal. 1:15–17; 2:20; 1 Cor. 9:1; 15:8). What "they" (the Jerusalem leadership and their Gentile sympathizers) "reject" and "do not understand" is not belief in Jesus, but Paul's version of it. Contrary to the traditional view (Paul's theology as grounded in his theological confrontation with establishment Judaism),[51] I see the integrity of the Jesus movement and its fidelity to Torah as the central issues at stake.[52] As to the Jewish dimension, I see no quarrel between the historical Paul and mainstream Judaism. Paul's confrontation was with the Jewish leadership of the movement,[53] not with "external" Jews.[54] It seems to me that what Gentile followers of Paul did or did not do would be of no interest to mainstream first-century Jews, unless Paul's proselytizing among Jews threatened Jewish identity and integrity. We have noted that Jews and Jewish followers of Jesus accused Paul of luring Jews away from the Torah, and we learn from Paul's letters and from Acts that Paul proselytized to Jews (Rom. 7:1–5; Gal. 4:21–29; 1 Cor. 9:20–22; Acts 18:4 and 21:21).[55] According to Paul he was flogged five times in the synagogues (2 Cor. 11:24). This type of punishment was dispensed in extreme circumstances, that is, when individuals violated sacred boundaries. Paul's words and activities suggest that he did attempt to lure Jews and God fearers away from Judaism. These are affronts that no religion, modern or ancient, would accept. This behavior would have led him to conflict with Jews everywhere. Furthermore, Paul's attacks on Torah observance and on Judaism while addressing mixed audiences may have become common knowledge, and would have triggered retaliation.[56]

Due to the contingent nature of his Epistles, each student of Paul has to assign to this extraordinary figure a center of gravity, a defining focal center. In Galatians Paul is beyond himself with fury and resentment at "those from James" that require Gentiles to keep Jewish traditions. In Romans (9–11, 11:1) Paul is conciliatory and thoughtful. Those that emphasize Galatians tend to see anger, resentment, and conflict. The existence of a relatively good relationship between Paul and the Jerusalem leadership, as portrayed by Acts (J. B. Lightfoot and others), is countered by the argument that the Acts rendition is an attempt to cover up the tensions (The Tubingen school—F. C. Bauer and others). We have seen that the supporters of the "revised" Paul contend that the debate was about Judaism, not with Judaism, that the traditional understanding of Paul as anti-Jewish stems from a misinterpretation by Paul's followers. Stendahl, Gaston, Gager, and E. P. Sanders emphasize that the process that led to the canonization of the Pauline letters has also determined an anti-Jewish reading of them in subsequent orthodox theology. For them the question is whether the anti-Judaism is truly Paul's own or whether it belongs to the interpretative assumptions of his readers. The claim is that the majority of Paul's followers misunderstood Paul's attitudes toward Judaism, and interpreted his conflict with the Jewish leadership and his opposition to Torah observance among Gentiles as one of ambivalence and rejection toward Judaism per se. Whether a true interpretation of Paul's thinking or not, we will see that as the confrontation with the Jewish faction and its Gentile sympathizers unfolds, anti-Judaic sentiment became endemic among Paul's followers. Regardless of one's understanding of Paul,[57] his (intended or unintended) legacy was understood by his immediate followers to be one of ambivalence toward Jesus's disciples, toward Torah observance, and toward Judaism.

Both, Pauline-Marcionites and Pauline-Lukans, were very close to Paul in time, location, and predisposition. It is interesting that they, who probably knew him best, considered him the apostle of the rejection of Judaism.

How far can the leader's ideas be from those espoused by his immediate and most fervent followers? The argument that Paul's immediate theological descendants misunderstood him, as put forward by supporters of a non-anti-Jewish Paul, is difficult to accept. I am not fully convinced either that Paul's anti-Judaic and anti-Law statements can be explained solely as techniques or as limited to Gentile audiences. Paul's letters are indeed addressed to Gentiles, but I do not concur that this fact determines his true understanding of Torah observance as it pertains to Jews, as argued by the proponents of the "revised" Paul. A "non-anti-Jewish" Paul may fit modern sensibilities and minds, but may have little in common with the first-century charismatic and exclusivist Paul.[58] Moreover, and unfortunately, since literal readings of Paul tend to yield an anti-Jewish Paul, the arguments that support the revised Paul may feel counterintuitive, complex, and inaccessible to lay audiences. My understanding of Paul stands on socio-theological arguments. It emphasizes an understated personal conflict with the Jerusalem leadership over his interpretation of Jesus's legacy, his marginal standing among them, the rejection of his claims to direct revelation and to pre-eminence, and his luring of Jews away from the Law.[59]

The founding fathers of the Jesus movement wanted to remain a sect within Judaism. Paul, on the other hand, attempted to craft a rationale for a Gentile, and de-Judaized, strand of belief in Jesus. Paul was a charismatic theologian that laid down the foundations of the Christian edifice as-we-know-it. He was the pivot and the trendsetter that paved the pathway that led his Gentile followers to a religion, distinct and separate from the beliefs and traditions of the descendants of Jesus's disciples and first followers. Paul was a visionary that was propelled by great emotional stamina, militancy, enthusiasm, and a deep personal yearning for recognition and legitimacy. Overall "my Paul" comes out high on theological creativity and synthesis, high on polemical skills, problematic on coherence and consistency, ambivalent in his attitudes toward the Torah, Jews, and Judaism.[60] Paul is the most intriguing persona in the New Testament, a theological thinker, a charismatic itinerant visionary, a grassroots organizer, and a turf nurturer and protector. Paul's trajectory, from a rather extreme and enthusiastic persecutor of the Jewish followers of Jesus, to his extreme and militant defense of his de-Judaized mission to the Gentiles, point to an intense personality. He is willful, gutsy, temperamental, and explosive. Paul was a theological innovator and a rhetorical acrobat, as well as the dominant, most engaging and enigmatic character of the New Testament.[61]

Chapter 4

The Anti-Judaic Strand in Mark: The Need to Explain

Introduction

Most modern scholars consider Mark to be the earliest canonical Gospel.[1] Some are opposed to the majority view.[2] Throughout the ages Matthew was believed to be the earliest Gospel and was, therefore, placed at the beginning of the New Testament. Theories about the positioning of the Gospel of Mark in the Synoptic sequence abound.[3] Despite noted resonances, the Synoptics (Mark, Matthew, and Luke) diverge widely in their renditions of Jesus's ministry. Each Gospel has a substantially different Jesus and a distinct Christology. Mark's Jesus is a Jewish preacher, an unrecognized and misunderstood Messiah who dies in agony and despair (Mark 8:29–30). According to Mark, no one seems to understand Jesus. The people closest to him, his family and his disciples and first followers, "do not understand."[4]

The Synoptic Gospels were written at a time when anti-Christian sentiment throughout the empire was rising. From Jesus's death onward, for the next three hundred years, Gentile believers in Jesus were considered by the Romans to be a seditious and potentially rebellious sect. At the time of Mark's authorship the first Roman persecution may have already taken place (Nero 64 CE) and the early communities of Gentile believers needed reassurance and guidance.

Standing on Mark, the synoptic tradition seems to shadow the embryonic stages of a Gentile challenge to the authority and to the legitimacy of the descendants of Jesus's disciples and first followers as the exclusive guardians and interpreters of his legacy. At the time of authorship, Pauline communities seem to have experienced dissonance, anxiety, and doubt caused by the estrangement from the descendants of the Jewish founders. They needed reassurance and guidance. They needed a legitimating foundational discourse, a dissonance-reducing narrative. Mark attempts to reassure the rank and file that they are rightful followers of Jesus despite their rejection of the beliefs and religious traditions espoused by Jesus and by those chosen by him to be the custodians of his legacy. He does so by denigrating the disciples and by casting Jesus as trespassing traditions associated with the descendants of his disciples and first followers.

When reading Mark in the narrow context of our attempt to decipher the anti-Jewish phenomenon, and with the intent of identifying underlying and unstated agendas, we have grounds to suspect that his narrative operates on three levels. First, Mark uses the Gospel platform to denigrate the founding fathers, casting them as not understanding Jesus's ministry and as abandoning him. He does so in an attempt to explain to his congregation their estrangement from the descendants of Jesus's disciples and first followers. Second, he casts Jesus as violating purity law, dietary law, the temple, and the Sabbath—signaling to his community that they are rightful followers of Jesus despite their rejection of the beliefs and traditions of those chosen by him to be the guardians of his legacy. Third, he intensifies or invents a rumor about the involvement of "Jewish authorities" as instigators of Jesus's death. By casting Jesus's crucifixion as caused by a Jewish conspiracy Mark exonerates the Romans and casts followers of Jesus as respectful of Roman authority. He may have done so in an unsuccessful attempt to alleviate Roman persecution.

Denigrating the Disciples

Mark seems to stand on a tradition of opposition to authority that resonates with Judean sectarian traditions that may have originated among the founding fathers. Mark's adversaries are specific groups (scribes, elders, chief priests, Pharisees) within Judaism, not "the Jews," pointing to a probable Jewish sectarian source for his anti-establishment rhetoric, most probably the lore of the Jewish founders. Throughout his Gospel, Mark criticizes the Twelve Apostles, the special Three, and Peter—the theological ancestors of those that are seen by Mark as his adversaries. Throughout the ancient Middle-East denigration of the ancestors of one's opponents was common. In line with this tradition, the ancestors of Mark's adversaries, Jesus's closest associates and companions, "do not understand."—implying that their understanding of Jesus's legacy is wrong,—a stealth message that is of great interest to us. Hindsight derived from our knowledge of what was to come helps us retroject and identify the belittling of Jesus's disciples and first followers as the first salvo in the confrontation between the Jewish faction and their Gentile sympathizers on one side, and Pauline believers on the other.

Mark writes the earliest, and still tentative, Gentile challenge to the legitimacy of the descendants of Jesus's disciples and first followers as the exclusive guardians and interpreters of Jesus's legacy.[5] The author of Mark implies that the Jewish followers of Jesus did not understand Jesus's messiahship (they rejected Paul's understanding of his ministry) and he denigrates them for that—a first sign of the upcoming debates about who Jesus was and about what belief in Jesus should be.

Mark's depictions of the disciples are complex and ambivalent, almost of two minds. On the one hand, they were Jesus's chosen companions and successors. On the other, they are the target of a puzzling torrent of innuendo. We are informed by Mark that they "do not comprehend" (e.g., 4:13; 6:52; 7:18; 8:14–21), "do not understand" (e.g., 6:37; 8:31–33; 9:38–41), are "hard of heart" (e.g., 8:17; cf. 3:5; 10:5), blind and deaf (8:18; cf. 4:12), that they abandoned him in his moment of dire need (14:50; 14:66–72). Contrary to the almost universal veneration of the disciples of the founder in other world religions, Mark (and the Synoptics that stand on his work) is unique in his denigration and belittling of the first disciples, those that Jesus chose as custodians and guardians of his legacy. The few that knew him best, the ones that shared his ethnicity, his religion, his journey, and his worldview, are the targets of Mark's belittling and ridicule.[6] The denigration and vilification of the "founding fathers" of the movement is a peculiar motif that will reverberate throughout the canonical texts and throughout the tradition.

A crisis of identity and of legitimacy facing new converts underwrites the Markan narrative. At the time of authorship (*ca.* 60–80 CE) Paul's mission to the Gentiles appears to have been successful in attracting new Pagan sympathizers and recruits. However, shortly after conversion, these new recruits must have realized that they had joined a beleaguered faction at odds with the "founding fathers" of the movement. Yearning for recognition and for legitimacy as rightful believers in Jesus, some of these new converts would be attracted to the Jewish faction. Most of these converts, however, seem to have remained loyal to the Pauline perspective but needed a legitimating foundational discourse. Mark seems to address the yearning of Paulines to be acknowledged as rightful followers of Jesus, a theme that will take center stage in later canonical and non-canonical texts. However, the earliest of the Gospels addresses the issue of the inclusion of Gentiles implicitly, not explicitly and overtly. The juxtaposition of the disciples that deny and abandon Jesus at his moment of need with the centurion that recognizes Jesus as the "Son of God" (15:39) is the only textual hint at the inclusion of Gentiles.

The Markan narrative is, on the surface and according to traditional readings, about a conflict between Jesus and Jews in positions of authority. However, skeptical readers can detect a crisis of identity and of legitimacy among Gentile believers in Jesus, as seen from a Pauline perspective. Mark's critique of purity law, dietary law, the temple, and of Sabbath observance while acceptable commentaries, interpretations, and valid discussion topics among Jews became potentially malignant when harnessed by Gentiles to undermine opponents that were Jews. Furthermore, positioning the Pauline and Gnostic missions to the Gentiles in opposition to the founding fathers is our first indication that Mark's rhetoric would be directed against them, and not against Judaism, as traditionally understood. Indeed, along the way we shall encounter cumulative evidence that attacks by Gentiles on external-establishment Judaism should be considered a later, distinct, derivative, and secondary phenomenon.

"Their" Beliefs and Traditions

Mark seldom states unequivocal positions. Rather, the text seems to hint, imply, and subvert—a stance characteristic of those opposing established and revered authority. Mark casts Jesus as trespassing certain behavioral markers of Judaism with the apparent purpose of signaling to Gentile believers that their non-observance of the Torah does not disqualify them from being rightful followers of Jesus, contrary to the views of some among the Jewish faction. Although Mark stresses the issue to the breaking point, we do not find in the Gospel an unequivocal statement on Jesus's rejection of Torah observance. Mark avoids casting Jesus as severing the link altogether; he stops short of casting him as explicitly rejecting Torah observance. Characteristic of Mark's often ambivalent positioning and despite traditional readings, Mark's Jesus seems to affirm the Law (7:1–13; 12:28–34) and the Temple cult (1:40–45).

The Temple is a focal point in Mark's depiction of Jesus's final journey (11:15–17, 27; 12:35; 13:3; 14:48–49; 15:29; 15:38). Jesus's statement in 11:17 stands on a typological decontextualization of Isaiah 56:7 and Jeremiah 7:11. His actions in 11:15–16, seen in the context of the cursing of the fig tree (11:12–14), seem to imply a divine verdict against the Temple. Mark's anti-Temple rhetoric resonates with the anti-Temple rhetoric of Judean sectarians and may be an emulation of it. This is another variant in his attempt to justify the break with the beliefs and traditions of the founding generation. By claiming God's judgment on the Temple, Mark signals that it is no longer the cultic center and dwelling of God. Whether this points to the Temple's destruction in 70 CE or reflects the effort to undermine Mark's opponents by challenging their continuing affiliation with the Levitical priesthood associated with it is debatable.

Believers have read Mark as pointing to Jesus's rejection of the Law, table fellowship, purity laws, and Sabbath observance. Mark seems to be signaling to his Gentile audience that some beliefs and traditions of the founding fathers are of human origin and may be debated (2:23–28; 3:4), a position that would not be seen by contemporary Jews as rejection of the Torah. Jesus's rejection of "the traditions of the elders" and his declaration that all foods were clean (7:1–13) would be seen by contemporary Jews as a radical critique, but would not signal to them Jesus's dismissal of the Torah. Mark seems to target adversaries who are Torah-observant and who may have negated table fellowship to Gentiles. Mark's logic seems to be that if Jesus is cast as eating with "toll collectors and sinners" (2:13–17), eating with unwashed hands (7:1–23), and eating unclean foods (7:14–23),[7] the demand of the descendants of the founding fathers that Gentile believers should adhere to their traditions is delegitimated. The evangelist's message to believers experiencing the distress associated with the estrangement from the descendants of the Jewish founders is: don't pay attention to "their" claims as to the inadequacy of our form of belief in Jesus. Jesus's actions prove that they are wrong. They misunderstand his legacy, they never understood it.

The Jewish Responsibility for Jesus's Death

Throughout the Middle East, from the Persian conquests (first half of the sixth century) onward, the removal of local dynasties required their replacement with an alternative local oligarchy that would do the conqueror's bidding. From that point forward high priests were, for the most part, appointed by the conquerors and lost their religious legitimacy in the eyes of most among the local populations. Most of these traitors and collaborators with Persian, Greek, and Roman conquerors were opportunists that collected taxes and ruled the provinces on behalf of foreign oppressors. In Judea this process was accelerated by the Hashmonean usurpation of the high priesthood and its transformation into a quasi-monarchical role. By the time of the Roman conquest, the High Priest had little religious legitimacy among the people. During the turn of the era, the Romans imposed draconian measures against any and all forms of dissent or subversion throughout the empire. Any activity that could potentially challenge the Roman occupation was harshly uprooted. The Roman occupiers did consider messianic groups a security threat and would have persecuted them mercilessly. Jesus's arrival at Jerusalem was staged to create messianic resonances among the populace. It could not but trigger a Roman reaction. Furthermore, "[i]t is noteworthy that in every known case (of) action against the Jerusalem church or its leaders (it) was taken when the reigning high priest was one of those who belonged to the powerful Sadducean family of Annas (Ananus),"[8] a clan of notorious traitors, hated for its ties with the Roman occupiers.

The shift in the identity of the culprits in Jesus's death from the Romans to Mark's perpetrators (The high priests, the scribes and the elders—14:53) and the later gradual expansion of this accusation to a libel about the 'Jewish responsibility for Jesus' death,' would seem to parallel the ever-growing intensification, escalation and expansion of the Pauline antagonism towards the descendants of the founding fathers that we will encounter throughout. Pauline leaders and intellectuals exonerated the Romans and fused and confused the Judean people and the hated traitors that ruled Judea on behalf of foreign occupiers. They created an atmosphere of undifferentiated anti-Jewish incitement that could not but contribute to severing the influence that the descendants of Jesus's disciples and first followers had among Gentiles, ushering their decline as the exclusive guardians and interpreters of Jesus's legacy.

Given this background, Mark's often contradictory and ambivalent positioning is noteworthy. Mark informs us that Jesus's identity as the messiah is both; the trigger for his death sentence (14:61–65; 15:26) and part of God's will and plan (8:31; 9:11–13; 14:21, 27). This position, however, does not restrain Mark from placing at the core of his work a seemingly contradictory claim. Namely, that Jesus's death was not a consequence of Jesus's messianic claims or of Roman charges of sedition, but the result of a conspiracy by wicked priests and scribes who opposed him. Thus, according to Mark, the trial was a Jewish conspiracy to put Jesus to death (14:55). Furthermore, according to Mark, Pilate was a "reluctant" crucifier[9] who did not want to crucify Jesus. Pilate was "forced." He tried to save Jesus, to no avail (15:9–10, 12–14). Pilate, a ruthless and notoriously cruel Roman prefect, is cast by Mark as indecisive and subject to the influence of those ruled by him. The chief priests (11:18; 14:43, 53–65; 15:31–32) and the scribes (1:22; 9:11–13; 11:18, 27; 12:35–40; 14:1, 43, 53; 15:1, 31) are, according to Mark, the main culprits in Jesus's death.[10] Mark's casting of "the crowd" as asking for Jesus's crucifixion (15:12–14) implicates the Jewish people too. By casting Jesus's crucifixion as caused by a Jewish conspiracy, Mark may be attempting to signal to internal and external constituencies that Jesus's followers are not a threat to Roman society. By emphasizing Jewish culpability, he may be attempting to exonerate the Romans of responsibility for Jesus's death, an unsuccessful attempt to alleviate persecution. Mark may have also aimed at addressing concerns among prospective converts, some of which would be reluctant to join a sect at odds with the Roman authorities.

We do not know whether Mark invented or inherited his claim about the involvement of some Jews in Jesus's death. This theme may have originated with him or may reflect an intensification or decontextualization of traditions originating in the anti-Jewish-establishment lore of the descendants of the founding fathers. There is no consensus as to which elements are incorporations or intensifications of previous attitudes and which are original. It is plausible that following Jesus's death, a variety of accusations and rumors may have originated among his followers. Whether fact, rumor, or grounded on a pre-existing Essene template,[11] these accusations may have been part of the folklore of the Jewish followers of Jesus. We know, moreover, that the "Jewish culpability theme" was central only in one of the strands of belief in Jesus that we encounter at the turn of the first century—pointing to a factional origin.

We do not know the demographics of the movement at each decade following Jesus's death. However, we can say with relative certitude that the Markan casting of Jesus's death and resurrection, the intense focus on culpability that this belief entailed, and the libel about the "Jewish responsibility for Jesus' death" were not embraced by all early believers in Jesus. Anticipating the road ahead we may state that to all strands of belief in Jesus, his death was a matter of record, but not the pivotal focus of belief. In sharp contrast to the proto-orthodox view that came to be dominant among later believers in Jesus, the founding faction (focused on Torah observance) would not have considered Jesus's death the focal point of belief. Furthermore, some Gnostics believed that Jesus's death was a positive event signaling the end of his suffering. The Gnostic Gospel of Judas instructs us that, for some early believers in Jesus, Jesus's death was a welcome event. Under most Gnostic belief systems[12] the material world is the dominion of demonic forces and life is to be escaped so that the divine spark within may join the divine realm, where it belongs. Marcion had a different perspective: Jesus's death was divinely ordained (Marc.3.24; 5.6).[13] Marcion's outlook did not need the scaffold of the "Jewish responsibility for Jesus' death" either. That event was ultimately the responsibility of the creator and of the principalities and powers working under him (Marc.3.24; 5.6). Moreover, the Jewish rejection of Jesus was understandable since he was an alien and unprecedented figure who did not fit Jewish messianic expectations (Marc.3; 6).[14]

Significantly, blaming "the Jews" seems to have been expeditious in the Pauline quest to de-Judaize belief in Jesus and to demote the Jewish followers of Jesus. The symbiotic nature of the focus on Jesus's death and on the Jewish responsibility for Jesus's death could not but damage the prospects of the Jewish descendants of Jesus's disciples and first followers to lead the Jesus camp, and did strengthen the Pauline-Lukan drive for ascendancy. Furthermore, of the two possible culprits (the Romans and the Jews), the Romans were the acknowledged executioners of Jesus and were inhumanly oppressive. Significantly, they also offered great prospects in patronage and converts.[15] From 64 CE forward they were also engaged in an ongoing persecution of Gentile believers in Jesus that was to be responsible for the martyrdom of thousands.

The fact that the faction that strove to supersede, demote, and replace the Jewish followers of Jesus as the authoritative custodians and interpreters of Jesus legacy also embraced the libel about the Jewish responsibility for Jesus's death and made it into a central theological motif is intriguingly self-serving. Deciphering why and how this trajectory took place is central to understanding the evolution of the anti-Jewish strand that permeates the canonical and the authoritative lore. This theme and its corollaries will resurface with increasing intensity, and in a variety of configurations, in most of the canonical and authoritative texts. Moreover, the intensity surrounding the "Jewish culpability" theme increases as time passes, a peculiar and intriguing trajectory that seems to parallel the growing anti-Judaic pitch in the Pauline-Lukan lore. Indeed, as the crusade of the Pauline-Lukan faction for ascendancy enters into high gear, so does the de-Judaizing impetus. The anti-Judaic pitch increases as we move from Mark to Matthew, from Luke/Acts to John, and from the canonical to the authoritative texts of the second and third centuries,[16] leading us to suspect that unstated factors and agendas shadow this tradition.

As we travel forward in time we will see that the drive to de-Judaize belief in Jesus resulted in a sequence of escalating anti-Jewish rhetoric: it will engender an ever-growing tradition of emotional and theological anti-Judaism. Each phase in this sequence will incorporate, and intensify previous layers. Standing on the anti-Jewish-establishment lore of the Jewish founding fathers, Mark crafts a rendition of Jesus's ministry that includes the denigration and vilification of those chosen by Jesus to be the guardians of his legacy; Mark's Jesus is misunderstood by his disciples, his family, and by fellow Jews. Mark also plants the seeds for the future expansion of blame onto all Jews (15:12–14).

The emergence of an almost perfect match between the agenda of the Pauline-Lukan faction (the demotion of the Jewish followers of Jesus and the de-Judaizing of the Jesus tradition) and theology (the focus on Jesus's death and on the Jewish responsibility for it) is intriguing. Is it a coincidence that the group that staged the takeover and the de-Judaizing of belief in Jesus was also the group that embraced wholeheartedly the theme of the Jewish responsibility for Jesus's death and made it a central theological tenet? Did the focus on Jesus's death nurture attitudes that enabled and facilitated the de-Judaizing drive? Or was it the other way around?

My Mark

Mark may have been the first Gentile to use Jesus's life as a platform to claim a "truer" understanding of Jesus's ministry and legacy vis-à-vis the views of the Jewish founding fathers. Articulated long before the end of the mission to the Jews,[17] the Markan "rejection" of Jesus by "the Jews" is an anachronism and one of the clues to his unstated agendas. Thus, Mark's casting of Jesus as rejected by the Jews may tell us more about the author's goals and about the Jesus movement at the end of the first century—than about Jesus's ministry. Mark's peculiar texture has led scholars to suspect that his anti-Jewish bent originates in conflicts and tensions that afflicted the movement decades after Jesus's death. It seems that tensions between Gentile and Jewish followers intensified as time passed, and that the anti-Jewish escalation reflects this trajectory.

Mark addresses a community of Gentiles and conveys the following message: we are true and rightful followers of Jesus. Don't let anyone cast any doubt on your legitimacy as believers in Jesus. Despite the fact that "the Jews" (i.e., the Jewish followers of Jesus) are the descendants of Jesus's disciples and first followers—they do not understand the true meaning of Jesus's ministry. Nor did their ancestors; the disciples. The disciples not only misunderstood Jesus's true identity and message, they abandoned and betrayed him at the moment of his greatest need. They have forfeited any prerogatives they may have had. Whatever they say you should do is no longer valid or necessary. We have the true and right understanding of Jesus's legacy, and we are his rightful followers. The Jewish faction interprets Jesus's life and legacy differently than us due to the fact that Jesus's ministry was deliberately hidden. The disciples did not realize the true nature of his mission, "they did not understand." The people closest to him, his family, his disciples, his neighbors, and fellow Jews, misunderstood who he was and what was the true meaning of his life and legacy. We are the true guardians of his heritage.

What is it that the disciples, who shared Jesus's ministry as well as his ethnicity, religion, and socio-cultural background, did not understand? What is it that Mark, who did not know Jesus and whose background and life experience were alien to his, did know that his disciples did not? Unfortunately, Mark does not present his "bonafides"; he does not disclose the source of his detailed knowledge of the events. It seems that what the disciples "did not understand" is not belief in Jesus, but Mark's version of it. Mark is our first hint that the Gospel tradition shadows the embryonic stages of a Gentile challenge to the authority and to the legitimacy of the descendants of Jesus's disciples and first followers as the exclusive guardians and interpreters of his legacy. As we progress we will accumulate corroborating clues on this effort, although (for the most part) during the canonical era it seems to have been put forward in implied and veiled formats. Whether intended to open the door to Gentiles as rightful followers of Jesus or aimed at eroding the authority of the descendants of the founding fathers and furthering the de-Judaizing of belief in Jesus, Mark's Gospel paved the road for both. Under skeptical scrutiny, the Markan disciples that did not understand Jesus's ministry and abandoned him in his moment of need may emerge as a clever move to explain to recent Gentile converts the conundrum posed by the rejection of the beliefs and traditions espoused by Jesus and by those chosen by him to be the custodians of his legacy.

As stated previously, and as it pertains to the evolution of the anti-Jewish strand, we can identify three Markan legacies:

1. Jesus the unacknowledged messiah, a stranger among his family, his friends, and followers—an alien among fellow Israelites.
2. The denigration and vilification of the disciples, Torah observance, purity law, dietary law, the temple, and Sabbath observance.
3. The exoneration of the Romans and culpability of the high priests, the scribes and the elders.

This repertoire will be expanded upon by later leaders and intellectuals in their quest to de-Judaize belief in Jesus. However, although Mark is the cornerstone of the Synoptic edifice, he does not deploy the intense anti-Jewish invective of later writers. Mark's tone and demeanor are those of a community leader that attempts to craft a foundational saga of Jesus ministry that may bestow recognition and respectability on Gentiles experiencing the distress and anxiety engendered by the estrangement from the descendants of the founding fathers. The rhetorical aim of Mark is to shore-up Gentiles undergoing this painful estrangement and to articulate a rationale for it. Mark's writing craft is superb. Mark's foundational saga of Jesus's ministry signals to his Gentile audience that their being non-Torah observant does not impede their being rightful followers of Jesus. By casting Jesus as defying traditional identity markers of Judaism, Mark signals that demands on Gentiles, by some among the descendants of Jesus's disciples and first followers, to observe the Torah and to embrace a Jewish lifestyle are contrary to Jesus's own actions and deeds. Mark is moderate when compared to Matthew, Luke, and John. The rhetorical demons are still under control. In Mark the Gentiles are not yet YHWH's new favorites and the Israelites are not yet an apostate people. Furthermore, in Mark, "The Jews" occurs only in the non-Jewish designation "King of the Jews" (15:2, 9, 12, 18, and 26) and in 7:3 where "all the Jews" signals Mark's unfamiliarity with Jewish rituals. None of these instances are derogatory of Judaism. It is not obvious whether Mark weighed alternative renditions against specific goals. However, the intricacy and the delicate balancing of the apparent intended messages suggest, to me, thoughtful intent.

As we move forward in time, the main Markan themes will recur and resurface in varying guises and with increasing intensity throughout the emerging tradition. We will concentrate our attention on those elements, motifs, and themes that seem to reflect the concerns and the agendas of the authors of the canonical texts. We will use these texts to attempt to decipher what were the circumstances that brought about the composition of this unique literature. To what extent Mark's basic themes and story line, on which the Gospels according to Matthew and Luke elaborated, are historical renditions or are reflective of the confrontation between Jewish and non-Jewish followers of Jesus will be at the core of our quest.

Chapter 5

The Anti-Judaic Strand in Matthew: The Saga of the Jewish Followers of Jesus

Introduction

The emergence of Gentile forms of belief in Jesus did challenge the status of the descendants of Jesus's disciples and first followers as the exclusive interpreters of his legacy. The Jesus movement was becoming an unprecedented mix of Jews and Gentiles that threatened the Judean ethnic and religious identity markers. By the end of the first century the descendants of Jesus's disciples and first followers[1] may have become a minority in the Jesus movement and a problematic sect within Judaism. There is great urgency and an agonizing undertow in the Gospel according to Matthew.[2] Among the Synoptics, Matthew is simultaneously the most anti-Judaic and the most knowledgeable about Jewish traditions.[3] Its location at the beginning of the canon creates a potent anti-Jewish start. Many of Matthew's stories stand on Mark. Variations from Mark may be indicative of setting and intent. In Matthew the attacks on the Judean authorities intensify. The chief priests and elders are in power (16:21; 21:23; 26:3, 47; 27:1, 3, 12, 20; 28:11–12). Scribes and Pharisees are associated with the synagogues and tend to be antagonists in disputes over the law (3:7; 5:20; 6:1–18; 15:1–20; 19:3; 21:33–46; 22:15; 23:13– 33).[4] Matthew's polemic is mostly aimed at the leadership, especially the Pharisees, but he also draws his opponents' followers into his polemic (10:12–15, 20–24; 26:57; 27:24– 25). The central role that the Pharisees play as the archenemies in Matthew contrasts sharply with the marginal role they play in Jewish literature and may be indicative of their being polemical proxies. An intriguing possibility is that the Pharisees stand in as proxies for the descendants of the founders in the Gentile quest to de-Judaize belief in Jesus and to demote the Jewish leadership. Overall, the emphasis is on increased anti-Jewish sentiment and on variation from Mark.[5] Matthew tends to bundle all "figures of authority" and insinuates a monolithic Jewish opposition to Jesus. Matthew also broadens the blame: "all the people" take the responsibility for condemning Jesus to death. There is increased and widened malevolence in Matthew's picture (Judas's 30 pieces of silver, the field of blood, Pilate's wife dream, and most importantly—the first unequivocal articulation of Jewish collective responsibility).[6] For Jewish readers large segments of Matthew (5, 6, and 23) are unacceptable, disconcerting, and distressing, if read literally.[7]

Authorship and Setting

Stendahl, probing the similarity between the Matthean and Qumranian use of scripture, concluded that the Gospel of Matthew was the product of a school.[8] Echoing this conclusion "a consensus that the Matthean community went through several stages of interaction with the Jewish communities close to it, and that these stages have left fossils in the strata of tradition and redaction may be in place."[9] The canonical Matthew is peculiar among the Synoptic Gospels in that it contains an odd mixture of themes and emphases that do not fit later orthodox views. The Matthean enigma stems from the coexistence of Markan themes (culpability of the Jews, exoneration of the Romans, and an enhanced Passion Narrative), anti-Pauline themes (strict Torah observance 5:17–20, 22:35–40, and 23:2–3), anti-Jewish-establishment rhetoric (attacks on Judean figures of authority 16:21; 21:23; 26:3, 47; 27:1, 3, 12, 20; 28:11–12),[10] and socially subversive motifs (10:35–37).[11] Given the overall trajectory of increasing anti-Jewish sentiment and the growing gentile ascendancy within the movement, Matthew's defense of Torah observance is most intriguing. Whereas, according to the majority of scholars, Gentiles authored Mark and Luke, Matthew defies classification.[12] Tradition (Irenaeus and Eusebius) asserts that the original text of Matthew was written in Hebrew. Others have supported Arameic as the original language of the earliest strata.

Was Matthew authored within one community that underwent change and transformation? Or, did a later Gentile community incorporate earlier traditions originating among the Jewish founders and containing pro-Torah observance elements that could not be subverted? If the canonical Matthew is an integral text authored by a community of Jewish followers of Jesus, how does a text authored by Gentile believers (Mark) become authoritative to descendants of the Jewish founders, an apparent reversal in the flow of theological legitimacy?[13] Those that argue for a proto-Matthean[14] text authored by a community of Jewish followers of Jesus that was appropriated by a later and Gentile community, provide a plausible explanation for this Matthean enigma.

Ferdinand Christian Baur (1847) first proposed the existence of a proto-Matthew. Flusser, somewhat in the footsteps of Bauer, has claimed a non-Greek original, a proto-Matthew. More importantly, he claimed that the non-Greek sections of the text do not contain anti-Judaic elements and that the polemical sections are all distinguishable as later and Greek in origin.[15] In proto-Matthew, the new people of God are the Jewish followers of Jesus. Torah observance, the Law, and the prophets are not abolished, they are embraced. Proto-Matthew is firmly anchored in Judaism. Jesus brings salvation and renewal to Israel. For the proto-Matthean writer, a Jewish follower of Jesus, the Messiah would be an exalted human, not a divine savior. Written at a time when the mission to the Jews was only a couple of decades old, proto-Matthew's rhetoric is reflective of a strident dispute among Jews about Jesus messiahship, a legitimate and recurring question that has surfaced throughout Jewish history whenever claimants to messianic status emerge.

Matthew and Judaism

Using the authoritative texts of preceding cultures as templates to fashion new religious narratives is an ancient technique deployed to vest contemporaneous protagonists with the legitimacy and the authority of ancient traditions and figures. The biblical flood story, the Moses infancy story, the Jesus Passion, and Matthew's Jesus seem to have been molded on pre-existent religious lore (the Gilgamesh Epic, the legend of Sargon II of Akkad, Israelite traditions,[16] and the Moses story, respectively). In the canonical Matthew Jesus is cast as mirroring Moses,[17] the towering Jewish figure. Matthew's infancy narratives (Matt. 1:18–2:22) and Jesus's earlier ministry are emulations of Moses's life story. Jesus is no longer Mark's unrecognized Messiah. In Matthew, Jesus is the clear and obvious fulfillment of Jewish messianic expectations. Proto-Matthew's teachings about Jesus are firmly rooted in Jewish traditions.[18]

Proto-Matthew also seems to be among the earliest originators of the predictive nature of the "Old Testament" and of prophecy fulfilled (4:14; 8:17; 13:14, 35; 21:4; 26:54), a theme that will be appropriated by Lukan authors in their quest to de-Judaize belief in Jesus and will take center stage in Barnabas and in the Epistle to the Hebrews. In proto-Matthew, followers of Jesus are cast as perfect Jews, Jesus as the most Jewish of preachers:

> Think not that I have come to abolish the law and the prophets; I have come not to abolish them but to fulfill them. (Matt. 5:17)

> Whoever then relaxes one of the least of these commandments and teaches men so, shall be called least in the kingdom of heaven; but he who does them and teaches them shall be called great in the kingdom of heaven. (Matt. 5:19)

> For I tell you, unless your righteousness exceeds that of the scribes and Pharisees, you will never enter the kingdom of heaven. (Matt. 5:20)

> He answered, I was sent only to the lost sheep of the house of Israel. (Matt. 15:24)

It seems that wherever the context reflects a debate among Jews, or when Jesus is seen as the realization/fulfillment of Jewish expectations and traditions—we may be facing traces of the lore of the Jewish founders (Jesus the Messiah, son of Abraham and David [1:1–17; 5:17–20; 21:33–46) or Jesus the new Moses [l:18–2:23; 5:1–2; 8:1–9:34; 11:25–30; 17:2–9; 28:16–20]. Moreover, due to their being diametrically opposed to the de-Judaizing thrust of the Synoptics, calls to Torah observance in Matthew are our best indicators of the incorporation-appropriation of a proto-Matthean text into the canonical version. Some scholars consider that pro-Torah observance segments in Matthew may be true representations of Jesus's views, on the grounds that they go counter to the anti-Jewish tendency otherwise apparent in the canonical Gospels. Apparently, these verses represented old and revered traditions that could not be easily erased; a Jewish proto-Matthew.

Most scholars support the integrity of the canonical version.[19] According to Saldarini, a supporter of an integral text, Matthew's discussions of Jewish law, customs, and practices fit within the acceptable range of debates in first-century Judaism. Saldarini's Matthew defends his positions with sophisticated arguments comprehensible to the Jewish community, and he sees himself as an authoritative teacher within the Jewish community, not as the spokesperson for a new religion.[20] However, Saldarini's integral text comes at the cost of assigning Jewish authorship to segments that denigrate the disciples, the ancestors of Saldarini's designated authors—creating a significant conundrum. It also comes at the cost of assigning Jewish authorship to segments that contain condemnations of the Jewish people that would be unacceptable to any Jew, to the inclusion of the descendants of the Jewish founders. Those supportive of an integral and coherent Matthew face the need to harmonize Matthew's dissonant messages about the disciples and about Judaism.[21]

The footprints of the proto-Matthean layer, if identified, presented, taught, and read as an example of Judean anti-Jewish-establishment rhetoric (without the imposition of later superssesional and/or orthodox connotations or resonances), would be a Qumran-like sectarian text that should not be part of our conversation about the anti-Jewish strand. However, its appropriation-incorporation into the canonical text and the reading of the canonical Matthew as an integral Pauline-orthodox text does place the canonical Matthew at the center of our concern.

Matthew's Anti-Judaic Rhetoric

"You brood of vipers! How can you speak good, when you are evil? For out of the abundance of the heart the mouth speaks" (Matt. 12:34). The Jews are accused of Jesus's crucifixion and damned for eternity (Matt. 23–24:33–36). The Jews assume the guilt for the death of Jesus (Matt. 27:25–26). In the parable of the weeds the Jews are demonized, they are "sons of the evil one." "The weeds are the sons of the evil one, and the enemy who sowed them is the devil" (Matt. 13:38–39). The canonical Matthew seems to draw from two pre-existent streams of anti-Judaic sentiment: the anti-Jewish-establishment tradition of the founding faction (proto-Matthew) and the Pauline-Markan rejection of the beliefs and traditions of the founding fathers. Although the canonical Matthew may feel anti-Jewish to a twenty-first-century literal reader, significant portions seem to originate among the Jewish followers of Jesus and may reflect their sectarian posturing toward the Judean establishment. Matthew's pro-Torah observance segments, and Jesus's casting as emulating Moses, stand in sharp contrast to the significant anti-Judaic bent elsewhere in the text. The seemingly contradictory juxtaposition of pro-Jewish and anti-Jewish elements may indicate a situation where the exaltation of Torah observance is simultaneous with rejection of mainstream Judaism, a traditional Jewish sectarian posture.

Reading Matthew as an integral text creates dramatic circumstances: family and community links are being severed. The way back is being shut. The descendants of the founding fathers may preserve their Jewish identity but their choice is clear: sinfulness and eternal damnation among the Jews, or salvation among non-Jews. Several enigmatic passages that may fit this context:

Matthew 12:30—He who is not with me is against me, and he who does not gather with me scatters.

Matthew 10:22—and you will be hated by all for my name's sake. But he who endures to the end will be saved.

Matthew 10:35—For I have come to set a man against his father, and a daughter against her mother, and a daughter-in-law against her mother-in-law.

Matthew 10:36—And a man's foes will be those of his own household.

Matthew 10:37—He who loves father or mother more than me is not worthy of me; and he who loves son or daughter more than me is not worthy of me.

In the context of an integral text, these extreme utterances must be connected to critical circumstances. Even if (as argued by some) these segments reflect an eschatological outlook, the intense emotional pitch points to extraordinary conditions. Families and communities are being torn apart. Members are told to find solace in Jesus's anticipation of their circumstances. The writer is saying to followers of Jesus of Jewish origin: Jesus foretold your suffering; this is all part of the divine plan. Jesus is the Jewish messiah who fulfills the Jewish scriptures. You cannot go back. If necessary, you must leave your community, your family, and your past.[22]

A reading of Matthew as a layered text yields very different insights. The dispute as to which Jews were the true Israel, those who believed in Jesus or those who rejected him,[23] would reflect the sectarian anti-Jewish-establishment tradition of a proto-Matthean community. Proto-Matthew would address an audience of followers of Jesus of Jewish origin, and would be aimed at segregating the community from establishment Judaism, while calling for strict Torah observance. According to Wilson the break was not yet a clean one, since the obsession with Jewish matters and the polemic against other Jews show that the ties were still strong. Oversimplifying for the sake of clarity, we may say that when the Synoptics attack specific Jewish groups or individual Judean figures of authority, when Israel is deemed sinful and unrepentant, when Israel is threatened with the loss of God's favor—we have a good chance that we are looking at residues of a Jewish proto-Matthew, in a tradition edited-incorporated-appropriated-subverted by later Gentile authors, editors, and compilers. The conflict between the proto-Matthean group and other Jews suggests that the larger community sees this group as deviant. Proto-Matthew's posture against his opponents and their positions is typical of Jewish sectarians. His accusations of hypocrisy against his opponents are an attack on their integrity. In matters of substance proto-Matthew claims the high moral ground. By stressing love, mercy, justice, and faith, the text implies that the community's opponents neglect or oppose these fundamental principles of biblical life and theology. Needless to say, the text does not give a fair picture of proto-Matthew's opponents, but testifies to the intensity of the struggle.

A Gentile Editor/Compiler

Scholars differ on the socio-theological background that brought about the creation of a canonical text in which a Jewish proto-Matthew, Q, Mark, and some instances of pro-Gentile redaction are identifiable. Whereas proto-Matthew's intense rhetoric against the Judean establishment is a Qumran-like call to all Jews to recognize Jesus as the Messiah of the Jewish tradition, the canonical editor/compiler created a complex document that stands on a layered trajectory. The Gentile author/compiler of the final text may have also added hints on the inclusion of Gentiles in God's plan: the Magi (2:1–12), the centurion at the cross (27:54), the nations (28:16–20), the Great Commission (21:33–46; 24:14, 28:16–20, 31) and possibly 8:5–13; 15:21–28.

Obviously, the Gentile editor/compiler that incorporated-appropriated the Proto-Matthean anti-Jewish-establishment rhetoric embedded in the parent community's lore, could not anticipate the long-term implications of his actions. However, the unintended consequences of this clever move were vast and horrific. As he combined the Markan text, Q, and the harsh proto-Matthean anti-Jewish-establishment rhetoric of the founding fathers he had a wide spectrum of possible choices. His selection of ingredients and their proportions provide us some clues as to his mindset and intentions. Although crafted in the context of a Gentile challenge to the establishment of the Jesus movement, the canonical text was to be read by later believers from within a Pauline-orthodox hermeneutic and was interpreted throughout the centuries as sanctioning and sanctifying anti-Jewish attitudes. By incorporating the proto-Matthean diatribe against establishment-Judaism without clarifying its original context, the author/compiler of the canonical text created a particular mix that, when read as an integral text, conveys an incendiary anti-Jewish message. Thus, proto-Matthean lore that argued that the Jewish followers of Jesus were the new people of God (21:43) was subverted by later Gentiles to claim their right to being the newer people of God and to marginalize all Jews, to the inclusion of the descendants of the founding fathers. From the same quarry: the suspension of national privilege (21:43), a staple Judean sectarian warning against Jewish adversaries, was subverted to claim the unqualified loss of God's favor by the Jewish people.

As the arguments of Jewish sectarians against establishment-Judaism were appropriated-incorporated by Gentiles intent on de-Judaizing belief in Jesus, they became tools in the marginalization of the Jewish faction. Whether intended or accidental, the incorporation of the piercing proto-Matthew into the final text created an anti-Jewish climate that could not but weaken the founding faction. Furthermore, the reading of the anti-Jewish-establishment lore of the early Jewish followers of Jesus through the Pauline-Lukan lens could not but bring about the perception of a conflict between "Judaism" and "Christianity." These phenomena will be at the center of our journey and will preoccupy us throughout. Eventually, Pauline believers in Jesus embraced Matthew as authoritative and read this text as "Christian," despite its call for strict Torah observance and ambiguity regarding the stance of proto-Matthew toward the inclusion of Gentiles.[24] The Pauline orientation of most of the texts included in the New Testament

and dogmatic reading did camouflage and mitigate the anti-Pauline outlook of Proto-Matthew.

My Matthew

I have suggested that the survival of pro-Torah and anti-Pauline elements may
indicate that proto-Matthew had become authoritative before the Pauline
ascendancy, and could not be rejected, nor fully re-edited to comply with
the Pauline-Lukan emerging narrative. Indeed, the pro-Torah segments in
Matthew and in the Epistle of James provide us unique windows into the
mindset of the descendants of Jesus's disciples and first followers. However, the
canonical Matthew also contains elements that cannot be said to originate with
followers of Jesus of Jewish origin. This would indicate that proto-Matthew
migrated from a community of Jewish followers of Jesus to a community of
Gentile believers. A Gentile group that incorporated pre-existing materials, to
the inclusion of Mark, proto-Matthew, and the Q source, may have compiled
the canonical Matthew. This argument is based on the following:

1. If the community that produced the final version of Matthew included
   sons and grandsons of the Jewish founders, the denigration and vilification of the disciples (their ancestors) cannot be assumed to originate
   with them.[25] This observation is reinforced by the consensus that, in
   the ancient Middle-East, denigration of the ancestors of adversaries
   and enemies is intentional and reflects later conflicts and agendas.[26]
2. The final text expands Mark's circle of those responsible for Jesus's
   death to the Jewish people. Matthew 27 would be unacceptable to any
   Jew, follower of Jesus or not. Even those followers of Jesus of Jewish
   origin that may have come to believe that the Roman appointed traitors, collaborators, and minions paraded by the canonical Gospels as
   "Jewish authorities"—may have acquiesced or collaborated in Jesus's
   death—would not have authored such an expansive accusation.
3. Exoneration of the Romans is a related but separate component of
   the author's positioning. The idea that the descendants of the founding fathers would participate in exonerating hated conquerors and
   oppressors can only originate in a later, and Gentile, perspective.[27]
4. Since Mark is acknowledged by most scholars as earlier and of Gentile
   provenance, how would his anti-Judaic passion narrative end up in
   the sacred texts of a community of followers of Jesus of Jewish origin?
   This migration seems to violate the expected flow of beliefs from the
   older and authoritative lore of the founding group, to the still-evolving
   views of Gentile believers in Jesus. Under what circumstances would
   the descendants of the founding fathers, who saw themselves as the

keepers and inheritors of Jesus's ministry and legacy, incorporate elements from Mark—a later, adversarial, and Gentile interpretation of Jesus's legacy? The implausibility of this countergravitational flow seems to support the existence of a Jewish proto-Matthew that was incorporated by a later Gentile community into its lore.[28]

Thus, in my view, the arguments enumerated here, and the odd mixture of Markan and anti-Pauline themes cannot be reconciled with a whole and integral Matthew.[29] As I have argued earlier, a single author would have to be a staunch observant of the Torah who would embrace the disparagement of his biological and theological ancestors, the exoneration of the Romans, and the culpability of all Jews—an unlikely combination.

Nonetheless, I can visualize one scenario for a whole and integral text. If the final author/editor is a Gentile who addresses an audience of Gentile sympathizers with the founding faction in an attempt to sever the affinity between them and the descendants of Jesus's disciples and first followers, the text could originate from a single author that combined various sources to address this peculiar target audience and this particular purpose. This audience, non-Jewish but close to the descendants of Jesus's disciples and first followers, could be the recipient of the dissonant messages enumerated earlier.

If the canonical Matthew is the product of the incorporation of a proto-Matthew by a later and Gentile community of believers in Jesus, it may be the earliest instance of the incorporation-appropriation of the heritage of the descendants of Jesus's disciples and first followers into Gentile dominated traditions, a trend that will intensify thereafter. This layered Matthew would explain the odd coexistence of the Pauline-Markan hallmarks with pro-Torah themes and motifs, including some of the most enigmatic thematic textures and some of the more baffling verses of the New Testament. Early Gentile authors and compilers attempted to grapple with the fact that belief in Jesus was originally Jewish and that, originally, Gentile forms of belief in Jesus represented an anti-establishment element within the Jesus movement. The editor/compiler of the Matthean canonical text is part of the Synoptic chain that argues, in a subdued and almost covert manner, against the imposition of the beliefs and traditions of the founding fathers on Gentile converts as a precondition to being considered rightful followers of Jesus. Thus, the appropriation/incorporation of the anti-Jewish-establishment invective of the Jewish founders seems to be designed to carry a complex agenda that argues for the recognition of a Gentile form of belief in Jesus as a valid dispensation. At the hands of the Gentile editor/complier and assisted by the Markan material, the proto-Matthean claim that rejection of Jesus's messiaship is rejection of God's salvation and incurs God's judgment, an argument among Jews, morphs into hints that that rejection of the author's Gentile form of belief in Jesus is tantamount to rejection of God's salvation and incurs God's judgment—on all Jews, to the inclusion of the Jewish followers of Jesus. In the final text we encounter in an embryonic form the tools that will bring about the de-Judaizing of belief in Jesus and the demotion of the descendants of Jesus's disciples and first followers from their status as the guardians of Jesus's legacy: the disciples that "did not understand" (therefore the Jewish followers of Jesus do not understand Jesus's legacy) the Jewish loss of God's favor (therefore the founding faction cannot claim to be the new people of God) and the "Jewish" responsibility for Jesus's death (an expansion of the Markan culprits to include all Jews).

The destiny of the proto-Matthean Jewish followers of Jesus was tragic and ironic. Members of the proto-Matthean community that found themselves estranged from Judaism did find themselves, within two–three generations, at the epicenter of a religious struggle that engulfed the Jesus movement during the next two hundred years. At the end of this strife, their identity, and lore sequestered and their Torah vilified and superseded, they will become marginal, isolated, and inconsequential. The irony here is Machiavellian: some among the descendants of the Jewish founders, whose beliefs were the closest to those of Jesus and his disciples, may have been lured away from Judaism by the Matthean promise to fulfill the Torah. Within a generation or two, Gentile followers of Paul will oppose, denigrate, and eventually marginalize and demote them, on the grounds that *their* practices were heretical.[30]

Chapter 6

The Anti-Judaic Strand in Luke/Acts: Yearning for Respectability

Introduction

> In as much as many have undertaken to compile a narrative of the things which have been accomplished among us, just as they were delivered to us by those who from the beginning were eyewitnesses and ministers of the word, it seemed good to me also, having followed all things closely for some time past, to write an orderly account for you, most excellent Theoph'ilus, that you may know the truth concerning the things of which you have been informed. (Luke 1:1–4).

Why did the author(s) of the Gospel according to Luke consider that a new telling of the short history of belief in Jesus was necessary? Who's telling needed correction? Mark's? Matthew's? Both?

Most scholars have concluded that the Gospel of Luke and the book of Acts were authored during the second–third decade following the destruction of The Temple (70 CE). A minority[1] supports authorship during the first decades of the second century.[2] Whereas during the later decades of the first century the Jesus movement was torn by tensions between Gentiles and the descendants of the founding fathers, during the first decades of the second century a multilateral socio-theological confrontation dominates the period. Thus, if the later date is embraced, the protagonists impacting the author's world could include not only the Jewish faction and their Gentile Sympathizers but the various Gentile factions that surfaced following the success of the Pauline and the Gnostic missions to the Gentiles.

The Jewish Faction and Luke/Acts

We have seen that Mark's denigration and vilification of the disciples may signal the embryonic stages of Gentile opposition to the imposition of the beliefs and traditions of the Jewish founders of the Jesus movement and the opposition to their status as the exclusive interpreters of Jesus's legacy. The status of the descendants of Jesus's disciples and first followers as the guardians and interpreters of Jesus's legacy seems to have been a central, although unstated, concern for Luke/Acts. Compared with what is to come during the second century, the anti-Judaic pitch in Luke/Acts is relatively restrained. Jesus's subversive social teachings, originating in the founding faction, are downplayed. Significantly, Luke continues the Markan framing of the events as "the rejection of Jesus by the Jews" at a time when the mission to the Jews was ongoing and followers of Jesus of Jewish origin were active among fellow Jews. At the time, a definitive end of the mission to the Jews was still in the future, an outcome unknown to the protagonists. This Synoptic misrepresentation became later on an ingrained misperception among later believers due to the fact that the mission to the Jews did eventually die out and due to the effort to erase the drive to de-Judaize belief in Jesus.

Similar to the other Synoptics, the Luke/Acts narrative puts forward, in narrative form, the claim of Gentiles to the guardianship of Jesus's legacy. The author of Luke/Acts refined the Markan myth of origins: he transfers the mantle of leadership and of legitimacy from the descendants of the Jewish founders to the Pauline-Lukan faction, without calling attention to the deep implications of this shift. Paul's maverick and controversial ministry is legitimized by casting Paul as submissive to James's authority. The Roman maxims of order, hierarchy, continuity, antiquity, and legitimacy are catered to. The disciples and Jesus's followers, subtly denigrated by Mark and Matthew, enjoy "slightly better press."[3] Luke/Acts give us non-Jewish believers in Jesus as the rightful heirs of Jesus's ministry and legacy and a submissive and Roman-friendly Jesus movement. The Lukan narrative signals the focus of 'Christianity' (i.e., the Pauline mission) on Rome. It faces forward, toward a Roman future.

Some scholars consider Luke to be the culmination of the anti-Jewish motif in the Synoptics. According to others, the Jewish people fare a bit better than in other canonical texts. We find scholars at both ends of a spectrum: those impressed by Luke's leniency[4] and others impressed by his anti-Judaic stance.[5] Some identify segments in Luke/Acts that seem to preserve non-anti-Judaic attitudes toward the Pharisees and toward the Jewish people. Given the Roman veneration for legitimacy, ancestry, and antiquity, the better Jewish imagery that some scholars detect in Luke/Acts may be part of a self-serving presentation. Strangely, and anticipating

future developments, in Luke/Acts the rejection of the beliefs of the founding fathers is embedded in a claim to harmony with Jewish traditions.[6]
However, Luke's "continuation" with Judaism[7] is no continuity at all. The
descendants of the founders are offered the olive branch of continuity with
the caveat of self-negation. The Lukan positioning vis-à-vis Judaism seems
to be a public relations effort of self-promotion, not an articulation of a
less anti-Judaic theological stance. The improvement is therefore illusory;
it disguises a profound negation, deployed in a more sophisticated manner.
That said, in Luke/Acts the Pauline rejection of Judaism (i.e., worldview
of the descendants of the Jewish founders) does not come from the gut.
Whereas the author of the canonical Matthew incorporated-appropriated
the anti-Jewish-establishment focus of the Jewish followers of Jesus and fashioned an intense and resentful text, the Lukan author is seemingly deliber-
ate and cerebral—less visceral.[8] Among the Synoptics, Luke/Acts brings the
anti-Jewish theme to new temporary heights by widening its scope: "Jews"
had tried to kill Jesus prior to his crucifixion (4:28–29). Scribes, elders, and
Pharisees plotted against Jesus all along (6:7, 11, and 9).[9] The enemies of
Jesus are satanic (10:18–19). Contrary to Mark and Matthew, the people
who arrest Jesus are Jewish (22:52–53). Pilate pronounces Jesus innocent
three times and three times "the Jews" demand his execution.

Marcion and Luke/Acts

Similar to the Pauline-Lukan faction, Marcion understood himself to
be "the" true interpreter of Paul's legacy. However, contrary to his opponents' reject-but-appropriate approach, Marcion advocated a complete
and radical rejection of any affiliation with the legacy of the founding faction,[10] and strived for a thorough de-Judaizing of belief in Jesus. Both the
Pauline-Lukan and the Pauline-Marcionites attempted to erode and discredit the legitimacy of the descendants of Jesus's disciples and first followers as the exclusive custodians of Jesus's legacy. However, whereas the
Pauline-Lukan supported appropriation-supersession, Pauline-Marcionites
supported rejection-separation. It seems that Marcion presented a formidable challenge to those who opposed his theology and practices. His opponents made extraordinary efforts to combat his influence and attack his
theology. Marcion's opponents understood that the very definition of belief
in Jesus was at stake.
    While most scholars support a first-century date of authorship, a minor-
ity view by Knox-Tyson-Townsend[11] advocates a second-century date and
sees Luke/Acts as reflective of an effort to address the Marcionite threat.
John Knox's analysis of Acts suggests that the Acts rendition of Paul was
aimed at rescuing the Pauline legacy from Marcion's appeal.[12]According to

Knox, Paul's letters are supportive of Marcion's theology and they do suggest, as Marcion claimed, that Paul was the only apostle and that he was completely independent of the group in Jerusalem. Knox also suggests that the Luke/Acts author may have reached the conclusion that unless provided with a proper commentary, Paul's letters would lead readers to Marcion's camp. Knox maintained that to accept Paul and at the same time repudiate Marcion "meant to affirm with all possible vigor that the Apostle to the Gentiles, far from being independent of the Twelve, had acknowledged their authority, had been gladly accredited by them, and had worked obediently and loyally under their direction." However, since Paul's letters gave only scant support to this view, "some book which, without reducing or disparaging Paul, subordinated him to the Twelve was obviously required."[13] That, according to Knox, is the intent of the Luke/Acts narrative. For Tyson, Luke/Acts are early chapters in the response to Marcion and played a major role in what turned out to be a defining struggle among competing second-century Gentile forms of belief in Jesus.[14] While supportive of Knox, Tyson wrestled with the fact that there are no explicit references to the Marcionite controversy in Luke/Acts and that it avoids attacking Marcion openly. Townsend provided further support to the Knox-Tyson-Townsend view by pointing out that only after 170 CE we find definite citations and allusions to Luke/Acts, that there is no conclusive evidence that Luke/Acts was written in the first century, and that citations and allusions to the Gospel of Luke do not require us to date the canonical version before *ca.* 120–125 CE.[15]

If the Knox-Tyson-Townsend view is correct, the author(s) of Luke/Acts may have reacted to Marcion's growing success by fashioning a narrative that does not seem to address the Marcionite opposition overtly. Instead, it showcases the Lukan outlook as if authoritative and unchallenged— two hundred years before the actual triumph of orthodoxy. Significantly, by supporting the existence of a confrontation among various forms of belief in Jesus, the Knox-Tyson-Townsend reading would make Luke/Acts a precursor of themes that loom large in the next section, and are center stage in this monograph. Furthermore, Tyson's observation that Luke/Acts avoids attacking Marcion openly is supportive of my suggestions on the modus operandi of the Pauline-Lukan faction in its struggle with the founding fathers and their descendants. In both fronts the Pauline-Lukan seem to have fashioned strategies that attempted to bypass and avoid direct textual confrontation with their adversaries. It would appear that as the Pauline-Marcionite threat emerged, the Pauline-Lukan faction used the strategy they had previously deployed against the descendants of Jesus's disciples and first followers. In both conflicts they seem to have created narratives where conflict is insinuated but not explicitly stated, where adversaries are dealt with by ignoring them, and where the Lukan account is showcased as the only legitimate and authoritative version. It is noteworthy that, at the time of authorship, the decline of the Pauline-Marcionites, the Gnostics, and of the mission to the Jews were centuries away and unknown to the participants.

Thus, somewhat surprisingly, my suspicions about the modus operandi of the Pauline-Lukan faction in its confrontation with the descendants of the founding fathers, and the Knox-Tyson-Townsend perspective on Luke-Acts, turn out to be mutually supportive. Furthermore, Knox's analysis of Paul's relationship with the Jerusalem leadership is compatible with "my Paul." Thus, Luke/Acts may emerge as an effort to address three concerns that may have dominated the socio-theological context of its authorship:

1. The influence of the Jewish faction—the continuing Gentile struggle against the influence of the descendants of Jesus's disciples and first followers, the original guardians and interpreters of Jesus's legacy.
2. Marcion's influence—the continuing struggle against Marcion's theology[16] and ecclesiastical organization.
3. Respectability and legitimacy—increasing Roman persecution of Gentile believers in Jesus and theological chaos and dissent required a narrative that would bestow respectability and legitimacy on Pauline communities.

Respectability and Legitimacy

The Lukan saga is both a Pauline account of the origins of the Jesus movement and the introduction of "Christianity" (i.e., the Pauline-Lukan interpretation of Jesus's legacy) to the Roman world. In Luke/Acts unresolved tensions between the needs of internal and external constituencies yield a text that seems to be both: more lenient toward Judaism (catering to the Roman expectation for respect of religion, antiquity, authority, and hierarchy) and more anti-Jewish (reflecting the growing militancy of the non-Jewish majority against the descendants of the Jewish founders). The author's craft is remarkable; he walks a difficult line between continuity and discontinuity, and between veneration and rejection of authority. In the Lukan narrative we can detect two incompatible needs and expectations. Part of Luke's constituency seems to yearn for recognition from the founding faction as rightful believers in Jesus, while on a collision course with them. Other elements in his constituency seem to be critical of any affront to tradition, authority, or hierarchy and therefore of any affront to the Jewish leadership. Whereas some expected continuity, discipline, and respect toward the Jewish leadership of the movement, others anguished for the opposite message: the validity of discontinuity. The resulting ambivalence has been noted[17] but not clarified, or set in a socio-theological context.

The author of the Gospel according to Luke may have also considered that a new telling of belief in Jesus was necessary due to intensifying Roman persecution. Romans had to be persuaded that the persecution of Gentile believers in Jesus was unwarranted. Anti-Christian sentiment in the empire was rising. To the Romans authorities, Gentile believers were an odd and suspect lot: non-Jews that claimed to be the followers of a Jew crucified on charges of sedition. The common prescription for subversive claims of this sort was execution. Luke does not hide the fact that the charges are sedition (19:38; 23:2, 11, and 38). To the Romans, as to first-century Jews, the Jewish messiah was a liberator from oppression. Luke/Acts (in the footsteps of Mark) seems to hope that if Roman involvement in Jesus's death is deflated[18] and Jesus's death can be recast as due to a Jewish conspiracy, Gentile believers in Jesus would no longer be seen as members of a seditious sect and could be seen as respectable members of Roman society. Despite the fact that Luke/ Acts looks inward, the author also has an eye on the broader Roman stage. He edifies and informs the faithful but also aims at a larger horizon. Luke/ Acts is an effort by a highly educated individual to present to his constituency, and to a wider Roman audience, Paul's ministry at its Roman best. Acts is concerned with the fate and reputation of Paul.[19] Submission to hierarchy being a Roman must, this maverick individualist is cast as a subservient team player. The author fashioned a submissive and disciplined Paul to fit the expectations of a Roman audience that venerated tradition and ancestry, valued discipline and submission to authority. The Jesus movement started off as a messianic, apocalyptic, and socially subversive movement of Jews.[20] Luke seems to be repositioning the Jesus movement to meet the Roman "checklist." He may be addressing the needs of conservative elements within his audience by complying with entry requirements to the Roman religious marketplace. In the Roman mind novelty was suspect. Continuity, antiquity, and legitimacy were the gateway, a precondition, to social acceptance. Thus, despite difficulties in the relationship between Paul and the Pillars, the Lukan Paul emerges as a "team player," a controversial visionary that is, nonetheless, embraced by the leaders of the movement.

Whereas Luke is presented to the reader as an update and a correction of the earlier Gospels accounts (Mark and Matthew), Acts is a Pauline-Lukan manifesto. Seen from this perspective, the Lukan texts seem to have been fashioned as a legitimating narrative for a faction posturing for ascendancy. We do not know whether any Romans in positions of authority ever read the Lukan apologia. Luke's efforts to cast a Roman-friendly image fail, and persecution persists for another four–five generations.

My Luke/Acts

It would appear that the author(s) of Luke/Acts crafted a new telling of the short history of belief in Jesus to address a complex reality that included theological and factional strife within the Jesus movement and growing Roman persecution. Luke/Acts is a masterful attempt to find the middle ground between struggling factions that advocated differing attitudes toward the beliefs and traditions of the founding fathers, a precursor of the later proto-orthodox theological compromise-building. The texts also attempt to strike a balance between the internal need to explain and to justify the estrangement from the founding fathers, and the Roman veneration for antiquity and authority.

Casting Paul as a law-abiding Jew[21] and as a submissive member of the hierarchy presided by James is a tactical masterstroke in a narrative that navigates the tricky transition from a sect within Judaism to a non-Jewish religious movement. Luke/Acts is a claim to Pauline-Lukan pre-eminence, an outcome that did come about only several generations later. At the time of authorship this was a claim, not a reality. The protracted struggle among contending interpretations of belief in Jesus did not run its course until the fourth or fifth centuries. We do not know the demographics of the Jesus movement at the turn of the first century, but Luke/Acts are dominated by a Pauline-Lukan agenda, at a time when differing Gentile forms of belief in Jesus were gaining momentum, and the descendants of the Jewish founders were still recognized by many as the true keepers of Jesus's legacy. Luke/Acts hints that Pauline-Lukans are the legitimate inheritors and custodians of Jesus's ministry and legacy, at the time that the campaign against the descendants of the founding fathers is bursting to the surface. The Pauline-Lukan dilemma was how to explain to the internal and external constituencies the circumstances of Jesus's death and the double discontinuity (from Judaism and from the descendants of Jesus's disciples and first followers). The author's claim to the transfer of legitimacy from the descendants of the Jewish founders to the Paulines signals to Luke's audience that those embracing Luke's interpretation of Paul's legacy are the legitimate inheritors of Jesus's ministry.

Luke/Acts, experiencing a reality of theological conflict, chaos, and flux, anoints centrist Paulines as the new guardians and interpreters of Jesus's legacy, without addressing the growing tensions within the movement. Luke is casting a shift that has not yet taken place, as if it already did. Luke/Acts provided a curtain of legitimacy behind which the proto-orthodox push for compromise, unity, and ascendancy took place. These texts attempt a compromise between continuity and discontinuity vis-à-vis the founding faction while explaining and justifying the estrangement from them. This positioning is a window into the embryonic stages of the Via Media, the theological compromise championed by the Pauline-Lukan faction from the second century onward. Significantly, at the same time that the Pauline-Lukan faction is engaged in an "all-out" assault on Jesus's disciples and first followers, and while conducting a smear campaign against their doctrinal children and grandchildren, Luke/Acts embraces the tribulations of the early Jewish followers of Jesus with no apparent discomfort at the obvious dissonance and contradiction.

Luke/Acts leaves the reader ignorant of the reality confronting the Jesus movement at the time of authorship: internal dissent among Gentile believers, growing estrangement from the founding fathers, and increasing Roman persecution. Luke/Acts project an imaginary, consensual, and almost idyllic transfer of legitimacy, authority, and guardianship from the descendants of the Jewish founders to the Gentile followers of Paul.[22] A literal-traditional reading of the Lukan narrative would not make us aware of the existential crisis between Jewish and Gentile factions, nor of the existence of conflicting and incompatible Gentile interpretations of Jesus's ministry and legacy. At a time when belief in Jesus is chaotic and diverse, the author of Luke/Acts states a premature claim to Pauline-Lukan ascendancy and pre-eminence that does not seem to correspond to the facts on the ground. It anticipates and hopes for a reality that did materialize only generations later. Luke/Acts goes as far as it can in the circumstances dictated to him.

Chapter 7

The Anti-Judaic Strand in John: Estrangement

Introduction

In John's Gospel we encounter the loftiest, most ornate, and most sublime exaltations of Jesus in the New Testament: "If Jesus is painfully human for Mark, he is serenely transcendental for John."[1] In John we also find the most explicit declarations about the divinity of Jesus in the canonical Gospels, the closest affirmations of Jesus's divinity (i. e., John has the "highest" Christology). When read literally, John's Gospel is also the most anti-Jewish Gospel.[2] This tragic co-occurrence has magnified the impact of John's anti-Jewish bent:

> 8:42 Jesus said to them, "If God were your Father, you would love me, for I proceeded and came forth from God; I came not of my own accord, but he sent me. 43 Why do you do not understand what I say? It is because you cannot bear to hear my word. 44 You are of your father the devil, and your will is to do your father's desires. He was a murderer from the beginning, and has nothing to do with the truth, because there is no truth in him. When he lies, he speaks according to his own nature for he is a liar and the father of lies. 45 But, because I tell the truth, you do not believe me. 46 Which of you convicts me of sin? If I tell the truth, why do you not believe me? 47 He who is of God hears the words of God; the reason why you do not hear them is that you are not of God.'

There exists somewhat of a consensus that John's Gospel was written in the last decade of the first century, and that the Gospel and the Johannine Epistles were part of the literary corpus of one community. Most date the

Epistles later, to a period of schism within the community. Standing on Martyn,[3] the consensus identifies two dramas that were fused into one by the author(s)/editor(s): Jesus's conflict with the "Jewish authorities" and the conflict of the Johannines with differing believers in Jesus, decades later.

In John we find traces of several debates. Disputes among Jews (about who Jesus was; whether messiah or not),[4] disputes within the Jesus movement (was Jesus human, divine or both), and disputes about what theological worldview should be adopted (Jewish, Pauline, or Gnostic) lay fused and intertwined in the text.

Who were the "Ioudaioi"?

Whereas the lore of the Jewish followers of Jesus, on which the Synoptics stand, chastises Judean figures of authority (the scribes, the chief priests, and the Pharisees) the "Ioudaioi" are the utmost adversaries in John, and reign supreme as the arch-enemies of the author(s) of the canonical text. The Latin term Iudaeos, later translated as "Jews," emerged out of the Greek Ioudaioi. In John we encounter the term Ioudaioi seventy times, most often in negative connotation. This compares with five times in Matthew, six times in Mark, and five times in Luke. In addition, we encounter often the implied denigration of the "Ioudaioi." The various possible meanings of the term in John can be derived from context and stand in stark contrast to the uniform, intriguing, tendentious, and monolithic later translation into "the Jews." Who were the Ioudaioi?[5]

> John 11:54; 19:12—his enemies
> John 12:9—Jesus's own people
> John 12:9, 11—these people
> John 11:19, 31, 33, 36, 45—their friends
> John 18:31; 19:7—they
> John 18:36—my enemies
> John 18:38—Jesus's accusers
> John 4:9 and probably 4:22—Jesus
> John 4:29—salvation is from the Jews
> John 8:31; 11:45; 12:11—believers in Jesus
> John 8:39–44—children of the Devil

According to some scholars, up to half of the occurrences of Ioudaioi in John are best translated as the Jewish authorities. Urban C. von Wahlde[6] studied ten previous studies on the subject and found that they agreed unanimously in identifying 31 instances of hostile use of Ioudaioi in John

(1:19; 2:18, 20; 5:10, 15, 16, 18; 6:41, 52; 7:1, 11, 13, 15; 8:22, 48, 52, 57; 9:18, 22a, 22b; 10:24, 31, 33; 13:33; 18:14, 31, 36; 19:7, 31, 38; 20:19). Von Wahlde also argues that, with the exception of John 6:41 and 52, all the hostile uses of Ioudaioi refer to Judean authorities, not to the common people. In John 6:41, 52; 7:1; 8:22, 31; 10:19; 11:19, 31, 33, 36, 45, 54; 12:9,11; 18:20; and 19:20–21 the term seems to mean "the people." On the other hand: salvation is from the Ioudaioi (John 4:22). Some Ioudaioi, apart from his disciples, believe in Jesus (John 8:30–31; 11:45; 12:9–11; cf. 7:31, 40–43; 9:16; 10:19–21). The inconsistent and disharmonic deployment of the term is puzzling and consequential: "this produced the multiple meaning of the name Jew that is so confusing, and which, when read synchronically, is so utterly contradictory."[7] A large number of attempts to explain this phenomenon[8] has not yielded a consensus. Recognition of the multivalent character of the term Ioudaioi in John is now a majority view that is, unfortunately, not properly reflected in the popular editions of the New Testament nor fully understood by lay believers.

There is some evidence that the term Ioudaioi was also used for Gentiles who observed Jewish practices. According to Wilson, Dio Cassius, writing at the turn of the second and third centuries, says: "This title 'Ioudaioi' is also borne by other persons who, although they are of other ethnicity, live by their laws."[9] This is also the meaning implied by Epictetus.[10] J. D. Cohen informs us that by the second half of the second century BCE, the term Ioudaioi was used to identify Judeans, Jews, and people who were not ethnic or geographic Judeans, but who had political or religious affinities with them. It appears that at the time of John's authorship the term would mean "Judeans and their Gentile sympathizers."[11] It is plausible, therefore, that Gentile believers in Jesus would identify the Jewish followers of Jesus as Ioudaioi. Thus, the emergence of the Ioudaioi as a derogatory term for the adversaries of the Johannines may have started off as internal labeling and "name calling" by an opposing faction. De Jounge and De Ruyter[12] have concluded that in John, the Ioudaioi are Christians of non-Johannine persuasion. De Jounge claims that John uses the term Ioudaioi to aim at a group of Christians whom he perceives as under strong influence of "Judaism." I agree, but we can go further. Using the terminology advocated here, the intended adversaries behind John's deployment of the term Ioudaioi could be the Jewish faction or their Gentile sympathizers.

John seems to reflect a transition from the implied and tentative belittling of the descendants of Jesus's disciples and first followers that we encountered in Paul and in the Synoptics, to the more self-assured and vitriolic tone against the Ioudaioi in the generations to come. With John we seem to be at the threshold of a shift in the intensity of the anti-Jewish rhetoric. This acceleration in the anti-Jewish trajectory reflects an underlying socio-theological reality that is not unique to John[13]: at the dawn of the second century several Gentile interpretations of Jesus's legacy were entering a process of adversarial self-definition.

John's vitriolic rampage against the Ioudaioi stands unique in the context of the New Testament corpus: John contains the most emotional and visceral attacks on opponents that are Jewish and may have contributed more than any other text to the saturation of the hearts and minds of later believers with anti-Jewish sentiment. The various interpretations of Ioudaioi (the Jews, some Jews, some Judeans, the people, some people, the descendants of the Jewish founders, differing Johannines, differing Gentiles) in John may indicate that confusion regarding the historical ministry of Jesus was widespread, and that the second or third generations after Jesus's death already had blurred and stereotypical views of who the Ioudaioi were. Significantly, and anticipating the journey before us, it seems that it was not uncommon for early Pauline-Lukan writers to characterize opponents within the Jesus movement as "Ioudaioi"[14] pointing at the internal context of John's ire. Thus, the massive use of the multivalent Ioudaioi in a dissonant and incoherent manner agglomerates and blurs adversaries across generations (Jesus's life is used to stage later conflicts),[15] across religious and ethnic boundaries (Jews, Jewish followers of Jesus and their Gentile Sympathizers), and across social categories (the Jewish authorities, the people, the crowd).

It seems that at the dawn of the second century a tidal wave of anti-"Ioudaioi" sentiment and incitement swept through many Gentile communities. We will witness a crescendo of undifferentiated anti-Ioudaioi disparagement that flooded the hearts and minds of the Pauline-Lukan leadership and literati, a phenomenon that needs deciphering. However, the intensification in anti-Jewish rhetoric during the second and third centuries cannot be attributed to the influence of John due to the fact that the Gospel of John was favored by Gnostics, and was not embraced by the Pauline-Lukan leadership until the fourth century.[16] Therefore, the explanation for the transition (from the second century forward) to "the Jews" as the ultimate adversaries requires a different perspective, a turning point of wider scope. What triggered the widespread use of "Ioudaioi"? What caused the tidal wave of anti-Ioudaioi sentiment and incitement that we will witness during the second and third centuries? What was the socio-theological context that led to the later misinterpretation and mistranslation of the multivalent Ioudaioi into "the Jews"?

Evolution of the Text

As we turn our attention to the evolution of the Johannine text, we may start by pointing out that there seems to be a tentative consensus among scholars that the canonical text took shape through stages or phases[17] although the details and characteristics of the trajectory are debated.[18] Brown identified seven groups of protagonists,[19] a significant departure from the traditional juxtaposition of "Jews" versus "Christians." Standing on Carroll,[20] Brown's scenario for the Johannine saga, one of the foundational analyses on which the current consensus stands, may be summarized as follows:[21]

Phase One—the pre-Gospel community: The original group were Jewish followers of Jesus. They included disciples of John the Baptist and a later group of anti-Temple persuasion with some Samaritan converts (4:21, 23–24). This assortment of pre-Gospel believers was affiliated to a synagogue of "mainstream Jews." According to Brown, the newcomers may have influenced some among the founding faction to embrace a Christology unacceptable to Judaism. This group "had been expelled from the synagogues (9:22; 16:2) because of what they were claiming about Jesus."[22]

Phase Two—the writing of the Gospel: The Gospel was written following the expulsion of the pre-Gospel believers from a host synagogue. At the time the Gospel was written (*ca.* AD 90) "the expulsion from the synagogues is now past, but persecution (16:2–3) continues, and there are deep scars in the Johannine psyche regarding the 'Jews.' The insistence on a 'high' Christology (made all the more intense by the struggles with the 'Jews') affects the community's relations with the other Christian groups…"[23]

Phase Three: The writing of the Epistles occurs in the now-divided Johannine communities, presumably *ca.* AD 100 (I John 2:19)…the struggle is between two groups of Johannines who are interpreting the Gospel in opposite ways in matters of Christology, ethics, and eschatology…the secessionists are having the greater numerical success (I John 4:5) and the author is trying to bolster his adherents against further inroads by false teachers (2:27; II John 10–11). The author feels that it is "the last hour" (I John 2:18).

The antagonists of I John seceded and moved rapidly toward Docetism[24] and Gnosticism. This explains why the Fourth Gospel, which they continued to revere, is cited earlier and more frequently by heterodox believers than by proto-orthodox ones. During the next decades, adherents of the author of I John may have gradually merged with what Ignatius of Antioch calls "the church catholic," as exhibited by the eventual acceptance of Johannine Christology among the Pauline-Lukan. The use of the Epistles as a guide to interpret the Gospel eventually won for John a place in the canon of the church.

A weak link in Brown's model is the assertion that descendants of the founding fathers worshiped in mainstream synagogues. It seems to me that, similar to other Judean sectarians, Jesus's followers would have worshiped in their own synagogues, where Jesus would be exalted, not in mainstream synagogues where Jesus's messiahship was rejected. Whereas Brown, and Martyn see Jewish followers of Jesus seceding from a community of mainstream Jews accompanied by a group of Gentiles that had joined that community, I see in the Gospel two layers and two secessions. I position the Gentile Johannines as joining, and later seceding from, a community of Jewish followers of Jesus:

1. *First secession-estrangement*: Establishment of self-segregated communities of Jewish followers of Jesus following Jesus's death, or very soon thereafter.

2. *First layer—The proto-Johnnines*: A community of followers of Jesus that understands itself to be part of Judaism. The polemic is vis-à-vis establishment-Judaism. Whether Jesus was the messiah—a dispute among Jews is the subject of contention (12.34; 7.41–42, 52, 12–13, 27, 15, 40–43, 5–18; 9.16; 5.41–47; 10.24). At some point, Gentile believers join this community. In this new environment, a new dispute about what kind of messiah Jesus was would have surfaced. This debate would have taken place between members of the founding faction and Gentile believers. Whether Jesus was an exalted human, a divine being (10:24, 30; 6.38, 60–66, 26–27; 8.17–18, 30–59),[25] or both, would be the subject of contention.

3. *Second secession-estrangement*: Gentile believers in Jesus would be alienated by the Jewish milieu of the proto-Johannines and would oppose the imposition of the beliefs and traditions of the founding fathers on Gentiles. They secede and create a community that gravitates toward a "higher" Christology. In this second secession-estrangement, a proto-Johannine text may have transited from the Jewish milieu of the descendants of Jesus's disciples and first followers, to a non-Jewish context.[26]

4. *Third layer—The Johannines*: A community of Gentile believers authors the Gospel of John by incorporating traditions and/or texts that originated in the founding community they had seceded, or had been expelled, from. This Gentile community, having undergone a process of separation-individuation, and in need to reduce the emotional and theological dissonance caused by the estrangement from the descendants of Jesus's disciples and first followers, generates the high emotional pitch of the anti-Ioudaioi vitriol in John (9:22; 12:42; 16:2).

For the Jewish proto-Johannines, the adversaries are the high priests, the scribes, and the Pharisees, that is, the Judean establishment from which they seem to have self-segregated-seceded. For the Gentile Johannines the main intended adversaries behind the deployment of the Ioudaioi curtain seem to be the Jewish faction and its Gentile sympathizers; the establishment from which they found themselves estranged. Thus, despite the deployment of the multivalent term Ioudaioi we can say: first, the negative use of the term is characteristic of the later and Gentile layer and should not be attributed to the proto-Johannine (and Jewish) first layer.[27] Second, the term is never used in connection to a person that is a Johannine believer. An intriguing exception is 4:9 where it seems to apply to Jesus.[28]

Using the template suggested by Brown as a benchmark, the alternative scenario outlined earlier may be expanded as follows:

Layer one—first secession-expulsion and the traditions of proto-John: discussions about whether Jesus was the messiah or not, not about whether he was divine or not, triggered the split between the proto-Johannine Jewish followers of Jesus and mainstream Judaism (1:35–49). Both parties were Jewish and viewed Jesus as a human. This layer contains the stridency (1:11, 35–51; 17:14–16)[29] characteristic of Jewish sectarian posturing against establishment-Judaism and is similar to the hyperbole of other Jewish sectarians (Qumran, Enoch, Jubilees etc.). The first secession-expulsion-estrangement may have taken place sometime circa 80 CE. Similar to most Jewish sectarians, the proto-Johannines would have formed communities and synagogues of their own.

A dualistic juxtaposition of diametrically opposed poles was characteristic of turn-of-the-era Jewish sectarian attacks against the Jewish establishment. Befitting Jewish anti-establishment posturing, the most extreme rhetoric in John is characteristically dualist. In John, whoever does not accept the Johannine interpretation of Jesus's legacy (8:12–59) is a child of the devil. When the Ioudaioi are cast as untrue to their own beliefs and traditions and do not keep the Torah (7:19), when they are cast as not understanding their own Scriptures (5:39–41; 10:31–38), when their leaders are accused of serving the Roman occupiers (19:15) and are children of the devil (8:39–44; 12:31; 14:30; 16:11; 17:15; 1 John 2:22 and 2 John 7) we may be encountering the fossilized remains of sectarian anti-Jewish-establishment rhetoric or its subversion-appropriation by Gentile believers. The descendants of Jesus's disciples and first followers may also be behind the Ioudaioi that are supportive of Jesus (7:15; 10:24; 12:9) and those that believe in Jesus (8:31; 11:45; 12:11). Whereas in proto-Matthew we find several calls to Torah observance, in proto-John we have none.

Layer two—second secession-expulsion and the writing of John: The fellowship, the co-existence, of Gentiles and Jews in the Jesus movement seems to have failed throughout. First, the Jewish milieu of the founding fathers was alien to Gentile newcomers. Second, the various and conflicting Gentile interpretations of Jesus's ministry and legacy would be considered inadequate and lacking by the descendants of Jesus's disciples and first followers—most of whom seem to have conditioned fellowship on strict Torah observance. The second stratum seems to originate in seceding Gentile believers and targets the Jewish leadership of the movement and their Gentile sympathizers. Here Gentile secessionists deploy against the descendants of Jesus's disciples and first followers a variant of the sectarian invective originally deployed by the founding fathers against fellow Jews. It is clear that at the time of the Gospel's writing, estrangement or secession-expulsion had already taken place (9:22; 16:2). When we add the belittling of the disciples (6:60–66) and the attitude of the canonical text toward the Jewish faction (8:30–59), we are on relatively strong grounds to argue that the community that gave us the final version of John was demographically Gentile. I concur[30] that when claims to the divinity of Jesus appear, the estrangement from a synagogue has apparently occurred. However, contrary to most interpretations, I posit that the estrangement-expulsion that incenses the author(s)/editor(s) of the second layer is from a synagogue of Jewish followers of Jesus, not from a synagogue of mainstream Jews.

To the editor/compiler of the final text, the Ioudaioi and their traditions and institutions are not "us" or "ours" but "they" and "theirs" reflecting his Gentile perspective. His alienation from the Jewish context is visible also in "the Passover of the Jews" (2:13; 11:55) and "a feast of the Jews" (5:1; 6:4; 7:2). This stratum centers on arguments about whether Jesus was divine or not (5:18; 10:33; 16:2).[31] The debates about the divinity/humanity of Jesus are omnipresent in the second layer of the Gospel and in the Epistles. The main conflict in the second Johannine layer is Christological. In 5:18, 10:33, and 19:7, the Ioudaioi (in this case the descendants of the Jewish founders) seem to oppose equating Jesus to God. The adversaries of the Gentile Johannines were Ioudaioi that considered Jesus a human and Docetic-Gnostic Gentiles[32] that believed that Jesus was only divine, his human form being an illusion. Although there is no unequivocal articulation of a proto-Nicean stand in the Gospel, we may infer the Johannine position as standing in the mid-range between their adversaries. The Johannines seem to have embraced the middle ground. They seem to have gravitated toward a proto-orthodox understanding of Jesus's ministry and legacy: Jesus as both, human and divine. The Fourth Gospel's assertion that rejection of its claims about Jesus is sin[33] (8:21–24; 31–34; 9:39–41; 15:22–24; 16:7–11; 19:10–11) attempts to encapsulate both: the human messiah of the Jewish followers of Jesus (made flesh), and the divine savior of the Docetists (Jesus is the *logos*, the Word). This positioning of the Johannines is an early precursor of the upcoming "Via Media"; the compromise creed forged by the Pauline-Lukan during the second and third centuries. There is also a proto-supersessionary[34] element in the second layer. The Johannine supersessionary posture toward the Ioudaioi is implicit in the claim that the Johannine understanding of Jesus's life and legacy replaced and made obsolete the traditions of the descendants of Jesus's disciples and first followers. The Gentile Johannines of the second layer affirm that their understanding of Jesus's ministry and legacy replaces all that was before, i.e., the beliefs of the Jewish founders (1:9; 2:1, 19–22; 4:10–14, 23, 21; 5:39; 7:28–29; 8:16, 19, 58; 15:1, 21; 16:3; 17:25; 19:19–22).

By internalizing the aberration Ioudaioi= the Jews, and by fusing and confusing the two layers of the Johannine saga, traditional and many current readers see "the Jews" as hostile and violent toward Jesus and his followers (5:16, 18; 7:1; 8:31, 37–38, 44, 47, 9:22, 16:2–3, 18:36, 19:38, 20:19). This is a bizarre claim. If understood literally, end-of-the-first-century Gentile believers in Jesus would be chastising "the Jews" for persecuting the Jewish followers of Jesus, at the same time that they were engaged in a derogatory campaign against them—that is, mounting an assault on their authority and legitimacy. Is it possible that two–three generations after Jesus lifetime Gentile believers had already forgotten that the original followers of Jesus where the great-grandfathers of their adversaries in the present? Were internal and external Jews already fused and confused in the minds and hearts of Gentile believers?

Layer three—The Johannine Epistles tell us of a third secession. This time the debate was about the nature and the details of Jesus's divinity, an argument that could take place only among Gentiles. This third polemic, against Gentile believers that "went too far" and understood Jesus to be non-human and wholly divine, is hinted at (1:14, 18 and 19:34–35).[35] The Johannine Epistles reflect the Johannine struggle with differing Gentile believers in Jesus. Neither the Ioudaioi nor Israel are mentioned specifically in the Johannine Epistles. Contrary to the central role they play in the Gospel, written one or two generations prior, the Ioudaioi are not the main adversaries in the Epistles. A group of differing Gentiles seems to be the target of the wrath of the author(s). I follow Brown's analysis of the Epistles as reflecting the other facet of the Johannine struggle, this time against those that rejected Jesus's humanity and claimed his unequivocal divinity. The struggle of the Pauline-Lukan faction against the refusal of the descendants of Jesus's disciples and first followers to embrace Jesus's divinity and against the refusal of Docetics and Gnostics of all kinds to embrace Jesus's humanity anticipates the remainder of our journey. Despite the fact that 1 John 2:22–23; 3:10; 4:3; 5:10–12; and 2 John 7 can be considered offensive to Jews, the polemic in the Epistles seems to target differing Gentiles, not "the Jews."[36]

Estrangement

When the author(s)/editors(s) of the canonical John criticize or downplay the disciples, they are attempting to explain and justify to their audience the estrangement from the heritage of the Jewish founders, not their estrangement from "Judaism." By John's time, the theological dissonance

and the emotional distress caused by the estrangement from the leaders of
the movement were existential matters for the author's audience. The tensions between the parties had become an open confrontation. The implied
and somewhat cautious criticism of the disciples that characterized the
Synoptics was no longer sufficient. The influence that the descendants of
Jesus's disciples and first followers exerted over the flock had to be curtailed
with blunter tools.

For most scholars, the religious institution being attacked by the
Johaninnes is Judaism.[37] My contention is that the Ioudaioi against which
Johannines are lashing out are the Ioudaioi that infuriate them: the Jewish
followers of Jesus. They seem to be the establishment in the community
from which the Gentile Johannines have seceded, and in the movement
as a whole. They are the ones that consider the Johannines' beliefs about
Jesus inadequate and lacking. They were, and will remain thereafter, a
threat against which Gentile believers will struggle with for the next two
hundred years. My suspicion that the Johannines underwent a process of
secession-estrangement from the descendants of Jesus's disciples and first
followers, and not from "Judaism," is based on multiple clues, themes, and
motifs (some already embryonic in the Synoptics) that take center stage in
John and anticipate much of our journey ahead. The context and background that support the argument:

- John used the life-story of Jesus to explain and justify to his community the estrangement from the descendants of the founding fathers.
  The estrangement from the Jewish leadership, not from Judaism,
  underwrites Johannine anti-Ioudaioi fury.
- Being the establishment in the community from which the Johannines
  were expelled or seceded, the descendants of the founding fathers
  would draw the dissenting fire of the Johannines.[38]
- The denigration and the vilification of the disciples that did "not
  understand," that "abandoned" and "denied" Jesus, and "drew back
  and no longer went about with him" is the creation of Gentile believers stating a claim against the descendants of Jesus's disciples and first
  followers, not against Judaism.
- The leap from Gentile belief in Jesus to establishment Judaism is too
  great to be assumed. Synagogues of descendants of the Jewish faction, where Jesus would be exalted and venerated (instead of rejected)
  would be a more obvious and emphatic place of worship for Gentile
  Johannines prior to the secession-expulsion.
- Some Gentiles were attracted to the Jewish faction because they were,
  at the time, the acknowledged guardians of his legacy. They were
  influential despite their Judaism, not on account of it.
- There was no fellowship, and consequently no estrangement between
  Gentile Johannines and "mainstream Judaism."

- The debate about Judaism (not a debate with Judaism) became a "wedge issue" that was used to sever the attraction that the Jewish founders had over some among the rank and file.
- Whereas there was no theological incompatibility between followers of Jesus of Jewish origin and fellow Jews, there was an unbridgeable incompatibility between them and Gentile believers in Jesus—who rejected Judaism and gravitated toward the divinity of Jesus.

Further support for the contention that Jewish followers of Jesus were the targets of the later layer of abuse dispensed against the Ioudaioi in the Gospel:

1. The attacks on Peter (13:23–26; 18:15–16; 20:2–10; 21:7, 20–23).[39] In most current scholarship these attacks are understood as targeting the Apostolic Church, an entity of unclear identity and unclear theological characteristics. The Apostolic Church, the term used to describe the Apostolic Synagogue may have surfaced to bypass and obscure the Jewish grounding of the founders of the Jesus movement.

2. The upstaging of the Jewish followers of Jesus by the Johannines, one of the most explicit and direct corroborations we have for the argument that the descendants of Jesus's disciples and first followers were an imminent threat underwriting the Gospel:[40]
   i. "The Community of the Beloved Disciple," rather than Jesus's disciples and first followers were in intimate contact with Jesus (13:23–26). It is the Johannine community that accompanied Jesus into the dangers of the court of the high priest. The Jewish followers of Jesus enter the court with the help of the Johannine community (18:15–16).
   ii. The Johannine community claimed that it had been present at the cross and was given privileges and responsibilities upstaging Jesus's disciples and first followers who, according to John and the Synoptics, denied Jesus and fled (19:26–27).
   iii. The Johannine community out runs the Jewish followers of Jesus in a theological race to the empty tomb and they "believe." By implication, their Jewish opponents do not. (20:2–10).
   iv. The Johannine community recognizes the risen Jesus standing on the shore of the lake, and tells the Jewish followers of Jesus who Jesus is (21:7).
   v. Finally, the risen Jesus wishes the Johannine community to remain where it is theologically, until he returns (21:20–23).
   This upstaging of Jesus's disciples and first followers by the Johannines is not a peculiar oddity; it is reflective of a Johannine challenge to the descendants of the Jewish founders. The segments cited here are

unique in the canon in that the estrangement between the descendants of Jesus's disciples and first followers and Gentile believers is rather explicit.

3. In John 6:41–71 we have an intriguing story where the Johannines seem to acknowledge the fact that their claims about Jesus would be unacceptable to "The Twelve." The Johannines were aware that their beliefs, as reflected in 6:41–60, were unacceptable to the Jewish leadership, and they enlist Peter to defend their position. The casting of "after this many of his (*Jesus*) disciples drew back and no longer went about with him" is designed to enhance the claim that the disciples "abandoned" Jesus. By casting those that did not agree with their theology as "not understanding," "denying" or "abandoning" Jesus, the Johannines (and Gentiles elsewhere in the canon) successfully obscured their opposition to the legacy of those chosen by Jesus to be his successors.

4. The debates about whether Jesus was closer to the divine savior of the Pagan and Zoroastrian heritage or to the human messiah of the Jewish tradition—would have taken place between followers of Jesus of Jewish and Pagan origin. The divinity of Jesus was an argument between the Johannines and the Jewish sectarians from which they had seceded, or by whom they had been rejected—not with "establishment Judaism.'" "After chapter 4 the reader encounters a 'high' Christology and a sharp conflict with the 'Ioudaioi' (i.e., followers of Jesus of Jewish origin) who, according to their Jewish heritage, object strenuously to the deification of the Johannine Jesus."[41] "Mainstream" Jews would not be interested in the views of Gentiles about the divinity of a Jew whose messianic claims they had rejected. Therefore, an argument between Gentiles advocating the divinity of Jesus and "Jews" opposing them may be deemed to have occurred only if these Jews were the descendants of the founding fathers.

5. If we divest the adversarial casting of the text, we find that the debate at the core of the Gentile layer of the Gospel is about Jesus's divinity. When the author of the canonical John seems to make Jesus equal with God: "making himself equal with God" (5:18), and makes him God "you, being a man, make yourself God" (10:33), he is presenting to his audience, in narrative form, the "higher" Christology of the Johannines as against the "low" Christology of the Jerusalem faction.

6. References to "people who believe but fear to confess" (John 7:12–13; 9:22; 12:42; 16:2; 19:3) seem to chastise Gentile sympathizers with the Jewish followers of Jesus. From a Johannine perspective, they are seen as hypocrites that know in their hearts that they are wrong about Jesus's divinity, but remain attached to the beliefs and traditions of

the Jewish founders. This Johannine perspective rejects the possibility that some Gentiles were genuine sympathizers with the views espoused by the descendants of Jesus's disciples and first followers.

A Strong Undertow

In the next chapters we will encounter a steep escalation in anti-"Ioudaioi" rhetoric. Why, and as a consequence of what socio-theological context, did an anti-"Ioudaioi" flood burst at the threshold of the second century and became an anti-Jewish deluge?

The transition in John to an undifferentiated deployment of the term Ioudaioi to designate the Jewish opponents of the Johannines (and their Gentile sympathizers) is idiosyncratic to John, but is not unique. It seems that at the dawn of the second century a strong undertow was sweeping many Gentile believers in an anti-Jewish direction. As we transit into the second century, we will encounter this phenomenon throughout the literature of that period. We have already noted that this peculiar shift is too sweeping, and too broad, to be assigned to John's influence due to the fact that John's Gospel was at first popular among Gnostics, and shunned by the Pauline-Lukan. Anticipating later conclusions, I will suggest that the end of the first century was the threshold to the central and pivotal process of the second and third centuries: the eruption onto the surface of a multilateral struggle about identity, legitimacy, and ascendancy that was brewing in the hearts and minds of believers and followers of Jesus since the emergence of the Pauline and Gnostic missions to the Gentiles. This protracted and inconclusive conflict will dominate the second and third centuries, and will fade away gradually during the fourth and fifth. In John we encounter in embryonic form some of the protagonists that will take part in the debates of the next three centuries: the descendants of the Jewish founders and their Gentile sympathizers, and Pauline-Lukan and Docetic-Gnostic Gentiles.

Rensberger and others have noted the sectarian origins of proto-John,[42] but lacking an alternative socio-theological narrative, the yield of these insights has not been fully harvested: "It has simply not seemed apparent that the group conflicts and social patterns that were formative for the Johannine writings might have theological meaning not only for the Johannine community itself but also for modern readers."[43] From my perspective, Rensberger is headed in the right direction, but he does not harvest the full bounty of his insight due to the Pauline-Lukan narrative that still dominates the field. Thus, when he states that "the Fourth Gospel represents a heretical offensive against orthodoxy, i.e., the orthodoxy of the synagogue authorities."[44] I would rephrase: the first layer of the Fourth Gospel reflects anti-Jewish-establishment sentiment among Jewish followers of Jesus. The second layer of the Fourth Gospel represents a sectarian offensive by Gentile Johannines against orthodoxy—this time the orthodoxy of the Jewish founders of the movement, from which they have found themselves estranged.

Current Scholarship and Current Dilemmas

Many attempts have been made to understand John's anti-"Ioudaioi" invective. However, most scholars have not fully freed themselves from the Pauline-Lukan narrative and the conflict between the Johannines and Judaism remains the consensus background for the Fourth Gospel.[45] During the last decades Johannine scholars have attempted a variety of strategies to deflate the theological implications of the Johannine anti-Jewish rhetoric[46]:

> Explicitly or implicitly, all the authors who discuss the alleged anti-Judaism of the Fourth Gospel use certain reading strategies that allow them to safeguard the authority of the sacred text despite the presence of ethically problematic content.[47]
>
> The critical theological issues, therefore, revolve around the question of whether supersessionism, with its attendant rejection of Judaism, is essential to Christianity.[48]
>
> The first results about the anti-Judaism it contains were produced by a comparison of his account of the passion with the accounts in the Synoptic Gospels. The result was: (a) the Gospel of John emphasizes the innocence of Pilate more than any of the other New Testament Gospels; (b) hand in hand with this it incriminates the Jews most over their responsibility for the death of Jesus.[49]

Many scholars argue that the Gospel's negative comments about the Ioudaioi are not a reflection of anti-Judaism but rather an expression of a prolonged and violent controversy between the Johannine community and "the Jews" in the wake of the "expulsion from the synagogue."[50] J. L. Martyn, followed by other scholars, argued that the expulsion from the synagogue of those who confess Jesus to be the Christ is related to the insertion of a curse into the twelfth benediction of the Amidah, a central daily prayer.[51] The argument is that the inclusion of this curse, known as Birkat Haminim, was intended to expose Jewish followers of Jesus and to force a decision on their part. Reinhartz[52] surveys the proponents of this view[53] as well as the growing number that oppose the basic premises of this position, that is, the connection between the Johannine expulsion-secession and the "benediction against the heretics."[54] De Jonge's analysis of John seems to be remarkably close to the views advocated here. Namely, that John's polemic does not seem to reflect a dispute with traditional Jews. Rather, it seems to reflect a controversy with followers of Jesus of Jewish origin or with their Gentile sympathizers, who maintain a different Christological understanding from John's own group.[55]

The conundrum that John forces upon scholars is daunting and reverberates throughout the discourse: "It would be incredible for a twentieth-century Christian to share or justify the Johannine contention that 'the Jews' are the children of the devil, an affirmation which is placed on the lips of Jesus; but I cannot see how it helps contemporary Jewish-Christian relationships to disguise the fact that such an attitude once existed."[56] The dilemmas posited by the anti-Jewish attitudes that surface in a literal reading of the Gospel of John are showcased by the conclusions reached by the editors of *Anti-Judaism and the Fourth Gospel*[57]:

1. There are some dimensions in the way in which the Fourth Gospel treats Judaism and the Jews that we consider to be expressions of anti-Judaism (against those who propose escape routes). We find it impossible to relegate anti-Judaism to the marginal aspects of the text and to deny that, in one way or another, it reaches to the core of the Christian message. We find it hard to escape the conclusion that the anti-Judaism in the text of John is intrinsically oppressive, that is, we are convinced that in these cases human sinfulness has in some way touched the core of biblical texts. The expression intrinsically oppressive is not intended to mean that the scriptures contain nothing but oppressive aspects. Rather, as we shall see, despite the all-pervasiveness of the consequences of human sin, we are convinced that the scriptures transcend their own intrinsically oppressive aspects.

2. We count the anti-Judaism that we find in the scriptures among the intrinsically oppressive dimensions and not among the revelatory dimensions, invested with divine authority. They are therefore totally unacceptable from a Christian point of view (against neo-Nazis).

3. Because of the all-pervasiveness of human sin, we do not find convincing any solutions that try to eliminate the anti-Jewish statements from scripture by ascribing them to later redactions (against literary-critical solutions). We reject attempts to create a canon within the canon by ascribing revelatory authority only to the words of Jesus or to the texts of the original writers (as eyewitnesses?) and none to the later redactors.

We thus affirm three convictions: (i) the Fourth Gospel contains anti-Jewish elements; (ii) the anti-Jewish elements are unacceptable from a Christian point of view; and (iii) there is no convincing way simply to neutralize or to remove the anti-Jewish dimensions of these passages in order to save the healthy core of the message itself. Thus, despite the impressive progress in deconstructing the anti-Jewish strand in John, the fundamental dilemma still stands. The hermeneutical challenge for Christian interpreters is to find a way to interpret the Gospel as a document of faith for contemporary Christian communities that recognizes its indebtedness to Judaism and responds to its anti-Jewish polemic."[58]

My John

John targets the Ioudaioi, a multivalent phantom whose peculiar deployment and multiple identities need deciphering. Scholarship is still attempting to calibrate its observations to meet the demands of this complex, elusive, and most peculiar phenomenon. The shield that protects religious dogma, the complexities of the texts, the intricacy of the circumstances, the fog of history, active obstruction by the guardians of orthodoxy, and the multivalency of the terms Ioudaioi, Jew, and Christian all conspire to make this quest difficult.

We have noted that the writers of the canonical Gospels used the setting of Jesus's ministry to convey to their audiences important messages about their own circumstances and tribulations.[59] Similar to the other canonical Gospels, the setting in John is Jesus's lifetime, but issues and arguments relevant and contemporary to the author(s)/editor(s) and to their audiences dominate the text. Thus, not altogether dissimilar from the situation in the Synoptics, there is a growing consensus around the suspicion that the experiences of the Johannine Jesus, and the expulsion from "the synagogue," reflect the tribulations of the Johannine community, rather than those of the historical Jesus. In John, the Ioudaioi seem to be a proxy for their Jewish opponents within the Jesus movement, a rhetorical and metaphorical mirror against which the (Gentile) Johannines defined themselves. Our overriding concern is to understand why, and due to what circumstances, they did come to stand in front of a mirror, why was it a "Jewish" mirror, and why they saw the reflections that they did.

"The Evangelist uses the category of 'the Jews' as a watershed term to characterize followers and believers in Jesus who are anti-Johannine."[60] The Ioudaioi phantom may have allowed the Gentile leadership to drive a wedge between followers of Jesus of Jewish origin and the rank and file, without appearing irreverent toward the founding fathers. Whether intentional or unintended, this "bundling" by the Gentile literati and ideologues of Jews of all sorts, Gentile sympathizers with the Jewish faction and of differing Gentile believers[61] into the multivalent Ioudaioi eventually fostered a militant, intense, and undifferentiated antagonism against all Jews.

The later translation of Ioudaioi to "Jews," exacerbated and intensified the consequences of the deployment of the term in John.

Older traditions that originated among the founding faction were claimed and incorporated by Gentiles that may have been affiliated with their synagogues at first, but at a later stage established communities of their own. Such spin-offs would display the double-layered "anti-Jewish" anger that we encounter in John: rhetoric by Jewish sectarians against the Jewish establishment intertwined with rhetoric by Gentiles against the Jewish establishment of the Jesus movement. Thus, in John we witness a variant of a phenomenon we already encountered in Matthew: the migration of Judean anti-Jewish-establishment hyperbole to the hearts and minds of Gentiles where, unrestrained by the mitigating and restraining effect of kinship, it metastases and becomes virulent. The theologian Peter Tomson reached similar conclusions when he stated that in John, an internal polemic against fellow-Jews is transposed to an explicit non-Jewish framework and acquires a strong anti-Jewish effect.[62]

The suggested trajectory of the Johannine community and their literary corpus clarifies the odd coexistence of pro-Jewish segments as "salvation is from the Ioudaioi" (4:22) that may have originated in the Jewish proto-John, with the anti-Jewish intensity of the second layer. Beck, Tomson, and Townsend reached similar conclusions on this subject. In their view, the Gospel's relatively pro-Jewish elements seem to belong to the earlier stages of its development, while the more anti-Jewish aspects would have entered the text with later editing,[63] a conclusion not dissimilar from my observations on proto-Matthew. However, contrary to James's and Matthew's call for Torah observance, the theology of the second layer of John reflects a shift toward the divinity of Jesus, a development that would be anathema to the disciples. This may be an indication that whereas the canonical Matthew may reflect yearnings for continuity vis-à-vis the legacy of the Jewish founders, the circumstances of the Gentile Johannines seem to have precluded such continuity—propelling them toward the threshold of appropriation and supersession.[64]

Our ability to recapture the original context, the intended audience, and the identity of the adversaries is compromised by the fact that the two layers, proto-Johannine and Johannine, are now inexorably intertwined in the canonical text. Most scholars see the Johannines as a community that underwent transformation from the Jewish theology of the Jewish founders to a proto-orthodox understanding of Jesus divinity (the current consensus). My understanding is that the Johannines are Gentiles that seceded from a community of Jewish followers of Jesus, laid claim to their lore, and made them into the targets of their ire. This phenomenon will shadow not only our discussion of John, but of the next two centuries. In my view, the wide consensus about the secession of the Johannines from "the synagogue" is reflective of a wide misconception of great consequence: it obscures a complex trajectory, and distorts our understanding of the first three centuries of the Jesus tradition. The anti-Judaism of the Fourth Gospel has also been associated with processes of self-definition by some. Religious self-definition is a socio-theological process underpinned by factional struggles for identity, legitimacy, and ascendancy that are grounded in a specific experience. Therefore, communities, like Matthew's and John's, that may have experienced secession and estrangement from the descendants of Jesus's disciples and first followers would be expected to fashion an intense, militant, and double-layered text.[65]

Before we take leave of John, and standing on Paul and the Synoptics, we may want to recapitulate:

1. Wherever the adversaries are "Judean authorities" (high priests, Pharisees, scribes etc.) the internal setting indicates that proto-Johannine Jewish followers of Jesus might be the protagonists.
2. Since the proto-Johannines were descendants of Jesus's disciples and first followers, denigration of the disciples, of Judaism, and of Torah observance cannot be said to originate with them.
3. The leaders and literati of the growing Gentile majority strived to create a wedge between the descendants of Jesus's disciples and first followers and the rank and file, to whom Judaism was alien.
4. As claims about the divinity of Jesus grow increasingly explicit and unequivocal, we are moving farther away from the proto-Johannine Jewish followers of Jesus.
5. The univalent interpretation and translation of the multivalent Ioudaioi as "the Jews" anticipates, and later facilitated, the emergence of the mythical "conflict between Judaism and Christianity."
6. John was authored at a time when the Johannine position was a minority view. The fact that later Pauline-Lukan believers embraced John obscures that fact.

The anti-Jewish message that emanates from literal readings of John is of great concern because of its impact on the souls of believers. The unfortunate entanglement of sublime and anti-Jewish motifs in John has contributed to the emotional attachment of Christian audiences with the anti-Jewish strand throughout the ages.[66] Throughout many centuries, believers have developed a deep bond with the Gospel of John and have counted on it to nurture their faith. However, throughout history John has also been used to legitimate, nurture, enable, and facilitate anti-Semitism. Given the content, it is no surprise that so many acts of violence and discrimination were inspired by the perceived anti-Jewish message of John.[67] With the probable exception of Matthew 27:24–25, no other text has incited more anti-Jewish hatred and violence than this sublime and disturbing rendition of Jesus's life and death.

Beck, and others, have concluded that because the members of the Johannine community expressed their strong anti-Jewish feelings not in their own name but in words-of-Jesus and ministry-of-Jesus vehicles, it is difficult for us as late-twentieth-century believers to make this distinction, especially because the distinction has not been made during the past 19 centuries.[68] The anti-Jewish motif in John epitomizes the dilemma of modern believers: should sacred lore contain and legitimate denigration, vilification, and hatred of Jews and of Judaism, even if these attitudes originate in misreading, mistranslation, misperception, and misinterpretation?

Chapter 8

The Anti-Judaic Strand in Revelation: Judaism within

Introduction

> I know your tribulation and your poverty (but you are rich) and the slander of those who say that they are Jews and are not, but are a synagogue of Satan. Do not fear what you are about to suffer. Behold, the devil is about to throw some of you into prison, that you may be tested, and for ten days you will have tribulation. Be faithful unto death, and I will give you the crown of life. (Rev. 2:9–10)
>
> Behold, I will make those of the synagogue of Satan who say that they are Jews and are not, but lie—behold, I will make them come and bow down before your feet, and learn that I have loved you. (Rev. 3:9)

From the Reformation to modernity, the Book of Revelation has captured the imagination and the emotional allegiance of countless believers. Favored by enthusiasts, its fascination with violence and suffering has been viewed with suspicion by those concerned with the impact of fiery and extreme imagery. Traditionally, Revelation 2:9–10 and 3:9 have been read as attacks on Judaism. Traditional scholarship has read Revelation 2:9–10 and 3:9 as targeting local Jews, instructing us that the community reflected in the Apocalypse of John struggled with "Jews" *ca.* 80–100 CE. James and the Book of Revelation are considered by many to be the most Jewish-Christian texts in the New Testament. Revelation uses gematria (Hebrew numerology) and the Greek in this document contains more Hebraisms than any other New Testament writing,[1] hinting that John and the congregations addressed to in

Revelation had been influenced by Judaism, whether directly or through the agency of the Jewish followers of Jesus.

The enigmatic accusations in Revelation 2:9–10 and 3:9, part of two letters to believers in Jesus in Smyrna and Philadelphia, have baffled scholars for centuries. These verses target those "who say that they are Jews and are not" during the last decades of the first century. As it pertains to our survey of the anti-Jewish strand in Revelation, our main query is whether these segments originate with the Jewish followers of Jesus (where audience and adversaries are Jews), in an internal debate within the Jesus movement (where both parties are followers of Jesus),[2] or in Jewish Christian inter-religious tensions.[3] Whether Revelation 2:9 and 3:9 represent a Jewish sectarian view of mainstream Judaism, a Gentile view of Judaism or an internal struggle within the Jesus movement is the question before us. There are four theoretical possibilities as to the identity of the intended adversaries:

1. Mainstream Jews (Jewish non-believers in Jesus).
2. Gentile sympathizers with Judaism (Gentile Judaizers)
3. Gentile sympathizers with the descendants of Jesus's disciples and first followers.
4. The descendants of Jesus's disciples and first followers.

Mainstream Jews

The view that the adversaries of the author of Revelation were the Jews is compatible with the current meta-narrative about the "conflict between Judaism and Christianity." This view sees the Jewish Christian saga as resulting from tensions between the two faiths. Some scholars have concluded that the intended adversaries are worshiping at "Jewish synagogues," an interpretation supported by a literal reading of the text. The arguments put forward by supporters of the traditional reading are: first, they are called a "synagogue of Satan" (2:9–10), a curious nomenclature for any other than Jews. Second, there seems to be an attempt to associate the adversaries with persecution and imprisonment[4] of Gentile believers, an accusation later voiced against 'the Jews.' A neotraditionalist reading of Revelation may be plausible if we assume that the anti-Jewish-establishment rhetoric that characterized the posturing of Jewish sectarians toward the Jewish mainstream could be operative here. If we assume that an earlier version of Revelation originated in a community of Jewish followers of Jesus, 2:9–10 and 3:9 may be read as "Qumran-like" classical Jewish sectarian posturing toward mainstream Jews, who may be seen by the author as unworthy and false Jews.

Gentile Sympathizers with Judaism

According to current scholarship, Paul provides evidence for the existence of Gentile sympathizers with Judaism in the same geographical area, a few decades prior to Revelation's authorship.[5] This evidence would be supportive of the identification of Revelation's immediate adversaries as Gentile Judaizers. Indeed, the author of Revelation seems to deploy the term "Jew" in the same way that the Gospel of John and Epictetus do; to refer to Jewish ethnicity and to affinity to Judaism. The opponents referred to in 2:9–10 and 3:9—identified as part of the "synagogue of Satan" in Smyrna and Philadelphia—are claiming to be Jewish but are not. Therefore, John's vitriol may be aimed at Gentiles who falsely claimed to be Jews and followed a Jewish lifestyle.[6] It has also been suggested that some Gentile believers in Asia Minor were identifying themselves as Jews in order to escape Roman harassment, given that the Jews had a unique and prestigious position in the Roman world and were not required to sacrifice to the Roman Gods. By claiming to be Jews, Gentile believers in Jesus would avoid the fate that some were experiencing at the hands of the Romans. Therefore, if Gentile sympathizers with Judaism are in view in Revelation, a further motive for Judaizing may be operative here: fear of persecution by the Romans.[7]

Gentile Sympathizers with the Jewish Followers of Jesus

Those who (in the author's eyes) falsely claimed to be Jews could, of course, have been Gentile sympathizers with the Jewish faction, some of which may have converted to Judaism.[8] As noted in our discussion of the Gospel of John, this argument is strengthened by the observation that the leap from Gentile belief in Jesus to establishment Judaism[9] is too great to be assumed, especially when synagogues of descendants of the Jewish founders (where Jesus would be exalted and venerated instead of rejected) would be a more obvious and more emphatic place of worship. Therefore, contrary to the current consensus, Gentile believers would be attracted to the synagogues of the descendants of Jesus's disciples and first followers because they were perceived by many to be the true guardians of his legacy, not on account of their Judaism. That Gentile sympathizers with the Jewish faction are involved may be supported by Ignatius in his letter to the Philadelphians, at approximately the same time of Revelation's authorship. Thus, if Revelation 2:9–10 and 3:9 aim at Gentile sympathizers with the descendants of the founding fathers, these accusations would not reflect a struggle between Jews and Christians.

Rather, they point to a conflict among Gentile followers of Jesus, one side favoring a strong Jewish affiliation, the other calling for rejection of the beliefs and traditions of the founding fathers. In this case the main motivating factor behind worship at the synagogue would be fellowship with the descendents of the founding fathers, not attraction to Judaism. Attraction to Judaism would be a consequence, not the cause, of this behavior.

The Descendants of Jesus's Disciples and First Followers

In Revelation the immediate targets seem to be those whose attendance of Jewish synagogues is suspect, not those who would normally worship there. However, Revelation's author may be seen as targeting the influence of the descendants of the founding fathers among his congregants. Thus, despite the fact that the text seems to aim at Gentiles (those who say that they are Jews and are not), its intended and ultimate adversaries seem to be the descendants of the founding fathers, whose influence among Gentile converts seems to exasperate the author and would be the trigger for the author's ire.

Conclusions

Revelation is cryptic and enigmatic and does not yield the identity of its adversaries. My inclination for setting Revelation's authorship within the Jesus movement stems from the fact that no intrinsic Jewish issues (Torah observance, dietary law, Sabbath observance, the covenant, etc.) are addressed by the text. Furthermore, the final text of Revelation seems concerned with both; believers attracted to the descendants of Jesus's disciples and first followers, and those with Pagan inclinations and affiliations—strengthening the internal setting option. Revelation not only rallies against "those that say they are Jews and are not," it also rallies against believers in Jesus with Pagan inclinations and affiliations in the letter to believers in Pergamum (Rev. 2:14) and in the letter to believers in Thyatira (Rev. 2:20). Thus, Revelation showcases a conflict between the author/editor of the canonical text and followers of Jesus with varying degrees of Jewish and Pagan affinities, affiliations, and inclinations—pointing to a debate within the Jesus movement. Therefore, the debate would not be with Paganism and Judaism. Rather, the debate seems to be about Paganism and Judaism. It seems to me that we can detect an external enemy (the Romans)[10] and internal foes (the descendants if the Jewish founders and differing Gentiles). I am inclined to think that at this early stage, and for most of the texts presented in this section, the underlying and defining socio-theological process is a struggle about identity, authority, and legitimacy between the Jerusalem faction and the Gentile forms of belief in Jesus that surfaced following the Pauline and Gnostic missions to the Gentiles. As it pertains to our goal of tracking the evolution of the anti-Jewish strand, whether the religious opponents are "Jews," Jewish believers in Jesus, or Gentile sympathizers with the Jewish faction,[11] the historical context does not favor a conflict between "Judaism" and "Christianity." Revelation may reflect a setting not dissimilar to Matthew and John, where a tradition of anti-Jewish-establishment rhetoric that originated with the founding faction may have been appropriated-subverted and turned against them, as the establishment group within the Jesus movement. The text reflects a period of significant instability and lack of theological integration. Similar to the situation we encountered in John, Revelation seems to reflect the emotional, theological, and social consequences of the estrangement of Gentiles from the descendants of Jesus's disciples and first followers. I agree with Wilson, Murray, and others as to the de-externalization of the conflict and its re-placement within the Jesus movement. I differ in that, to me, the epicenter of Revelation is the hold that the descendants of Jesus's disciples and first followers had over new converts, not the attraction that mainstream Judaism exerted over them.

Chapter 9

The Anti-Jewish Strand—The Embryonic Stage Summary

Introduction

During the first three hundred years of belief in Jesus there was no consensus on which texts should be considered authoritative.[1] The Synoptic Gospels, divergent on narrative and theology, are renditions of the life and ministry of Jesus of Nazareth that became canonical among Pauline orthodox believers some three hundred years after their authorship. The full current canon first emerges in a list compiled by Athanasius, the bishop of Alexandria (*ca.* 367 CE). The understanding that factional agendas underpin the writing of the canonical texts is increasingly accepted among New Testament scholars. The NT texts are windows into the conflicts and debates of the authors' generation. When a scribe sat down to write an account of Jesus's ministry, he had goals and alternatives. The paths chosen were not inevitable; they reflect the writers' circumstances, concerns, and agendas.

Missionary and Secessionist Trajectories

We can identify throughout the lore two main trajectories for the emergence of communities of Gentile believers in Jesus, a conceptual distinction that may be useful in understanding the evolution of different strands of anti-Jewish rhetoric. The distinction between missionary and secessionist trajectories seems useful in our attempts to decipher the curious coexistence of intense rhetoric against the beliefs and traditions of the founding fathers in texts that seem to reflect significant Jewish influence and/or some knowledge of Jewish traditions. Most communities seem to have emerged out of one of these pathways. However, some communities may have experienced a layered or mixed trajectory.

> *Missionary communities*—members of Pauline and Gnostic missionary communities would have limited knowledge of Judaism and would have encountered the Jewish faction and its Gentile sympathizers as external adversaries who considered their beliefs inadequate and insufficient. Their grievances and their vitriol toward the descendants of Jesus's disciples and first followers would be less intense and personal (candidates—Mark, the later and Gentile layers of Matthew and John, Luke/Acts, and Justin).

These are communities that emerged from the Pauline and Gnostic missions to the Gentiles. This seems to have been the main thrust behind the demographic growth of the Jesus movement. These communities would have little or no interaction with the Jerusalem faction during the embryonic stages of community formation. However, tensions arose as these new converts encountered the descendants of Jesus's disciples and first followers or their Gentile sympathizers in the public arena, and became aware of their claims that Gentile forms of belief in Jesus were "insufficient" and "lacking." Often, members of these communities did not differentiate between followers of Jesus of Jewish origin and mainstream Jews, and may have understood the Pauline legacy as one of confrontation with, and negation of, Judaism.

> *Secessionary communities[2]*—Gentile believers that seceded from, or were rejected by, communities of the Jewish followers of Jesus would display the most strident and extreme "anti-Jewish" bent. Their sense of grievance, their anger, and their rancor would be personal and gut wrenching (possible candidates: proto-Matthew, proto-John, Barnabas, and Hebrews). These communities or individuals would incorporate-appropriate-emulate elements of the identity and lore of the parent community.

During the decades following Jesus's death, and in areas and towns where there was a strong presence of the Jewish faction, Gentile individuals or groups may have joined the synagogues or communities of the descendants of the founding fathers. This would be a natural consequence of the sway that the descendants of Jesus's disciples and first followers exerted over recent converts. Some of these Gentiles may have integrated successfully into the host communities. Others may have felt alienated in the Jewish milieu of these Jewish sectarians, rejected Judaism, seceded, and formed Gentile communities. This short-lived fellowship between Jewish and Gentile followers of Jesus may explain the existence of Gentile leaders and intellectuals with some exposure and knowledge of Judaism; the agents in the upcoming selective incorporation-appropriation of the identity, lore, beliefs, and traditions of the founding fathers into Gentile forms of belief in Jesus. This seems to have been a smaller, but militant and influential, evolutionary track that produced some of the most resentful "anti-Jewish" rhetoric.

*   *   *

It seems to me that, for the most part, Jews and Gentiles did not enjoy a cordial fellowship within the Jesus movement. For a while, some among the Jerusalem faction and small numbers of Gentiles may have attempted full fellowship and may have coexisted in an asymmetrical relationship. However, it appears that most Gentiles found the Jewish milieu of the descendants of the founding fathers alien and yearned for recognition and legitimacy as rightful followers of Jesus—despite their rejection of the beliefs and traditions of the founding generation. On the other hand, members of the Jewish faction may have remained ambivalent and equivocal about the many forms of Gentile belief in Jesus that surfaced following the Pauline and Gnostic missions to the Gentiles, resulting in self-segregation and mounting tension.

As time passed the anti-establishment posturing, characteristic of secessionist communities, merged with the milder strand originating in the Pauline and Gnostic missionary communities. If we add the pro-Torah but anti-Jewish-establishment rhetoric of the Jewish founders, we have the anti-Jewish collage that we encounter in the New Testament. This mix yields the confusing, ambivalent, and seemingly contradictory signals about Jews and Judaism that we encounter in the lore. The fusion and the confusion of these rhetorical layers and groups in the hearts and minds of Pauline-Lukan believers may have become an ingrained tradition before the turn of the first century. It seems that the distinction between three types of "Jews" (mainstream Jews, the Jewish followers of Jesus, and their Gentile sympathizers) started to fade quite early too. The use of the identifiers "they/them" and "Ioudaioi" to address and identify a variety of Jewish antagonists is present already in the Gospel of John and in Barnabas, and may have been commonplace at the time,[3] adding further confusion and ambivalence to the mix.

A Growing Tension

Following the destruction of the Temple and the decimation of Judea during the Jewish War of 70 CE, the strongholds of the Jewish faction fade away and the center of gravity of the Jesus movement gradually shift from Torah-observant Judaism to Gentile variants of belief in Jesus.

Several Gentile strands of belief in Jesus, with competing proto-theologies, gospels, and embryonic organizational structures, gain definition in the post-70 CE era.[4] Most Gentile believers in Jesus were inhabitants of the Roman Empire but were culturally and ethnically diverse. Creedal confusion, organizational chaos, ceremonial improvisation, and religious experimentation were rampant.[5] Therefore, it is not surprising that differing accounts of the life and ministry of Jesus were written during the first and second centuries reflecting the transitional and tentative nature of this period. A number of Gospels have survived, four of which are included in the New Testament canon. The Jewish followers of Jesus with their vast historical and religious heritage and Gnosticism with its diverse and fascinating esoteric theologies were the two poles that set the range for the second-century identity-forming crucible. As Gentiles grew increasingly assertive in their opposition to the descendants of the founding fathers they began using Jesus's life story, epistles, homilies, and sermons to address issues of concern to their rank and file, and to provide guidance to their beleaguered communities:

1. Should Gentile belief in Jesus be Jewish, Pauline, or Gnostic?
2. Could Gentiles follow Jesus without becoming Jews?
3. How did Gentiles fit in the ministry of a Jewish Messiah?
4. Why did the disciples reject Paul's interpretation of Jesus's ministry?
5. How to explain the estrangement from the descendants of the founders?

During the period between the two failed Judean uprisings (70–135 CE), emboldened by the success of the Pauline and Gnostic missions and by the decimation of the strongholds of the Jewish faction in Judea, Gentile intellectuals and leaders deployed a variety of literary platforms to put forward their claim as rightful believers in Jesus. However, lacking the means to impose an outcome, the internal struggle within the Jesus movement will linger through two–three centuries of stalemate and attrition. The battle about "what belief in Jesus should be" degenerated into a protracted struggle in which the weapons of choice seem to have been defamation and bitter and derogatory vitriol.

The canonical Gospels were authored during this transitional period. Gentile believers, diverse and lacking a coherent and normative theology, had to navigate the counter-currents of continuity and discontinuity vis-à-vis the legacy of the founding fathers. The disciples that "did not understand, denied and betrayed," and the rejection and denigration of the beliefs and traditions of the Jewish followers of Jesus seem to shadow the Pauline-Markan intent to claim a superior understanding of Jesus's ministry vis-à-vis that of the founding faction. These mutually sustaining polemical tools seem to signal to Gentile converts that opposition to the imposition of the beliefs and traditions of the descendants of Jesus's disciples and first followers is legitimate. The dilemma of the Pauline-Lukan literati was how to de-Judaize belief in Jesus, without appearing irreverent toward the founding fathers and to Jesus's religious beliefs. In pursuit of these goals they gradually gravitated toward a strategy that had two components: to place a wedge between Jesus and his disciples and first followers, and to build on the aversion of most Gentiles to the beliefs and traditions of the founders. The Synoptics gave their communities, beleaguered by dissent and self-doubt, a legitimating narrative: the Jewish faction may be the descendants of Jesus's disciples and first followers but their ancestors did not "understand" Jesus's true message. Moreover, his messiahship was hidden to "them" but clear to "us." As proven by their scriptures, the Jews were sinful and had lost God's favor. Consequently, the descendants of the founding fathers can no longer claim to be the custodians and interpreters of Jesus's legacy.

Moreover, the Qumran-New Testament connection seems to support a major thesis of this manuscript, namely, that in their quest to de-Judaize the Jesus movement, Pauline believers subverted-emulated-appropriated the anti-Jewish-establishment traditions, attitudes, and rhetoric of the founding fathers toward the Jewish mainstream, and converted them into an anti-Jewish-establishment tool within the Jesus movement. This "second generation" anti-Jewish-establishment rhetoric was aimed at the descendants of Jesus's disciples and first followers, who were (at the time) the establishment of the Jesus movement and the authoritative guardians and keepers of Jesus's legacy. In the New Testament these two anti-Jewish-establishment layers are intertwined and provide the scaffold for the anti-Jewish strand. In other words, the "Jews" of the canonical Gospels seem to reflect the fusion and confusion of two types of Jews, the antagonists of two distinct struggles. In the most ancient strata, the protagonists are the Jewish followers of Jesus and their antagonists are Judeans in positions of authority (i.e., the Pharisees, the scribes, the elders, the High Priests). In the later strata, the protagonists are Gentile believers in Jesus and their antagonists are the founding faction and their Gentile sympathizers. The earlier stratum reflects the debate among Jews about who Jesus was (messiah or not).[6] The later one reflects the debate among Gentile believers about "what belief in Jesus ought to be" (Jewish, Pauline-Lukan, Pauline-Marcionite, or Gnostic), and about who Jesus was (human, divine, or both). The texts and the tradition reflect the fusion and confusion of these distinct debates and their misinterpretation by later believers as a conflict between Judaism and Christianity. The misperception about the existence of a conflict between Judaism and Christianity was for the most part a consequence, not the originating cause, of anti-Jewish attitudes among early Gentile believers in Jesus.

In summary, in the canonical texts we find hints that a challenge to the legitimacy of the descendants of Jesus's disciples and first followers, the original guardians of his legacy, was brewing up. The main clues that did steer our inquiry in that direction are:

1. Denigration of the beliefs and traditions of the founding fathers.
2. The denigration and vilification of the disciples.
3. Family, friends, and disciples that "do not understand, deny and abandon."
4. Shift from "the chief priests, the scribes and the elders" (Mark 14:43) to "the Jews."
5. Appropriation and decontextualization of the identity and lore of the founders.
6. Intensification of the anti-Jewish incitement as time passes.
7. Exoneration of the Romans and culpability of "the Jews."
8. Embrace of the biblical narrative while divesting beliefs and traditions demanded by it.

It seems to me that the vacuum of leadership, and of authority, created by the decimation of the communities of the descendants of the Jewish founders in Judea during the Jewish War may have opened a window of opportunity for the non-Jewish majority, triggering and facilitating the transition to an overt confrontation about identity, legitimacy, and authority. In the anti-Jewish-establishment traditions of Judean sectarians, Pauline-Lukan believers found a "ready to deploy" arsenal that could be used to demote the establishment of the Jesus movement: the descendants of the founding fathers. This throve of anti-Jewish-establishment lore will become a tool to sever the influence of the founding faction and to de-Judaize belief in Jesus. By appropriating and by decontextualizing the Judean anti-establishment lore of the founding fathers and other Judean sectarians, and by decontextualizing the Judean prophetic tradition and the Judean tradition of self-criticism, Lukan believers embedded the campaign to de-Judaize belief in Jesus in seemingly authoritative and venerated claims.

In light of these conclusions I found it necessary to suggest a modified and expanded version of Hare's terms and categories of anti-Judaism[7] as follows:

1. Prophetic anti-establishment criticism, as found among the Jewish prophets.[8]
2. Judean anti-Jewish-establishment rhetoric.[9] The anti-Jewish-establishment lore of Jewish sectarians (Enochic, Jubilean, and Qumran rhetoric as well as the rhetoric of the messianic followers of Jesus).
3. Gentile anti-Jewish-establishment rhetoric. Gentile rhetoric directed against the establishment of the Jesus movement, that is, the Jewish followers of Jesus.

4. Gentile anti-Judaism, the rhetoric that emerged out of fusion and confusion of the previous layers and the transformation of a conflict about Judaism, into a conflict with Judaism.
5. Anti-Semitism, the later culture of disenfranchisement, hatred, and persecution that emerged out of the sacrosanct status of the anti-Jewish strand.

The Road Ahead

Why does the anti-Judaic ire increase as the distance (in time, geography, and cultural background) between the author and the events grow? Why is it that as we transit from Mark to later authors, the claims about the responsibility regarding Jesus's death widen and ultimately encompass the Jewish people? Why does the canonical anti-Judaic bent pale in comparison to what is to come in the second century? Why does the defamation of "Jews" and of "Judaism" intensifies as we travel further away from Jesus's lifetime?

It seems that throughout the trajectory from Paul forward, anti-Jewish sentiment is symptomatic of an underlying crisis; it is the barometer by which we can gage the intensity of the emotions associated with the estrangement between Jews and Gentiles in the Jesus movement. At the dawn of the second century the tensions that had been brewing under the surface between the "founding fathers" and most Gentiles did reach a boiling point and did erupt into the open in a flurry of unrestrained anti-Jewish sentiment. It seems that Gentiles who were attracted to the descendants of the founders provoked strong anti-Jewish reactions from ecclesiastical leaders who, through their criticism of Jews and Jewish customs, sought to dissuade members of their congregations from such behavior.[10] As texts containing the rhetoric and the polemic accompanying these conflicts became increasingly authoritative, anti-Jewish attitudes were exacerbated, legitimized, and sanctified. Given the ingredients, the outcome is hardly surprising.

Eventually, the struggle against the descendants of Jesus's disciples and first followers had to be erased from the collective memory of the movement. Misinterpretation, misrepresentation, and loss of context also contributed to transforming this conflict against internal opponents that were Jews, into a struggle against external Judaism—thereby shielding the emerging orthodoxy from the embarrassing implications of the de-Judaizing of belief in Jesus and the demotion and delegitimating of the descendants of those chosen by Jesus to be the custodians of his legacy.

A Personal Note

The first draft of this monograph was entitled "Re-Reading the New Testament" and was intended as a report on my encounter with the unsettling anti-Judaic polemic in Paul and in the Synoptic Gospels. However, as my excursion progressed, I became aware of more extreme levels of anti-Jewish incitement at the historical downstream (John, Hebrews, the church fathers, and other second- and third-century authoritative texts). I soon realized that Paul and the Synoptics were only the preamble, the foundation, of what was to come. As I reached the periphery of the original range, I realized that the project was incomplete, that the issues had not been fully engaged and had not been brought to proper closure. The gap between the anti-Judaic mindset I had encountered in Paul and in the Synoptics and later anti-Semitism was too wide. Gradually, I came to the realization that I had surveyed the first floor of a towering edifice. Without yet having an understanding or a conceptual map of where I was going, I crossed the gateway into the second phase of this work.

My encounter with the anti-Jewish intensity of the texts ahead of us was disconcerting and gut-wrenching. Compared to the texts ahead of us, the original causes of my outrage felt tame, almost harmless. However, as I attempted to processes these new texts, paralysis took hold of me. I could not digest the new material; I could neither process it, nor write about it. Somehow, my verbal skills were inadequate to cope with the ever-increasing escalation. After many months of stalemate, I gradually realized what had happened: I had exhausted my emotional and expressive range. I had no conceptual space, no cognitive range, to accommodate the next phase of virulence. I had exhausted my ability to describe and grade the ever-growing levels of abuse.

When the reality you encounter overwhelms your cognitive and verbal range, what terms do you use to describe further denigration? Eventually I had to recalibrate and tone down my descriptions of the previous phase to create cognitive space for the more intense and virulent literature of the second and third centuries. In other words, I had to scale down the terminology used to describe the Pauline and the Synoptic challenge to the beliefs, authority, and traditions of the founding fathers, in order to free "derogatory range" to accommodate the upcoming and more strident anti-Jewish phase.

For our purposes, it is important to point out that the phase we are about to enter is the continuation, not the beginning, of a process. Partisan enthusiasts authored and edited the authoritative texts that we will encounter in the next section. Significantly, this next phase would not have come about without the foundation provided by the texts we have surveyed. Strangely, we are both—fortunate and unfortunate. We are fortunate that the majority of the texts that were eventually canonized belong to the earlier phase and that most of the texts that were authored during the second century did not become part of the New Testament. We are also unfortunate: the texts that were eventually canonized were written during the embryonic stages of belief in Jesus, a period of tensions between believers with pro- and anti-Jewish inclinations and affiliations. This tragic coincidence embedded a footprint of anti-Jewish sentiment in the lore of the victorious faction and in the hearts and minds of believers.

Chapter 10

Supersession

Introduction

It is probable that we will never know with certainty what Paul's true attitude toward Judaism was. We know, however, that when Gentile believers needed a foundation for their rejection of the beliefs and traditions of their Jewish opponents, they found in Paul the theological and polemical support they needed. Whether this exegesis was based on a true and correct understanding of Paul's intent (the traditionalists) or on its distortion (the revisionists) is an open debate. By the dawn of the second century, the antagonism between followers of Jesus of Jewish ancestry and believers in Jesus of Pagan ancestry was a few generations old, and intensifying. Within a couple of generations after Jesus's short ministry, the Pauline and Gnostic missions to the Gentiles and the descendants of the Jewish founders created a tripolar reality that made a confrontation about identity, legitimacy, and authority inevitable. Christianity-as-we-know-it emerges from the melting pot of the religious "civil war" that ensued. The texts before us were authored during this period and reflect the factionalism, confusion, anxiety, and heightened emotions that characterized the early phases of this struggle.

Supersession

Supersession theology provides the rationale for the de-Judaizing of the Jesus movement. It sustains the Pauline-Lukan claim to the custody and to "the" true interpretation of Jesus's legacy. The articulators of appropriation-supersession theology (Hebrews, Barnabas, and Justin) built on the selective and embryonic appropriation-incorporation of elements of the lore, traditions, and beliefs of the Jewish founders, by earlier Gentile believers.

To claim continuity with Jesus's ministry, and to keep the members of the contending factions in the fold, the emerging "orthodoxy" retained some elements of the beliefs and traditions of the founding fathers but rejected the core customs and traditions of Torah observance, circumcision, and dietary law—and rejected the Levitical priesthood. Flanked on all sides of the theological spectrum, the Pauline-Lukan faction opted for the midway between the rejection of, and continuity with, the Jewish faction. Given the proto-orthodox inclination to appropriate the identity and the lore of the Jewish founding fathers, the choice of the Israelites as YHWH's beloved had to be annulled, to undercut the claim of the descendants of the Jewish founders to being "God's chosen," the "New Israel," and the legitimate custodians of Jesus ministry.[1] To vest the Pauline-Lukan faction as God's new favorites, YHWH had to be "freed" from his particularistic commitment to the Jewish people. Thus, supersession theology emerged to explain to Gentile believers in Jesus the de-Judaizing of belief in Jesus via the "loss of God's favor" by all Jews, to the inclusion of the descendants of Jesus's disciples and first followers.

The alleged Jewish "loss of God's favor," which sustains supersession theology, is an elaboration (by non-Jews) of a traditional Jewish sectarian attitude toward establishment-Judaism. The claims "you have forfeited God's favor," "we are the new Israel," and "you are irredeemable" echo similar claims by the Enochic, Jubelean, and Qumranic texts. Indeed, the arguments and the language deployed by the Pauline-Lukan faction against the establishment of the Jesus movement emulate the language, the arguments, and the imagery that we encounter among Jewish sectarians and, we assume, would encounter among the Jewish followers of Jesus. Said differently, from the second century forward, the Pauline-Lukan will "turn the tables" and will confront the descendants of the founding fathers with Jewish-sectarian-like claims they harvested from the founders' texts and traditions. This identity emulation-transformation is unique in world history, is fascinating in its dynamics, tragic in its consequences.

Supersession-appropriation theology was necessary to justify the transfer of the Jewish God's favor to its new, non-Jewish and self-appointed, beneficiaries. By internalizing elements of the identity and lore of the descendants of the Jewish founders, the Pauline-Lukan faction emerged from this process thinking and feeling as a persecuted Jewish sect. Thus, the descendants of Jesus's disciples and first followers became the involuntary agents and facilitators in the transformation of non-Jewish believers in Jesus into militant pseudo-Jewish sectarians. The tension between the rejection of core beliefs and customs of the founding fathers and the wish to claim continuity with them, embedded a permanent ambivalence toward Judaism at the core of the emerging theology and teachings. Although this theological ploy was originally aimed at the descendents of the founding fathers, it eventually led to the disenfranchisement of Judaism.

The Forfeiture of God's Favor

Since time immemorial humans have attempted to decipher the ever-present and turbulent oscillations of reality and fate. The efforts to understand the vicissitudes of health, fertility, wealth, and survival populate the traditions of human civilizations since the dawn of history. All civilizations have attempted to grapple with divine favor and divine wrath. Throughout the Near East the Mesopotamian, Egyptian, Hittite, Canaanite, and Israelite cultures pondered the divine enigma in search for answers to these fundamental questions. The loss of God's favor, God's wrath, and God's chastisement are recurring motifs in ancient Near Eastern cultures. In many ancient civilizations, divine wrath and misfortune were often understood as originating in non-compliance with the sacrifices and ceremonies instituted to court the favor of the divine realm. The Mesopotamian "Gilgamesh Epic" and "Enuma Elish," the Egyptian "Deliverance of Mankind from Destruction," the Israelite flood story, the Canaanite "Epic of the Gods," and the Hittite "Myth of Telepinu" all attempt to grapple with these fundamental questions.

Judean Self-Criticism

Prophets were an integral part of the Israelite nation and often served as an ethical, political, and religious counterbalance to the monarchy and the religious establishment. Not all biblical prophets were alike; some were subservient to the crown,[2] while others confronted the monarchy and the people. Most demanded ethical conduct from both. Some prophets were political insiders; others were from the political fringes. Some prophets were part of the cultural elite; others were uneducated. Most biblical prophets exhorted the flock to repent and return to the ways of the Lord. The often-adversarial prophet-king relationship that we encounter throughout much of the Israelite texts reflects not only the tensions between secular and religious elites, but also a tradition of opposition to power and despotism that originates in the pre-monarchical tribal setting.[3] However, in "real-time" it was impossible to identify true prophecy from the many seers, fortune-tellers, political doomsayers, and false prophets that crowded the biblical marketplace of divination.[4] At any given time, there were many "prophets," some supporting one side of a controversy, others supporting the opposing view.

The biblical standard for true prophesy is Deut. 18:22: "[W]hen a prophet speaks in the name of the LORD, if the word does not come to pass or come true, that is a word which the LORD has not spoken; the prophet has spoken it presumptuously, you need not be afraid of him." Canonization of prophets came during the second Temple period and was a retroactive exercise by scribes and religious functionaries aimed at furthering religious interests and agendas. It is no surprise that among the many prophets and seers active in the Israelite marketplace of divination, the Jewish cannon favors prophets that challenged the monarchy and therefore laid the ground to legitimate the transition from Davidic to priestly rule.

It is noteworthy that Israelites developed a remarkable and unparalleled inclination and predisposition for self-criticism and introspection that may have originated in the dialectic between the monarchy, the tribal structure, and the religious establishment. The anti-establishment stance of the canonical prophets, and the recurrent chastisement of the nation, became part of the nation's psyche and a by-product of the priestly ascendancy following the end of the monarchic period. Cycles of favor and disfavor and of grace and sin, engendered by this tradition and probably inserted by priestly editors, were seized upon by later Jewish sectarians to chastise establishment-Judaism. Ruether is correct when she claims that prophetic exhortation is significantly different from the Christian claims about Israel's apostasy and forfeiture of God's favor due to the emotional and national loyalties of the critics. The former are members of a group articulating an edifying call to the flock, the latter is an attempt to divest a nation of its heritage.[5] Evans probes further and concludes that in-house prophetic criticism, no longer understood as challenge from within the community of faith, was understood as condemnation of a particular people outside of the faith—the people who had rejected Jesus, his apostles, and the church. In light of this truncated hermeneutic, Gentile polemicists could cite scripture from both Testaments as a weapon against the Jewish people.[6] Beck adds that the self-criticism that Judaism did permit made it particularly vulnerable to the polemical attacks of its offspring and later competitors.[7] However, despite the recurrence and the pervasiveness of anti-Jewish arguments, themes, and motifs throughout the texts before us, the deep well of Jewish ethics has also nurtured and edified Gentile believers in Jesus for almost two millennia.

Judean self-criticism and Judean anti-establishment rhetoric, the quarry where many Pauline-Lukan anti-Jewish stones originate, do reflect Jewish humility and the traditional Judean inclination to chastise and humble the people and its leaders. The Israelite tradition of self-criticism was harnessed by Pauline-Lukan thinkers to "justify" the Jewish "forfeiture of God's favor" (i.e., the transfer of God's favor from the founding faction to the Gentile followers of Paul). This takeover of the Jewish scriptures became one of the most formidable tools in the proto-orthodox quest for ascendancy. When the nation's prophets add the burden of guilt and sin to the consequences of a national calamity or defeat it may be considered a benign effort to edify the nation, a call for renewed commitment to Torah observance. This manipulation of suffering may be acceptable (although ethically questionable) in the context of internal self-criticism. However, the harnessing of this unique and admirable Judean capacity for self-criticism to demote the Jewish founders of the Jesus movement had momentous consequences. In the next chapters we will witness how these assertions gradually morphed into claims to the supersession of "Judaism" by "Christianity." Centuries later, the projection onto Judaism of this rhetoric (originally aimed at the Jewish founders) did create an untenable situation for a militant and exclusivist church aiming for worldwide ascendancy and claiming to exclusive status as YHWH's chosen. Following the projection onto Judaism of the arguments used to demote the descendents of the founding fathers, the continuing existence of Judaism eventually became a threat to the church's legitimacy and hegemony.

God's Wrath, Calamities, and Defeat as God's Retribution

The idea that misfortune is a sign of God's displeasure comes from an equation common to most ancient cultures and religions: good fortune = divine favor. In the ancient world, appeal to historical events to legitimate religious claims was common. Victory in war or a long and peaceful reign were considered signs of divine favor. Defeat was a sign of divine displeasure.[8] This axiom has been the legitimating creed of the victors, the powerful, and the mighty since times immemorial. Moreover, ethical monotheists tend to see victory as a sign of righteousness and predestination, thereby making critical and rational historical analysis difficult and rare. The unjustifiable suffering of the innocent and the recurrence of "righteous but vanquished" and "evil but victorious" should have challenged ethical monotheists since law, religion, and ethics first merged, apparently in King Hammurabi's law code (Babylonia 1795–1750 BC). Unjustifiable evil and suffering, in a world created by a benevolent, omniscient, and omnipotent deity, posit a daunting challenge to ethical monotheists. Under the construct of ethical monotheism, suffering, and defeat are signs of God's displeasure or the consequence of sinful behavior. At the national level, this corollary of ethical monotheism turns national defeats or disasters into signs of retribution for sinfulness. This axiom transforms victims into accomplices in their own suffering and inculcates in them inner doubt, self-loathing, and a sense of "deserving" their tragic circumstances. The mechanism at play is a double jeopardy of the victim. The victim, individual or nation, not only suffer the calamity and its consequences; it is also driven to accept the burden of guilt and sin. When the poor, the meek, and the victim are made responsible for their predicament, they are also made guilty of their circumstances, thereby "freeing" society of responsibility.

Sin, Guilt, and Ethical Monotheism

When the Jewish God entered the Pauline pantheon he had been the traveling companion of the Judean nation for many generations (3,500 years according to Jewish scripture, some 1,500–2,000 years according to historical research). By the turn of the era, the Judean understanding of the divine already embodied a long mythical and historical journey whose origins can be traced back to Canaanite deities. The first-century Judean understanding of its God may be described as henotheistic,[9] anthropomorphic, and idiosyncratic. Contrary to popular misperceptions, the Judean journey from the henotheistic outlook of its tribal origins to monotheism was protracted and complex. Only after the return from the Persian exile and the ascendance of the priestly class, Israelites gradually moved ever closer to unequivocal monotheism.[10]

According to Jewish scripture, YHWH is a just and severe God who is also inscrutable, wrathful, vengeful, zealous, capricious, and temperamental. Furthermore, the Jewish God is omnipotent, omnipresent, and omniscient but not necessarily benevolent. This complex and seemingly contradictory persona may facilitate the believer's coping with the reality of evil. In Judaism, evil, suffering, and injustice are part of the complexity of reality. Thus, Jews can accommodate evil without processing it into personal sin and guilt, avoiding the devastating effects that this internalization has on ethical monotheists. Gentile believers in Jesus, free from the ethnic and historical "baggage" of the Jewish faction, did gravitate toward a fully benevolent, omnipotent, omnipresent, and omniscient God. However, since an omnipotent and benevolent God is incompatible with the recurring suffering of the righteous and the fortune of sinners, and evil cannot be attributed to God, believers have to internalize evil by processing it into individual sin and guilt—theirs or their enemies.

The Destruction of the Temple

The destruction of the Temple looms large in the canonical and in the authoritative lore.[11] The failed revolution of 70 CE and the destruction of the Temple were a great tragedy for the Judeans. With the loss of sovereignty, hopes for independence were dashed and the loss of life was great. However, the impact and the implications of the destruction of the Temple were not as dramatic, nor as definitive, as implied by the authoritative texts of the Pauline-Lukan faction or by Christian theology since. The destruction of the Temple as the pivot of Jewish decline, and as the turning point in Jewish-Christian relations, has been questioned by reevaluations that downgrade the devastation of 70 CE[12] and upgrade the impact of the Bar Kochba revolt of 135 CE.[13] Loss and decimation were great during the Jewish War, but the Judeans had a long record of survival on which they could draw. The nation had rebounded from many reversals and the Temple had been rebuilt before.[14] Within Judaism the destruction of the Temple did not signal an irreversible loss of God's favor. Nor do Jewish sources endorse the Gentile claim that the loss of the Temple invalidated the observance of the Law or signaled the end of the covenant.[15] Furthermore, the legitimacy of the Herodian Temple had long been controversial among Jews and its destruction was not seen as a definitive blow to Judean national aspirations.

Jesus's attacks on the Temple are often presented in the authoritative lore as unique and as "proving" the existence of unbridgeable differences between Jesus and fellow Jews. However, anti-Temple sentiment and the belief that it had been defiled and desecrated were rather common in first-century Judea:[16] the Temple had been built by King Herod, whose Jewish ancestry was questionable and unacceptable to many traditionalists, and was therefore considered by many to be sacrilegious and impure. Herod was a Roman vassal who had been imposed and sustained by the Roman conquerors. His pro-Roman orientation made him and his actions suspect and controversial. He was hated by the populace. The murder of all the descendants of the Hasmonean Dynasty (the ruling family since the Maccabean revolt)[17] further alienated most Judeans. Furthermore, the decline in the status and in the prestige of the high priests (not rightful Zadokite priests but rather traitors, collaborators, and Roman appointees) fueled anti-Temple sentiment. At the time the Temple, the priesthood, and the cult were the focus of intense debates. Not all Jews were satisfied with the conduct of the Jerusalem cult, and some boycotted it.[18] Many[19] considered the priesthood in power and its liturgy blasphemous. Furthermore, the Qumranites, whose sacred texts are available to us in the Dead Sea Scrolls, were virulently "anti-establishment" and considered the Temple priesthood "the sons of darkness," the Temple defiled. E. P Sanders[20] regards Jesus's attitude toward the Temple as prophetic in nature. Craig Evans supports the thesis that Jesus's actions, similar to the Qumran position on this subject, were directed to the cleansing of the Temple[21] not to its destruction. Dunn sees Jesus's attack against the Temple as symbolic of his alienation from the ruling elite.[22]

From the Epistle to the Hebrews forward, the destruction of the Temple became a central theme in the lore of the Pauline-Lukan faction, distinct and separate from the actual impact it had on the Judeans. We have seen that, in accordance with the ancient understanding of the divine impact on military affairs, opponents would interpret the destruction of the Temple as a theological omen. It is no surprise, therefore, that the non-Jewish factions understood the loss of the Jewish cultic epicenter as supportive of their campaign to delegitimize the beliefs and traditions of their opponents. It seems that the defeat of "the Jews" was seen as synonymous to the defeat of the Jewish faction, and it was embraced as a trove in the propaganda war against them. In other words, the attempt to discredit, demote, and disenfranchise the descendants of Jesus's disciples and first followers was "corroborated" by God's unequivocal rejection of the Jews as illustrated by the destruction of the Temple.

It seems that plans to rebuild the Temple, first by Nerva and later by Trajan, caused great anxiety among the proto-orthodox. The jubilation over the weakening of the Jewish leadership was brought to a temporary halt when news of the upcoming rebuilding of the Temple spread. Suddenly, the great theological-rhetorical investment in the destruction of the Temple as "proof" of God's displeasure with the "Ioudaioi" was in jeopardy and a great embarrassment seemed to be imminent. Although these plans came to naught, they may have caused an increase in the intensity of the attacks by "Christians" against "Judaism" (i.e., attacks of the proto-orthodox against the descendants of the Jewish founders and their sympathizers) due to the implications of a sudden Jewish renaissance on the internal struggle. If the destruction of the Temple was a core element in the arguments that "proved" YHWH's abandonment of its favorites, its reconstruction would have been a great polemical blow to the Pauline-Lukan faction, the champions of the forfeiture theme. Wilson observes that Nerva's and Trajan's apparent support for the rebuilding of the Temple made Jewish hopes for a restoration seem more than a dream. However, with the devastating Jewish defeat under Hadrian, the future must have seemed, from a Pauline-Lukan perspective, secure.[23] I fully agree with Wilson's analysis but would place the argument and its consequences within the Jesus movement.

A recapitulation of the arguments that point to a needed reevaluation of the overstatements concerning the destruction of the Temple:

1. High priests were, for the most part, appointed by the conquerors and lost their religious legitimacy in the eyes the local population. Most of these traitors and collaborators with the Roman conquerors were opportunists that collected taxes and ruled the provinces on behalf of foreign oppressors. The decline in their prestige contributed to the decline in the status of the Temple prior to its destruction.

2. Many Judeans considered the edifice that was destroyed in 70 CE a sacrilege. It had been built by Herod who had murdered all the legitimate descendants to the throne under the patronage of foreign occupiers. The Herodian high priests were considered by most to be traitors and collaborators with the Romans. Many, sectarian and

mainstream alike, considered the Herodian Temple an abomination and prayed for its destruction.

3. The destruction of the Herodian Temple was seen by most Jews as a temporary setback that called for repentance and renewal, not a sign of a permanent rift between YHWH and his chosen.

4. By 70 CE, the transition from Temple-based to Synagogue-based Judaism was already underway and the destruction of the Temple did not end Jewish continuity. Rabbinical Judaism did emerge following the failed Judean revolutions due to the fact that by that time synagogues and prayer houses provided a foundation for Jewish life in Palestine and in the Diasporas.[24]

5. In the ancient world the military defeat of small nations often led to the elimination of the vanquished party as a political, religious, and cultural entity. However, by the turn of the era, Judaism had a collective history that spanned many generations and included many victories and many defeats. Military defeat or the destruction of the Temple, although great national tragedies, were not understood by Jews as "the end of the road."

In the aftermath of the Jewish War and emboldened by the Jewish defeat and by the decimation of the communities of the Jewish followers of Jesus in Judea, Gentile believers stepped up their de-Judaizing effort. However, it was only after the Judean defeat of 135 CE that the Pauline-Lukan faction launched a more overt crusade against the descendants of Jesus's disciples and first followers. Wilson and others have concluded that the Bar Kochba rebellion may have spurred Christian thinkers to recognize that the outcome of the Jewish War was final and God's judgment irrevocable.[25] Thus, the Judean defeats (the Jewish War 66–74, the uprisings in Cyrene and Egypt in 115–117 CE, and the Bar Kochba revolt 132–135) became rhetorical ramps that facilitated the de-Judaizing of the Jesus movement and the assault on the legitimacy of the Jewish elite. With the Bar Kochba revolt, the slow decline of the descendants of the Jewish founders accelerated, and the slow ascendancy of the Pauline-Lukan faction was enabled and facilitated. The emphasis is on slow, for despite the decimation of their Judean stronghold, the Jewish faction and their Gentile sympathizers remained a formidable opponent. Not until Theodosius I (379–395 CE) did the demotion of the descendants of the founding fathers and the ascendancy of the Pauline-Lukan faction reach an irreversible turning point.

In summary, Jewish suffering was seen by the Pauline-Lukan faction as a reflection of God's wrath and was deemed to support and justify their claim to being the new guardians of Jesus's legacy. The suffering of the Jews, to the inclusion of the descendants of the founding fathers, was showcased as proof of their "loss of God's favor." The supporting rationale seems to have been that if the Jews were no longer God's chosen, the Jewish followers of Jesus could no longer claim to be the guardians of Jesus's legacy either. Accordingly, to Pauline-Lukan leaders, the Judean defeats and tribulations were punishment for: the death of God's servants (Matt. 22:7), the persecution of Christians (Justin Dial, 16), the death of Jesus (Luke 23:37–41; Justin Dial. 16; Tertullian Marc. 3.23; Origen Cels. 1.47; 4.22, 32; 8.42), the death of James (Origen Cels. 1.47), God had spoken (Matt. 22:7; 23:37–39 = Luke 13:34–35). We also find that it was a fulfillment of prophecy (Justin Dial. 16, 110; I Apol. 47; Tertullian Marc. 3.23) and the disinheritance of the Jews (Justin Dial. 40,46).

Afterthoughts

The appropriation-supersession move by Pauline-Lukan leaders and intellectuals seems to have emerged to counter the arguments of their adversaries that Jesus was a Torah-observant Jew and that his beliefs and traditions should anchor belief in Jesus. Since the Pauline proto-orthodox rejected Judaism but did not want to reinvent themselves outside the Jewish narrative, they had to articulate a rationale for their rejection of the beliefs and traditions espoused by those chosen by Jesus to be the custodians of his legacy. It seems that, in order to confront this dilemma, Pauline proto-orthodox intellectuals and leaders gravitated to the deployment of a variety of means to erode the status of the descendents of the founding fathers (use of Jesus's life story to denigrate the disciples, the subversion-appropriation of pre-existing anti-Jewish-establishment lore and rhetoric, the de-contextualizing of the Hebrew Scriptures and of Judean self-criticism). By harvesting the anti-Jewish-establishment lore of Judean sectarians, these authors gathered an assortment of "off-the-shelf" rhetorical arrows that they could harness to argue for the de-Judaizing of belief in Jesus. This collection of polemical arrows included an array of Pauline-Lukan anti-Jewish staples that were originally deployed by Jewish sectarians against the Judean establishment (you have lost God's favor, we are God's new chosen, we are the new Israel, we embody a new covenant, the Temple and the priesthood are defiled and no longer authoritative, etc.). However, contrary to Judean sectarians who used this rhetoric to reform Judaism, the proto-orthodox wanted to eradicate Judaism from the Jesus movement—inclining them to decontextualize, expand, and intensify the appropriated polemic. Whereas the rhetoric of Judean sectarians was aimed at correcting the behavior of fellow Jews and allowed for a benevolent future for the Jews, Pauline-Lukan rhetoric evolved to negate a future for their Jewish opponents. To them, eradicating the beliefs and rituals of their opponents was critical and existential.

We also need to consider the implications of the fact that Hebrews and Barnabas, the earliest explicit articulations of supersession theology, were roughly contemporaneous with the canonical Gospels. During the same period that the Gospel authors crafted their texts and incorporated subdued hints[26] about the inadequacy of Jesus's disciples and first followers (and therefore of their descendants), the authors of Hebrews and Barnabas were crafting more explicit and virulent challenges to their legitimacy and authority. Although this divergence in intensity and in degree of explicitness could be due to regional, personal, or factional differences, I am more inclined to see them connected to the delivery platform (the genre) chosen by each author. Said differently, it seems plausible to me that the differences in the intensity of the anti-Jewish strand between the canonical Gospels vis-à-vis Hebrews and Barnabas reflect differences in genre and tactics, rather than in aims and ultimate purpose. Therefore, the implied criticism of the disciples and of their beliefs and traditions in the canonical Gospels may be due to their being authored to function as foundational accounts of the Pauline strand, not as overt and explicit polemical tools.

If supersession theology emerged to provide an ideological grounding for the drive to de-Judaize belief in Jesus, its theological validity collapses. The unintended consequences of this unfortunate theological turn remain tragic beyond measure, but supersession theology no longer needs be an insurmountable theological anchor. Only the embrace of multiple, separate, and equally valid tracks to the Divine[27] will diffuse the ever-present danger of supersession theology. All else is derivative.

Chapter 11

The Anti-Jewish Strand in Hebrews

Introduction

The author of Hebrews is viewed by many scholars as one of the fore-most theologians of the New Testament, second only to Paul. The author's Greek is widely acclaimed as the most elegant in the NT.[1] Among the canonical texts the author's language skills are unsurpassed indicating that he was a highly educated and accomplished individual. Contemporary scholarship on Hebrews and its stand on Judaism is highly nuanced and differentiated. Many Anglo-Saxon scholars consider that the primary aim of Hebrews was to prevent a relapse to "Judaism." Others, mainly German scholars, emphasize a general lassitude caused by the delay of the Parousia, persecution, and waning enthusiasm.[2] Although admittedly simplistic and introductory, scholars may be divided into those that are critical of the Epistle's supersessionary message (N. Beck, L. Freudman, J. Gager, and S. Sandmel), those supportive-sympathetic to his theological message (D. DeSilva, D. Hagner, L. T. Johnson, W. Lane, B. Lindars, R. W. Wall), and those attempting a middle ground (H. W. Attridge, S. Lehne, S. G. Wilson, C. Williamson).[3] Among contemporary approaches, socio-rhetorical models seem to have great promise for they emphasize the importance of approaching the text from multiple perspectives (analysis of narrator, plot, characters, setting, inner texture, and other aspects of the narrative or discourse).[4] The "structure/anti-structure" model of Victor Turner,[5] which views society moving back and forth between structure and antistructure, is supportive of my suggestions. When Turner's model is applied to Hebrews, the rhetoric of the author is seen as aimed at sub-verting the parent group and reinforcing the norms and values of the new belief structure. In Hebrews, and throughout the tradition, the framework being subverted is the belief system of the descendants of Jesus's disciples and first followers, and the countercultural alternative is the author's inter-pretation of belief in Jesus.[6]

As it pertains to our effort to understand the emergence of the anti-Jewish strand, Hebrews is a unique window into events "on the ground" a couple of decades after Paul. The author of Hebrews, roughly contemporary with the Gospels' authors, offers us a distinct glimpse into the Jesus movement during the second half of the first century. Whereas Gospels are intended as foundational narratives of Jesus's ministry and therefore tend to insinu-ate and veil their agendas, Hebrews provides us an overt articulation of the tensions that accompanied the "push-and shove" of theology in the making. The author of the Epistle to the Hebrews, following in the footsteps of Paul, argued that Jewish Law, the cornerstone of the beliefs and traditions of the descendants of the founding fathers, had played a legitimate role in the past but was superseded by a new covenant (cf. Rom. 7:1–6; Gal. 3:23–25; Heb. 8, 10).[7] However, Hebrews goes beyond Paul and seems to attempt a more complex and nuanced definition of this relationship. As we move forward, and as we discuss the emergence of anti-Jewish attitudes among some Gentile believers, the question at the forefront will be: why would Gentiles of Pagan origin feel the need to engage in a contentious and con-temptuous dialectic with "Judaism"? What was the driving force behind the ever-increasing escalation of anti-Jewish rhetoric that we will encounter as we move forward in time? What necessitated the elaboration of an intri-cate rhetorical, ideological, and theological edifice vis-à-vis Jewish traditions and beliefs? Was it a conflict with Judaism? Was it to fend off attraction to Judaism? Or was it to disenfranchise fellow believers in Jesus that were Jews, as I have come to suspect.

Hebrews is a seminal text; the precursor of several currents that will become authoritative among some later Gentile believers. Hebrews is the earliest canonical text to engage openly and explicitly the battle against those that advocated continuity with the beliefs and traditions of the found-ing fathers. Thus, contrary to ingrained perceptions, the author of Hebrews is opposing continuity. Anticipating a later and more detailed engagement of the subject, it is important to note that at the time of authorship there was no consensus among Gentiles as to what belief in Jesus was, or should be. Somewhat simplifying a rather complex reality, we may say that during the second half of the first century we can see the embryonic stages of four groups that will vie for Jesus legacy, two of which (the Jewish followers of Jesus and their Gentile sympathizers) advocated continuity with Judaism. Other believers, Pauline-Marcionite and Gnostics, advocated severing all ties with the beliefs and traditions of the founding fathers. The Pauline-Lukan faction advocated an appropriate-supersede approach.

Within the broader authoritative tradition, Hebrews and Barnabas are viewed by many as the cornerstones of supersession theology.[8] The theme

of supersession, the view that the beliefs and traditions of the Jewish founders was superseded, replaced, and rendered irrelevant by Paul's interpretation of belief in Jesus, is present in many canonical and authoritative texts.
However, in most of the New Testament this peculiar phenomenon, which
will occupy our attention from here onward, manifests itself in implied and
subtle forms. In two documents it is a central theme: Hebrews and Barnabas.
Whereas the Synoptics restrained, veiled, and subdued their attacks on the
descendants of the founding fathers, the authors of Hebrews and Barnabas
offer us unfiltered views of the friction "in the trenches" between Jews and
Gentiles in the Jesus movement. Somewhat different in style and theology,
Hebrews and Barnabas also allow us seemingly independent attestations
on this struggle. Whereas Hebrews originates in an educated mind and his
theology and arguments are cerebral and clever, Barnabas's originate in a
hypermilitant, idiosyncratic, and bizarre mind. Due to the importance of
Hebrews for the formation of future attitudes toward Jews and Judaism, we
must differentiate the author's intent from the way in which the text was
interpreted by future generations. Future believers, guided by the guardians
of dogma and orthodoxy, and impacted by the anti-Jewish strand in their
lore, will tend to read the text in anti-Jewish ways. The gap between intent
and consequences is especially disheartening in Hebrews.

Addressees and Context

Most scholars have concluded that Hebrews was written during the second half of the first century (60–90 CE).[9] The author writes with authority
and seems to be a leader, probably one of the founders of the community
to which the Epistle is addressed. The text contains hints about the circumstances of the author and his audience, but scholars have not reached
a consensus on authorship, context, or intended audience. Obviously, the
author and his audience knew who the protagonists were, but their identity is implicit—not explicit. The vast majority of scholars, both traditional
and current, adhere to the view that the author of Hebrews juxtaposes
"Christianity" to "Judaism." Significantly, the author does not use the terms
"Christian," "Christianity," "Jews," or "Judaism." Rather, he juxtaposes "us/
ours" to "them/their." Thus, Hebrews has been traditionally seen as reflective of a breach with Judaism, despite the fact that there is nothing in the
epistle that necessitates the assertion that the author's concerns, adversaries,
audience, or horizon are outside the Jesus movement.

Most scholars agree that the author is a Pauline pro-orthodox believer
and, consequently, the author's views are commonly identified as "Christian."
However, the use of this term to discuss this period is inappropriate. At
the time of authorship, the author's opponents considered themselves

Christian too. The socio-theological circumstances of the Jesus movement at the time of authorship and a variety of clues and hints (which we will discuss in some detail) seem to point to an internal debate about Judaism—not to a confrontation with it. I agree with Salevao's deployment of a conflict model.[10] However, whereas Salevao (in line with the consensus) juxtaposes Judaism to Christianity, I see the author's universe and horizon as limited to the Jesus movement. A minority of scholars acknowledges that the descendants of the founding generation might be among the author's antagonists.[11] Speaking of the addressees, Lehne's observation is among the closest to my reading: "[T]heir faith is being threatened by a group (or groups) of conservative Jewish-Christians from within (or from without) their number."[12] Scholars are split on the core impetus driving Hebrews. The author seems concerned with a variety of issues: low participation in community life (10:25), "strange teachings" and " unprofitable foods" (9:10; 13:9), consciousness of sin (9:14; 10:2, 22; 13:18), covenant issues (8:1–13), priesthood (7:1–19), sacrifice (10:1–18), the tarrying of the Parousia (10:25, 37), and danger of apostasy (2:1; 3:12; 6:6; 10:29). The combined weight of several factors, perhaps coupled with a disappointment over the delay of the Parousia[13] may be the best description of the "wedge issues" put forward by the author.

For our purposes and as it pertains to our subject (the emergence of the anti-Jewish strand among Gentile believers) the socio-theological impetus behind the anti-Jewish escalation seems to be the need to articulate a theological grounding to justify to the rank and file the estrangement vis-à-vis the descendants of the founding generation. This need took center stage as the communities founded by Pauline missionaries encountered differing believers in Jesus and questions about legitimacy surfaced. Foremost among them seems to have been the estrangement from the descendants of Jesus's disciples and first followers and the debate about whether their beliefs and traditions should be observed or rejected. As corroborated by the obsession with "all things Jewish," and the intense resentment that permeates the texts authored during this era, the "Jewish question" seems to have become a contentious and painful concern for second- and third-generation Gentile believers in Jesus.

According to most commentators, the community was in danger of apostasy to Judaism.[14] I think this framing of the issues is incorrect for there is no evidence in the text that would point to external-mainstream Judaism. According to my reading, the 'apostasy' in question is the natural attraction that some believers felt towards the beliefs and traditions of the founding fathers. Unfortunately, we do not know the cultural-ethnic origin of the addressees. Nor do we know if they were the majority or a minority in the community.[15] Nonetheless, our identification of the addressees and of the implied adversaries may be assisted by the author's choices of language: "Do not be carried away by diverse and strange teachings. For it is good for the heart to be made firm with grace, not foods, whose observers were not benefited. We have an altar from which those who serve the tabernacle have no right to eat" (13:9–10). The author also alludes to "strange teachings" and "unprofitable foods" (9:10; 13:9), a peculiar choice of words if the addressees were present or past Jewish followers of Jesus. This language and the view that adherence to the beliefs of the founding fathers is apostasy (6:6) would be counterproductive if addressing Jewish followers of Jesus or their Gentile sympathizers, but might have been useful in shoring up vacillating Gentiles that were in danger of succumbing to the influence of the Jewish faction. The imminent danger seems to originate from believers who may have advocated a stronger continuity with the founding fathers (7:11; 9:8–10, 13–14; 10:1–2; 13:9–13). Unfortunately, we are unable to ascertain whether the adversaries are the descendants of the founding fathers or Gentiles attracted to them.[16]

The setting seems to be a debate among Gentile believers in Jesus about continuity-discontinuity vis-à-vis the founding fathers of their movement (9:11–14; 10:1–2; 13:9–10). We need remember that, the attraction to the founding fathers was a natural consequence of their being the descendants of those chosen by Jesus as the custodians of his legacy. At the time of authorship, a couple of decades after Jesus's death, they would have been seen by many, probably by most, as the legitimate guardians and interpreters of his ministry. In these circumstances, distancing the addressees from attraction to the founding fathers would require extreme means, precisely what we encounter: intense and negative rhetoric and the deployment of an array of "wedge issues."

Somewhat similar to the situation in Paul's Galatians and I Corinthians, the community addressed by the author seems to be on the brink of apostasy from the author's interpretation of Jesus's legacy. In both cases the danger seems to be the sway of the founding fathers. In both cases, the authors use a variety of rhetorical tools and techniques to persuade recently evangelized believers to hold firm to the authors' strand of belief in Jesus. Overall, it seems to me that we are on strong ground when arguing that the community in question is a Gentile "missionary community."[17] At the time of authorship (centuries before attaining formal canonical status) Hebrews reflects the reaction of a Pauline believer that sees the work of the founders of his community being undone by the influence of his opponents within the Jesus movement. This situation seems to have emerged as Pauline evangelists organized new communities and moved on. Sooner or later these new converts would have encountered believers that embraced differing interpretations of Jesus's legacy and would have realized that they had been evangelized into a version of belief in Jesus at odds with the beliefs of Jesus's disciples and first followers—a volatile situation that could ignite a variety of outcomes. Most scholars also advocate a recent separation from "the Synagogue."[18] However, I have argued elsewhere that affiliation of Gentile believers in Jesus with mainstream synagogues should not be assumed.

Rather, if estrangement from a synagogue is suspected, a synagogue of the founding faction should be the assumed option.

The understanding that the community is living in the last days may be driving and exacerbating the author's pitch and choice of words too. His eschatological outlook seems to inspire and intensify the boldness of his claims. His quotation of Jeremiah 31:31 begins with an understanding that the new covenant will be completed in the coming days. For the author of Hebrews, the "coming days" have arrived. He refers to his own time as the "last days" (1:2; 9:26).[19] And yet, there is a sense that the final consummation of all things is still in the future (4:9; 6:11; 10:26–30; 13:14).[20] An eschatological mindset may have provided a context in which a radical change of the covenant would make sense, for it enables the author to cast the old and new covenants in redemptive terms. An imminent eschatological framework may contribute to our understanding of the deployment of the claim to God's annulment of the first covenant at the inauguration of the second.

Theology

Hebrews clearly belongs to the earliest phase of the evolution of Pauline theology. It seems that prior to Hebrews, the theology inculcated to the community (2:3–4; 13:7–8) would have included the basic Pauline kerygma (1 Cor. 15.3) but probably not much more. Overall, nothing in Hebrews is contradictory of Paul. Indeed, there are many things in common between Paul and our author, suggesting that the author was associated with the Pauline circle.[21] The author is the main architect of Pauline-Lukan theology. The need to decide whether Paul was the originator of the supersession of Judaism (the traditionalists) or was only defending the right of Gentile believers to reject the beliefs and the traditions of the founding fathers (the revised Paul)[22] resurfaces when trying to decipher Hebrews. If we embrace the "traditional Paul," and read Hebrews as derivative of it, the anti-Jewish strand in Hebrews would target Judaism. However, if we embrace the "revised Paul," and read Hebrews as derivative of it, the anti-Jewish strand in Hebrews would target the descendants of the founding fathers and their Gentile sympathizers.[23]

Hebrews, following Paul's Colossians, sees Jesus as God's adopted son and does not claim incarnation. The Christology of Hebrews is eclectic. The proliferation and the seemingly indiscriminate agglomeration of titles and attributes bestowed on Jesus cannot but reflect anxiety about legitimacy often visible in groups challenging established authority,[24] in this case the authority of the descendants of Jesus's disciples and first followers. The author's claim that his form of belief in Jesus originated from Jesus himself (2:3), would be opposed by the Pillars and by their descendants (the author's opponents). By the time of authorship, the critique by Judean sectarians of the Temple, the priesthood, and the covenant stood on established anti-Jewish-establishment traditions. Thus, the polemic in Hebrews may be best seen as the subversion, emulation and appropriation by a Gentile believer, of the anti-establishment rhetoric and lore of the descendants of the founding generation, deployed to demote them from their position as the authoritative custodians of Jesus's legacy.

The main argument of Hebrews stands on his elaboration of three principal themes: Jesus's priesthood in the order of Melchizedek, the advent of the new covenant and the sacrificial-atonement theme. These three pillars are deemed to provide a compelling argument for the superiority of the author's strand of belief in Jesus. In other words, these three arguments are deemed to provide a compelling argument that justifies the rejection (by Gentiles) of the beliefs and traditions of the founding fathers, while nonetheless bestowing upon them YHWH's favor. From Hebrews onward Pauline-Lukan Gentiles perceived themselves as replacing "the Jews" as YHWH's chosen.

Priesthood

The Hebrew Scriptures, last edited by the priestly class, give us the establishment's description of the Israelite priesthood as ordained by God[25] and assigned to the tribe of Levi.[26] The role of the priesthood evolved over time, was part of ongoing debates within Judaism, and was not exempt from sharp critique. Following the Persian conquests (first half of the sixth century) and throughout the Near East, the scions of venerable and legitimate priestly families were often coerced into cooperating with the conquerors or were silenced by other means. I have already noted that high priests were, for the most part, appointed by the conquerors and lost standing in the eyes the local populations. Most of these traitors and collaborators with Persian, Greek, and Roman conquerors were hated opportunists that collected taxes and ruled the provinces on behalf of foreign oppressors. By Jesus's lifetime, the decline in the legitimacy of the priesthood was widely acknowledged and a staple of Jewish anti-establishment rhetoric.[27] Although the institution of the priesthood is seldom openly criticized, abuse or disgrace of the office and illegitimate ancestry were the subject of intense polemic.

The author of Hebrews expands a short, enigmatic, and obscure biblical story about Melchizedek, the priest-king of Salem (Gen. 14:18–20) to anchor his challenge to the Jewish elite of the Jesus movement (7:1–9). The Israelite Scriptures do not know of any predecessors to Melchizedek and are silent concerning any successors. The biblical story is somewhat of a dead end and consequently there were no limitations to where Melchizedek speculation could go, an opening used by Qumran and by the author of Hebrews. According to the author of Hebrews, Melchizedek (a rather marginal character in Judaism)[28] founded an unprecedented non-Levitical priestly line and placed Jesus as its inheritor and its culmination. The author used Genesis 14:18–20 to claim that Melchizedek antecedes Abraham, making him a superseding figure "Without father, without mother, without genealogy, having neither beginning of days nor end of life, but resembling the Son of God" (7:2–3). Although Melchizedek's priesthood seems to emerge ex nihilo from the author's expansion of Genesis 14:18–20, there are some interesting external antecedents. The most probable influence on Hebrews might be Qumran's 1QMelchizedek, although Attridge instructs us on other instances of Melchizedek speculation (Philo, the fragmentary Nag Hammadi tractate Melchizedek [NHC 9, 1], 2 Enoch, and 3 Enoch).[29] 1QMelchizedek, discovered at Qumran Cave 11,[30] asserts that the coming judgment is to be performed by a representative of God who is called Melchizedek.[31] Some scholars argue that there is no direct connection between 1QMelchizedek and Hebrews, despite that in both writings the Melchizedek figure has comparable eschatological functions and despite Hebrews' other resonances with Qumran, which will be discussed in each segment of this chapter.[32] Attridge concludes that "[t]he inspiration for Hebrews's treatment of Melchizedek probably derives from one or another of these speculative trends."[33] Wilson is more definitive: "We can conclude without doubt that Jewish speculation provides the immediate context for these chapters, and yet there is no precise parallel to the particular analogies or the overall scheme that the author develops."[34]

The author's deployment of the Melchizedek figure, whether built on the Qumran model or the author's independent creation, seems to be aimed at achieving a specific goal. According to the author (a) Melchizedek blesses Abraham (7:1), (b) Abraham offers Melchizedek a tithe (7:2), (c) Melchizedek is linked to the "Son of God" motif and his priesthood is eternal (7:3). On this anchor, the author develops his argument in tight sequence: since Melchizedek receives the tithe, blesses Abraham, and lives eternally, he is superior to Abraham (7:4–5, 6, and 8). This opening of chapter 7 points to the author's purpose: he is creating a pathway, a bypass, to argue the supremacy of his brand of belief in Jesus over that of his Jewish opponents within the Jesus movement. The Melchizedek move allows the author to claim that his newly created priesthood is superior to the Levitical priesthood that stands on the Abrahamic tradition. If Melchizedek is superior to Abraham, so is the tradition that emanates from him. The author proceeds with his gallant reconfiguration: "The Levitical line is useless (10:2–10), and annulled. The hereditary principle is no longer relevant, the law abrogated (7:16–19), the Levitical priesthood was defective (7.20–1). There is no longer a need for a succession of priests (7.23–4)."[35] The author attempts to undermine allegiance to the descendants of the founding fathers

by belittling the priesthood associated with them and by replacing it with a
new, and superior, one. Some two thousand years after the establishment of
the Israelite priesthood, the author argues for the existence of a previously
unknown "legitimacy bypass" that supersedes a venerated religious tradition
spanning many generations. The rationale for the battering of the Levitical
priesthood seems to have been that if the Levitical priesthood is superseded,
those that the priesthood serves are diminished. If the beliefs of the descendants of Jesus's disciples and first followers stand on the legitimacy and
sanctity of the Levitical priesthood, the author's beliefs (that stand on the
priesthood of Melchizedek) are superior.[36]

According to first-century Judaism, the messiah was a descendant of King
David and a member of the tribe of Judah, necessitating the New Testament
casting of Jesus as Judah's descendant (7:4) and his birth in Bethlehem.
However, a descendant of Judah would be disqualified from the priesthood,
which was hereditary and was the privilege of the tribe of Levi. The author
seems to be aware of this contradiction but seems to have believed that
priestly status was required to designate Jesus's death as an atoning sacrifice
for all sins and for all times. Therefore, "Hebrews has to argue that Jesus is a
priest, because according to the Law only a priest may offer sacrifice."[37] To
that effect the author bypasses the traditional priesthood and makes Jesus a
priest according to his enhanced order of Melchizedek (7:17). The author
questions the priestly institutions of the dominant group (the descendants
of the disciples and their followers) and creates an earlier and superseding
priestly succession that has two high priests over a span of some two thousand years, Melchizedek and Jesus.

Covenant

Whereas the author's attack on the Levitical priesthood targets the institutions and traditions of his Jewish opponents, the author's denigration of
the covenant aims at eroding their standing as God's chosen altogether.
Furthermore, whereas the author's critique of the Levitical priesthood and
of the sacrifices associated with them had antecedents among Judean sectarians, the assault on the Israelite covenant is a radical and sweeping claim—a
move to supersede-appropriate the identity of his opponents and to delegitimize them. With this foray into the core of Jewish identity, the author's
theological rhetoric became a transgression of the most sacred identity
markers of Judaism. With this theological move, the author articulates the
first cornerstone of identity annihilation theology, the gravest component
of supersession-replacement theology.

The author "demonstrates" to its readers why the new covenant is better than the "old."[38] The first covenant is declared "imperfect" (8:7–8a)

and the imperfection is "proven" (8:8b-12). The argument is framed by a self-referential argument: "For if that first covenant had been faultless, there would have been no occasion for a second" (8:7). Throughout the text we encounter a pattern of "correspondence, contrast and superiority."[39] Despite the fact that the author focuses his rhetorical fire on institutions and traditions, he also aims at the people: "For he (God) finds fault with them when he says..." (8:8). Hebrews 8:1–13 is part of the author's argument against the exclusivity of the beliefs and traditions of the founding group as the means to be a rightful believer in Jesus. The author's argument that the "old" covenant was replaced-fulfilled by the "new" is a platform to argue the superiority of his understanding of Jesus's legacy against "their" interpretation of it.

Judean sectarians routinely claimed the need for the renewal of the people's commitment to its covenant with YHWH. The possible attestations of "new covenant" language in the texts of the Second Temple period (Jub. 1.16–25 and Ezra 6.26b–28, and Qumran)[40] are best understood as metaphors that call for the reinvigoration of the people's commitment to the covenant, not to its replacement. The Hebrew Scriptures' use of the people's failings and of "new covenant" rhetoric[41] to inspire and edify the nation were inclusive exhortations within the Jewish journey, not calls to deny or replace Judaism. Hebrews' development of this theme, unique among the NT texts,[42] is the first attempt at a comprehensive and methodical deployment of this argument from without the Jewish camp. The author's "anti-Judaism" reflects a countercultural drive to delegitimate the elite of the Jesus movement. By faulting the Israelite covenant, the author attempts to convince his readers to reject any affiliation with the Jewish faction. The shift of emphasis does not seem to be unintended; demoting the covenant between the Jews and God seems to be a means to an end. Hebrews' appropriation of Judean anti-establishment themes and motifs to degrade adversaries that were Jews is the forerunner of a future and all-encompassing transgression of sacred boundaries that will have grave consequences. By his gratuitous and gallant "voiding" of the "old" covenant, the author is attempting to undermine his opponents' legitimacy as the guardians of Jesus's legacy, in the eyes of the Gentile rank and file: if "their" covenant with God is seen as superseded, "their" beliefs and traditions cannot be the vehicle to belief in Jesus either.

In this context, the author's use of Jeremiah 31:31–34[43] in Hebrews 8:8–12 requires our attention. We find that the author's interpretation of this prophetic exhortation to revitalize the Israelite commitment to the covenant is subverted to support the advent of a new covenant with non-Israelites (8:8), the collapse of the "old" (8:9), and the superiority of the new (8:10–11). By decontextualizing Jeremiah 31:31–34,[44] the author "proves" that God himself had called for the replacement of the "old" covenant, six hundred years before the author's lifetime. Unfortunately, the author does not offer us any support for his claim that Jeremiah's call anticipates his particular interpretation of Jewish history and of Jesus's legacy. Although throughout the Second Temple period Jeremiah's call had been echoed by countless anti-establishment figures, Hebrews is the first non-Israelite to claim a standing in this matter. By quoting Jeremiah out of his historical context, the author makes one of the most radical anti-Jewish statements in the New Testament: "When He said, "a new covenant, In speaking of a new covenant he treats the first as obsolete. And what is becoming obsolete and growing old is ready to vanish away" (8:13). "What is implied is that the very purpose of the second covenant was to fulfill what the first covenant could not. There is no room or reason for the first covenant to continue, once the second has been established. The emergence of the second or new covenant renders the first old, null, and void."[45] The supersessionary message of Hebrews, which in large measure stands on this argument, became integral to the self-perception of many theologians, scholars, and believers since.

Hebrews seems to have been the first to articulate the strategy and the arguments for the demotion of the descendants of Jesus's disciples and first followers as the custodians of his legacy. The annulment of the Israelite covenant became a necessary move for Gentiles that rejected the beliefs and traditions of the founding fathers but did not want to sever all links with the Jewish grounding of the Jesus movement and did not want to build their theological edifice outside the Jewish narrative. Whereas earlier proto-orthodox authors cast the founding fathers as "misunderstanding" and "abandoning" Jesus, Hebrews escalates the challenge and lays the theological foundation to the replacement of their legacy as the driving force of the Jesus movement.

Sacrifice

From early on, Israelites developed a nuanced appreciation of their sacrificial traditions. Standing on the archaic view that proper cosmic maintenance required sacrifices to the Gods, First and Second Temple Israelites developed a complex awareness of the spiritualization of the Levitical sacrifices.[46] Opposition to a mechanical view of sacrifice can be tracked to the biblical tradition.[47] "There was an old Palestinian tradition extending to the psalms and prophets which had condemned any belief in the automatic efficacy of sacrifices, demanding in its place a 'sacrifice of thanksgiving' or deeds of mercy."[48] The sacrificial traditions were a focus of considerable attention at Qumran too.[49] However, the community did not believe the sacrificial cult was null and void. Rather, they believed that it would eventually be practiced properly. The Qumranites thought that

the contemporaneous priesthood was illegitimate but hoped for a legitimate one. The Israelite sacrificial traditions and Jesus's sacrifice occupy a
large portion of this letter (7:1–10:8) pointing to their centrality for the
author.[50] The theological effort surrounding Jesus's sacrifice seems to originate in the author's wish to reinforce Paul's interpretation of Jesus's death
as an atoning sacrifice. Therefore, the author invests great effort to "prove"
the inadequacy of "the Law" and the Levitical offerings (10:1–10) and the
superiority of Jesus's sacrifice (10:11–18). In his discussion of the Israelite
sacrificial tradition, as elsewhere, the author of Hebrews seems to feed on
Judean sectarian anti-establishment traditions and rhetoric. The sacrifice
of Jesus as replacement and annulment of the Levitical sacrificial tradition
that atoned for sins would be unacceptable to Jews to the inclusion of
the Jewish followers of Jesus, who rejected human sacrifices,[51] but would
resonate with believers with Pagan affiliations and inclinations. The use
of Psalm 39:7–9 (LXX, MT 40:6–8) in verses 10:5–7 to argue that the
Levitical sacrifices have been nullified and to "demonstrate" that God himself acknowledged the inadequacies of the Levitical sacrifices (10:8–10),
despite the dissonance of such interpretation with Jewish exegesis, is seen
by many scholars as grounding the authors' claims in the authority of
Hebrew Scripture.

The view that Jewish sacrificial traditions were ceremonial and lacked
spiritual meaning is deeply embedded in the proto-orthodox lore and in the
minds of Gentile believers since. The practice, by Pauline-Lukan believers,
of subverting and appropriating biblical traditions to legitimate their interpretations of Jesus's legacy seems to originate in the decontextualization
and emulation of Qumran's Pesher[52] exegetical method, a procedure that
was rejected by establishment Judaism. Overall, the authors' decontextualized use of the Hebrew Scriptures to support his arguments may have
been favorably received by Gentiles who were superficially acquainted with
these texts, but would not convince believers better versed in them—to
the inclusion of the descendants of Jesus's disciples and first followers. The
Israelite religion took shape during the axial era, when sacrifices were seen as
a means of cosmic maintenance and the servicing of the Gods. According to
the axial era's understanding of the universe, the divine realm requires sacrificial offerings in exchange for victory, abundance, and fertility. However,
the understanding that sacrifices were not believed to act "ex open operate,"
and were not a ceremonial act devoid of spiritual meaning, has deep roots
in biblical Judaism. Discomfort among Israelites with a mechanical view of
the sacrificial system antedates Paul, Hebrews, and belief in Jesus. Contrary
to Hebrews' simplistic juxtapositions, Israelites emphasized the need for
devotion, pure intent, and atonement when giving offerings. The author's
appropriation-incorporation of significant traditions within Judaism, and
their deployment as an insight on the comparison between his interpretation
of belief in Jesus and his opponents', showcases the recurring phenomenon

of the quarrying of Judean sectarian lore to argue anti-establishment claims within the Jesus movement.

The Jewish Background

We have seen that the use of the Hebrew Scriptures is prominent throughout the book (although the author follows the Greek Septuagint, rather than the Hebrew text).[53] The author of Hebrews attempts to legitimize his interpretation of belief in Jesus by appropriating and decontextualizing a variety of forward-looking passages in the scriptures of his opponents. Harnessing Qumran's Pesher exegetical method, the author appropriates-subverts the lore of his adversaries to "prove" his interpretation of Jesus's legacy (Psalm 8:4–6, in 3:12–4:1–Psalm 95:7–11, in 5:11–6:12 and 7:1; Jer. 31:31–34 in Chapter 8; Psalm 40:6–8 in Chapter 10; Jer. 31:33–34 and Habakkuk 2:3–4 in Chapter 12). The author of Hebrews attempts to bestow on his interpretation of Jesus's legacy the authority of the "Old" Testament (about 30 actual citations and over 70 allusions have been counted). Although Hebrews seems to invoke the Hebrew Scriptures at every stage of his argument, his interpretations of the Torah, the Prophets, and Psalms are often alien to their historical context and service his typological aims (to prove that the Hebrew Scriptures anticipate his interpretation of Jesus's ministry).

The author uses a superior/inferior dialectic and a decontextualized reading of Psalm 110:4 and Psalm 39:7–9 (LXX) to delegitimate the priestly institutions and traditions associated with his opponents within the Jesus movement. The author's argument that God himself acknowledged the inadequacies of the Levitical sacrifices (10:8–10) and his use of Psalm 110:4 to argue that God called for the replacement of the "old" priesthood by the "new" priesthood are far reaching. New covenant rhetoric and a decontextualized interpretation of Jeremiah 31:31–34 were also used by the author to dissuade congregants from fellowship with his Jewish opponents and to infuse greater commitment to his interpretation of belief in Jesus. Harnessing Jeremiah's call to revitalize the Israelite commitment to YHWH to denigrate opponents that were Jews may have seemed a clever rhetorical ploy at the time. However, as the original context was lost and standing on Eusebius's misinterpretation (or misrepresentation) of the evolution of belief in Jesus,[54] seemingly harmless claims aimed at adversaries within were projected onto external Judaism with horrific consequences.

Unable to challenge the legitimacy of his opponents, the author frames the argument around their perceived weakness: their idiosyncratic beliefs and traditions. To challenge the influence of the descendants of the founding fathers, the author emulates long-standing traditions of sectarian critique and rhetoric within Second Temple Judaism, most probably by subverting-appropriating the lore of the founding faction. The author articulates severe warnings of the dire effects of "apostasy," that is, attachment to the beliefs and traditions of his opponents (6:6–8; 10:26–31). By "borrowing a page" from his opponents' anti-Jewish-establishment lore (or from other Jewish sectarian anti-establishment rhetoric) the author attacks the Levitical priesthood, the Law, the validity of the Israelite covenant with YHWH, and the Temple sacrifices—all traditional targets of Judean sectarians and the subject of heated debates among Second Temple Jews. The author's views and arguments on these subjects are best seen as the deployment of Judean sectarian rhetorical staples against the establishment he opposes, the Jewish elite within the Jesus movement. Hebrews harnesses and develops pre-existing rhetorical themes and traditions originating in the Jewish sectarian milieu to claim the superiority of his strand of belief in Jesus over the traditions of the founding fathers. "There is, finally, a constant thread in the Christological argument that needs to be singled out: the radical contrast between old and new, good and better, sketch and reality, earthly and heavenly, spiritual and physical, outer and inner, repeated and unique."[55] The terms of contrast vary considerably, but they all serve the same purpose: to assert the superiority of the author's form of belief in Jesus over that of his opponents. In conclusion, little of Hebrews' hyperbole about the beliefs and traditions of his opponents is original. The most that can be said about the author's anti-Jewish creativity is that he was the first to apply some of these themes and motifs to the circumstances of the Jesus movement. One theme, however, is elaborated well beyond its Judean roots; the priesthood of Jesus after the order of Malchizedeck (7:1–10).[56]

There is also an effort by the author of Hebrews to appropriate the identity, history, and legacy of the founding fathers by claiming that Gentile believers, of his particular persuasion, are the true heirs and the righteous inheritors of YHWH's promises to the Israelites (a claim most probably put forward by his adversaries vis-à-vis mainstream Judaism). Thus, the God of the Israelites is cast as declaring the obsolescence of the "old" covenant and the inauguration of the new. The selective appropriation of the sacred scriptures of his opponents to champion his form of belief in Jesus was one of the author's hallmarks and became deeply ingrained in the tradition and in the hearts and minds of later believers. The raiding and decontextualization of Jewish sacred scripture to "prove" the superiority of the Pauline worldview became a trademark of the Pauline-Lukan strand.

Supersession

Appropriation and supersession are two distinct components of Pauline-Lukan theology. Appropriation theology reflects the mindset of some Gentile believers who vested themselves as the inheritors of the identity and lore of the founding fathers. Supersession theology is the view that the Pauline-Lukan interpretation of Jesus's legacy replaced and annulled the beliefs and traditions of Jesus's disciples and first followers. However, despite the fact that the author's concerns, horizon, and adversaries were within the Jesus movement (once the text was canonized and the original context forgotten-obscured) the resulting projection onto Judaism transformed Hebrews into the unintended cornerstone of the supersession of the Jewish people. The appropriation and supersession of the identity and beliefs of the Jewish founders, embryonic in Paul and in the Gospels and expanded upon by the author of Hebrews, reach their peak as Gentile proto-orthodox and orthodox believers gradually gravitate to the view that their interpretation of belief in Jesus constitutes the replacement-annulment-fulfillment of Judaism,[57] a process of grave and tragic consequences. Supersession theology is couched in extreme and unequivocal terms and has two main components: The Jewish loss of God's favor and the supersession of Judaism in all things religious and ethical.

At the turn of the century we encounter within the Jesus movement a full spectrum of attitudes toward the beliefs and traditions of the founding fathers—from continuity to rejection. From among all the New Testament writers, Hebrews moves furthest in the direction of a breach with the traditions of Jesus's companions, a process that did take place over the next three centuries. The future impact of the deployment of supersession theology by later orthodoxy is hard to grasp. The horrible consequences of this clever theological move by this first-century religious enthusiast eventually led to the negation and disenfranchisement, first, of the descendants of the founding fathers, and, later, of all Jews—paving the way for later anti-Semitism.

However, despite being deeply entrenched in the lore and in the hearts and minds of some believers, the denigration of cultural and theological ancestors is by no means necessary, in theory or in the experience of other cultures. Communities can, and have, emerged from preceding cultures without carving their path with derogatory polemic and making it sacrosanct.[58] Seemingly oblivious to the impact that appropriation-supersession theology has had on the soul of believers, on their attitudes toward Jews and Judaism and on Jewish lives—some scholars emphasize Hebrews' "continuity with Judaism." However, continuity with the caveats of appropriation-supersession and identity annihilation is no continuity at all.

Modern Dilemmas

Post–World War II scholars have attempted to reduce the dissonance between the anti-Jewish sentiment that emanates from traditional and literal readings of the Epistle to the Hebrews and modern ethical values. Some have labored to salvage Hebrews from its supersessionist impetus. A variety of approaches have been suggested to tame the text's anti-Jewish impact, rehabilitate its image, and accommodate modern sensibilities.[59] The challenge is daunting. Some modern interpreters have attempted to minimize the supersessionist and derogatory implications of the author's statements by arguing that Hebrews' negative theology functions as a foil for the writer's theological edifice. Others advocate the replacement of the term "supersession" with the term "fulfillment,"[60] despite the fact that the theological implications of both terms are similar and despite Hebrews 8:7 and 8:13, which seem to impede such efforts. Other scholars absolve the author of supersessionary intent vis-à-vis the Jewish people,[61] while acknowledging his claim to the supersession of Jewish institutions and beliefs. This strategy seems to emerge out of a wish to neutralize the anti-Jewish strand embedded in the text, while salvaging its canonical status. The strategies vary but the aim is similar—to rescue Hebrews from its association with supersession and anti-Judaism.

However, the candor of the author is hard to reconcile with any attempt to deflate the impact of the text: terrible consequences will follow the rejection of the author's views (4:11–13), and mercy will be available only to those that persevere in the path advocated by him (4:14–16). The derogatory parade is wide ranging: Jewish atonement traditions are deemed superseded, sacrifices under the Law "cannot perfect the conscience of the worshipper" (9:9) since "the law has but a shadow of the good things to come" (10:1), sacrifices that are repeated cannot have permanent effect (10:2), the ceremonies of the Law are only "regulations for the body" (9:10) and for "the purification of the flesh" (9.13), just to point out a few of the author's "contributions." The author's contrasts and derogatory juxtapositions (old/new, sketch/reality, earthly/heavenly, spiritual/physical, outer/inner, repeated/unique) are applied to many arguments and polemical themes. The repertoire and the terms of contrast vary, but they serve the same purpose: to assert the superiority of the author's strand of belief in Jesus and the inferiority of those advocating a close affiliation with the beliefs and traditions of the founding faction. In Hebrews, "[t]he contrast between first/second and old/new could in principle be neutral, an expression of temporal order that allows that both elements have intrinsic value. But in this case it is not; their purpose is to elevate the new and denigrate the old."[62]

My Hebrews

Why would some Gentiles, recently converted to a non-Jewish form of belief in Jesus, be obsessed with the need to justify their rejection of Jewish beliefs and traditions and to prove the superiority of their still-evolving belief structures? What is the socio-theological context behind the author's assault on the Levitical priesthood, on the covenant between the Israelites and their God, and on their sacrificial traditions? What circumstances would explain, or necessitate, the emergence of this discourse of anti-Judaism?

In previous texts we identified themes, motifs, segments, or fragments that may be residues of the shift from the anti-Jewish-establishment polemic of the Jewish founders to rhetoric against them. In Hebrews the author seems to articulate for the first time the arguments to support such a shift. The Epistle to the Hebrews, roughly contemporary with the canonical Gospels, signals the imminent eruption onto the surface of the overt phase of a centuries-long struggle about what belief in Jesus should be. The defensive language deployed in Hebrews indicates that a significant threat loomed over the legitimacy of the author's belief system. It seems that some members of the author's community were attracted to the beliefs and traditions of the founding faction. That attraction posed an existential threat to believers that advocated Paul's interpretation of Jesus's ministry and the de-Judaizing of belief in Jesus.

By the time Hebrews was written, the estrangement between Gentile and Jewish followers of Jesus seems to have intensified. Whereas in the canonical Gospels the de-Judaizing of belief in Jesus is understated, obscured, and implied, in Hebrews and Barnabas it is explicit and overt. The author of Hebrews attempts to provide, to a community evangelized by Pauline missionaries, the arguments to deflect criticism as to lack of continuity with the religious worldview and traditions embraced by Jesus and by those chosen by him as custodians of his legacy. The author and contemporary Pauline leaders and intellectuals were anxious to provide Gentile believers a theological narrative that would reassure them that they were rightful believers in Jesus despite their rejection of the beliefs and traditions of the founding fathers.

The current consensus seems to be that the author of Hebrews had several concerns that included the danger of a relapse to "Judaism" among a group of converts to "Christianity." Some modern scholars identify the intended addressees as Jewish followers of Jesus or as a community with a mixed composition. However, there is little that points to the ethnic background of the readers and some sayings fit a Gentile audience better than a Jewish one (e.g., 6:1; 9:14). Furthermore, the view that disrespectful and derogatory comments on Judaism would be used, or would be effective, to persuade the descendants of Jesus's disciples and first followers to sever their affiliation to their ancestral traditions is beyond my comprehension and seems to stand on the continuing bondage to the orthodox hegemony over the discourse. Furthermore, despite the fact that the author's arguments and knowledge of the Hebrew Scriptures has impressed scholars, I suspect that he would fall short of convincing committed Jews—to the inclusion of the descendants of Jesus's disciples and first followers. Although the text would underwhelm readers with deep and intimate knowledge of the Jewish tradition, it may have impressed Gentiles with little or no grounding in the Hebrew Scriptures.

Gentile believers, "caught in the crossfire" between those advocating continuity with the beliefs and traditions of Jesus's companions and those advocating a selective appropriation-supersession, could be the audience for this text. Hebrews' anti-Jewish rhetoric would have been most effective on Gentiles that belonged to Pauline congregations, had limited knowledge about Judaism, and had concerns and anxieties about their estrangement from the descendants of the founding fathers. The author argues throughout that Gentile converts need not embrace the beliefs and traditions of the descendants of Jesus's disciples and first followers, apparently against a strong lobby of Gentile sympathizers that was inclined to do so. These Gentiles apparently felt a natural attraction to those that, at the time of authorship, were known to be the descendants of Jesus's disciples and first followers and would be considered by many to be the legitimate heirs of his ministry.

Hebrews' author may have been the earliest systematic articulator of the strategy that did eventually bring about the demotion of the founding faction. By shifting the debate away from the weak flank of the Pauline argument (the fact that their adversaries were the descendants of Jesus's disciples and first followers, and therefore the presumptive guardians of his legacy) and framing the debate around beliefs and traditions that most Gentiles found strange and idiosyncratic, early Pauline-Lukan intellectuals crafted a strategy that eventually led to a growing alienation of Gentile believers from the founding faction. This tactical positioning helps us understand the author's choice of emphases, themes, motifs, and rhetorical ploys. Later writers will expand on this foundation by attacking a wide range of institutions, beliefs, and traditions associated with the founding fathers (Torah observance, the Temple, circumcision, dietary laws being the "wedge issues" of preference). However, one peculiar thread will remain constant throughout the efforts to demote the founding faction; they are seldom acknowledged as the descendants of Jesus's disciples and first followers and they are seldom attacked explicitly and frontally—although, from nuance and context, the addresses would know the identity of the intended adversaries. This demotion by proxy will become an ingrained tradition that, with the passage of time and loss of context, will be projected, misinterpreted, and misrepresented as a conflict with Judaism—obscuring the theologically embarrassing demotion and marginalizing of the descendants of those chosen by Jesus to be the custodians of his legacy.

The author does not disclose the source of the authority by which he "annuls" and "abrogates" the vast religious heritage of his adversaries. Nor does the author inform us whether his insight originates in direct revelation or in authoritative precursors, although he does make ample use of decontextualized quotes from the "old" testament that, according to the author, anticipate his interpretation of Jesus's ministry. An intriguing but weak claim to authority and indirect access to the historical Jesus is made by the author when he states, "[H]ow shall we escape if we neglect such a great salvation? It was declared at first by the Lord, and it was attested to us by those who heard him" (2:3). These claims are put forward despite the fact that most scholars concur that none of the theological predecessors of the author of Hebrews was an eye witness to Jesus's ministry, and that the descendants of those who were, rejected the authors interpretation of Jesus's legacy.

Unfortunately, we do not know whether the author was part of a minority or a majority in his geographical area, among Gentiles or in the Jesus movement as a whole. At the time of authorship, Gentile believers espoused a variety of embryonic and non-Jewish forms of belief in Jesus and were attempting to assert themselves as valid alternatives to the descendants of the founding fathers of the movement who stood on the vast heritage of Judaism. The author exalts belief in Jesus but he does not deploy or elaborate a comprehensive theology about those beliefs. Rather, the author's form of belief in Jesus seems to stand on the Pauline Kerygma and on the negation, denigration, replacement, and supersession of the beliefs of the founders. Hebrews seems to have been authored at the pivotal moment when proto-orthodox believers embark in an appropriation-supersession journey that will last a couple of hundred years and will transform them from an ill-defined group lacking a coherent and comprehensive definition of what belief in Jesus was or should be, into militant, self-assured, and exclusivist believers. We should note that the author uses the "Old" Testament's authority to legitimize his interpretation of Jesus's ministry while at the same time he claims the supersession and invalidation of beliefs and traditions anchored in it. This peculiar midway positioning will emerge during the second century as the proto-orthodox "Via Media" and will require our attention and scrutiny. The tensions inherent in the continuity-discontinuity conundrum engendered by this positioning, and the appropriation-supersession choice, will embed in the tradition an ambivalent and resentful attitude toward the beliefs and traditions of the descendants of Jesus's disciples and first followers. Whereas Gnostics and Pauline-Marcionites will reject the lore of the founding generation, and will build new theological edifices disconnected from the founders' beliefs and traditions, the author of Hebrews stands at the threshold of a journey into the labyrinth of appropriation-supersession.

Since the theological strand to which the author seems to have belonged chose to perceive itself as the continuation and the replacement of the beliefs and traditions of the founding generation, it had to weave intricate arguments that would support a continuity-discontinuity strategy. These theological choices led to the decontextualization of the Hebrew Scriptures and their conversion into a platform to legitimize the author's understanding of Jesus's legacy. The author of Hebrews, the main architect of the Pauline appropriation-supersession edifice, set the markers of the theological construct that was later to be the central anchor of "orthodoxy." This strategy seems to have included three elements: (a) to accept the Jewish meta-narrative; (b) to gut out most of its institutions, beliefs, and traditions; and (c) to appropriate the remaining shell to vest a non-Jewish edifice with legitimacy and antiquity.

I have argued that the obsessive and systematic denigration of the beliefs and traditions of the Jewish founding fathers seems to emerge out of intense debates among Gentile believers in Jesus about the movements' affiliation with Judaism, which was one facet of a multilateral confrontation among Gentile believers with varying degrees of affiliations with, and inclinations toward Judaism, Paganism, Platonism, and Gnosticism. Vicious attacks against the beliefs and traditions of the descendants of Jesus's disciples and first followers are best seen as indicative of a rising tide of confusion, tension, and anxiety about identity and legitimacy among Gentile believers. Hebrews and Barnabas reflect in their tone and pitch a transition to an overt confrontation about the movements' identity that burst into the surface, first against the beliefs of the founding generation and later on against differing Gentile interpretations of Jesus's ministry and legacy. The Jewish facet of this struggle looms large in the tradition due to the unfortunate fact that the founding fathers were Jewish and that the failed fellowship with them occurred during the canonical era, exacerbating the impact that the estrangement that ensued has had on the attitudes of Gentile believers toward Judaism throughout the ages.

At a time when a cacophony of Gentile forms of belief in Jesus vied for the allegiance of Gentile believers, the addressees are being asked to choose between two forms of belief in Jesus—one Jewish and one Pauline. Overall, the combative demeanor of the Epistle to the Hebrews does not reflect the serene and thoughtful theology of a self-assured thinker. His defensive and resentful tone is characteristic of sectarian challenges to established authority. Hebrews reflects intense emotions originating in a community leader anxious to preserve and protect the gains of the Pauline mission to the Gentiles. Written from the perspective of the de-Judaizing camp, the Epistle is highly abusive to Jewish sensibilities. Although the author does not aim at Judaism per se, its abuse of adversaries that are Jews created a potent anti-Jewish legacy. Hebrews deploys a mostly self-referential argument about the inferiority of the beliefs and traditions of the descendants of the founding fathers that encompasses all aspects of Jewish life. This type of serial denigration of an opponent's religious tenets has little theological merit and can easily be turned around.

The possibility that some believers had a genuine interest and affection for the descendants of the founding fathers and for their traditions and beliefs seems to challenge ingrained intellectual and emotional predispositions, engendering among some scholars a tendency to explain this rather plausible reality in loaded and negative terms (fear of persecution, failure of resolve, political pressure, marginalization, etc.). Despite the slowly growing realization that the descendants of the founding fathers persisted in their embrace of Judaism, and despite the growing awareness about the existence and importance of Gentile sympathizers with the Jewish faction, the adherence to the beliefs of the founding fathers is still cast by some scholars as weakness, defection, apostasy or return. Given that, throughout the centuries that concern us, we witness a persistent drive to de-Judaize belief in Jesus (not a drive to Judaize it) this casting of the issues is intriguing. Indeed, the self-referential and recurring inference that continuity with the beliefs and traditions of the founding fathers is tantamount to apostasy from belief in Jesus is dominant throughout the text and throughout the tradition. This is a peculiar argument given that, at the time of authorship, the author's interpretation of Jesus's legacy championed discontinuity (apostasy) from the beliefs and traditions embraced by Jesus and by those chosen by him to be the guardians of his legacy. Therefore, and contrary to most presentations, attraction to the beliefs and traditions of the founding fathers among Gentiles should be seen as affinity to things "as they were," as opposition to change—rather than a relapse or apostasy. Furthermore, reading traditional scholarship one gets the impression that the choice was between "Judaism" and "Christianity." However, at the time of authorship, the choice for recent converts was between nascent Gentile forms of belief in Jesus and the beliefs and traditions of the founding fathers of the Jesus movement.

The author's strategy of demotion by proxy, embryonic in Paul and Mark, will be refined further during the next two centuries as authors will target the priesthood, the covenant, the people, the Law, circumcision, the Temple, and dietary traditions in their quest to de-Judaize belief in Jesus. The author of Hebrews was among those Gentile believers that did not want to reinvent belief in Jesus in full discontinuity from the beliefs and traditions of the founding fathers. Therefore, in order to retain and appropriate the rich history of his opponents' religious heritage, the author had to thread a delicate line between denigrating these traditions and his wish to clothe his creation with the legitimacy that emanated from them. Thus, and paradoxically, although the author wishes to sever the influence that his Jewish opponents had on his congregants, he also wanted to bestow on his interpretation of Jesus's ministry the authority inherent in their ancient and venerated traditions, and in the legitimacy intrinsic to their being the descendants of the founding fathers. Significantly, despite the wholesale battering of the beliefs and traditions of his adversaries, the author does not place himself outside the Jewish universe altogether and attempts to remain within the umbrella of the Jewish narrative. The author quarries his opponents' sacred scriptures to supply all the necessary definitions and templates to which Jesus's high priesthood and sacrifice must conform. (Jesus as a Davidic descendant, Jesus as a rightful priest, Jesus's sacrifice as a rightful sacrifice, the author's interpretation of Jesus ministry as emanating from the "Old" Testament, the "Old" Testament as anticipating the author's interpretation of Jesus ministry, etc.).

With Hebrews we are only midway in the ever-escalating anti-Jewish trajectory of the Pauline-Lukan authoritative texts. Within an edifice of sanctified and authoritative anti-Jewish invective, the author of Hebrews is one of the central contributors for he provided a cerebral and elaborate theological platform on which a forthcoming torrent of abuse fed. The author of Hebrews, in line with the proto-orthodox narrative, opted for strengthening the case for the validity of his strand of belief in Jesus by disparaging and abusing the beliefs and traditions of his opponents. It seems that the author concluded that if the addressees are to be motivated to remain faithful to his interpretation of Jesus's legacy, they must be persuaded that his views are true and superior vis-à-vis those of the descendants of the founding fathers, which stood on Judaism. Given this background and the future trajectory of the anti-Jewish strand, it is imperative to differentiate the author's intent and circumstances from later interpretations of the text. However, and unfortunately, our re-placing of Hebrews' horizon within the Jesus movement does not alleviate its impact, nor does it change the fact that traditional readings of the text have enabled, facilitated, and exacerbated anti-Jewish attitudes among Gentile believers in Jesus throughout the ages. Hebrews deploys with significant skill a number of themes, arguments, and motifs that provided the theological scaffold that has been used since to denigrate, marginalize, and persecute Judaism—despite the fact that this outcome seems to have been unintended by the author. The tension between the wish to sever and the wish to appropriate-inherit, and the inherent inconsistency and dissonance in building a new edifice on the denigration of Jewish beliefs and traditions, could not but embed in the lore ambivalent attitudes toward Jews and toward Judaism. This continuity-discontinuity conundrum (how to sever the appeal of the founding fathers while at the same time claim to be their theological heirs) required great linguistic, polemical, and rhetorical ability. For two millennia, believers have bonded with the arguments put forward by the author as to the inferiority of the "old" and the superiority of the "new," embedding and ingraining ambivalent attitudes toward

Judaism in the hearts and souls of believers. Hebrews is the cornerstone of supersession theology and has been embraced and acclaimed for almost two millennia as a theological anchor. The author of Hebrews was indeed clever and educated. His arguments, however, stand on the decontextualization and degradation of a tradition that at the time of authorship was already a widely respected and venerated religion.

At this stage in our journey it is important to note that Hebrews is among the earliest proto-orthodox texts where these phenomena are visible, and that we will encounter in the texts ahead of us a large variety of elaborations of his theological platform. We will also encounter the footprints of differing Gentile interpretations of Jesus's ministry and legacy, and differing Gentile approaches to the beliefs and traditions of the founding fathers. As we move forward in time, and as more components and layers are added to the anti-Jewish strand, the tragic implications of the author's choices will become increasingly clear. As we move into the second century and to our next section, we will see the internal conflict among differing interpretations of Jesus's legacy explode and become an all-out confrontation. By the first decades of the second century, the subtle and seemingly inconsequential denigration of the disciples in the canonical Gospels will have morphed into an overt and vicious attack on all things Jewish, Marcionite, Pagan, and Gnostic. Within that trajectory, Hebrews represents a midway point between the implied and embryonic tensions hinted at in the Gospels and the extreme viciousness ahead, as represented by the texts of Melito, Chrysostom, and the Adversus Judaeos literature of the next centuries. Many influential Pauline-Lukan leaders and intellectuals will follow the pathway created by the author of Hebrews.

Chapter 12

The Anti-Jewish Strand in Barnabas

"When they strike down their own shepherd then the sheep of the flock will perish" (5:12), and *"then the men are no more, no more is the glory of sinners"* (8:2).

Introduction

The Pauline and Gnostic success among non-Jews laid the ground for the demise of the Jewish leadership of the Jesus movement. The weakening of the Jewish and Torah-observant leadership that followed the devastation and the loss of life inflicted upon Judea during the failed uprising of 70 CE further exacerbated this process. From this catastrophic revolt to the reign of Emperor Nerva,[1] Judeans experienced one of their darkest periods. Barnabas lives and writes in the preamble to the forthcoming confrontation among competing forms of belief in Jesus that will dominate the next two centuries, and whose Jewish Gentile facet had been brewing since Paul's days and permeates the New Testament. Barnabas, Hebrews, and John are early variants in the transition to undifferentiated anti-Jewish polemic. Barnabas and Hebrews are the earliest texts to venture the transition from implied opposition to the Jewish elite to its theological articulation. They are considered by many to be the first seeds of supersession.[2]

New Testament writings are not used in Barnabas, neither explicitly nor tacitly, which would argue for an early date. The consensus is that the letter was written sometime between 70 and 170 CE[3] with a majority supporting a date prior to the end of the first century. Whether the writer was Jewish or Gentile is still debated. There is evidence supporting either side with a preponderance pointing to a Gentile origin (3:6; 16:7). Many scholars consider 16:5 an allusion to the destruction of the Temple, and date Barnabas to the last decades of the first century. A minority advocates the post–Bar Kochba era (post-135 CE). The text of Bar 16 could imply a planned rebuilding of the Temple with Roman permission. The historical evidence points to Nerva as the most likely to have supported this project (96–98 CE).[4] We have noted that Nerva's reign may have ignited hopes for a Judean reconstruction and revival despite the fact that Jewish hopes for the rebuilding of the Temple did not materialize. A period of Jewish resurgence and enthusiasm would have strengthened the weakened Jewish faction. A reinvigorated Judaism would have dented the sense of upcoming ascendancy among Gentile believers in Jesus.[5]

Clement of Alexandria, Eusebius, and others saw Barnabas as an important early text; it was considered authoritative by many and it was revered accordingly.[6] Barnabas's argumentation is viciously anti-Jewish and derogatory—an "honor" it shares with Melito and Chrysostom. Scholars give Barnabas low marks on consistency and quality of argumentation. Some of Barnabas's anti-Jewish argumentation is widely acknowledged as fantastic, peculiar, bizarre, and internally incoherent.[7] In the most detailed analysis by a Jewish scholar, Alon[8] concludes that Barnabas's knowledge of what he quoted was rather superficial, in sharp contrast to those that advocate a Jewish author on the basis of the author's use of the "two ways" motif, familiarity with a variety of Jewish traditions and with Gematria.[9] Couched in crude Greek, Barnabas's arguments are often clumsy, disconnected, and contradictory. Reading Barnabas is a journey to a chaotic time through the eyes of a most peculiar mind. Barnabas's idiosyncratic and occasionally bizarre views could be dismissed as inconsequential if we could dismiss the fact that his views and arguments are foundational for future Pauline-Lukan supersession theology and if we could overlook the wide use of his arguments by later apologists, theologians, and clergy.[10] Barnabas's militant and confrontational style and content (2:10; 3:6; 4:6b; 14:1–4; 8:1; 7; 9:4; 10:2, 9, 12; 12:10f; 15:8; 16:2f) has spawned countless anti-Jewish sermons and exhortations throughout the centuries. Read by later Gentile believers standing within an anti-Jewish hermeneutic, Barnabas's stereotypical views of his adversaries became embedded in the hearts and minds of many among the faithful.

In an attempt to delegitimize the descendants of Jesus's disciples and first followers, Barnabas attempts to nullify, denigrate, and ridicule their beliefs and customs. Although his exegesis is rudimentary, many of his inflammatory "creations" did resonate with believers whose exposure to, and knowledge of, Judaism was limited to the Pauline-Lukan prism. Many of Barnabas's arguments did become staples despite the fact that "the extent of his obsession, the radicalness of his claims, and the general defensiveness and rancor of his tone would normally be thought to position the author of Barnabas on the margins of Christian opinion."[11] Barnabas has a proto-Orthodox outlook, although somewhat of an idiosyncratic one.

Barnabas places the "old" Covenant, the Temple, and Jewish beliefs and customs (Torah observance, dietary law, and circumcision) center stage. In Barnabas, Jewish "literal" misunderstandings are superseded by new proto-orthodox "spiritual" interpretations. Barnabas's caricature of Judaism did become integral to the lore.

Barnabas's Adversaries

Barnabas does not show any affinity to the Jewish people. Historical Israel is not "us" or "we" but "them" or "they" (Bar. 3:6; 4:6; 8:7; 10:12; 13:1, 3; 14:5). The author does not use the term "Jews." Most of the references to Israel are to the distant past (5:2; 6:7; 9:2; 11:1; 12:2), or to the time when Jesus and his disciples worked among the Jews (5:8; 8:3). In Barnabas the adversaries are not some Jews (elders, scribes, Pharisees, high priests, etc.) or "the Jews" but rather "they." It is unclear whether "they" are all the Jews, establishment-Judaism, the Jewish faction, or their Gentile sympathizers. Later proto-orthodox staple anti-Jewish themes are expressed here with stark simplicity.[12] The extensive usage of we/they, them/us, ours/theirs in negative and hostile contexts (2:9–10; 3:1–3, 6; 4:6–8, 14; 5:1; 8:7; 10:12; 13:1–6; 14:1, 4–8) exacerbates the polemical impact of the text. Who are "us" and who are "they" is implied, not explicitly stated or clarified.[13] "Us" seems to refer to converts to the author's form of belief in Jesus—apparently a Pauline-Lukan strand. "They," on the other hand, are deceived (2:9), conversion to "their law" is equivalent to shipwreck (3:6), "they" are perfect in sin (8:1), things are clear to "us" but obscure to "them" (at 8:7), "their" failure to understand the food laws is a consequence of their "lust of the flesh" (at 10:9), "they" are wretched men who erred in putting their trust in the temple (16:1–2). Barnabas's deployment of the term "they" resonates with John's confusing and inconsistent deployment of the term "Ioudaioi" and may be aimed at the same internal adversaries. Furthermore, it is increasingly apparent that it was not uncommon for early proto-orthodox writers to identify and characterize Jewish opponents within the Jesus movement as "Ioudaioi."[14] It may be that for some, or most, Gentile believers in Jesus the boundaries between these groups were blurred to start with.[15] Indeed, we will encounter a persistent lack of differentiation throughout the textual tradition between the different possible Jewish antagonists.

Deciphering who are the immediate and the ultimate adversaries at the epicenter of Barnabas, and of the other texts of the period, is crucial for our understanding of the underlying crucible that brought about the emergence of the anti-Jewish strand. Throughout the text the author argues that "they" are sinful and misguided, "they" misunderstand their religious heritage, lost or never had the covenant, and lost God's favor. The author and his immediate audience knew the identity of the intended adversaries. However, to us, their identity is obscured by loss of context, the orthodox narrative, and the fog of history. It is quite clear that Barnabas addresses behavior occurring among Gentile believers within his own community. Furthermore, if we divest the Pauline-orthodox hegemony over the discourse, there is nothing in the text that would indicate that the immediate targets are outside Jews or that the author's horizon is beyond the Jesus movement. The text seems to reflect an internal dispute about Judaism—not a conflict with external Judaism. Furthermore, why would Gentile believers obsess about "their" beliefs, traditions, and institutions—unless "they" are the descendants of Jesus's disciples and first followers and the underlying conflict is about legitimacy and identity within the Jesus movement?

Barnabas seems to build on Mark's deprecation of the disciples (i.e., they did not understand Jesus's true legacy, denied, and abandoned him). He is among the first to imply that his opponents' understanding of Jesus's life and ministry, anchored in Judaism, must be erroneous. For Barnabas the true meaning of Israelite history is to be understood and deciphered by non-Jews. The argument seems to be that if the Israelites are incompetent to properly interpret their own theological heritage, Barnabas's Jewish opponents cannot understand Jesus's legacy either. The tension inherent in Barnabas's appropriation of the self-perception of the Jewish founders as the new people of God and "God's chosen" on one hand and the rejection of their beliefs and traditions on the other exacerbates Barnabas's anti-Jewish vitriol. The stress inherent in Hebrews' and Barnabas's appropriate-but-reject answer to the continuity-discontinuity dilemma vis-à-vis the founding fathers required and triggered the emergence of the appropriation-supersession phenomenon, with horrific consequences. The exasperation of Barnabas, and of later Proto-orthodox believers, would be a measure of the influence that the descendants of Jesus's disciples and first followers exerted among Gentile believers, not of the influence of, or attraction to, Judaism. According to Murray, Barnabas is also concerned with the possible recognition, by members of his congregation, of the validity of a joint covenant (Bar. 3:6 and 4:6).[16] Concern about the possible conversion of some of the members to Torah observance (Bar. 3.6) is also present.[17]

The Covenant

A major theme, found in several chapters, is possession of the covenant. The opening salvo is:

> [B]e on your guard now and do not be like certain people; that is, do not continue to pile up your sins while claiming that your covenant is irrevocably

yours, due to the fact in fact the covenant is both theirs and ours. (4:7) It is ours, but those people lost it completely in the following way, when Moses had just received it. For the Scripture says: "And Moses was in the mountain fasting for forty days and forty nights, and he received the covenant from the Lord, stone tablet's inscribed by the fingers of the hand of the Lord" (4:8). But by turning to idols they lost it. For thus says the Lord: "Moses, Moses, go down quickly, due to the fact your people, whom you led out of Egypt, have broken the Law." And Moses understood and hurled the two tablets from his hands, and their covenant was broken in pieces, in order that the covenant of the beloved Jesus might be sealed in our heart, in hope inspired by faith in him.[18]

Barnabas addresses, what he considers to be, a disturbing attitude held by some members of the community to which he writes (Bar. 4:6; 13:1; and 14:1). Barnabas's adversaries seem to favor a closer affiliation with the traditions and beliefs of Jewish founding fathers. It is also possible that some members of Barnabas's community may have thought that the covenant belongs to the descendants of the Jewish founders and to Gentile believers in Jesus, and therefore were not differentiating sufficiently between the two. Barnabas warns the addressees against being influenced by these individuals.[19] The debate is framed as an argument about "their" claim to the covenant. Barnabas argues that "they" never "truly" did possess the covenant (chapters 13 and 14). It was given, Barnabas declares, "but they were not worthy to receive it due to the fact of their sins" (14.1). Barnabas's distinctive doctrine is that the Jewish Law never did have any validity; it was nothing but a misunderstanding on "their" part. Pauline believers in Jesus must make sure, by being accurate, that they do not make a similar mistake (2.10).[20] According to Barnabas only the church is blessed and "they" never were the chosen people.[21] The author rejects the notion that the covenant could be shared. He argues that it never was "theirs" and was always (in God's intention) "ours." The Gentile followers of Paul became the "people of inheritance" (14:4) and received the covenant (14:5) and that was what God always intended. As God's true people, Pauline believers are a light to the nations fulfilling the role of the servant in Isaiah (14:7–9). It is "us" who, as "another type" of people (6:11) and a new creation (6:14), will inherit this promise—if not in the present, then certainly in the future (6:18–19).

The Temple

Most scholars seem to agree that Barnabas reflects fear among Gentile believers in Jesus about the impact of the rebuilding of the Temple (16:3–4). However, they disagree on the importance of this hope in fueling Barnabas's furor against "them."[22] From Hebrews and Barnabas on, an explicitly apologetic use of the Jewish War and the loss of the Temple become integral to the discourse.[23] Destruction of the Temple in 70 CE is deployed by Barnabas as testimony to "their" loss of God's favor. For Barnabas, "they" are like Pagans in their attitudes toward the Temple. "Their" relationship to the Temple is paganized" in the service of Pauline apologetic: "Moreover I will tell you likewise concerning the temple, how these wretched men being led astray set their hope on the building, and not on their God that made them, as being a house of God" (16.1).[24]

It has been argued that the threat that the Temple might be rebuilt profoundly disturbs Barnabas's convictions about the meaning of recent historical events and is one reason for his particularly negative account of the beliefs and traditions of his Jewish opponents.[25] The growing emphasis on the destruction of the Temple as signaling "their" demise would be proven void by the rebuilding of the Temple, which is perceived as a major threat. The prophecy in 16.3–4 should be taken in conjunction with that in 4.3–5, as indicating a peril that is about to break upon the church.[26]

Wedge Issues, Stumbling Blocks

Torah observance—Barnabas warns his readers not to imitate those who stray from proper behavior (Bar. 4:6). He aims to negate the validity of the traditions and rituals of the Jewish followers of Jesus (Bar. 5:4) by taking an adversarial interpretation of the Jewish law and arguing that the Mosaic Law was never supposed to be interpreted literally. Therefore, those who lived according to the literal understanding of the law (i.e., the descendants of Jesus's disciples and first followers) were wrong. According to the author, Gentile believers in Jesus, who found the customs and traditions of the founding fathers attractive and practiced them, were misguided and mislead.[27] He warns Gentile believers against becoming "shipwrecked by conversion" (3:6).

The dietary tradition—According to Barnabas, the food laws were never intended for literal use, but for allegorical instruction regarding correct ethical behavior (Chapter 10).[28] In the last verse of Chapter 10 he states: "But how was it possible for them to understand or comprehend these things? But we having a righteous understanding of them announce the commandments as the Lord wished" (10:12). What is forbidden refers to forms of immoral behavior. What is allowed refers to the superior spiritual focus of the author's form of belief in Jesus. It is only "them" who cannot grasp or understand this, who insist that these prohibitions refer to actual foods.[29] Barnabas disparages "them" by suggesting that their incorrect understanding of the law originates in moral deficiency[30]: "Moses received three doctrines concerning food and thus spoke of them in the Spirit; but they received them as really referring to food, owing to the lust of their flesh" (10:9). Some of the author's arguments on Jewish dietary law are particularly bizarre and strange. The segments on his opponents' dietary traditions are worth reading as a gateway to the peculiar mind of this first-century enthusiast.

Sabbath observance—Barnabas attempts to encourage Gentiles to worship on Sunday instead of Saturday. The Sabbath is understood as an eschatological parable (Chapter 15). The eschatological Sabbath replaces the weekly Sabbaths. This will occur after six thousand years (15:3–6) for in these present evil times the Sabbath cannot be sanctified (15:6–7).[31] Gentile believers at any rate have their own day of celebration, Sunday (15:9).

Circumcision—Some Gentile believers in Jesus, under the influence of the Jewish faction, would understand circumcision to represent participation in the covenant with God and, hence, an integral part of being followers of Jesus.[32] However, for the author "they" misinterpreted the commandment to circumcise by interpreting it literally (Chapter 9) and "[h]e circumcised our hearing, so that we might hear the word and believe" (9:4). The circumcision in which "they" have placed their confidence has been brought to nothing. What God commanded was not circumcision of the flesh: "They transgressed, due to the fact a wicked angel instructed them" (9:4).[33] Barnabas's metaphorical view of circumcision originates within Judaism (Lev. 26:41; Deut. 10:16; 30:6; Jer. 4:4; 6:10; 9:26). Jewish exhortations of the faithful to see beyond the literal observance of the Torah, a staple of Jewish spirituality and of Jewish mysticism, become in Barnabas arguments against "them."

The author's thinking is shot through with powerful eschatological convictions. The present age is an evil age, controlled by the evil one (2:1, 10; 4:1, 13), but time is running out and the last days are here (4:3, 9; 16:5; 21:3) preceded by certain judgment (15:1–3; 21:6). The writer's sense of urgency is unmistakable and it was presumably either shared by his readers or something he wished to inculcate in them. And, in striking parallel with Hebrews and John, it is suggested that some were dropping out of communal gatherings (4:10), while others might even have abandoned their faith.[34]

> Now to us indeed it is manifest that these things so befell for this reason, but to them they were dark, because they heard not the voice of the Lord. (8.7)

> But whence should they perceive or understand these things? Howbeit we having justly perceived the commandments tell them as the Lord willed. To this end He circumcised our ears and hearts, that we might understand these things. (10:12)[35]

Barnabas and Qumran

Qumran aims its anti-establishment arrows at the Judean religious establishment and calls for the return of the Jewish people to righteousness.

Barnabas, on the other hand, seems to appropriate Qumran-like sectarian rhetorical idiosyncrasies, to the inclusion of the Pesher exegetical method,[36] to delegitimize the religious establishment of the Jesus movement and to negate the validity of Judaism—its theological anchor. Barnabas seems to emulate-incorporate-appropriate a pattern of religion we find in Qumran, characteristic of other Judean sectarians, to the inclusion of the Jewish founders of the Jesus movement:[37]

1. God has given a covenant at Sinai.
2. That covenant, as a result of the intervention of an extraordinary individual, is the possession of the community and not those outside it, who have forfeited their right to it through their sins.
3. The correct interpretation of the commandments, which are intimately bound up with the idea of the covenant, of the scriptures generally, and of the prophets lies with the community.

Anti-Jewish-establishment rhetoric is the designation I have used throughout to encapsulate various types and manifestations of Jewish sectarian posturing against the Jewish mainstream-establishment, to the inclusion of the "Two Ways" imagery. We have already noted that the "Two Ways" theme[38] is the label given by scholars to a Judean sectarian worldview that sees this world as the battleground between the forces of good and evil. This is contrary to the traditional Israelite view that creation was good and benign. The resentful, righteous, and militant posturing of Jewish sectarians is oftentimes intertwined and undistinguishable from the "Two Ways" material. Nonetheless, the distinction is useful to separate the polemical from the theological aspects of this separatist subculture. In Barnabas we find shadows of anti-Jewish-establishment posturing and of the "Two Ways" material that we encounter in the texts of Judean sectarian communities (Qumran, I Enoch, Jubilees). These themes and attitudes characterized Jewish sectarians and may have migrated to Gentile settings through the agency of the descendants of the founding fathers—most probably through a community (or individual) that seceded from a community of Jewish followers of Jesus.[39]

Barnabas's "two ways" motif has angelic powers, and "the ruler of this present lawlessness" (18.2). The times are evil, and there is evil lurking to "sling us out from our life" (2.10).[40] By using Pesher exegesis and the "two ways" motif, Barnabas seems to mimic Qumran and other Judean sectarians where the official Jewish cult is seen as displeasing to God, idolatrous, and evil. Another area of similarity and difference between Barnabas and Qumran is the covenant. We have already noted that Barnabas: (1) holds to the view that there is one covenant; (2) regards the covenant as containing the right laws if only interpreted correctly; and (3) is strongly opposed to the idea that the covenant is anything other than the possession of those espousing the author's interpretation of Jesus's legacy. Although the Qumran covenanters regularly speak of a "new covenant" (CD 6:19; 8:21; 20:12; IQpHab 2:3f.), there does not seem to be so great a disjunction between this new covenant and the covenant that it seems to replace. In Qumran, what is new in the "new covenant" are secret teachings, present in the law from eternity, but only revealed to the community through the teacher of righteousness (IQpHab 7:4f.), or in another formulation the Zadokite priests (see IQSb 3:24; IQS 5:21f.).[41]

Barnabas's incorporation-appropriation of the identity and lore of the Jewish founders into a Gentile narrative is one of the earliest and clearest instances of the supersessionary trajectory. Barnabas is also one of the earliest, explicit, and crude articulations of the attempts to Gentilize belief in Jesus by delegitimizing the beliefs and traditions of the founders. This ambivalent and seemingly contradictory approach (incorporation-appropriation while superceding-Gentilizing) to "the Jewish question," found in embryonic form in Paul and in the Synoptics, will be deployed during the next three hundred years against the descendants of the Jewish founders and their Gentile sympathizers in a variety of configurations. Barnabas's weapon of choice is the erosion, through vilification and disparagement, of the high esteem that their beliefs, traditions, and institutions had among some Gentile believers.

My Barnabas

Barnabas's claims, and the "anti-Jewish" claims we found in the NT, were made at a time when the Pauline mission to the Gentiles was a few decades old and still uncertain of its theological footing. The debate about what belief in Jesus was or should be was in its embryonic stages. This, however, does not seem to encumber Barnabas. The author claims that the covenant was "our" possession, that it had never belonged to "them" in the first place.[42] Barnabas also claims that his strand of belief in Jesus had the key to the correct understanding of a national and religious tradition spanning, at the time, at least one hundred generations—a religious tradition that enjoyed the respect and admiration of the ancient world. In the context of the late first century, these were astonishing statements. These claims, put forward by recent converts still uncertain of what their beliefs were, or should be—would be considered extraordinary and odd by contemporary intellectuals and thinkers.

In Barnabas, in the footsteps of Mark, the people that shared Jesus's life and ministry as well as his religious and ethnic affiliation "do not understand." "We" are the only truly ethical people, the true inheritors of the covenant and the rightful interpreters of the Jewish sacred scriptures. Thus, "their" understanding of their own traditions is wrong and their covenant is an illusion: God did give the covenant to the Israelites, but their transgressions made them unworthy to receive it: "Moses received it, but they were not worthy" (14:1–3).[43] The implied message seems to be: Judaism misinterpreted and misunderstood its heritage. Therefore, the Jewish faction cannot have it right either.

That Jewish observances, the Temple, the covenant, and the Land are the central themes of Barnabas's polemical exegesis is widely recognized.[44] Traditionally, scholars have seen the purpose of Barnabas as bound up with Judaism, either directly, or indirectly. Some have argued that Barnabas is fighting Judaistic tendencies among his addressees. Others have drawn the conclusion that Barnabas perceives Judaism itself as an actual threat. For many modern scholars the author is reacting to the attractiveness of Judaism and answers are to be found in the conflict between the synagogue and the Church.[45] During the last decades some scholars[46] have begun to differentiate intended adversaries from literary or metaphorical ones and have rediscovered the internal setting of these debates. Gentile Judaizers, Gentile sympathizers with Judaism, are increasingly seen as the intended targets. Murray, in the footsteps of Wilson and others, suggests that the targets are Christian Judaizers.[47] The scenario advocated here suggests that the Christian Judaizers in question are Gentile sympathizers with the founding faction. Accordingly, Barnabas's vitriol is to be understood as anger about the influence of the Jewish faction among Gentile congregants and about the attraction to their beliefs and traditions. Regardless of the identity of the immediate or intended adversaries, many elements of the author's response to the attraction to Jewish beliefs and traditions among his flock are offensive to Jews and, read literally, are anti-Jewish.[48]

It seems to me that the author of the Epistle could be a Gentile that joined, and later seceded from, a community of Jewish followers of Jesus (and therefore had some exposure to Judaism). This profile could fit this peculiar text and its many idiosyncrasies. Barnabas's superficial acquaintance with Judaism and his crude argumentation signals that his intended audience was Gentile. In this setting, Judaism could be made into whatever the author's rich imagination concocted it to be. My analysis de-externalizes the conflict and re-places it in what I consider to be the original, and internal, context. In Barnabas, the adversaries are not the Synoptic High Priests, Jewish authorities, Elders, Pharisees, scribes, nor John's Ioudaioi, but "they"/"them." However, I suggest that the deployment of "they"/"them" is essentially similar in intent to John's deployment of the term "Ioudaioi" and aims at the descendants of Jesus's disciples and first followers or their Gentile sympathizers—directly or through "the Jews" as a proxy. The author of the Epistle of Barnabas criticizes Jewish interpretations of scripture and Jewish religious practices in order to dissuade members of his community from attraction to the descendants of the founding fathers and from observing their customs. In reaction to what he perceived to be the excessive influence that they exerted over members of his community, Barnabas targets the Jewish faction—who were, at the time and to many, the acknowledged inheritors, guardians, and interpreters of Jesus's ministry. Barnabas argues that the Mosaic Law was never supposed to be interpreted literally. Therefore, the descendants of the Jewish founders, who lived according to the traditional Jewish understanding of the Torah, were wrong, and Gentile believers who found Jewish customs attractive and practiced them were also wrong.

Any attempt to understand the anti-Jewish turn among early non-Jewish believers in Jesus needs to provide a context, and a socio-theological pathway, to how and why recent converts to Gentile forms of belief in Jesus started denigrating the beliefs and traditions of the descendants of the founding fathers, using language, imagery, and arguments that seem to emulate the anti-Jewish traditions of Jewish sectarians. Barnabas "turned the tables" against the establishment of the Jesus movement and claimed that Gentiles that embraced his interpretation of Jesus's legacy were the new holders of God's franchise; the new people of YHWH, the God of the Jews. Judean sectarian traditions, prophetic chastisement, self-criticism, allegory, and metaphor, most probably originating with the descendants of Jesus's disciples and first followers, are turned against them. In Barnabas, and throughout the texts of early Gentile believers, attacks on Judaism by some and attraction to it by others may be understood as symptoms of an identity crisis within the Jesus movement. It is not Judaism per se that is center stage. Rather, debates about Judaism reflect a struggle about identity, ascendancy, and legitimacy within the Jesus movement. Judaism got dragged into the whirlwind as a consequence of the fact that the movement was originally Jewish and that the shift to a Gentile majority led to a de-Judaizing thrust. Centuries later, misinterpreted and misrepresented, the resentful and derogatory rhetoric of this de-Judaizing thrust was to become the seed of anti-Semitism.

Barnabas's outlook must be intimately linked to the background against which it was written: context-shaped theology.[49] Barnabas seems to be part of a chain of sectarian affront to a group in position of authority. Barnabas's understanding of the covenantal relationship and his claim to the Hebrew Scriptures, although extraordinary at the time, make sense when understood as an attempt to address the internal conflict with the Jewish faction. Barnabas's peculiar theological position, that the Jewish followers of Jesus misunderstood their own sacred texts and that God's covenant with "them" was a temporary measure (9:4), seems to be reasonably fitted to the erupting struggle within the Jesus movement. This position shadows the claim of the Pauline-Lukan faction that the legitimacy and the leadership of the descendants of Jesus's disciples and first followers was temporary and that their understanding of Jesus's ministry was mistaken. Barnabas's anti-Judaism[50] is proto-orthodox; it is the anti-Judaism inherent in appropriation-substitution, as distinct from the anti-Judaism of rejection (Pauline-Marcionites and Gnostics). The full measure of Barnabas's vitriol is difficult to convey. Barnabas is relentless: "They" are Pagan-like (16.1–3), demonized (7. 10), Jesus's sacrifice completed the full measure of the sins of those who persecuted the prophets and put him to death (5:11–12). In addition, misreading of God's will, diabolical inspiration, and an endless array of derogatory rhetoric are dispensed without the slightest restraint.

Barnabas's extreme disparagement of the beliefs and traditions of his opponents and his often-bizarre arguments did eventually relegate it to the margins of canonicity.[51] Although Barnabas's claims and choice of words are unacceptable to Jewish readers, we need emphasize the socio-theological context of authorship. First-century Gentiles, still evolving toward a clear understanding, definition, and consensus about what Jesus's legacy was or should be, often produced texts characterized by overstatement and intense militancy. If this type of disrespectful and presumptuous trespassing and disparagement would have remained an internal hyper-enthusiastic debate about Judaism, its abusive tone and content would be inconsequential and might be disregarded. Unfortunately, many of Barnabas's arguments became normative among later believers. They did become staple supersessionary views that did permeate homilies and sermons, and the hearts, minds, and souls of believers.

Chapter 13

The Second-Century Protagonists

Introduction

Walter Bauer (1934) is credited with the rediscovery of the diversity and the complexity of the early Jesus movement, a conclusion that emerged out of a survey of the texts and traditions found in the different geographical areas of the Roman Empire. Although his methodology and some of his findings have been questioned, a growing group of modern scholars agree that the proto-orthodox were not the only strand of belief in Jesus at the dawn of the second century and that the Jesus movement evolved from diversity to uniformity, contrary to traditional accounts. Recent work and insights on the diversity of the early Jesus movement have triggered a qualified rehabilitation of the work of Bauer,[1] setting the stage for a conceptual revolution in New Testament studies.

The diversity of the early Jesus movement is further supported by 1 Corinthians 1–4, Q,[2] James, and the pro-Torah segments of proto-Matthew—where we encounter early Gentile believers in Jesus not grounded in the Kerygma of the cross and resurrection.[3] Q, used by Matthew and Luke, does not consider Jesus's death part of the core message and it is not interested in stories and reports about the resurrection. Furthermore, one of the most striking features of the Gospel of Thomas is its silence on the matter of Jesus's death and resurrection—the keystone of Paul's missionary proclamation. These deviations from Pauline-Lukan dogma signal that Jesus's significance lay in his words and in his words alone.[4] The existence of early non-Pauline Gentile understandings of Jesus's legacy is further corroborated by the opponents of the Johannine community. These non-Pauline traces challenge the assumption that early Gentile believers in Jesus were unanimous in making Jesus's death and resurrection the fulcrum of faith. In addition, thanks to the discovery of the Nag Hammadi library (1959), scholars gained direct access to a variety of Gnostic forms of belief in Jesus, undistorted by the orthodox filter. The traditional perception of the adversaries of Paul and of the later opponents of the Pauline-Lukan faction as heresies has given way to a growing acknowledgment of the great variety of early Gentile forms of belief in Jesus. Finally, acknowledgement of the diversity of the early Jesus movement requires freeing Marcion from the stigma of heresy and his rehabilitation as a rightful Pauline believer in Jesus.

It seems that as the Pauline and Gnostic missions to the Gentiles grew, Gentile believers harnessed the main cultural currents that predominated in their environment (Judaism, Paganism, and Gnosticism) to articulate the uniqueness of Jesus's ministry and the purpose of his early death. Of the four factions or strands that gradually emerged, three represented opposing and irreconcilable theological stands (the Jewish followers of Jesus, the Pauline-Marcionite, and the Gnostics). A fourth faction, the Pauline-Lukan, strived for unity and struggled to define and articulate a compromise middle ground that came to be known as the "Via Media." A multilateral struggle between these factions engulfed the Jesus movement well into the fourth century. All the participants in this religious "civil war" understood themselves to be the only "true" Christians and viewed their adversaries' beliefs as heretical, misguided, or inadequate.[5] The doctrinal and theological descendants of the Pauline-Lukan strand gradually became the dominant faction and were later identified as "orthodox." The later fusion of the term Christianity with the Pauline-Lukan interpretation of belief in Jesus reflects the success of the proto-orthodox push for ascendancy and perpetuates the traditional representation of the Jesus movement as evolving from unity to diversity. Therefore the use of the term "Christianity"[6] to discuss the first centuries of belief in Jesus is problematic. Clarity is added when we refrain from doing so.

Significantly, Judaism, Gnosticism, and Paganism were not participants in the second-century religious "civil war" within the Jesus movement—they were the themes, the subject matter, of the dispute. Therefore, when the canonical Gospel tradition and the authoritative texts denigrate Torah observance and Judaism, they reflect an internal conflict with followers of Jesus that advocated that belief in Jesus be Jewish, not a conflict with Judaism. Similarly, when the canonical and authoritative texts denigrate Gnostics and Pagans, they reflect an internal conflict with opponents advocating that belief in Jesus be Gnostic or Pagan, not a conflict with Paganism or Gnosticism.

In the chapters ahead we will discuss texts authored after the canonical era and reflect a new phase—a higher level of anti-Jewish invective. We will also survey the persistent, but declining, influence of the Jewish faction. The period covered by this second section encompasses more than two hundred years and straddles the postcanonical era at one end and the council of Nicea (325 CE) at the other end. This period is characterized by diverse, opposing, and incompatible interpretations of Jesus's ministry and legacy. The main strands had different theological centers of gravity (Torah-observance, Jesus's sayings, secret knowledge, and Jesus's death and resurrection) and varying degrees of affinity to the external forces without (Judaism, Paganism, mystery religions, Platonism, and Gnosticism). The shift to the upcoming overt, intense, and vicious anti-Jewish rhetoric is "fog-like." The trajectory is not linear, nor homogeneous. Change seems to have been gradual and subject to local, regional, and factional variation. Transitions "on the ground" are often unclear, tentative, ambiguous, and complex. The rate of change along this trajectory is not always clear, but the atmosphere at the two ends of the spectrum is distinctly different. We may not know exactly when shifts occur, but we know when we are beyond them.

Background

The era that we are about to enter, the second and third centuries, was a period of great religious excitement, enthusiasm, militancy, and fervor. The Roman world was in spiritual and religious turmoil. A variety of cults and sects vied for the interest and affiliation of a large number of spiritual seekers. Not dissimilar to the emergence of the twentieth-century eclectic "New Age," the Second Century Christianities[7] reflected the variegated theological spectrum of the era, and attracted large numbers of converts dissatisfied with the official Roman cult. These circumstances give the second and third centuries their special flavor—an extraordinary religious intensity and militancy. This period of great flux and vitality winds down by the fourth century. It is important to internalize the fact that the range and depth of the diversity that we encounter during the second century goes far beyond the diversity we encounter today. Today, a large number of Catholic, Protestant, Greek Orthodox, Coptic, and Mormon denominations and strands vie for Jesus's legacy. However, this diversity emanates from one strand, the Pauline orthodox. Consequently, today's diversity has a narrower theological range. Survival of the other second-century Christianities would have created a current landscape of much greater diversity.

Table 13.1 attempts to illuminate the transition from the "second-century Christianities" (i.e., the factions that surfaced during the second century) to the compromise creed that emerged from their struggle about identity, legitimacy, and ascendancy. This compromise creed, rightfully called the "Via Media," is the result of the victorious campaign of the Pauline-Lukan faction for unity and ascendancy. A detailed analysis of the table brings to the surface the fact that the "Via Media," the theological synthesis of

Orthodoxy, was a compromise. Indeed, the "Via Media" attempted to hold the middle ground between three distinct and incompatible theological strands represented by the Jewish followers of Jesus, the Pauline-Marcionites, and the Gnostic strands.

The Jewish Followers of Jesus

After the decimation of their communities during the failed Judean revolutions (70 CE and 135 CE) and following the success of the Pauline and Gnostic missions to the Gentiles, the descendants of Jesus's disciples and first followers gradually became a controversial minority within the Jesus movement.[8] To their probable surprise and discomfort, they had become the unintentional founders of an increasingly non-Jewish religious movement, while simultaneously being anti-Jewish-establishment sectarians. The descendants of the Jewish founders were under great pressure to renounce Judaism or renounce Jesus. Caught between two worlds, they were marginalized and coerced by their Jewish brethren and by fellow followers of Jesus. They faced a two-front confrontation: against other Jews in defense of the messiahship of Jesus, and against Gentiles in defense of Judaism and in opposition to the deification of Jesus. We must assume a full spectrum of outcomes, ranging from those that may have severed their links with Judaism, to those that renounced Jesus. Deciphering the genealogy of anti-Jewish tendencies among early Gentile believers in Jesus requires an understanding of this crucible. As to the "parting of the ways" between the Jewish followers of Jesus and the Jewish mainstream, most scholars have argued for 80–120 CE.[9] The date for this estrangement-transition is debated. I am inclined to support the arguments pointing to the Bar Kochba (132–5 CE) era as the pivot in a possible estrangement between these parties.

Most of our knowledge about the descendants of the Jewish founders comes from the writings of heresiologists and apologists,[10] and from pre-Synoptic sediments in the New Testament. Scholars have also gained some knowledge about the early Jewish followers of Jesus from James, the Didache, and from their footprints and traces in Matthew, John, and Revelation. Additional insights have emerged from studies of Q and the pre-Synoptic era, and from the writings of the Greek and Latin Fathers.[11] Scholars have also gained important insights by studying the Qumran, Enochic, and Jubelean texts. Using the Qumran material as representative of the broader phenomenon of turn of the era Jewish sectarianism and standing on the traces of the pre-Synoptics in the canonical texts, we can speculate on what the theology of the descendants of Jesus's disciples and first followers may have looked like.[12] In Acts, the Jewish followers of Jesus are the bridge between Jesus's ministry and the investiture of the Pauline-Lukan faction

Table 13.1 The Emergence of a Compromise Creed

	Jewish Followers of Jesus	Pauline-Lukan Compromise	Pauline-Marcionite Believers in Jesus	Gnostic Believers in Jesus
YHWH/Jewish god	Severe/just	Benevolent	Renegade/vengeful	Renegade/creator of an evil world
Jewish bible	Sacred scripture	Keep, reinterpret, and supersede	Reject/disregard	Bad/disregard
Jewish law	Keep	Supersede	Disregard	Disregard
Number of gods	One	One/trinity	Two	Several
Attitude toward the Jewish people	Positive	Ambivalent	Negative	Ambivalent/negative
Purpose of belief	Serve God by keeping the law	Salvation	Salvation	Release from evil world
Route to salvation	By faith and God's law	By faith alone	By faith alone	By secret knowledge
The nature of creation	Good	Good / ambivalent	Ambivalent	Bad
The source of evil	Not keeping the law	Human sin	Human sin	Cosmic flaw
Human nature	Ambivalent	Sinful	Sinful	Good/divine spark within
The chosen people	Jews	Jews originally/ Christians now	Christians	All that receive secret knowledge
Should Jews keep the Jewish law	Yes	Ambivalent	Irrelevant	Irrelevant

as the legitimate heirs to Jesus's ministry. Communities with varying affinities to the descendants of Jesus's disciples and first followers are attested to
in Irenaeus, Epiphanius, and in the Pseudo-Clementine literature. Labeled
Nazarenes, Ebionites, or Ekliesates they surface in the literature as bizarre,
eccentric, and heretical oddities. However, once their role as legitimating
agents for the Pauline-Lukan ascendancy and for the orthodox myth of
origins is accomplished, they disappear from the historical record to resurface as marginal and disenfranchised "heretics." Significantly, despite the
fact that some New Testament texts seem to build on the heritage of the
descendants of the Jewish founders, and that their existence and influence
are palpable throughout, they are not acknowledged as the rightful successors of Jesus's ministry and legacy. Throughout our journey they will remain
the unacknowledged antagonists of the writers and editors of many of the
canonical and authoritative texts.

The Pauline-Lukan Faction

The Pauline-Lukan were one of two factions that claimed Paul's legacy. Their
theological evolution is reflected in the doctrinal lineage that includes Paul,
Mark, Luke/Acts, Hebrews, Ignatius, Justin, Polycarp, Tertullian, Irenaeus,
and Eusebius. The traditional interpretation of Paul's theological legacy was
shaped by the views and mindsets of these leaders and thinkers. This is the
theological chain that carries and develops the "orthodox" outlook to its
maturity as the post-Constantine orthodoxy. Eventually, the proto-orthodox
faction became the dominant group and is therefore often labeled Christian,
Christian orthodox, or Orthodox. Central to the proto-orthodox success was
the Christian community of the city of Rome. This community, large in size,
rich, and influential, had a significant impact on the direction of belief in
Jesus. Bauer (1934) first championed the centrality of the Christian community of Rome. Today, it seems appropriate to assign to this community a
significant impact, but not the overwhelming influence that Bauer implied.
      According to the majority view, Justin was one of the first thinkers and
intellectuals to consolidate the main themes and tenets of this faction and the
first Pauline-Lukan writer to have explicitly responded to Marcion's threat.[13]
We have noted that the proto-orthodox strand attempted to hold the middle
ground demarcated by the theological triangle created by the descendants of
Jesus's disciples and first followers, and by Pauline-Marcionite and Gnostic[14]
Gentile believers. The Pauline-Lukan faction placed itself in the middle of
this theological range and confronted adversaries from all sides. The socio-
theological trajectory of the Jesus movement and the proto-orthodox theological positioning as depicted in table 13.1 led me to characterize their
theological narrative as a compromise creed. The proto-orthodox were the

main driving force in the unification of the church's creed and organization, and in the eventual Christianizing of the Roman Empire—requiring the main share of our interest and scrutiny. The implications of the fact that their adversaries, Jews and non-Jews within the Jesus movement and oftentimes within the author's community, are not properly acknowledged and represented in the tradition have not yet fully permeated the discourse. Christian-orthodox theology was born out of this process of self-definition.[15] It had to navigate a narrow path through a maze of contending arguments. The attempt at holding the middle ground enjoyed broad appeal but was burdened with ambivalences and unresolved "mysteries"—the tensions and unresolved dissonances characteristic of a compromise.

As it pertains to the proto-orthodox drive to de-Judaize the Jesus movement, some consistent themes emerge out of the authoritative texts of the Pauline-Lukan faction. These themes and motifs surface, resurface, and morph throughout our inquiry:

1. Denigration of the disciples, who "did not understand" and who forsook Jesus.
2. Denigration of the beliefs and traditions of the founding fathers.
3. Jesus as alienated from fellow Jews. Jesus, a stranger among his people.
4. Exoneration of the Romans and the culpability of the Jews.
5. Intensification and expansion of the anti-Jewish rhetoric as time passes.
6. A militant and exclusivist compromise creed.
7. The mysteries—unharmonized appropriated theological elements.

The Pauline-Marcionites

Marcion was born and raised in Sinope, a port on the Black Sea, in the province of Pontus in Asia Minor (Epiphanius, Panarion 42.1.3). Although scholars differ on Marcion's dates, we can safely place his ministry in the first half of the second century.[16] Marcion was a rich merchant who gained great influence through his wealth and charisma. He was eventually expelled from Rome and transferred his activities to Asia Minor, where he became very popular. Marcion's ecclesiastical organization lasted for several centuries and had an extensive network of affiliated communities. Marcion was an enthusiastic and literalist champion of Paul. He understood himself to be "the" true interpreter of Paul's legacy. Most modern scholars acknowledge the contribution of Marcion to orthodoxy by creating one of the templates against which it defined itself. By creating the first canon, apparently centered on a revised version of Paul's Epistles, Marcion prompted the Pauline-Lukan to self-definition. He was a main motivator for the pro-to-orthodox "rescue" of Paul from his interpretations.[17]

Marcion made the earliest and most radical attempt to sever the link between the Gentile followers of Jesus and the descendants of Jesus's disciples and first followers. Contrary to the orthodox complex and ambivalent reject-but-appropriate approach to the beliefs and traditions of the founding fathers, Marcion advocated a complete and radical rejection of any affiliation with their legacy[18] and strived for a thorough de-Judaizing of belief in Jesus. Unencumbered by the intricate and ambivalent theological fine threading characteristic of the proto-orthodox drive for compromise, Marcion's radical solution was attractive to many Gentiles and became a formidable stumbling block to the proto-orthodox push for ascendancy. By severing the link between Gentile believers and the Jewish faction, Marcion rejected the Pauline-Lukan wish to stand on Hebrew Scripture and lore. Marcion's rejection of the beliefs and traditions of the founding fathers was complete and unqualified[19] and, according to his opponents, was also derogatory. To Marcion the Jewish god is righteous and just, but also capricious and prone to anger (Marc. 2.16, 20, 23). Marcion's rejection of the Jewish "baggage" of the descendants of the founding fathers, whether intrinsic to his worldview or directed at fending off the proto-orthodox attacks against him,[20] could have eliminated the rancor, resentment, and ambivalence that accompanied the reject-but-appropriate trajectory of his adversaries. A clean rejection of the beliefs and traditions of the founding faction also liberated the Pauline-Marcionites from recurring charges leveled against the Pauline-Lukan and their theological descendants. Most notably, that they claimed the Jewish heritage but failed to follow through.[21] Marcion's outlook did not need the scaffold of the "Jewish responsibility for Jesus's death" either. That event was ultimately the responsibility of the creator and of the principalities and powers working under him (Marc. 3.24; 5.6). Moreover, the Jewish rejection of Jesus was understandable since he was an alien and unprecedented figure who did not fit Jewish messianic expectations (Marc. 3, 6).[22]

By providing an alternative to the descendants of the Jewish founders, Pauline-Marcionite and Gnostic believers framed the arena within which the compromise creed, the Via Media, was to emerge. Marcion addressed the dilemma of the relationship of the new faith to Judaism and of the origins of evil and suffering in one bold move: his beliefs in two deities. This Gnostic element allowed Marcion to see YHWH as a renegade creator of this evil world and to embrace Jesus as the son of the supreme and benevolent deity of the universe. Marcion's theology seems to have borrowed heavily from Gnostic motifs but seems to have stopped short of categorizing the universe as evil and corrupt.[23] The Marcionite Jesus was a new and unprecedented figure that revealed a previously unknown deity of love and mercy—in sharp contrast with the God of the "Old

Testament" that was viewed by Marcion as an inferior deity, lacking in wisdom and justice.[24]

Gnostic Believers in Jesus

Gnosticism, a controversial term, is a later designation for a variety of syncretic spiritual trends that flourished during the first centuries of the Common Era (Hermetica, Valentians, Mandaeans, and Manichaeans). The usefulness and the relevancy of the term have been criticized. However, an alternative term has not emerged.[25] In many Gnostic systems, the world is the creation of a lesser and evil God (the Jewish God). Despair and pessimism are pronounced and permanent. The world is evil and there is no hope for change. Salvation from this world is through secret knowledge taught by a divine savior (Jesus) and understood only by few, the elect. Various Gnostic schools evolved from the "Gnostic Fathers" Ptolomey, Cerinthus, and Valentius.

The origins of Gnosticism are shrouded in mystery and are hotly debated.[26] "The most influential current view is that Gnosticism arose among sectarian Jews on the outskirts of Judaism."[27] The Gnostic mission to the Gentiles may have originated with Simon Magnus (Acts 8) and Menander, both from Samaria (north of Judea). Magnus was a charismatic figure with messianic aspirations. Gnostic forms of belief in Jesus became one of the important second-century forms of belief in Jesus, competing with the founding faction and with the Pauline-Lukan and the Pauline-Marcionites for the future of the Jesus movement.[28] Gnostic cosmogony is a fascinating alternative to the Jewish understanding of creation as the work of a benevolent deity. Gnostic believers posited a transcendental, immutable, and unengaged deity. In most Gnostic systems, the world is the creation of a lesser and evil God (the Jewish God). Despair and pessimism are pronounced and permanent. Creation follows a cosmic catastrophe. The world is evil and there is no hope for change. From Jewish sectarians that may have been its precursors, Gnosticism derived the world as a battleground between dualistic forces (good and evil, soul and flesh, sin and righteousness, light and darkness). The divine spark within (that originates in the divine catastrophe) is to be freed by the redeemer-savior (Jesus) who provides secret knowledge to escape from suffering. Interestingly, Gnosticism seems to have fomented two radically opposing extremes: libertinism and asceticism. The Gnostic view of Judaism is mostly negative but does not necessitate the resentment-ambivalence inherent in the proto-orthodox appropriate-delegitimize pathway. Outright rejection does not create an emotional residue, the possessive impulse behind appropriation and supersession-replacement does.

The Gnostic library found at Nag Hammadi (1945) has been credited with intensifying the conceptual revolution initiated by Bauer. For the first time, one of the contending second-century Christianities emerged from the shadows and scholars have been able to study these early believers in Jesus unmediated by their opponents. Thanks to the findings at Nag Hammadi, the extent of the sectarian and polemical bias of the Pauline-Lukan apologists has been corroborated by a direct source.[29] Interestingly, the Nag Hammadi findings included the Gospels of Mary, the Savior, Thomas, Truth, and Phillip—none of which are dedicated to Jesus's life story. In the Apocryphon of John, probably the most philosophical and enlightening of all Gnostic treatises, Jesus is not mentioned at all. Secret knowledge, self-knowledge, and truth are the main focuses of these texts, highlighting the abyss between the proto-orthodox and the Gnostic worldviews. Gnostic speculation and imagery had great influence among many early thinkers and theologians with mystical inclinations, some of which attempted to harmonize the Pauline-Lukan and the Gnostic strands unsuccessfully.[30] From the fourth century forward Gnostics went underground due to Pauline persecution, became crypto-Gnostics and made central contributions to Western esoteric and mystical thought. Twelve- and thirteen-century Gnostics (Albigensians, Cathars, and Spanish Kabbalists) as well as many modern esoteric strands resonate with Gnostic imagery, motifs, and themes.

Gentile Sympathizers with the Founding Fathers

In most of the canonical and authoritative texts, the identity of the author's antagonists is, more often than not, implicit rather than explicit. This peculiarity may be due to the fact that many texts were written with specific audiences in mind, and that the audience knew the identity of the intended targets. Often, the enemy was within. The "enemy within" would be those members of the community that were attracted to the descendants of Jesus's disciples and first followers or to Gentile, but non-proto-orthodox, interpretations of Jesus's ministry.[31] Commitment, affinity, and affiliation with the Jewish faction varied greatly. Some among the Gentiles attracted to the descendants of Jesus's disciples and first followers converted to Judaism. Most seem to have embraced some of the beliefs and traditions of the founding fathers of the movement. These "Gentile Judaizers" drew some of the most vitriolic fire from Gentile leaders and literati who were incensed by their attraction to the beliefs and traditions of the Jewish faction. Furthermore, it seems to be the case that many Gentile believers in Jesus did not distinguish between different types of Jews. We can carve out of the texts a spectrum of "Jews" that includes Gentile sympathizers with the descendants of the

Jewish founders, both internal and external to the Gentile community in question, the Jewish followers of Jesus, the Jewish rank and file, the authentic Jewish religious leadership, and the Roman-appointed minions and collaborators that ruled Judea. Lack of clear identifiers for the various protagonists and the recurring use of the multivalent terms "Ioudaioi," "Jew," and "Christian" by the sources and by scholars contribute to our difficulties in deciphering, and discussing, this period.[32]

The Via Media

Whereas the original followers of Jesus were (and seem to have remained) Jews and therefore had an established religious worldview and lifestyle, the newer (non-Jewish) strands of belief in Jesus had to define a theological and creedal grounding to stand on. Thus, the non-Jewish factions evolved through a process of adversarial dialectic vis-à-vis the Jewish faction and among themselves. As Gentile believers in Jesus attempted to interpret Jesus's life and death and to transform this understanding into a mature and non-Jewish religious outlook, the protagonists of the second century started to emerge. This process did not reach closure until the fourth century. The existence of two sets of "apologies" by Justin and by Tertullian (each having written two "apologies," one against "the Jews," the other against Marcion) reflects the fact that the Pauline-Lukan confrontation with the descendants of the Jewish founders paralleled and mirrored their confrontation with the Pauline-Marcionites. In fact, in Tertullian's works the same charges are often laid against either antagonist, with only minimal adaptation.[33] Thus, it is important to internalize the fact that the anti-Jewish universe that we are about to enter emerged out of one of three fronts that the Pauline-Lukan faction did maintain throughout their crusade for ascendancy and unity (against the Jewish faction and against Pauline-Marcionite and Gnostic Gentile believers). Fighting on these three fronts engendered a highly nuanced, and somewhat inconsistent, orthodox position regarding a number of issues. When debating Gnostics, the Pauline-Lukan claimed that the Jewish scriptures are to be read literally. When debating the descendants of the founding fathers or their Gentile sympathizers, they claimed that the Jewish scriptures are to be read figuratively and allegorically. When confronting Gnostics and Marcionites they insisted on the relevance of the Jewish creator God and of the Jewish heritage. When confronting the Jewish faction they emphasized the divinity of Jesus and the rejection of Jewish beliefs and traditions.[34]

We have in the canonical and authoritative texts a unique window into the birth of a religion, including the fascinating "push and shove" of theology in the making. With the passage of time, the factions consolidated, the debates sharpened, the arguments became clearer and better defined, and the demarcations became more visible. As anticipated in the previous section, the Jesus movement will go through a period of self-definition and an all-out theological "civil war" will erupt as the earlier theological strands morph from proto-factions to factions. Throughout several centuries the pendulum swung between the Marcionite, Jewish, and Gnostic poles. Surprisingly, the difficult balancing act of bringing about a compromise creed was eventually successful. This consensus-building approach gained the centerfield for the Pauline-Lukan faction, the champions of "unity." The forging of "orthodoxy" out of the matrix of the second century is also unique in that the emerging creed was not the original belief system of the victorious party. Rather, the theology of the victorious party (the Pauline-Lukan strand) was a compromise between contending theologies and was crafted and promoted as a "Via Media," that is, a compromise. As we go forward through this momentous and tumultuous period, we need to keep in mind that although we can see crucial changes taking place, the participants were unaware of the eventual scope, impact, and direction of these processes.

Although the assimilation of the textual heritage of the descendants of Jesus's disciples and first followers by Gentile believers may have started as early as Matthew, the transition from conjectural to undifferentiated polemic is gradual, not uniform or homogeneous. The texts ahead of us represent variations of this transition. They provide us some insight into how the sequence appropriation-supersession[35] may have been ignited and enabled. Since a compromise required absorbing elements of the identity and the heritage of the Jewish faction into the compromise creed, the Pauline-Lukan identity markers were drawn inside Jewish territory. Claiming Jewish ground placed them on a future collision course with Judaism and caused frictions that generated intense antagonism. John Gager, comparing Paul's time to Jerome's, concluded that in both periods, and in between, the issue was the same—the legitimacy of orthodoxy. For whenever believers argued, in the name of the founding apostles, that Christianity could not claim to be the true Israel without also honoring Israel's covenant, the self-understanding of those who represented mainstream-orthodox Christianity must have seemed threatened.[36] The incorporation of Pauline-Marcionite and Gnostic elements into the "Via Media" runs parallel to our trajectory, but is beyond the scope of this work.

The Mysteries

By retaining elements of the theology of the contending factions, the predecessors of "orthodoxy," forged an appealing (although tension-ridden) theological compromise. This forging process embedded tensions and dissonances in the tradition. Some of the Christian "mysteries and paradoxes" appear to be the result of the attempts to absorb the theological variety that existed during the second century into a compromise creed. Centuries of theological work were required to craft harmonizing formulas that would accommodate the diverse components of the Via Media.

Pauline-Lukan theology placed itself as a midway compromise between contending extremes, emerged all inclusive, but burdened by the paradoxes inherent in holding the middle ground between contrary theological positions[37]: Jesus thus became fully human (the Jewish followers of Jesus) and fully divine (Marcion and Gnostics). The beliefs and traditions of the Jewish founders were to be observed (the Jewish followers of Jesus) and rejected (Marcion and Gnostics). God is one (the Jewish followers of Jesus) but also plural (Marcion and Gnostics). The Law was to be observed (the Jewish followers of Jesus) but depleted (Marcion and Gnostics). The Jews were God's chosen (the Jewish followers of Jesus) but no longer (Marcion and Gnostics). Although these dualistic pairs help us internalize the implications of "compromise building," they do not fully clarify the complex and profound theological dilemmas they engender. We may showcase the complexity of theological compromise-building by probing into a couple of theological challenges.

To the descendants of the Jewish founders Jesus was an exalted human. Some Gnostic believers believed that Jesus was fully divine (Docetists). Other Gnostics believed that he was human, but had a divine spark within and divine knowledge about how to free the soul from this evil world. Pauline-Marcionites thought that Jesus was the emissary of the supreme God of the universe and that YHWH was the creator of this evil world of pain and suffering. Still others thought that Jesus was born a human but had been chosen by God to be his son—his chosen (Adoptionists). The Via Media compromise: Jesus as both human and divine.

The proto-orthodox theological compromise is also reflected in attitudes toward suffering and evil. In biblical Judaism YHWH is a warrior God, a just, severe, and wrathful deity. Evil and suffering are part of reality. For the Gnostics the world is a place of evil and suffering. Salvation is the escape from it. For Marcion evil was the child of the lesser God of creation, a quasi-Gnostic view. The God of the Pauline-Lukans, on the other hand, was to be benevolent, omnipotent, and omniscient. Thus, if God and his creation are good, evil and suffering must originate elsewhere. To exonerate God from the evil and suffering evident in this world, human sinfulness had to be made into the root cause of all that had turned wrong. This theological compromise by the Pauline-Lukan faction necessitated the internalizing of evil and suffering as individual guilt and sin.

Summary

The first burst of growth of the Jesus movement was impressive. Estimates vary, but most scholars agree that within 250 years of Jesus's birth 10–15 percent of the population of the Roman Empire had some attachment to one of the second-century Christianities. We know little about the socio-metrics of these factions. It seems that during the second century the strands that we encountered in the previous century coalesced into proto-factions and then into factions. The degree of doctrinal cohesion of these groups is unknown and may have been minimal. The situation "on the ground" was, most probably, characterized by great fluidity, variety, and change. As attested by the texts surveyed in this monograph, confusion and chaos were rampant. It appears that local variants and improvisation were the rule.

It seems that, at first, belief in Jesus was very much a local affair with some degree of coordination with like-minded communities on a regional basis. It seems that the confrontation among the second-century Christianities was spearheaded by elites. Theologians and community leaders were the trendsetters in these debates. In a world of 5–10 percent basic literacy,[38] only 1–2 percent of the people could articulate and sustain an intellectual argument. Most were followers with daily and mundane concerns and interests and their allegiance was grounded on local affiliations and on emotional inclinations and personal ties. It is probable that the founding faction, having a shared and authoritative tradition, was more cohesive and organized than the other groups. Pauline-Marcionites, followers of a single leader, would also exhibit some unity and uniformity. The variants within Gnosticism are so diverse that the use of the term has been under attack. The Pauline-Lukans, the fourth faction, was characterized by great flux, anxiety, and confusion. The theological compromise they championed, the "Via Media," was at the time a "work in progress" rather than a systematic theological articulation. Following Ignatius, they viewed unity and uniformity (as opposed to division and diversity) as good and necessary. Unity, it was hoped, would weed out some of the more extreme variants and would bring some respectability and acceptance by Roman society.

Attempting to navigate through the fog of ancient "history" is an endeavor fraught with low resolution. Loss of memory and loss of context, and the protective walls that surround dogma, conspire to blur our sight. However, once we visualize the anti-Jewish strand as emerging out of an internal struggle among differing believers in Jesus, many otherwise mystifying puzzles, and previously disconnected phenomena, seem to find their place. A scenario where the estrangement from the descendants of the Jewish founding fathers would be center stage presents grave theological challenges to established truths, cherished for millennia. The existence of an effort to demote the descendants of Jesus's disciples and first followers would be theologically embarrassing. It is no surprise therefore that the traces of this trajectory have been obscured and are neither obvious nor plain to see. We would expect that the mere existence of these phenomena would barely percolate through the protective membrane of dogma. Precisely the situation we encounter.

Anticipating the chapters ahead, we may say that whereas the descendants of Jesus's disciples and first followers had a clear identity, doctrine, and theology, the non-Jewish strands entered the upcoming confrontation within the Jesus movement unprepared and in disarray. Throughout the second and third centuries Gentile believers in Jesus will gradually achieve some theological definition and clarity. It may be said that for Gentile believers, identity, doctrine, and theology matured as a by-product of the struggle over legitimacy and ascendancy. The period between the second to the fourth century may be described as an intermediate stage when anti-Jewish polemic becomes ingrained in the cultural fabric of proto-orthodox communities and expands to multiple friction points. It intensifies and becomes generic (undifferentiated). This is a transitional stage when undifferentiated anti-Jewish attitudes and expressions become prevalent as the result of persistent and increasingly authoritative anti-Judaic rhetoric. During this phase the internal conflict between the founding faction and the growing Gentile majority will be projected and externalized onto the inter-religious arena, and will be gradually transformed into a unilateral attack on "Judaism."

Chapter 14

The Anti-Jewish Strand in Ignatius

Introduction

Ignatius was the bishop of Antioch, the hub of Roman Syria, at the dawn of the second century.[1] It is speculated that Hellenistic Jewish followers of Jesus that fled to safety during the events that followed Stephen's death (Acts 6:13–14) founded the community at Antioch. According to Acts, it was in Antioch that some of them first began to preach also to the Pagans, evidently with considerable success (Acts 11:19–21). It was in Antioch that followers of Christ were first called "Christians" (Acts 11:26). Ignatius's episcopate was a triumph for the Pauline faction in the Antiochene community[2]—a community that would have been originally Torah-observant. His ascent, probably during the first decade of the second century, would have occurred in the face of considerable opposition from the founding faction and their Gentile sympathizers[3] and may reflect Paul's evangelizing success and the demographic shift to a Gentile majority. Ignatius emphasized Jesus's death and resurrection (not his life and ministry), championed church authority and hierarchy,[4] and strove for the de-Judaizing of belief in Jesus[5]—a cluster of themes associated with the faction I identify throughout as Pauline-Lukan. Eusebius informs us that Ignatius was the third Bishop of Antioch, following Peter and Evodius, apparently the first Gentile to rise to this status. Ignatius's episcopate, whose background and affinities were not Jewish, was a triumph for the Paulines. Insistence on unity and hierarchy, an Ignatian maxim, became characteristic of the emerging Pauline proto-orthodox strand.[6] Ignatius, free from Paul's complex relationship with the "Pillars" and from any emotional attachment to Judaism, articulates a more overt and unequivocal negative tone toward the beliefs and traditions of the founding fathers.

Tradition has focused on the figure of Ignatius as exemplary of true faith and religious conviction under the threat of martyrdom. Ignatius's letters are the foundational rock of "Imitatio Christi," a devotional inclination to glorify and seek suffering and martyrdom. Ignatius's journey to martyrdom is peculiar in that it is cast, in the letters assigned to him, as a triumphant journey from Antioch to Rome (Eph. 21.2). Most scholars acknowledge his letters as genuine. To me, the leisurely and almost royal transit of Ignatius through the cities of Asia Minor defies what we know about the inhumane conditions of the Roman prison apparatus. According to the traditional account, Ignatius was able to write elaborate letters at will (to Ephesus, Magnesia, Tralles, Philadelphian, Smyrna, and Rome), to receive and address delegations of fellow bishops (Eph. 1; Mag. 2; Trail. 1), and to address local audiences (Phld. 7.1). In addition, Ignatius's poise while awaiting martyrdom is astonishing, inhumane. Ignatius seeks martyrdom, welcomes death, requests fellow believers in Rome not to intervene on his behalf (Rom. 2), and argues that martyrdom allows believers to attain unity with God (2.1– 2). In Romans 4, he anticipates his death by wild beasts during the games at Rome providing us with one of the most graphic, yet exalted, depictions of this cruel form of martyrdom. Overall, the staging fits a promotional tour by a religious celebrity. The almost regal atmosphere does not fit the known viciousness of the Roman prison system, nor does it fit the journey of a convict through the brutal pipeline that supplied victims for the spectacles at the Roman capital. This leads me to speculate that the letters were composed (or heavily edited) by a supporter or admirer, rather than by Ignatius himself.

The Adversaries

Ignatius may be the earliest author to clearly reflect the upcoming second-century "religious civil war" among believers in Jesus. In Ignatius, similar to Barnabas and Hebrews, adversaries are marginalized and disenfranchised by inserting the duality us/them and by "labeling them out" of the reference group. Throughout his letters Ignatius defends the Pauline tenets against those insisting that true faith must be affiliated with the traditions and customs of the Jewish founding fathers. Although the descendants of Jesus's disciples and first followers are being marginalized, they remain an ever-present shadow. They are unacknowledged adversaries that cast their shadow over the scene. Following an already ingrained tradition, Ignatius does not target the descendants of the founding fathers explicitly. Rather, the arrows are aimed at their influence among their Gentile sympathizers. The immediate culprits are Gentile members of the community that are embracing Jewish ways (i.e., the beliefs and traditions of the Jewish faction). Thus, as Paul, Hebrews, and Barnabas struggled with the influence of the founding faction among Gentile believers, so did Ignatius of Antioch, decades later.

A small group of scholars (Strecker, Gager, Gaston, J. Sanders, Wilson, Murray, and others) has done pioneering work toward the recognition that Ignatius, and some of his contemporaries, were concerned with the influence, and the attraction, that "Judaism" exerted over some Gentile converts. These analyses did emerge out of the meta-narrative that emphasizes the conflict between Judaism and Christianity. These scholars contend that anti-Jewish polemic was the reaction of ecclesiastical leaders to attraction to Judaism and to observance of Jewish customs by certain Gentiles within their own communities.[7] I differ and suggest throughout that Gentiles would be attracted to the descendants of Jesus's disciples and first followers due to the fact that they were the original, and therefore authoritative, guardians of his legacy (not because they were attracted to Judaism). We can assume a spectrum of Gentile sympathizers that ranges from those that yearned for fellowship with the descendants of Jesus's disciples and first followers, to some that eventually converted to Judaism. The attraction to Judaism should be viewed as a consequence, not the cause, of this trajectory—creating a shift of emphasis and perspective.

In Wilson's words: "[W]hom Ignatius had in mind when, with grudging approval, he spoke of 'the circumcised expounding Christianity' is unclear; but whether they were the early disciples, Paul, or Jewish Christians active in his day, they serve mainly as a rhetorical contrast to those who were the immediate and pressing problem—Gentiles who expounded Judaism."[8] Wilson's articulation of the context seems to indicate that the attraction to Judaism was the core issue at stake, an analysis I disagree with. To me, the attraction to Judaism was a consequence of the yearning for fellowship with the descendants of the founding fathers, not attraction to Judaism per se. To most scholars the segment "For if we continue to live until now according to Judaism we confess that we have not received grace" (Magn. 8: 1) is a reflection of the "conflict between Judaism and Christianity." To me, it is a reflection of the influence of opponents within the Jesus movement, who were Jewish. As it pertains to the anti-Jewish strand, Ignatius is part of the transition from the subtle and often-inferred polemic that characterizes Paul and the Synoptics, to more overt and explicit attacks on the influence of the descendants of the Jewish founders and their Gentile sympathizers.

The Letter to the Philadelphians

But if any one propound Judaism unto you, here him not: for it is better to hear Christianity from a man who is circumcised than Judaism from one uncircumcised. (Phld. 6:1)[9]

This enigmatic segment is a "mind-twister." We seem to have two gradations of adversaries, one identified as worse than the other. My deconstruction:

First and foremost: If anyone expounds Judaism to you, do not listen to him.

Second: However, it is better to hear about belief in Jesus from a Jewish follower of Jesus,

Third: than to hear Gentile sympathizers advocate Judaism.

In other words, Ignatius is fighting the influence of the descendants of the Jewish founders over the rank and file and tries to do "damage control." He seems to recognize the existence and the legitimacy of the Jewish faction, but utterly rejects and denigrates Gentiles that sympathize with them.

> For I heard certain persons saying, If I find it not in the charters, I believe it not in the Gospel. And when I said to them, It is written, they answered me That is the question. But as for me, my charter is Jesus Christ, the inviolable charter is His cross and His death and His resurrection, and faith through Him . . . (Phld. 8.2; same theme in 9:1)[10]

In this cryptic segment Ignatius rebuts those that require that belief be grounded in Jewish scripture ("the charter"). Ignatius's position is that Christ is the new focus, the new charter, that supersedes Jewish scripture. In the Letter to the Philadelphians Ignatius's opponents are Gentile believers in Jesus with varying degrees of affiliations and affinities with the descendants of Jesus's disciples and first followers. The danger that he warns against comes from within—not from without.

The Letter to the Magnesians

Ignatius's zeal causes him to overreach and make seemingly bizarre and incoherent statements: "It is absurd to talk Jesus Christ and to practice Judaism. After all, Judaism believed in Christianity, not Christianity in Judaism" (Mag. 10.3). For Ignatius, biblical Jews were crypto "Christians" (i.e., crypto Paulines). For him, Jewish history is an anticipation of his version of belief in Jesus, and the Jewish prophets were crypto-Pauline prophets.[11] In Ignatius we have an example of the Pauline move to an overt and unequivocal claim to the heritage, and to the identity of the Jewish faction.[12] Ignatius claims that Christianity (i.e., Pauline-Lukan belief in Jesus) is the foundational faith, not Judaism (i.e., the beliefs and traditions of the founding fathers). Despite our difficulties in decoding Ignatius's rhetoric, his message seems to address Gentile believers who would understand the implied message: Pauline-Lukan believers in Jesus are God's chosen. The Jewish faction never was. Ignatius targets those living according to Judaism (8.1–2), berates the practice of "Sabbatizing" (9. 1), and refers to the monstrosity of those who "talk of Jesus Christ" and Judaize (10.3). If we read these passages without assuming a priori that they are combative vis-à-vis "Judaism," they appear to fit the internal struggle against the descendants of the Jewish founders.

It has been suggested that the attempt by some Gentile believers in Jesus "to be both Christians and Jews" was the heart of the matter. Thus, according to J. Sanders, Gentile believers "felt that the Jewish Christians should give up their Jewish ways."[13] Gentile sympathizers with the descendants of Jesus's disciples and first followers, who transgressed the boundaries between church and synagogue and sometimes defected permanently, blurred the distinction between the parties, causing confusion and a crisis of identity.[14] Isacson[15] suggests that whereas Magnesians addresses Generic Jewish followers of Jesus, Philadelphians addresses members of Ignatius's congregation. Furthermore, he suggests that the adversaries in Trallians, Smyrnaeans, and Ephesians may be Docetists, pointing to the fact that he was fighting differing believers within the Jesus movement and to the internal focus of his concerns.

Unity and Hierarchy

Ignatius, Bishop of Antioch, was the first writer known to have used the term "the Catholic church"[16] and the first Gentile believer in Jesus to attain a position of authority in the most important stronghold of the descendants of the Jewish founders outside Judea, suggesting a demographic shift to a Gentile majority and the transition to the overt phase of the de-Judaizing of belief in Jesus. Ignatius claims the superiority of Paul's understanding of Jesus's ministry and legacy over and against that of the descendants of Jesus's disciples and first followers. With Ignatius, the Pauline drive to demote the Jewish faction enters its overt phase. For Ignatius and his followers the struggle over legitimacy, identity, and authority is a struggle between "Christianity" and "Judaism," that is, between the Gentile followers of Paul and the Jewish followers of Jesus.

The unity of the church, on which Ignatius harps so much, is seen as an essential link in what we may call the chain of ontological validation.[17] Ignatius "circled the wagons," left all other forms of belief in Jesus outside the boundary of inclusion, and made them into heretics. This protective barrier stood firm for almost two thousand years and is the precursor of Eusebius's later myth about the Christian origins. Ignatius's relentless insistence on unity and hierarchy is the clearest indication that they did not exist, that they were a goal to be achieved—not a reality. From Ignatius forward the early church and its legitimacy depend on validating the hierarchical structure that claimed to originate in Jesus and flow through his disciples to the church.[18]

Chapter 15

The Anti-Jewish Strand in Justin: The Dialogue with Trypho the Jew

Justin was born, *ca.* 100 CE, of pagan parents in Flavia Neapolis (Shechem) in Samaria. It seems that he was converted at Ephesus. He founded a school in Rome during the reign of Antoninus Pius, who ruled from 138 to 161.[1] He was more or less a contemporary of Marcion and his best-known opponent. After an extended and active ministry, Justin was tortured and executed under the Roman prefect Junius Rusticus (162–168).

Genre, Protagonists, and Intended Audience

The *Dialogue* instructs us that during the mid-second century, the debate about Torah observance and allegiance to Judaism was still center stage. The debate about Justin's audience will not subside any time soon. Most modern scholars allow for various possible target audiences and purposes. Many possible constituencies have been championed. The intended audience seems to be Gentiles that, Justin fears, may succumb to the lure of the Jewish faction. Justin is aware that some Gentile believers were so attached to the descendants of the founding fathers that they did eventually abandon "their faith in Christ." Some Gentiles strayed beyond the limits of the Pauline community altogether. These individuals could not "in any way be saved" (47.4) and "succumbed" completely to "Jewish" ways. Despite the fact that Paul is never mentioned or quoted, Justin clearly stands within the tradition I refer to as "Pauline-Lukan." Compared to Paul and Ignatius, Justin is grudgingly tolerant toward Gentiles attracted to the beliefs and traditions of the Jewish faction (not committed to the Pauline-Lukan understanding of Jesus's legacy). Various groups have been recognized as either protagonists or intended audiences in the Dialogue[2]:

1. Jewish followers who insisted that Gentile believers maintain Jewish traditions.
2. Jewish followers (perhaps from the previous group) who refused fellowship with Gentile believers in Jesus.
3. Jewish followers who did not fully observe the Torah but were not fully Pauline either.
4. Gentiles, who became believers in Jesus, began observing the law, eventually converted to Judaism, and became Jewish followers of Jesus.
5. Gentile believers who observed some of the Torah (i.e., Christian Judaizers) but did not convert to Judaism.
6. Gentile Pauline-Lukan believers in Jesus, apparently the majority in Justin's audience.

Justin's *Dialogue with Trypho the Jew* does not "stand alone" and should be read and understood in the broader context of Justin's lifetime ministry and literary work. Despite the fact that the Dialogue seems to be cast as a debate with Judaism, the internal and external circumstances of the Jesus movement at the time of authorship and the nuanced depictions of followers of Jesus enumerated earlier do not favor a scenario where the dominant element could be an inter-religious (Jewish versus Christian) conflict. Similar to Tertullian and Chrysostom, Justin fought "heresy" on multiple fronts. He wrote against Marcion and against the influence of the Jewish faction suggesting that he saw himself holding the middle ground between these two interpretations of Jesus's legacy, that the context was internal, and that he was concerned about the influence of the descendants of Jesus's disciples and first followers—not about the influence of external Judaism. The Dialogue is a stage to battle "Judaism within." Rather than a dialogue with Judaism, the text seems to address a more immediate and internal concern: the sway that the founding fathers exerted over many among the rank and file.

Furthermore, it seems to me that Justin's *Dialogue with Trypho the Jew* is too adversarial, derogatory and rudimentary in Jewish matters to address an audience that would include Jewish followers of Jesus—as claimed by many.[3] Although Justin is sufficiently informed about Judaism to present a credible case to a non-Jewish audience, his knowledge and arguments are too simplistic and stereotypical to be effective on a Jewish one. Justin is unique in the literature of the period in that he provides explicit evidence on the struggle with the Jewish faction (Dial. 47:2–3). Justin is also unique in acknowledging the existence of a range and a variety of attitudes toward the beliefs and traditions of the Jewish founders.

It seems that Justin viewed Gentile believers, who observed Jewish customs, as dissidents rather than apostates and includes them (though reluctantly) in his Christian tent (Dial. 47:2–4). That is, he considers them as misguided members of the church but members nonetheless, and deems them worthy of being saved (Dial. 47:4).[4] Gentile sympathizers with the Jewish faction are personified in the Dialogue by Trypho's friends. They are described as "those wishing to become proselytes" (23:3) and "the fearers of God" (10:4). Of the defectors he says vaguely that they abandoned their "Christian" commitment "for some reason or another."[5] To later readers, Justin's struggle seems to be framed as a debate between "Judaism and Christianity." However, for Justin, "Judaism" stands for the beliefs and traditions of the descendents of the founding fathers. "Christianity" stands for the beliefs of his interpretation of Jesus's legacy. By Justin's time this framing of the issues, already embryonic in the Synoptics, seems to have become a persistent tradition.

Appropriation and Supersession

The proto-orthodox gravitated gradually to the view that the claim to the guardianship of Jesus's legacy required the appropriation-incorporation of the identity and heritage of the descendants of the founding fathers into a unifying creed. These proto-"orthodox" thinkers and community leaders maintained that Gentiles could not reinvent themselves and reject the religious narrative of the Jewish founders, as Marcion and most Gnostics argued. Justin is the first proto-orthodox author to attempt a systematic articulation and argumentation of the emerging "Via Media," the theological compromise championed by later Paulines. Although we do not find explicit connections between Justin's work and Paul's writings, his thinking is clearly Pauline-Lukan and it did become a cornerstone of the emerging Pauline orthodoxy.[6] As it relates to the Jewish facet of Justin's interests, many of the themes that will populate anti-Jewish condemnations throughout later centuries are laid down in Justin's *Dialogue*:[7]

> For the circumcision according to the flesh, that was from Abraham, was given for a sign, that you should be separated from the other nations and us, and that you alone should suffer the things you are rightly suffering now, and that your lands should be desolate and your cities burned with fire, and that foreigners should eat up the fruits before your face, and none of you go up unto Jerusalem. (Dial. 16:2)

> If we did not know the reason why it all was enjoined even on you, namely, due to the fact of your transgressions and hardness of heart. (Dial. 18:2)
> He charged you too to abstain from certain foods, in order that even in your eating and drinking you may have God before your eyes, since you are prone and apt to depart from the knowledge of him. (Dial. 20:1)

> For if before Abraham there was no need of circumcision, and before Moses
> none of keeping the Sabbath, and of festivals, and of offerings, neither
> in like manner is there any need now, after the Son of God, Jesus Christ.
> (Dial. 23:3)

The Adversaries

The unique role that the descendants of the founding fathers and their
Gentile sympathizers (Gentile Judaizers) played in this saga is currently
being rediscovered and recognized. Murray identified[8] in Justin four different types of believers in Jesus (of both Jewish and Gentile origin) who
follow "the Law":

- Jewish Christians who followed the Law and live with Christians
  without trying to convince them "either to receive circumcision like
  themselves, or to keep Sabbath, or to observe other things of the same
  kind" are to be accepted (Dial. 47:2).
- Jewish Christians who believe in Christ but "in every way compel
  those who are of Gentile birth and believe on this Christ to live in
  accordance with the law appointed by Moses, or choose not to have
  communion with them that have such a life in common" are not
  accepted (Dial. 47:3).
- Gentile Christians "who follow their advice and live under the law,
  as well as keep their profession in the Christ of God will, perhaps [or
  probably] be saved" (Dial. 47:4).
- Former Gentile Christians who "once professed and recognized" Jesus
  as Messiah but "for some cause or other passed over into the life under
  the Law" and deny Jesus "cannot, I declare, in any wise be saved"
  (Dial. 47:4)

The *Dialogue* is a debate between a Pauline-Lukan follower and a stereotypical and docile Jew that "stands in" as a proxy for the Jewish faction.
Justin's detailed description of, and engagement with, different types and
degrees of Gentile affiliations with the Jewish faction is further indication
that his concern was Judaism within, not without. Gentile believers would
be attracted to the synagogues of the Jewish followers of Jesus due to the
fact that they were the descendants of Jesus's disciples and first followers and
were perceived by many as the rightful heirs of his legacy. Significantly, for
Justin, Gentile sympathizers with the Jewish camp are dissidents, and may
be saved, but all other Gentile non-proto-orthodox believers (Gnostics and
Marcionites) are heretics. Justin's *Dialogue* is reflective of his concern to save
fellow believers from the influence of the Jewish faction. Thus, Justin directs

his animosity toward descendants of the Jewish founders who attract Gentile believers and "compel" them to observe Jewish practices.[9] Thus, there was no basis or reason for Gentile believers in Jesus to be attracted to "mainstream Judaism" when the synagogues of the Jewish faction would be a more obvious and emphatic choice. Furthermore, the view that "missionary competition between Jews and Christians over Gentiles was an important context for the *Dialogue* cannot be convincingly demonstrated from the text."[10]

According to tradition and to current scholarship, Justin's *Dialogue* is one of the earliest explicit and systematic deployments of the arguments for the replacement of "Judaism" (the beliefs and traditions of the founding fathers) by "Christianity" (the proto-orthodox strand of belief in Jesus) in a format accessible to all.[11] We have encountered earlier supersessionists (Barnabas and Hebrews) whose arguments resonate with Justin's, but he fashioned the first accessible argumentation of substance. "The law, explains Justin, has no permanent value, but was given by God as a temporary measure to restrain the sinfulness of the Jews. So, the argument continues, "the fact that this law was inferior and is now obsolete reflects badly, not on the God who decreed it of old, but on the people for whom it was decreed."[12] In other words, according to Justin, the Law, Torah observance, and Judaism, the rocks on which the descendants of Jesus's disciples and first followers stand, are no rocks at all. Nonetheless, Justin's tone is relatively tame, civil. His rejection and belittling of the beliefs and traditions of his opponents is persistent and sustained, but compared with his more extreme anti-Jewish "peers" (Hebrews, Barnabas, Melito's Pascha, Tertullian's Adversus Judaeos, Chrysostom, etc.) he is in the moderate range of the spectrum.[13]

My Justin

Why would Justin argue with "mainstream Jews" whether or not Jewish customs and traditions should be observed by Gentile believers in Jesus—unless "the Jews" are the Jewish faction and the core contention is about identity, legitimacy, and ascendancy within the Jesus movement? Several scholars[14] have concluded that Justin battles Gentiles attracted to Judaism. I differ in that, in my view, attraction to the descendants to the founding fathers infuriates Justin—not attraction to Judaism per se. To me, at the time of authorship, the setting and the socio-theological context seem to reflect an internal dilemma, not a theological rivalry vis-à-vis Judaism. Traditionally, the texts of this period have been read as reflective of a "conflict between Judaism and Christianity." However, the later externalization of the conflict obscures the fact that early Pauline-Lukan believers were battling adversaries that were Jewish, not Judaism without. The yearning for fellowship with the descendants of the founding fathers angered proto-orthodox leaders and intellectuals, prompting them to denigrate their beliefs and traditions, a reaction that has contributed significantly to anti-Jewish attitudes among members of the early Church.[15] Justin acknowledges that some Gentiles succumbed to persuasion by the descendants of Jesus's disciples and first followers and follow the Jewish law. He also accepts Gentile Judaizers (the Jewish followers of Jesus) as legitimate members of the ecclesiastical community.[16] Justin's *Dialogue* should be read in conjunction with his lifelong struggle against other interpretations of Jesus's legacy.[17] Reading Justin's *Dialogue* in isolation tends to overemphasize the Jewish facet of his apologetic efforts on behalf of the emerging Pauline-Lukan theology. It obscures the fact that Justin and his fellow proto-"orthodox" were engaged in an internal and multilateral confrontation with the descendants of the founding fathers and with differing Gentile believers.

Compared to what is to come, Justin is relatively civil and urbane. Nonetheless, Justin reflects a turn, a junction, in the ever-growing anti-Jewish trajectory whose beginnings we discussed in the previous chapters. As the crusade of the Pauline-Lukan faction for ascendancy enters into high gear, so does the de-Judaizing impetus. The disparagement of Torah observance and of Judaism becomes the highway to ascendancy and unity. The *Dialogue*'s plausibility has been discussed at length.[18] "Justin enjoys the lion's share of the debate and, enjoying authorial control, he does not wittingly present arguments that would embarrass or disadvantage himself."[19] Compared to some of his contemporaries, Justin is sophisticated and articulate, but he fails his title and presents us with a tendentious and condescending document. The *Dialogue* is best seen as a tendentious conversation where a Gentile audience would feel empowered and a Jewish one would remain unconvinced. Overall, there is nothing in Justin's *Dialogue* that requires us to expand its horizon beyond the Jesus movement.

As far as the reaction of mainstream Judaism is concerned, we can't say much. It is probable that at some point the arguments presented by Justin and his contemporaries filtered out and reached Jewish non-believers in Jesus. It is also probable that with time, as the anti-Jewish frenzy increased, we may speak of the emergence of a "conflict between Judaism and Christianity." However that conflict would be a consequence, a projection, of the internal strife within the Jesus movement, not an originating cause, as argued by most.

Chapter 16

The Anti-Jewish Strand in Melito

Introduction

The anti-Jewish texts of the second and third centuries did not appear on the scene "ex-nihilo." These writers were the third and more virulent wave in the continuous confrontation between the Torah-observant followers of Jesus and the Gentile majority within the Jesus movement. The gradual anti-Jewish turn among some Gentile believers becomes unequivocal with the emergence of this new generation of authors. What is, more often than not, implied and obscured in the New Testament, is now explicit and blunt. The targets are no longer the Pharisees, the high priest, the authorities, the elders, or the scribes. Nor are the adversaries the enigmatic "Ioudaioi" of John or the "they/them" of Hebrews and Barnabas. Melito projects and externalizes the conflict onto all Jews. It seems that by the time of Melito's writing, the externalized staging of the conflict that characterizes the second and third centuries had already taken hold of the minds and hearts of believers. In Melito we find no traces of an awareness of the internal origin of a now sacrosanct hatred. Wilson concludes that "no distinction is made between leaders and people, or between Palestinian and Diaspora Jews—as in some earlier writings, nor apparently between Jews of the past and the present. The crime is the crime of all Jews, past and present."[1] With Melito we are well into the third phase of the evolution of the anti-Jewish trajectory. Some scholars have pointed to the lack of evidence for a Jewish presence among Melito's adversaries.[2] Others see evidence that the adversaries are Gentile sympathizers with Judaism. Regardless of who were the intended adversaries, the language deployed has all the characteristics of later anti-Semitic incitement.

Melito, *ca.* 120–185 CE, lived through the long reign of Emperor Marcus Aurelius (161–180 CE). At the time, the Jesus movement was beleaguered by multilateral strife and multi-dimensional chaos within. It was also facing increasing Roman persecution. Eusebius describes Melito as a Quartodeciman[3] "who lived entirely in the Holy Spirit" (Hist. eccl. 5.24). Most of Melito's writings have been lost, except for a fragment from his Apology, which was addressed to the emperor, and the Peri Pascha[4]—authored *ca.* 170 CE. As a Quatrodeciman, Melito would be suspect of Judaizing, leading him to be all the more firm in his rejection of Jewish affinities among his flock.[5] The traditional assumption that Melito's attack on "Judaism" forms part of an active conflict between church and synagogue with religious as well as social and political dimensions is firmly entrenched.[6]

Melito's anti-Jewish rampage is widely recognized as the "opus maximus" of pre-Constantine anti-Jewish sentiment. The efforts to explain Melito's attitudes cover the full spectrum of theological, socio-theological, and social theories. Melito is clearly and unabashedly part of the third phase of our journey; his assault against Jews and Judaism is undifferentiated and unrestrained. The Peri Pascha (On Pascha) is an exercise in extreme demagoguery and unrestrained viciousness embedded in mediocre argumentation and superb literary skills. Written during the second half of the second century, this text is the most extreme rampage against Jews and against Judaism by a Gentile believer of the first and second centuries. Nothing can prepare the reader for the unrelenting denigration and incitement that permeate most of this long homily (105 sections, 804 segments). Reading Melito's Peri Pascha anticipates and renders trivial, and derivative, the worst anti-Semitic literature of the Middle Ages and of the modern era.

As we enter our time capsules and travel to the time and to the circumstances that originated this text, we must acknowledge that we know little about the impact that this text may have had at the time.[7] We know however that Melito's Peri Pascha is one of a long list of virulently anti-Jewish texts authored by Christian leaders (Tertullian's Adversus Iudaeos, Chrysostom's Homilies Against the Jews, Eusebius' Evangelical Demonstration, Aphrahat's Homilies, and Augustin's Adversus Iudaeos—just to name a few of the better known)[8] that facilitated and enabled the transformation of early tensions within the Jesus movement into Anti-Semitism.

Deicide in the Peri Pascha

Melito, Bishop of Sardis and a church father, is the first Pauline-Lukan writer to make an unambiguous accusation of deicide: the murder of God. The notion that "the Jews" were responsible for the death of Jesus is the result of a complex trajectory that stretches back to the canonical accounts of Jesus's Passion that originated in a proto-Synoptic strand or in Mark's creative mind. With Melito we arrive at the final phase of the libel about "the Jewish responsibility for Jesus's death," which we have been tracking since Mark.

Prior to Melito, however, no one had transformed the implied or explicit accusations of responsibility for the death of Jesus into the "Jewish responsibility for the death of God." For Melito, "the Jews" are culpable of deicide—an escalation of earlier claims:[9]

72. This one was murdered. And where was he murdered? In the very center of Jerusalem! Why? Because he had healed their lame, and had cleansed their lepers, and had guided their blind with light, and had raised up their dead. For this reason he suffered. Somewhere it has been written in the law and prophets,

73. Why, O Israel did you do this strange injustice? You dishonored the one who had honored you. You held in contempt the one who held you in esteem. You denied the one who publicly acknowledged you. You renounced the one who proclaimed you his own. You killed the one who made you to live. Why did you do this, O Israel?

74. Hast it not been written for your benefit: "Do not shed innocent blood lest you die a terrible death"? Nevertheless, Israel admits, I killed the Lord! Why? Because it was necessary for him to die. You have deceived yourself, O Israel, rationalizing thus about the death of the Lord.

75. It was necessary for him to suffer, yes, but not by you; it was necessary for him to be dishonored, but not by you; it was necessary for him to be judged, but not by you; it was necessary for him to be crucified, but not by you, nor by your right hand.

79. [A]nd vinegar, and gall, and a sword, and affliction, and all as though it were for a blood-stained robber. For you brought to him scourges for his body, and the thorns for his head. And you bound those beautiful hands of his, which had formed you from the earth. And that beautiful mouth of his, which had nourished you with life, you filled with gall. And you killed your Lord at the time of the great feast.

80. Surely you were filled with gaiety, but he was filled with hunger; you drank wine and ate bread, but he vinegar and gall; you wore a happy smile, but he had a sad countenance; you were full of joy, but he was full of trouble; you sang songs, but he was judged; you issued the command, he was crucified; you danced, he was buried; you lay down on a soft bed, but he in a tomb and coffin.

81. O lawless Israel, why did you commit this extraordinary crime of casting your Lord into new sufferings—your master, the one who formed you, the one who made you, the one who honored you, the one who called you Israel?

92. But you, quite to the contrary, voted against your Lord, whom indeed the nations worshipped, and the uncircumcised admired, and the foreigners glorified, over whom Pilate washed his hands. But as for you—you killed this one at the time of the great feast.

94. Pay attention, all families of the nations, and observe! An extraordinary murder has taken place in the center of Jerusalem, in the city devoted to God's law, in the city of the Hebrews, in the city of the prophets, in the city thought of as just. And who has been murdered? And who is the murderer? I am ashamed to give the answer, but give it I must. For if this murder had taken place at night, or if he had been slain in a desert place, it would be well to keep silent; but it was in the middle of the main street, even in the center of the city, while all were looking on, that the unjust murder of this just person took place.

96. The one who hung the earth in space, is himself hanged; the one who fixed the heavens in place, is himself impaled; the one who firmly fixed all things, is himself firmly fixed to the tree. The Lord is insulted, God has been murdered, the King of Israel has been destroyed by the right hand of Israel.

97. O frightful murder! O unheard of injustice! The Lord is disfigured and he is not deemed worthy of a cloak for his naked body, so that he might not be seen exposed. For this reason the stars turned and fled, and the day grew quite dark, in order to hide the naked person hanging on the tree, darkening not the body of the Lord, but the eyes of men.

99. Why was it like this, O Israel? You did not tremble for the Lord. You did not fear for the Lord. You did not lament for the Lord, yet you lamented for your firstborn. You did not tear your garments at the crucifixion of the Lord, yet you tore your garments for your own who were murdered. You forsook the Lord; you were not found by him. You dashed the Lord to the ground; you, too, were dashed to the ground, and lie quite dead.

Theology

Melito's claim to the Jewish heritage and his emphasis on the culpability of "the Jews," places him within the Pauline-Lukan strand, the doctrinal trajectory that also includes Paul, Mark, Luke/Acts, Hebrews, Ignatius, Justin, and Eusebius. After we express our astonishment and disgust at the writings of this second-century bishop, we must ask ourselves: since Melito is an example of a large literary corpus of anti-Jewish literature, are there circumstances that would explain the emergence of this kind of text? What was the social and emotional context within which this type of incitement would be part of the religious services of a community of believers? Can we imagine circumstances when a religious leader would read this kind of text to "edify" his flock?[10] What was happening in this writer's world that would induce him to author this extraordinary text?

Melito's assertive and unequivocal claims about Jewish collective responsibility for the death of Jesus are indefensible and theologically abhorrent.[11] However, despite the nausea that accompanies reading Melito, we must "bend backwards" and try to understand the genesis of this text. In spite of the emerging edifice of hate that we witness, and despite the heart's desire to react, we must analyze the socio-theological setting carefully. Melito's claim that Judaism may have served a purpose for a time but was a mere foreshadowing of the superior religion yet to come originates in Pauline-Lukan arguments against the Jewish faction. "You may have been God's chosen but no longer, we are now the true Israel and God's favorites" is the thread that sustains the Pauline-Lukan edifice of disparagement on which Melito stands. For Melito, once "Christianity" (i.e., Pauline-Lukan belief in Jesus) emerged, "Judaism" (i.e., the beliefs of the descendants of the founding fathers) lost its value; it no longer served a function.[12] For Melito, as expressed in the Peri Pascha, God loved only "Christians"; the church now has the honored position that once had belonged to "the Jews," the descendants of the Jewish founders.[13]

My Melito

The Peri Pascha unhinged my emotional floodgates and triggered demons, my worst emotions. After exposure to this kind of abuse, words lose their meaning and cognition disintegrates in profound dismay and rage. Unfortunately, and significantly, the texts that concern and outrage us were not authored by marginal or renegade believers. Contrary to modern misperceptions, texts like Melito's Peri Pascha were not the product of marginal "bad apples," nor were they the unfortunate indiscretions of otherwise admirable church leaders. Rather, they reflect a deep, sustained, and pervasive trend that, with the passage of time, will reach inconceivable scope and intensity. Melito and Chrysostom, cherished and prominent leaders and theologians, wrote the extreme anti-Jewish texts showcased here. From the mid-second century forward, and under an umbrella of sanctified legitimacy, anti-Jewish sentiment became endemic and extreme. It infected large segments of the clergy and laity during a period that will eventually span seventeen hundred years.

Contrary to earlier authors who are apologetic, in Melito, anti-Judaism seems normative. However, at the time, believers in Jesus were immersed in a fierce internal struggle about self-definition, legitimacy, and identity that makes their engagement of external enemies implausible. Until the post-Constantine era, beleaguered by internal strife and Roman persecution, believers in Jesus should not be seen as "taking on" external enemies gratuitously. The adversaries, the intended audience, and the goals are primarily internal. Only after the proto-orthodox emerge ascendant (fourth century) and after they reach minimal internal cohesion, they may be seen targeting external Judaism. Furthermore, it seems that by Melito's time, the distinction between Judaism and the descendants of the founding fathers had already faded. The fusion and the confusion of these two groups in the hearts and minds of Pauline-Lukan believers may have already become a deep-seated practice. Although at the time of authorship the socio-theological background and the context do not yet support attacks on "external Judaism," with Melito's undifferentiated anti-Judaism we are crossing over into the inter-religious arena. In Melito, the bias against the descendants of Jesus's disciples and first followers and their Gentile sympathizers is fully externalized and projected onto "the Jews." It is unclear whether this blurring of identities, which has accompanied us throughout, is intentional and conscious or due to loss of historical context. Regardless, the Peri Pascha showcases how the transition from internal invective against the Jewish opponents within the Jesus movement to attacks on Judaism came about: deep resentment toward adversaries that were Jewish gradually morphed into vicious attacks on Jews and Judaism. This oversimplification of a complex trajectory highlights an important point: religiously sanctioned incitement can become integral to the cultural and emotional fabric of a community of faith and can, eventually, turn genocidal.

It seems that we have sufficient corroborative evidence to suggest that by the end of the second century unrestrained anti-Jewish incitement was increasingly dispensed from the pulpits throughout the empire. However, Melito could not have written his On the Pascha without standing on pre-existing traditions. Therefore, Melito's excesses are the fruits, not the seeds, of the anti-Jewish phenomenon. Some scholars have argued that Melilo's oratorical success may have blurred his judgment, that his language skills facilitated contrasts and denunciations that were bolder than he might otherwise have created. Nonetheless, we cannot but see a pattern: Melito was part of a sequence of connectable dots. Slowly, gradually, an unintended trajectory is moving toward its final destination.

Chapter 17

The Anti-Jewish Strand in Chrysostom

Introduction

In the Christian tradition, John of Antioch (347–407 CE), archbishop of Constantinople and known as "Chrysostom,"[1] is revered as a saint who was driven from the patriarchate by the evil scheming of the empress Eudoxia and the plots of Theophilus, the patriarch of Alexandria. His courage in the face of persecution and abuse, his unselfish devotion to his flock, and the nobility of his death quickly caught the imagination of Christians...the reverence bestowed on him as a saint of the church has obscured the memory of his earlier years when he was a presbyter in Antioch. John's sermons are not only a compendium of many of the themes that emerged in the Christian anti-Jewish phenomenon, they have also had an enormous influence on later attitudes toward the Jews.[2] Chrysostom's anti-Jewish homilies "not only marked an important moment in the Church's polemics against Judaism, but they seem to have exercised an influence which went far beyond any specific occasion or local situation."[3] John's popularity as a preacher and his mastery of the Greek language also account for the fact that his writings have exerted a powerful influence on later believers.

The Sermons

Half-truths, innuendo, abusive and incendiary language, malicious comparisons, and, in all, excess and exaggeration[4] are the hallmarks of

Chrysostom's sermons against Gentile believers that were attracted to the beliefs and traditions of the founding faction. Chrysostom advocates extreme measures to contain the influence of "Jewish ways" among his congregants:[5]

> Even if those who did fall are in number, we make them a multitude by the multitude of our rumors; we weaken those who resisted and we give a push to those on the point of falling. If one of our brothers hears the rumor that a large number joined in keeping the fast, he will be more inclined to be careless himself; again, if it is one of weak ones who hears the story, he will rush to join the strong of those who have fallen. Even if many have sinned, let us not join with those who rejoice at this or any other evil. If we do, we make a parade of the sinners and say that their name is legion. Rather, let us stop the rumor mongers and keep them from spreading the story. (Jud. 8:4:8)[6]

In the first sermon we find:

> Another more terrible sickness beckons and our tongue must be turned to heal a disease which is flourishing in the body of the church...What is this sickness? The festivals of the wretched and miserable Jews which follow one after another in succession—Trumpets, Booths, the Fasts—are about to take place. And many who belong to us and say that they believe in our teaching attend their festivals, and even share in their celebrations and join in their fasts. It is this evil practice I now wish to driven from the church. (Jud. 4.1; 48.844)

In sermons or speeches dealing with the foes of the Church, another favorite ploy was to describe opponents as ravenous wolves surrounding the helpless flock of Christ:[7]

> Again those sorry Jews, most miserable of all men, are about to hold a fast and it is necessary to protect the flock of Christ. As long as a wild beast is not causing trouble, shepherds lie down under an oak tree or a pine to play the flute, allowing the sheep to graze wherever they want. But when they realize wolves are about to attack, they immediately throw down their flute, grab their sling, lay aside the shepherd's pipe, arm themselves with clubs and stones, and stand before the flock shouting with a loud and booming voice, often driving away the wild beast without casting a stone. So also we, in the days just passed, were frolicking about in the exegesis of the Scriptures as in a meadow not touching on anything contentious due to the fact no one was troubling us. But since today the Jews, more troublesome than any wolves are about to encircle our sheep, it is necessary to arm ourselves for battle so that none of our sheep become prey to wild beasts. (Jud. 4.1; 48.871)

The eighth homily on the Judaizers, probably Chrysostom's anti-Jewish opus maximum, showcases the effort to sever the influence that the descendants of the founding fathers had over some among his congregation:

> Gone is the fasting of the Jews, or rather, the drunkenness of the Jews. (Jud. 8:1:1)

> This, in fact, is the special danger of madness: those who suffer from it do not know they are sick. So, too, the Jews are drunk but do not know they are drunk. (Jud. 8:1:4)

> Indeed, The fasting of the Jews, which is more disgraceful than any drunkenness, is over and gone. (Jud. 8:1:5)

> ...For those who have just observed the fast have fallen among robbers, the Jews. And the Jews are more savage than any highwaymen; they do greater harm to those who have fallen among them. (Jud. 8:3:10)

> ...as is the case with circumcision, so, too, the fasting of the Jews drives from heaven the man who observes the fast, even if he has ten thousand other good works to his credit... (Jud. 8:5:5)

> ...When you see that God is punishing you, do not flee to his enemies, the Jews, so that you may not rouse his anger against you still further... (Jud. 8:5:8)

> ...Tell me this. When you stand indicted before God's tribunal, what reason will you be able for considering the Jews' witchcraft more worthy of your belief than what Christ has said?... (Jud. 8:8:5)

> ...You profess you are a Christian, but you rush off to their synagogues and beg them to help you. Do not realize how they laugh at you, scoff at you, jeer at you, dishonor you, and reproach you?... (Jud. 8:8:9)

> ...Suppose you had to suffer incurable ills; suppose you had to die ten thousand deaths. Would it not be much better to endure all that rather than have those abominable people laugh and scoff at you, rather than live with a bad conscience?... (Jud. 8:10:1)[8]

Elsewhere:

> Nothing is more miserable than those who kick against their salvation. When it was required to keep the law, they trampled it under foot; now when the law has been abrogated, they obstinately observe it. What could be more pitiful than people who provoke God's anger not only by transgressing the law but also by observing the law? This is why the Scripture says, You stiff-necked and uncircumcised in heart; you always fight against the Holy Spirit. (Jud. 1.2; 48.845–846)

> We must return again to the sick. Do you realize that those who are fasting have dealings with those who shouted, Crucify him! Crucify him!" and with those who said, His blood be on us and on our children"? If a band of would-be revolutionaries were apprehended and then condemned, would

you dare to go to them and talk with them? I certainly don't think so! Is it not absurd to be zealous about avoiding someone who had sinned against mankind, but to have dealings with those who affronted God? Is it not folly for those who worship the crucified to celebrate festivals with those who crucified him? This is not only stupid—it is sheer madness. (Jud. 1.5; 850)

The Context

From Chrysostom we learn that some members of his congregation saw no problem in participating in services and ceremonies at synagogues. Chrysostom attempts to draw the line between "us" and "them" but it is obvious that some congregants see no problem in participating in both forms of worship. Called "the most horrible and violent denunciations of Judaism to be found in the writings of a Christian theologian,"[9] the eight anti-Jewish sermons targeted Gentiles in John's congregation who worshipped at synagogues. John's rampages are lucid, engaging, and demonstrate great ability, but they aim for the visceral, not for the logical, spiritual, or theological core of his constituency. Chrysostom's attacks are mostly tactical, not strategic. In other words, they are sophisticated incitement. They aim to inflame by pandering to the lowest instincts.

Similar to other authors analyzed in this section, Chrysostom does not unequivocally identify "the Jews" that attract his congregants as followers of Jesus. Traditional literal readings have understood the targets of John to be generic "Jews." During the twentieth century the academic discussion gravitated to whether John's ultimate adversaries were Jewish non-believers in Jesus, the Jewish followers of Jesus, Gentile sympathizers with Judaism,[10] or Gentile sympathizers with the founding faction. Many modern scholars have gravitated toward Gentile sympathizers with Judaism as the focus of John's ire. There is a wide consensus that supports the identification of the target audience as Gentiles. Besides context, some statements point decisively to their Gentile origin:[11]

[T]hat we might not shipwreck ourselves by becoming, as it were, proselytes to their law. (3:6) Before we believed in God, our hearts dwelling-place was corrupt and weak, truly a temple built by human hands, due to the fact it was full of idolatry and was the home of demons, for we did whatever was contrary to God. (16:7)

"If you believe Judaism is true," … "why do you trouble the Church?" (Jud. 4.4; 876). "Go into the synagogues," says John, "and see if the Jews have changed their days of fasting, if they observe the Paschal Feast at the same time we do, whether they have ever taken food on that day?…When have they celebrated the Pascha with us? When have they celebrated the festivals of martyrs with us? When have they shared the day of Epiphany with us?" (Jud. 4–3; 375–376)

Israelite traditions of prophetic chastisement and self-criticism, and the Judean tradition of sectarian anti-Jewish-establishment rhetoric, are appropriated to erode the influence of the founding faction. Chrysostom is quite explicit in recognizing that the biblical prophets and authors are being subverted to challenge the legitimacy of Jewish opponents within the Jesus movement: "By God's grace, we made the prophets our warriors against the Jews and routed them. As we return from pursuing out foes, let us look all around to see if any of our brothers have fallen, if the fast has swept some of them off, if any of them have shared in the festival of the Jews..." (Jud. 8:1:6).[12] Antioch was the largest stronghold of the founding faction outside of Judea. It seems that the synagogues of the descendents of Jesus's disciples and first followers attracted Gentile sympathizers, to the inclusion of some among Chrisostom's flock. John's ire originates in his rage at congregants that embrace his opponents' traditions and rituals. Indeed, John's candor can be enlightening:

> "This is the reason I hate the Jews," he says, "due to the fact they have the law and the prophets: indeed I hate them more due to the fact of this than if they did not have them" (Jud. 6.6; 913). "If you admire the Jewish way of life, what do you have in common with us? If the Jewish rites are holy and venerable," says John, "our way of life must be false" (Jud. 1.6; 851). The Jewish Scriptures are "bait to deceive the simple," the Law a "snare for the weak" (Jud. 6.6; 913). "Don't say to me that the Law and the books of the prophets can be found in the synagogue. That is not enough to make the place holy" (Jud. 1.5; 850).

During the third and fourth centuries the declining but still powerful influence of the descendants of Jesus's disciples and first followers[13] called into question the truth of Pauline orthodoxy. It seems that in Antioch of the end of the fourth century, three hundred years after Jesus's death, many Gentile believers were still attached to the descendants of Jesus's disciples and followers, a fact that infuriated John beyond civility.

My Chrysostom

John's career started in Antioch, a city with a long connection to the Jewish faction and their most important stronghold outside of Judea. We have seen that Ignatius, bishop of Antioch[14] two centuries earlier, chastised Gentiles in his community who were attracted to the beliefs and customs of the Jewish faction (Magn. 8.1–2; Phil. 6.1). It is clear from the content and context of John's sermons that two centuries later the influence of the descendents of the founding fathers among Gentile congregants remained a challenge.

Chrysostom and the Apostolic Constitutions corroborate that the beliefs and traditions of the founding fathers continued to attract rank-and-file Gentiles in Antioch, well through the fourth century.[15]

When attempting to decipher what socio-theological context triggered the authorship of these incendiary sermons, we face the same possible answers that we have considered throughout our journey: was it a conflict with Judaism? Was it the attraction of some to Judaism? Was it the continuation of the centuries-long effort against the beliefs and traditions of those chosen by Jesus to be the custodians of his legacy? Unfortunately, the fog of history and the guardians of orthodoxy obstruct our view on this matter. The historical record does not enlighten us as to the demographics and status of the Jewish followers of Jesus at the time of authorship.[16] I place John's sermons at the end of the excruciating and protracted "religious civil war" that engulfed the Jesus movement for at least three hundred years. Whether Chrysostom is aiming at Gentile sympathizers with Judaism or with the Jewish faction, there is growing support for the view that his eight anti-Jewish sermons were preached against "Judaizers," not against external/mainstream Jews.[17] Thus, despite the fact that Chrysostom's assault on Jews and on Judaism is extreme, the context seems to be internal; the persistent influence of the Jewish followers of Jesus among his congregants.

Significantly, prior to his ordination to the presbyterate, John's primary intellectual preoccupation was the defense of the ascending Pauline-Ignatian strand of belief in Jesus from Pagan influences among his flock. His sermons against Gentile sympathizers with the descendants of the founding fathers came later, highlighting the internal nature of his concerns. Throughout his career at Antioch Chrysostom unleashed his rage against differing believers in Jesus, whom he does not acknowledge as legitimate Christians. Chrysostom's multifrontal warfare is not dissimilar from Justin's or Tertullian's. Chrysostom's concern with Jewish and Pagan influences among his flock resonate with Justin's and Tertullian's apologies against "the Jews" and against Marcion, reflecting the fact that throughout three centuries the Pauline-Lukan confrontation with the descendants of the Jewish founders paralleled and mirrored confrontations with other differing believers within the Jesus movement—strengthening the internal context advocated here. A dispute about Judaism was cast, or misperceived, as a dispute with Judaism. A challenge to the legitimacy of those chosen by Jesus to be the guardians of his legacy was successful following an unrelenting assault on their beliefs and traditions. The context is a resentful and vicious debate about Judaism among believers in Jesus, not a conflict with it. In Chrysostom's resentful, defensive, and abusive homilies the externalization-projection of resentment toward adversaries that were Jews onto all Jews is seemingly complete. The projection of the intra-religious abuse that we encountered in previous texts onto the inter-religious arena is now almost seamless. However, despite Chrysostom's apparent targeting of "external Judaism," I suspect that the influence of the descendents of the founding fathers is the cause behind his ire:

1. At the time of authorship, the Pauline-orthodox assault on the beliefs and traditions of the founding fathers was a few centuries old and already quasi-sacrosanct. I doubt that Gentiles would be attending synagogue services under this derogatory barrage, unless they were attending the synagogues of the Jewish faction.
2. Antioch was an important stronghold of the Jewish faction. Some Gentile believers seem to have remained under the influence of the Jewish faction despite the orthodox de-Judaizing campaign, and would have attended their synagogues (where Jesus was venerated) not "mainstream" synagogues where his messiahship was rejected.
3. John's resentful complaint about lack of reciprocity (Jud. 4–3; 375–376) makes sense only if "the Jews" are the descendants of the founding fathers, from whom reciprocity was hoped and desired.
4. Often, the imagery and the metaphors deployed against these "Judaizers" are the same as those deployed in Chrysostom's earlier sermons against "Paganizers" among his congregants, strengthening the argument that the texts reflect an internal struggle against the beliefs and traditions of the Jewish faction—not a struggle with external/mainstream Judaism.
5. Chrysostom's use of the generic "Jews" to identify Jewish opponents within the Jesus movement resonates with the deployment of the "Ioudaioi" in the Gospel of John, and the deployment of "they/them" in Barnabas and Hebrews. It may also reflect a persistent, intended or unintended, fusion and confusion of Jews within and Jews without the Jesus movement.
6. The self-segregation of the Jewish faction, an important underpinning of the thesis presented throughout, is reflected in the estrangement between Jews and Gentiles in the Jesus movement.

Overall, there is nothing in Chrysostom's homilies that necessitates the expansion of his horizon beyond the Jesus movement. It is also important to internalize the fact that the writings of Melito and Chrysostom, bishops and saints, are not windows into marginal minds. Their writings reflect how many, if not most, Pauline-orthodox religious leaders thought and preached. During his tenure at Constantinople, the epicenter of the Eastern Empire at a time when Rome and the West were beginning the descent into the dark ages, John was second to the Pope in nominal hierarchy but was second to none in religious power and influence. Moreover, Chrysostom's sermons were popular with the masses and were reflective and representative of a culture of denigration, incitement, and persecution that took hold of the orthodox mindset. With Chrysostom we have reached the zenith of early anti-Jewish incitement. That said, and due to my concentration on his anti-Jewish "contribution," we must also acknowledge that Chrysostom's sermons and concerns encompassed a wide-ranging spectrum of theological and pastoral issues not discussed here.[18]

Almost three hundred years after Mark's seemingly inconsequential denigration of the disciples and the launch of the "Jewish responsibility" motif, we find the beliefs and traditions of those chosen by Jesus to be the guardians of his legacy thoroughly discredited and freely abused. Under the ever-increasing escalation of the anti-Jewish strand Jews and Judaism are demonic, sinful—their lives deemed worthless. By the fourth century, the disparagement of Jews and of Judaism that originated in the drive to de-Judaize belief in Jesus seems to have reached endemic proportions. From here onward, with few exceptions, anti-Jewish incitement will ravage the souls, hearts, and minds of Gentile believers in Jesus. From here onward, a distinct genre of literature (*Adversus Judaeos*)[19] will disseminate and intensify anti-Jewish sentiment throughout Christendom. At this stage, the transition from conjectural bias to undifferentiated polemic becomes endemic and paves the way to genocidal inclinations. As it concerns Judaism, the Christian fleet enters an era of inconceivable darkness. The age of Christendom's rise is the darkest age of Judaism. From here onward full-blown anti-Judaism and its worst manifestations are derivative; the fruits of an unintended journey gone awry. Light will be sporadic and anecdotal—persecution and disenfranchisement the rule.

Despite the obvious importance of Chrysostom's writings, these disturbing sermons have attracted relatively little attention from scholars. Some modern scholars seem to find refuge in stressing that ancients thrived on visceral clashes and often cling to the "bad apples syndrome," acknowledging the existence of rotten trees while refusing to see the forest. Indeed, ancients could be vicious. However, neither ancient nor turn-of-the-era religious texts were permeated by denigration and vilification of other religious traditions with the intensity and the pervasiveness that we encounter in the lore of the Pauline-Lukan faction. Nor is the disparaging of others as central and as dominant, in any major religious tradition, as it is in that strand. We cannot know with certainty how Western history would have evolved in the absence of the Pauline-Lukan ascendancy. However, the fact that views like John's won out is significant for it shaped attitudes and emotions about Judaism.[20]

Chrysostom's vicious bias is undistinguishable from later anti-Jewish tractates in either content or intensity. From here onward, and until the early twentieth century, unrestrained anti-Judaism will become endemic, normative, and sacrosanct. It will consume millions of Christian souls and Jewish lives. When a defenseless minority is the target of a derogatory discourse, the souls that populate the margins of human societies feast on the victims as the ever-silent majority looks away. Thankfully, hope and human dignity were preserved by those few brave souls that ventured to deviate from the frenzy.

Chapter 18

Recapitulation

The Epicenter

We are the rightful heirs of his legacy. Your ancestors, Jesus's disciples and first followers, did not understand his ministry. They betrayed and abandoned him in his moment of need. You claim to follow his path, but it is we who seek martyrdom for his sake. You claim to be righteous, but according to your scriptures and your prophets Jews are sinful and irredeemable. You claim that you are God's chosen but in fact you have forfeited God's favor. You observe strange rites and customs and think that you are better than us. Jesus's sacrifice and resurrection void any value that your traditions might have had.[1]

The response: In order to be rightful followers of Jesus you need to embrace his ministry and his faith. To be a true follower of Jesus you must live like him and worship like him. Jesus and his closest associates were Jews. True, Israelites have sinned often, but Jesus came to bring redemption to his people. You follow Paul who was not a disciple and did not know Jesus. The Jerusalem leaders did not embrace Paul's views. We don't accept Paul's claims that Jesus revealed to him what he did not reveal to his disciples.[2]

This is the underlying debate that seems to shadow the proto-orthodox lore. This is not a debate between "Christians" and "Jews"; nor is it a conflict between "Judaism" and "Christianity." This was, mostly, a confrontation between Gentile followers of Paul and Gentile sympathizers with the descendants of Jesus's disciples and first followers.

Challenging the Disciples

The belittling of the disciples and their traditions in the canonical Gospels and in the authoritative texts is a peculiar and unique deviation from most religious legitimating narratives, where the disciples of the founding leader are universally venerated as the legitimate heirs of the founder's legacy and ministry.[3] Why did Paulines engage in a unique and peculiar disparagement and vilification of those chosen by Jesus to be the custodians of his legacy? Why do the canonical Gospels signal to believers that Jesus's disciples "misunderstood" his ministry and his message, that they abandoned and betrayed him, implying that their descendants do not deserve to be revered and respected, that their customs, traditions, and beliefs should be rejected?

The use of ancestral and authoritative figures and stories to chastise contemporaneous adversaries is a widely attested phenomenon within Judaism and in most ancient cultures. In the Hebrew Scriptures, denigration of the ancestors of adversaries is a clear indication of the agendas driving the texts.[4] Judeans deployed metaphors, allegories, and proxies to chastise internal adversaries[5] and external enemies[6] by disparaging their ancestors and their ancestral traditions. Thus, we may suspect that the criticism of the disciples, Jesus's alledged alienation from fellow Jews, and the battering of Jewish beliefs and traditions may reflect the emerging Pauline-Lukan effort to delegitimate "the Jews" (i.e., the Jewish faction) rather than the circumstances of Jesus's life. Furthermore, the anti-Jewish rhetoric that we encounter in the lore seems to emulate Judean polemical traditions and seems to target the immediate danger confronting the Gentile followers of Paul a couple of generations after Jesus's death—the influence of the descendants of the founding fathers.

Throughout his gospel and in line with the ancient tradition of denigrating the ancestors of one's opponents, Mark criticizes the Twelve Apostles, the special Three, and Peter. Peter seems to be the leader of those that are seen by Mark as his adversaries. The author of Mark implies that Jesus's associates and companions, his family, and fellow Jews did not understand his true mission. Mark, writing some four decades after Jesus's death and alien to his cultural, ethnic, and religious heritage claims that he "understands" what was obscure to those that shared Jesus's life, ministry, religious background, and ethnicity; those chosen by him to be the custodians of his legacy. Hindsight derived from our knowledge of what was to come helps us retroject and identify the disparagement of Jesus's disciples and followers as the first salvo in the emerging opposition to the authority and to the legitimacy of the Jewish faction as the exclusive guardians and interpreters of Jesus's ministry.[7] Therefore, the Markan narrative is not only about a conflict between Jesus and some Judeans in positions of authority, it also reflects the emergence of a conflict about identity and legitimacy among believers in Jesus, as seen from a Pauline perspective.

By the time of Mark's writing, Paul's mission to the Gentiles appears to have encountered success in attracting Pagan sympathizers and recruits.

These new recruits must have soon realized that they had joined a belea-guered faction at odds with the founding fathers of the movement. Mark's denigration of the disciples seems to have been crafted to counteract the claim, by some among the descendants of the Jewish founders, that Gentile forms of belief in Jesus were insufficient and lacking. It may have also come about to explain to the rank and file the estrangement from the descendants of Jesus's disciples and first followers. Mark attempts to reassure the rank and file that they are rightful followers of Jesus despite their rejection of the beliefs and religious traditions espoused by Jesus and by those chosen by him to be the custodians of his legacy. He does so by denigrating the disciples and by casting Jesus as trespassing tradi-tions associated with the descendants of his disciples and first followers. From Mark forward we encounter in the Synoptics a crescendo of deni-gration that shadows the growing tension and estrangement within the Jesus movement:[8]

The disciples "did not understand"	—1 Corinthians 10:25–27; Romans 4:14; Acts 10:15, Mark 6:52; 7:17, 8:17; 9:32; Matthew 13:10–15.
The disciples "will deny Jesus"	—Mark 14:30; John 13:36–38; 25:27.
The disciples "fail to keep guard"	—Mark 14:32–42; Matthew 6:13; 26:36–46; Luke 11:4; 22:40–46.
The disciples "abandon Jesus"	—Mark14:50; Matthew 26:47–56; Luke 22:47–53.
Peter denies Jesus three times	—Mark 14:66–72; Matthew 26:69–75; Luke 23:2–3, 18–25.

Although the synoptic phenomenon creates considerable redundancy in this summary, the fact that decades after Mark, Matthew and Luke chose to perpetuate and intensify Mark's denigration of the disciples is significant.

Opposition to the Disciples in John

John's deployment of the multivalent "Ioudaioi" and his intense anti-Ioudaioi rhetoric signal a turning point. It seems that for the Johannines, the denigra-tion of the disciples that characterized the Synoptics was no longer sufficient. The tensions between the parties had become an open confrontation-estra ngement-secession. Blunter tools were deemed necessary to sever the sway of the descendants of the founding fathers. When the author(s)/editor(s) of the canonical John criticize or downplay the disciples or Peter (12:16; 12:27; 13:23–26; 18:2–11; 18:11; 18:15–16; 19:26–27; 20:2–10; 21:7, 21:20–23) they are justifying to their audience the estrangement from the Jewish founders, not their estrangement from mainstream Jews, to which they would have been indifferent.

The Challenge to the Legacy of the Disciples in Hebrews and Barnabas

Hebrews and Barnabas, roughly contemporary with the Synoptics, represent a more strident and overt opposition to the descendants of Jesus's disciples and first followers. Whereas the Synoptics camouflaged their dissent, in Hebrews and Barnabas we encounter the first stages of a transition to overt and undifferentiated attacks deployed to batter the Jewish elite. Their arguments against the legitimacy of the descendants of Jesus's disciples and first followers have populated the tradition throughout the centuries and are deeply embedded in the theological discourse and in the culture. Whereas Mark seems to imply that Jesus's messiahship was deliberately hidden, causing the disciples to misunderstand his ministry, Barnabas and Hebrews are the first to insinuate that "their" understanding of Jesus's life and ministry was erroneous, misguided, and originated in sinful minds. Whereas Mark hints that the descendants of Jesus's disciples and first followers did not understand Jesus's legacy and abandoned him, Barnabas and Hebrews reach deeper; they claim that the true meaning of the Israelite journey is to be understood and deciphered by non-Jews.

Challenging Unassailable Legitimacy

Those intent on de-Judaizing belief in Jesus, on severing the influence of the descendants of the founding fathers and on demoting them from their position as the exclusive guardians of Jesus's legacy, could ill afford, at first, to state their aims. Not surprisingly, their claims were initially put forward in an implied and subdued manner; their ultimate aims were seldom stated overtly. Throughout this confrontation, and throughout the lore accompanying it, we did encounter a persistent reluctance to cast the conflict as a confrontation with the Jewish faction. Intuitively confident of their core arguments but facing the unassailable legitimacy of those chosen by Jesus to be the guardians of his legacy, Pauline leaders and intellectuals gradually gravitated to a strategy of demotion by ancestor denigration and demotion by proxy, that centered on using their opponents' lore, beliefs, traditions, and institutions as "wedge issues" to sever their influence in the Jesus movement. By shifting the debate away from the weak flank of the Pauline argument (the fact that their adversaries were the descendants of Jesus's disciples and first followers, and therefore the presumptive guardians of his legacy) and framing the debate around beliefs and traditions that most Gentiles found strange and idiosyncratic, the Pauline-Lukan faction gradually fashioned a strategy that led to a growing estrangement between Gentile believers and the founding faction. Success, however, came at the cost of embedding in the tradition and in the minds and souls of believers a pervasive anti-Jewish strand. Worded differently—most Gentile converts seem to have resented the attempt to impose Jewish beliefs and traditions as a requirement for being recognized as legitimate followers of Jesus. These beliefs and traditions, while integral and intrinsic to the descendants of the founders, were alien to most non-Jewish converts and consequently emerged as wedge issues in the drive to erode the status of the Jewish faction and to de-Judaize belief in Jesus. Moreover, by casting those that did not agree with their theology as "not understanding," "denying," or "abandoning" Jesus, the Pauline-Lukan faction successfully obscured a theological embarrassment: their opposition to the legacy of those chosen by Jesus to be his successors.

Challenging the legitimacy of the descendants of the disciples and first followers of a religion's founder would be a towering task, in any religious tradition. The strategy that won the day had several components: the denigration of the disciples and their beliefs and traditions, the appropriation of their identity as the new people of God (the new Israel, God's new chosen), and the subversion of their anti-Jewish-establishment lore and of the Jewish traditions of prophetic exhortation and self-criticism. By deploying this complex and multifaceted strategy proto-orthodox leaders and intellectuals waged a protracted and uncertain, but eventually successful, challenge to the descendants of Jesus's disciples and first followers. The struggle over identity, legitimacy, and ascendancy of which the de-Judaizing effort was a central facet was cast by the later guardians of orthodoxy as a confrontation with "the Jews." Intended or unintended, conscious or unconscious, this blurring of the identity of the adversaries was self-serving. It allowed the proto-orthodox leadership to erode the status of the descendants of the Jewish founders, to the point that two centuries later the descendants of the founders could be considered marginal and "heretical." The de-Judaizing of belief in Jesus was also facilitated by the weakening of the Jewish faction caused by the decimation in their ranks during the two failed Judean revolutions. The decimation of the Judean stronghold of the Jewish faction may have created an unexpected vacuum of authority that facilitated the proto-orthodox ascendancy.

The Postcanonical Era

Anti-Jewish sentiment among Pauline-Lukan believers reaches its zenith in the Apostolic Fathers and in the apologists of the second and third centuries. What in the New Testament was ambivalent, ambiguous, and implied, bursts to the surface in the blunt and undifferentiated anti-Ioudaioi polemic that accompanied the second- and third-century religious "civil war." Great resentment and pain underwrite the texts authored during this period. The extreme anti-Jewish tone of the post-canonical texts is indicative of great emotional and psychological stress, of great anxiety about identity and legitimacy. It appears that the need to explain and justify the estrangement from the Jewish founding fathers, internal dissent, theological confusion, and Roman persecution did exert a great toll on the proto-orthodox psyche. Were it not for the impact it eventually had on the minds and on the hearts of millions of believers, the claim put forward in these texts—that a religious tradition spanning two thousand years is unworthy of its heritage and is incapable of understanding its own inner meaning—could be smiled upon. However, the extraordinary audacity and affront of these claims are opaque to modern believers due to the fact that the challengers were eventually successful and did come to dominate the cultural and theological discourse of the West. Thus, what from a first-century perspective seems outrageous did eventually become normative and sacrosanct.

At first, the reader's immediate reaction may be to dismiss the more extreme of the postcanonical texts as marginal, as non-representative of the mainstream. However, it is crucial to internalize the fact that we have discussed authoritative works authored by individuals that were the acknowledged leaders and trendsetters of their time—venerated by millions, their texts later read and revered throughout Christendom during almost two thousand years. Melito and Chrysostom, the most extreme and strident of them all, were bishops and both were later sanctified. Chrysostom was bishop of Constantinople, second only to the pope in protocol, but at the time, the most powerful ecclesiastical position in Christendom. Melito was the bishop of Sardis, a cultural and economic hub.

The non-canonical texts we have discussed are the third stage of a polemical sequence, a pre-anti-Semitic level. However, due to the internal context of their writing and the identity of the intended adversaries we need to withhold categorizing their authors as anti-Semitic. Although the authoritative texts did become the anchors, enablers, and facilitators of anti-Semitism, their intended adversaries were, for the most part, the Jewish faction and its Gentile sympathizers. Thus, despite the fact that to a literal reader these texts feel anti-Semitic in content and impact, despite the fact that they were written in the context of pervasive denigration of Jewish beliefs and traditions, we must acknowledge that, technically speaking, the writers' intent was not anti-Semitic. Therefore, and not withstanding the hearts' desire and the fact that with these texts the demons of anti-Semitism entered their last gestational stages, we need to exonerate these writers from anti-Semitic inclinations. Given on narrow technical grounds, this exoneration must stand despite the fact that, enhanced by authoritative status, these texts were treasured by anti-Semites throughout the ages. This third level in the "edifice of sanctified hatred" is the gateway into a horrific future. No leap of imagination is required to see continuity between these texts and later anti-Semitism.

Projection onto Judaism

The pioneering work of Munck (1959), Stendahl (1976), Gager (1985), Gaston (1987), Lieu (1996), Murray (2004), and others has shed new light on the importance of "Gentile Judaizers" (Gentile sympathizers with Judaism) for our understanding of the anti-Jewish bias in the canonical and authoritative literature. However, I have questioned throughout the current views about "the conflict between Judaism and Christianity" and about "the attraction to Judaism" that emerge out of this body of scholarship and are the current favorite narratives deployed to explain the emergence of anti-Jewish attitudes among early Gentile believers in Jesus. I have argued that clarity and consistency emerge out of re-placing the "anti-Jewish" rhetoric of the first four centuries within the Jesus movement. Conflict with external-mainstream Judaism seems to be a later, derivative, and unilateral phenomenon that stands on a complex and multilayered trajectory. Moreover, I do not see socio-theological grounds for a conflict between first-century Judaism and the many Gentile strands of belief in Jesus that surfaced at the time. The texts authored during this period seem to originate in a relatively closed universe; their context, purpose, horizon, and protagonists seem to be within the Jesus movement.

It seems that by the second century, a gradual fusion and confusion of several rhetorical themes took hold of the hearts and minds of Pauline-Lukan believers. This melting pot of incitement included externalization, projection, fusion, and confusion of motifs and themes that originated in the anti-Jewish-establishment lore of the founding fathers, in the decontextualization and appropriation of their identity and lore, in the crusade to de-Judaize belief in Jesus, and in the need to explain and justify the estrangement from the descendants of Jesus's disciples and first followers. Thus, attacks on Judaism (distinct from attacks on the beliefs and traditions of the Jewish founding fathers) should be considered a later and derivative phenomenon. This argument stands despite the fact that we should acknowledge circumstances where Jewish-Christian tensions may have surfaced, mostly as later consequences or derivatives of the events within the Jesus movement,[9] and despite the fact that there seems to have existed a persistent fusion and confusion of "Jews within" and "Jews without."

Furthermore, I have posited that since the legitimacy of the Pauline-Lukan "orthodoxy" could not be based on the acknowledgment of an adversarial takeover of the Jesus movement, it was necessary to obscure and conceal the demotion of the descendants of the founding fathers. This deletion may have emerged out of the desire to project a consensual transfer of leadership and of legitimacy from Jesus's disciples and followers to the ascending Pauline orthodoxy. Whether Eusebius's deletion of this theologically embarrassing phase from his "Historia Ecclesiastica" was conscious or reflects an already authoritative tradition, his telling of the origins of the faith became the foundational myth of the new religion. Thus, it seems possible that Eusebius wrote at a time (three hundred years after Jesus's death) when the fusion and the confusion between Jews within the Jesus movement and Jews without was already an ingrained tradition, and that this misperception was retrojected onto past events. However, it is also plausible that Eusebius's "history" was crafted with other goals in mind. From his ecclesiastical "history" and from his apologia to Constantine (Vita *Constantini*) we can surmise that Eusebius had a strong sense of "where the political wind was blowing" and was keen to cater and ponder to the powerful and the mighty.[10] Whether Eusebius was intent on obscuring and misrepresenting the evolution of belief in Jesus or was misinformed, his work enshrined the myth about the evolution of belief in Jesus from unity to diversity and heresy. By veiling the confusion, chaos, and conflict that engulfed the Jesus movement well into the fourth century, Eusebius's work offered the Pauline victors a legitimating account of origins on which the exclusivist, triumphalist, and militant ascendant orthodoxy stood for the next sixteen hundred years.

We have seen throughout the persistent use of the term Ioudaioi to identify the Jewish faction.[11] The assignment of a derogatory identifier to a foe that is affiliated with an external group is a rather common practice in internal feuds[12]—explaining how "the Jews" may have become the unintended targets of the resentment generated during the protracted and rancorous struggle against adversaries that were Jews. Most importantly, after Eusebius, given his presentation of the genesis of belief in Jesus, the footprint of the rancorous struggle against the descendants of Jesus's disciples and first followers could not but be read as reflective of a conflict between "Judaism" and "Christianity." The vacuum created by the Eusebian erasure of the campaigns to demote the descendants of the founding fathers and to de-Judaize belief in Jesus enabled and may have necessitated the externalization of the anti-Jewish sentiment generated during the protracted second-century religious "civil war," onto all Jews. Disconnected from their original socio-theological grounding, the emotions, and the attitudes that accompanied the estrangement between the descendants of Jesus's disciples and first followers and their Gentile sympathizers on one side, and the Gentile majority on the other was read as reflective of a Jewish-Christian conflict. Gradually, hyperbole against the founding faction, often hidden behind multivalent phantoms (Ioudaioi, they/them, Jews) and mostly indirect and implicit to start with, morphed into endemic anti-Judaism. As time passed and Eusebius's account of belief in Jesus became authoritative, the projection of the rhetoric against the descendants of the founding fathers onto "external" Jews became seemingly seamless. The externalization of internal tensions onto the intra-religious arena became "history."

In addition, until the Pauline-Lukan faction emerged ascendant, the internal and external circumstances of the Jesus movement do not favor a scenario where the dominant element would be an inter-religious (Jewish versus Christian) conflict. A first stage of self-definition, consolidation, and integration must have taken place before the proto-orthodox would engage enemies beyond the boundaries of their movement. We should not expect a religious movement in the initial stages of identity formation, engulfed in a "religious civil war," and enduring persecution by the Roman authorities to engage external enemies gratuitously. During the second and third centuries Pauline-Lukan believers were not in a position to "take-on" mainstream Judaism. Nor was it their most pressing concern. This was a period during which the energies of believers must have been focused inward. Therefore, in the canonical and authoritative lore "Jews" and "Judaism" seem to be rhetorical and literary derogatory labels and phantoms—proxies for adversaries within, rather than external adversaries. Some of the texts we have encountered seem to have been created to appease distraught believers whose legitimacy as rightful followers of Jesus's was being questioned by those advocating adherence to the beliefs and traditions of the founding fathers. Other texts seem to have been created to fend off the influence that the descendants of the Jewish founders exerted over the Gentile rank-and-file, to shore-up the folk, to provide solace and to induce resiliency in beleaguered Gentile communities.

Polemical internal religious exhortation is attested in many religious traditions. However, when internal resentment against kin is subverted-appropriated by an alien group and resurfaces as an inter-religious derogatory discourse, a qualitative and unprecedented phenomenon has occurred. When internal rhetoric migrates from the hearts, minds, and lips of Jews to the hearts, minds, and lips of Gentiles, and is used to dehumanize and to disenfranchise opponents that are Jews, a major shift has taken place. Outside its original setting, Jewish anti-establishment rhetoric was transposed to an external environment and became virulent. Lacking the natural protection provided by kinship, the intense and militant vitriol that characterizes sectarian posturing metamorphosed and became undifferentiated polemic. This trajectory, from infighting among Jews to incitement against Judaism by non-Jews, has been a core concern of our inquiry. Identity appropriation, initially a seemingly harmless process of consolidation, turns malignant when the new identity breaches the protective shield of kinship. Similar to a virus that mutates and invades a new species, identity takeover is the vehicle through which the ire of Jewish sectarians toward the mainstream did migrate to an alien community and became endemic.

Scholars and theologians often cite exhortation by biblical prophets and Judean sectarian anti-Jewish-establishment rhetoric to explain and justify the anti-Jewish deluge that we encounter in the Pauline-Lukan lore. However, the issue is not whether "by the measure of contemporary Jewish polemic, the New Testament's slander against fellow Jews is remarkably mild."[13] Behavior that we accept from our kin is unacceptable in a stranger. Fraternal exchanges are often strident, buy they do not license strangers to trespass inter-religious markers. Moreover, the viciousness of internal feuds is unacceptable in the dialog between religious traditions. Non-Jews may not use the fact that Jews denigrated Jews, as licensing, or "justifying" their denigration of Jews or of Judaism. The fact that the insults of a stranger are similar to fraternal attacks does not make the former any more acceptable— or less dangerous.

The complex and theologically unsettling socio-theological processes that dominated the first centuries of belief in Jesus were thereafter hidden behind a monolithic and all-encompassing mega-stereotype about Jews and about Judaism and a largely mythical "conflict between Judaism and Christianity." The tensions that we encountered in the New Testament between the authors and their Jewish adversaries gradually morphed (in the memory and in the perception of later believers) into a conflict between the "synagogue and the Church." This deeply rooted misperception, nurtured, and exacerbated by later orthodoxy and by the misinterpretation, and later mistranslation, of the multivalent "Ioudaioi" into the univalent "the Jews" have distorted our ability to discuss, let alone understand, what transpired.

About Judaizing

Recognition of the importance, and of the impact, of Gentile sympathizers with the Jewish faction has been slow to emerge. This statement stands despite the fact that we have evidence about the survival and the enduring influence of the founding faction well into the fifth century. Michele Murray,[14] standing on Strecker, Wilken, Stendahl, Gager, Gaston, Wilson, Taylor, and Lieu, argued the case for identifying Gentile sympathizers with Judaism (Gentile Judaizers) as main targets of some of these texts. Her work focuses on Gentile sympathizers with Judaism and rejects the traditional identification of "the Jews" as "the" main adversaries throughout the tradition. Murray's conclusions support the existence of an influential Jewish faction through the first four centuries of belief in Jesus.[15] On this subject Murray concluded that

> certain Gentile Christians received encouragement and pressure to Judaize from fellow Gentile Christians already engaged in Judaizing behavior—as was likely the case in Galatians, in Ignatius's letters to the Philadelphians and the Magnesians, and in the Epistle of Barnabas. They also were likely influenced

by Jewish Christians, as reflected in Galatians, the Didache, in Justin Martyr's Dialogue with Trypho, the Kerygmata Petrou in the Pseudo-Clementine literature, and in Colossians.

She further elaborates that

> assuming that Judaizing was indeed occurring, there is no substantive evidence that Jews were the instigators of such behavior among Christians. Rather, as stated above, this study contends that fellow Gentile Christians more likely were the primary aggressors—as, for example, in Galatia and, possibly, in Philadelphia. In other cases—such as the Didache and, possibly, in Colossae—Jewish Christians were the propagating party. Sometimes both Jewish and Gentile Christians were involved—as in Galatia.[16]

The attempts by the descendants of Jesus's disciples and first followers and their Gentile sympathizers to fend off the de-Judaizing of the Jesus movement have been traditionally portrayed as offensive moves to Judaize it. However, these activities should not be considered proselytizing given that they would be directed to oppose change, not to bring it about. Whether the opponents of an author are members of the Jewish faction, their Gentile sympathizers, or Gentile sympathizers with Judaism is important, but either is reflective of the opposition to the proto-orthodox campaign to Gentilize the Jesus camp, not of a drive to Judaize it.[17] According to the thesis advocated here, Paul and later Pauline-Lukan believer authors were not fending off "Judaizers," they were de-Judaizing the Jesus tradition.[18] They were not fending off change, they were promoting it. Belief in Jesus was not in danger of being "Judaized"; it was Jewish. Much more than a squabble about semantics is at play here for "Judaizing" is an anachronistic term that has come to symbolize heretical change and is associated with a discourse tainted by anti-Judaism. Murray suggests that it was unlikely that Jewish followers of Jesus followed a policy of aggressive proselytizing learned from Jews, for there is no evidence in extant sources from antiquity for organized missionary activity by Jews, although we cannot rule out that individuals may have proselytized at certain times.[19]

Most scholars agree that a tradition of "Gentile-Judaizing" existed without interruption from the earliest times.[20] Lacking is the recognition that it reflects and corroborates the persistent influence of the descendants of Jesus's disciples and first followers and/or their enduring legacy. Furthermore, Gentile Judaizing is most often associated to the attraction to "Judaism," not to the affinity to the traditions of the descendants of Jesus's disciples and first followers, where it originates.[21] The pioneering work of Gaston, Gager, Wilson, and Murray highlights the importance of "Gentile Judaizers" (Gentile sympathizers with Judaism) in the canonical and authoritative literature. I suggest that the "Judaizing" phenomenon that infuriated Pauline leaders and intellectuals should be re-placed within the Jesus movement and that the Gentile Judaizers that concern us are attracted to the descendants of Jesus's disciples and first followers, not to Judaism. "Judaizing" is a tendentious term that reflects a Gentile perspective on the opposition to the crusade to de-Judaize the Jesus movement. Thus, the process that underwrites the term "Judaizing" is the emergence through conflict, dissent, chaos, and confusion of a compromise creed aimed at de-Judaizing the Jesus movement and at achieving unity under Pauline hegemony. The goal was to fashion a Gentilized version of belief in Jesus that would maintain some similitude to the tenets of the founding fathers, but would reject those features that were most foreign and alien to new converts from Paganism (i.e., Torah observance, circumcision, and food laws). The orthodox faction, intent on presenting its ascendancy as legitimate and as flowing from Jesus through his disciples and followers, did obscure the adversarial nature of this process.

An Elusive Response

If, as argued by traditional and current scholarship, the intended adversary was establishment Judaism, the almost total silence and lack of response is intriguing. Compared to the scope, centrality, and pervasiveness of the anti-Jewish hostility among early Gentile believers in Jesus, the Jewish side is intriguingly silent.[22] Throughout the first and second centuries Judaism would have been a formidable adversary for the Gentile followers of Paul. Not only was it vastly superior numerically but, despite Judean rebelliousness, enjoyed significant privileges including being the only foreign religion given official recognition by the Roman authorities. Faced with the intense anti-Jewish escalation that we have encountered, we may ask: Where is the reaction of Judaism? Was the Jewish side as silent as implied by the lack of evidence? Was there a reaction that was lost or edited out? Or, as I suggest: there was no significant Jewish response due to the fact that the original crisis was about Judaism, not with it. This conclusion is strengthened by an intensive, and mostly futile, search by theologians and scholars for the other side of the controversy. Despite great efforts by many scholars, the search for the Jewish response has yielded dismal results.

Indeed, scholars have noted the enormous disproportion in intensity and quantity—to the point of rendering insignificant the few segments that have been identified as possible Jewish responses. The absence of a commensurate Jewish response, if Judaism understood itself to be the intended adversary, is difficult to explain. This puzzling lack of symmetry is seldom addressed in the literature and, consequently, it is difficult to speak of a majority view or a consensus on this subject. A scholar assigned to present a report on the subject concluded: "It seems that searching for references to Christians and

Christianity among the documents of the early rabbis neither elucidates greatly the condition of early Christianity, nor its anti-Judaism, nor, for that matter, the conditions under which second century rabbinism developed...In view of such benign results we simply must ask different questions."[23] During the centuries much has been said about a single instance of suspected Jewish anti-Christianism: Birkhat Haminim, "the benediction against the heretics,"[24] an issue we addressed in our discussion of the Gospel of John. Here we need only reiterate that the benediction seems to be a later collective and generic repudiation of heretics that was expanded to include the Jewish followers of Jesus. The benediction is not concerned with Gentile believers in Jesus. It was (apparently) designed to dissuade Jewish followers of Jesus from leading Jewish religious services. There are also a few second-century citations of "Jewish" persecution. However, it is often unclear whether the persecuted are Jewish sectarians (the Jewish followers of Jesus) or Gentile believers in Jesus, and whether the instigators are Jewish believers in Jesus[25] or mainstream Jews. In addition, it is often difficult to discern whether the persecution refers to biblical times, Jesus's lifetime, or is contemporaneous.[26]

It has also been suggested that Jewish self-censorship, triggered by fear (following the orthodox ascendancy), may lie behind the silence at the Jewish end. However, during the first three centuries, Judaism would have had no reason to exercise self-restraint, or self-censure, of its reaction to the attacks by Gentile believers in Jesus. Furthermore, evidence of a Jewish reaction should have survived beyond the reach of the later church in the Jewish strongholds of Judea, Egypt, Syria, and Persia, which had an extensive cultural interchange. As indicated elsewhere, from Theodosius and until the sixteenth century, the Jewish center of gravity moved to Mesopotamia and later spread to Muslim Spain and Egypt, far beyond the reach of Christianity. The geographic dispersion of the Jewish people and lack of a centralized authority or hierarchy should have guaranteed the survival of literary evidence of a Jewish reaction, if existent. As it regards the period surveyed here, it seems that the anti-Jewish rampage that we have encountered was not addressed, or reciprocated. It was either unknown or disregarded by the Jewish side. By and large, mainstream Judaism seems to have remained uninformed, unconcerned, and unengaged. Wilson contributes corroborating support when he observes that while we know that for many Christians their relationship to Judaism was of central importance, we cannot assume that the same was true for the Jews.[27]

The search for the response of the descendants of Jesus's disciples and first followers to the challenge by the non-Jewish majority has also come to naught. The reaction of the founding faction to the de-Judaizing crusade eludes us.[28] It would appear that the lack of evidence for a reaction to the attacks on the Jewish faction is due to the fact that the literature of small and defeated adversaries seldom survives. Self-segregation of the descendants of the founding fathers from the cacophony of Gentile voices that emerged following the Pauline and Gnostic missions to the Gentiles may be a factor too. The Jewish followers of Jesus were the children and the grandchildren of Jesus's first followers and they understood themselves to be the true and legitimate heirs of his legacy and ministry. Self-segregating by nature, they may have distanced themselves from the large influx of new-comers espousing, from the perspective of the founding faction, "strange" views, and beliefs about Jesus. This scenario suggests that the descendants of the founding fathers may have been absent antagonists—self-segregated and uninvolved protagonists.

Despite the absence of evidence on the reaction of the Jewish side, we should not preclude specific local circumstances where boundaries may have been breached. It is plausible that the intense anti-Judaic attitudes that came to predominate in the hearts and minds of Gentile followers of Paul eventually filtered out and did impact relations with local Jewish communities. This, however, would not be the cause behind the emergence of the anti-Jewish strand. Rather, it seems to have been one of its consequences.

The Anti-Jewish Strand

The Jewish milieu of the founding fathers was alien to recent converts from Paganism. Jewish traditions and customs were a stumbling block for most. A situation where Gentiles of Pagan origin would be required to accept Jewish customs and traditions would be untenable. Eventually, it would exacerbate tensions between Jews and non-Jews within the Jesus movement and would precipitate a bitter estrangement between the parties. I have anticipated in chapter 1 that the trajectory from the anti-establishment rhetoric of a Judean sect, to a religion that made hatred of all Jews sacrosanct, is complex, multi-layered and has six main sources:

1. Polemic by the Jewish followers of Jesus against the Judean establishment.
2. Polemic by Gentile believers against the Jewish establishment of the Jesus movement.
3. Appropriation Theology—The claim that Pauline believers in Jesus replaced the Jewish followers of Jesus as the New Israel, as God's chosen.
4. Supersession Theology—The view that the Pauline interpretation of Jesus's legacy replaced and annulled the beliefs and traditions of Jesus's disciples and first followers.

5. Decontextualization of the Judean tradition of self-criticism and prophetic anti-establishment censure.
6. Loss of context, fusion, confusion, and misinterpretation of these rhetorical layers and their projection onto Judaism.

The earliest layer of rhetoric originates in the relationship between the Jewish faction and establishment Judaism (candidates: James, proto-Mark, proto-Matthew, proto-John, and maybe proto-Revelation). Rumors and accusations regarding cooperation or participation of the hated and illegitimate "Jewish authorities," traitors, and minions that administered Judea on behalf of the Romans may have surfaced following Jesus's death. Accusations against the "Jewish authorities," distinct from later generic attacks on "the Jews," may signal that we are reading textual traces of the descendants of Jesus's disciples and first followers—filtered through the prism of Gentile editing.

The second layer of rhetoric targets the descendants of the founding fathers as the "establishment" group within the Jesus movement. At this stage the antagonists were not the "Jews without" but rather "the Jews within." The Pauline mission to the Gentiles evolved in opposition to the founding faction and would have directed its sectarian and militant rhetoric first and foremost toward them, not toward Judaism—as commonly understood. Initially, the need, the frame of reference, the horizon, and the context seem to have been intra muros. The second layer includes many points of friction that surfaced as the protracted conflict within the Jesus movement lingered on. They included the tensions between Paul and the Pillars, the disparagement of the disciples and their beliefs and traditions, the rejection of Gentile forms of belief in Jesus by the founding faction, the Gentile gravitation toward Jesus's divinity, the self-segregation/elitism of the descendants of the founders, the exoneration of the Jewish faction from Roman persecution, and the influence that the descendants of the Jewish founders had among some Gentile believers. This second layer engendered the Gentile appropriation of the identity and lore of the founding fathers that resulted in the subversion, appropriation, and decontextualization of the Jewish lore to the inclusion of the tradition of prophetic exhortation, the Judean tradition of self-criticism, and the Judean anti-Jewish-establishment traditions. This wide-ranging subversion, appropriation, and decontextualization seems to emerge out of the claim to the supersession of the descendants of Jesus's disciples and first followers as the new people of God and out of the drive to de-Judaize belief in Jesus.

A third and more virulent layer of the anti-Jewish bias emerges as these first two layers become fused and confused in the lore and in the hearts and minds of later Gentile believers. Somewhere along the way, authors and audience seem to have lost the distinction between the founding faction, their Gentile sympathizers, and establishment Judaism. As this occurred, the two distinct layers surveyed above merged into an undifferentiated, and tumultuous, river of anti-Jewish incitement. Dynamics of fusion, confusion, extrapolation, and projection converted an internal debate about Judaism into undifferentiated anti-Judaism. It is reasonable to assume that this "melting pot of incitement" matured at different times and at different rates for different communities. We know, however, that by the fifth century the process was almost complete. Many junctures, themes, and motifs characterize the unintended journey we have tracked:

1. The descendants of the founding fathers, similar to other Jewish sectarians, and as reflected by their footprints in the New Testament, seem to have developed a militant anti-Jewish-establishment lore, would have perceived mainstream Judaism as "apostate and sinful," and would have claimed to be "the new people of God."

2. The anti-Jewish-establishment lore of Jesus's Jewish disciples and followers may have included accusations and rumors about participation or cooperation of the hated and Roman-appointed traitors, collaborators, and minions that ruled Judea, in Jesus's death.

3. The rejection, by the Jewish leadership, of non-Jewish forms of belief in Jesus as inadequate and lacking and the rejection of Judaism by most Gentile believers are the engines behind the estrangement between Jews and Gentiles in the Jesus movement.

4. The Pauline (proto-orthodox and Marcionite) and Gnostic interpretations of Jesus's ministry struggled for recognition and for equal standing with the descendants of Jesus's disciples and first followers despite their rejection of the beliefs and traditions espoused by Jesus and by those chosen by him as the custodians of his legacy.

5. A crisis about authority, legitimacy, identity, and leadership engulfed the Jesus movement as the success of the missions to the Gentiles (Pauline and Gnostic) engendered a non-Jewish majority. Believers with Jewish, Pagan, and Gnostic affiliations and inclinations were the protagonists in this crisis. Judaism, Paganism, and Gnosticism were not protagonists; they were the subjects of contention.

6. It would appear that the members of the Jewish faction were, for the most part, unengaged, self-segregated, and absent adversaries. The protagonists at the epicenter of the strife seem to be Gentile believers with affiliations with, and inclinations toward, Judaism, Gnosticism, and Paganism—each claiming to espouse the only "true" form of belief in Jesus.

7. As time passed, the challenge to the authority and to the legitimacy of the Jewish faction morphed into an attack on their identity, integrity, beliefs, and traditions that was eventually successful in de-Judaizing belief in Jesus. These beliefs and traditions became "wedge issues" that

were deployed to sever the attraction to the descendants of the Jewish founders among the rank and file. This attack by proxy became an ingrained tradition.

8. Pauline-Lukan believers championed a compromise that led to the subversion and appropriation of the identity and lore of the founding fathers. They developed a theology of appropriation and supersession that "transferred" God's favor from "the Jews" (the Jewish followers of Jesus) to the "Gentiles" (the Gentile followers of Paul).

9. The Pauline-Lukan literature of the second and third centuries reflects the uncertainty, anxiety, and resentment that characterized the long transitional period between the campaign to de-Judaize belief in Jesus to its realization. Demotion by denigration is a nasty, protracted, and frustrating endeavor. Success is uncertain, slow, and hard fought. Animosity and hatred became deeply ingrained in the hearts and minds of the protagonists.

10. Only after Constantine's patronage did the Pauline-Lukan faction have the political muscle to expedite and impose their ascendancy, but approached hegemonic status only decades after Theodosius's reign (379–395 CE).

The systematic consolidation of Pauline-Lukan thinking into the theological rejection and supersession of the beliefs and traditions of the Jewish founders occurs during the second and third centuries. The arguments elaborated during this period became the bedrock of later anti-Jewish attitudes. An odd mixture of clever, vicious, and bizarre arguments creates a crescendo of incitement that is fully anti-Semitic in tone and pitch. In addition to Chrysostom's infamous sermons, scholars point to the writings of Tertullian, Aphrahat, Ephrem, Cyril, Eusebius, Augustin, and several fourth-century church councils (including the council of Elvira 309 CE, Antioch in 341 CE, and Laodicea in 360 CE) as the most notable contributions to the transition to anti-Semitism. Without this layer of consolidation and systematization, the edifice of hate that looms in the horizon would have had no foundation to stand on. Influential leaders and intellectuals will follow the pathway created by the authors we have surveyed. They will harness the human propensity to fall prey to our darkest instincts in a misguided attempt to sever the influence of opposing interpretations of Jesus's legacy at first, and against other internal and external adversaries thereafter. The disparagement of religious adversaries is found in many religious traditions. However, within the proto-orthodox tradition defamation, vitriol, and abuse of adversaries within and without became a central modus operandi that left a significant footprint in the lore and had a tragic impact on the souls and hearts of believers and on the lives of opponents.

Undifferentiated and genocidal polemics originate in "normal" conflicts that take a "wrong turn." At what point did Pauline-Lukan believers in

Jesus make an unintended and irreversible turn into an ethical dead end? Genocidal tendencies emerge when the disenfranchisement and the dehumanization of internal adversaries or external enemies merge with a secular or religious delegitimizing narrative. Undifferentiated anti-Judaism is an intermediate phenomenon that matures when the proto-orthodox interpretation of Jesus's legacy becomes the imperial faith. It reaches full bloom when the conjectural anti-Judaism of the first century is distilled into a systematic anti-Jewish theology. Only when these elements are in place we cross the threshold and witness the gradual emergence of full-blown anti-Semitism. The evolution of anti-Jewish attitudes, from the fourth century onward, is well documented and is beyond the scope of this work. Suffice it to say that by the fifth century the most ferocious and longest-lasting persecution humans have known was fully in place. The spiral of denigration that starts with the anti-Jewish establishment rhetoric of the Jewish followers of Jesus, and culminates with modern anti-Semitism, is mostly the result of complex socio-religious and socio-theological processes and dynamics that originated within the Jesus movement.

Orthodoxies and Sacred Texts

Orthodoxies emerge to preserve, control, maintain, and dispense religious legitimacy. Dogmatic gatekeepers attempt to perpetuate structures of religious power and legitimacy, despite the fact that humans are not qualified to place limitations on the creator's transcendence, immanence, or on his dialog with his creation. Continuous divine revelation and a continuing dialog of believers with the divine are orthodoxy's worst nightmare. Furthermore, during the twentieth century we have come to suspect that "reading" sacred texts is an intricate phenomenon. It seems that when we consult our sacred lore a cyclical sequence is at work—an interactive process where one's worldview, mindset, and predispositions are the dominant factors in the interpretation that emerges. The religious beliefs, socio-political perspectives, and ethnic heritage that we "bring to the table" are reinforced when we reencounter them in the sacred literature—one of the wells they emanated from. A believer's reading of a sacred text may be seen as a ritual act of reassurance and reinforcement that yields a pre-existent set of beliefs and values.

The anxiety, confusion, enthusiasm, fervor, and exuberance of first- and second-century believers in Jesus are palpable in the canonical and authoritative texts we have surveyed. The dynamics and the processes that we have debated, surveyed, and speculated about were, most often, hidden from the participants. To the protagonists, reality was chaotic, the outcome uncertain. It is only with hindsight and through the filter of time and interpretational meta-narratives that we are able to discern and connect events into processes. From the vantage point of the participants, militancy, factionalism, dissent, turmoil, and uncertainty were the rule. Our relatively organized, systematic, informed, and rational environment would be utterly foreign to them. Reading the authoritative texts we can take the pulse of a religion at the cradle of its birth; we are able to see a major world religion emerging before our eyes. The "push and shove" of theology-in-the-making is fascinating; so is the transition from chaotic creativity to structure and normative orthodoxy.

What If?

Despite the fact that victory does not bestow ethical or divine validation, the "reality" it engenders becomes a template that is hard to shed off.[29] Pondering on alterative historical and theological paths goes against our conceptual "wiring" due to the fact that such exercises threaten the validity of "the world as we know it." Alternative historical scenarios require a "leap of imagination" for they force us to realize how dependent our worldviews (our "reality") are on conjectural outcomes. These scenarios are unsettling for they question, challenge, and threaten our innermost need to see "reality" as the victory of justice over injustice, of good over evil, of right over wrong, of what is true over what is not.

"History" has been, since time immemorial, the legitimating narrative of the victors. Up to the modern era victors had a monopoly on "history" and often reshaped the past to legitimate the present. The suspicion that "history" tends to reflect the agendas of the party that gained the upper hand is only a few decades old. It is no surprise, therefore, that for nineteen hundred years the orthodox account of the emergence of belief in Jesus was accepted as the original, and therefore "true," understanding of his ministry. Whether this outcome was providential or the result of socio-theological processes, we cannot but wonder what might have been the alternatives. Could belief in Jesus have remained Jewish? Could either the Marcionite or the Gnostic worldviews have emerged as the majority view? Would a Pauline-Marcionite, Gnostic, or Jewish Christianity have evolved free of the "conflict between the Synagogue and the Church"?

At the dawn of the twenty-first century there is a growing recognition that unity emerged out of diversity, contrary to the traditional account. It may be said, in a gross oversimplification, that prior to the fourth century theology was local, that Rome became predominantly proto-orthodox, that the communities of Asia Minor tended to go counter-Rome and were inclined toward Marcion, that the Syrian communities were influenced by Judean strands, and that in Egypt there was great sympathy for Gnostic views. Furthermore, we have seen that while the founding faction focused on Torah observance, Pauline believers in Jesus emphasized Jesus's death and resurrection. Other believers emphasized his sayings and teachings or secret knowledge (Gnosis). Some believed that Jesus's death was a sacrifice for the sins of the world (Paulines). Others believed that death is freedom from a world of suffering (Gnostics). Many believers did not see Jesus's death as central to his legacy. Significantly, James and his community, the Q community, and the communities behind the Gospels of Mary, the Savior, Thomas, Truth, and Phillip as well as the Apocryphon of John do not seem to share the Pauline-Synoptic emphasis on Jesus's death, Roman exoneration, and Jewish culpability.

The rediscovery of the second-century Jewish, Pauline-Marcionite and Gnostic variants has momentous consequences for our reconstruction of the evolution of belief in Jesus and invites us to speculate about alternative pathways. The existence of several early forms of belief in Jesus also allows us to speculate that Christianity could have evolved differently. If the New Testament had included only texts recognized as authoritative by the descendants of Jesus's disciples and first followers, it would have an anti-Jewish-establishment tone and would include a demand for strict Torah observance. A Gnostic New Testament is more of an enigma, since Gnosticism, more a trend and a state of mind than a theology, was extremely diverse. We also know with some certainty that the Pauline-Marcionite New Testament would have focused on Paul's Epistles and Luke, purged of "Judaizing" influences. Whether the victory of Marcion could have resulted in a less strident anti-Jewish stance is one of history's greatest enigmas. The descendants of Jesus's disciples and first followers would pose a challenge to a Marcionite Christianity, but the supersessionary impulses behind the crusade to lay claim to their identity and lore would not be there to fuel the anti-Jewish flame. By rejecting the Jewish heritage of the founding fathers, a Marcionite Christianity may have avoided the anti-Jewish trajectory inherent in the ambivalent Pauline-Lukan denigrate-but-appropriate model. Moreover, "Marcion's insistence on the literal interpretation of the Hebrew Scriptures potentially created a bond of understanding between him and at least some Jews that his opponents could not have achieved."[30]

Whereas the Pauline-Lukan faction claimed to supersede the beliefs of the founding faction and strived to demote them from their position as the guardians and interpreters of Jesus's legacy, Pauline-Marcionites and most Gnostic believers rejected their beliefs and traditions altogether.[31] This critical difference may explain the growth of more dangerous strands of anti-Judaism among the Pauline-Lukan.[32] Whereas Pauline-Marcionites and Gnostics recognized that by rejecting the beliefs and traditions of the founding fathers they were creating new interpretations of Jesus's ministry, the proto-orthodox strove to vest themselves as the rightful inheritors of the Jewish founders, setting them on the supersessionary trajectory that led to an ethical dead end. Whereas rejection-separation leaves ground for separate and respectful coexistence, claims to appropriation and substitution do not. They set in motion the sequence that led to the dead end of anti-Semitism:

Appropriation > supersession > disenfranchisement > persecution

Realizing that Christianity "as we know it" emerges out of one of several strands is also helpful in understanding where things may have gone wrong in the Jewish-Christian relationship. Is it possible that a non-orthodox Christianity, free of the need to supersede Judaism and to lay claim to its heritage, may have parted company with it and may have avoided the anti-Jewish dead end?

Furthermore, the incorporation of cultural and theological precursors does not need be adversarial, derogatory, or dehumanizing. Some ancient rhetoric was vitriolic, but not all ancients denigrated their precursors (see the benign integration of Greek culture by the Romans and of Hinduism by Buddhism). Moreover, the life stories of Jesus and the Buddha share striking similarities. Both aimed at reforming their native cultures (Judaism and Hinduism). Both were deeply touched by the human condition (poverty, suffering, and death) and both championed mercy and love. Interestingly, their legacies were extraordinarily successful among strangers but were rejected by the majority of their brethren. Christianity and Buddhism also differ significantly: whereas Christianity forged an alliance with power and despotism, Buddhism by and large shun power and wealth. Christianity became exclusivist and confrontational. Buddhism, by and large, emphasized inclusiveness and non-confrontation. Whereas Christianity built an edifice of disparagement and contempt toward Judaism, Buddhism incorporated the Hindu tradition without a discourse of denigration or supersession.

Exclusivism and Militancy

As it pertains to deciphering the evolution of the anti-Jewish strand, the traditional account of the origins of belief in Jesus emerges as a myth that:

1. Legitimates the de-Judaizing of belief in Jesus and projects a myth about a quasi-consensual transfer of leadership and of legitimacy from Jesus's disciples and first followers to later orthodoxy.
2. Obscures the marginalizing, the disenfranchisement, and the eventual persecution of the descendants of those chosen by Jesus to be the guardians of his legacy.

3. Justifies the claims to the appropriation of the identity and to the lore of the Jewish faction and to the supersession of their beliefs and traditions.
4. Externalizes and transforms a conflict among believers in Jesus into a conflict between "Judaism" and "Christianity."
5. Successfully deflects questions about the legitimacy of the ascendancy of the Pauline-Lukan mindset.

Proto-orthodox attitudes toward the descendants of Jesus's disciples and first followers, and toward their beliefs and traditions, evolved gradually during the four centuries that culminated in orthodox ascendancy. The subtext, the implied message, embedded in the proto-orthodox lore regarding the founding fathers seems to reflect a phased and escalating antagonism that seems to have intensified along the following hypothetical sequence:

From "you have no right to impose Judaism on us," to
"we are rightful followers of Jesus too," to
"You are not the only legitimate guardians of Jesus's legacy," to
"You misunderstood Jesus's message, you abandoned him," to
"You are no longer the legitimate guardians of Jesus's legacy," to
"We are the exclusive interpreters of Jesus's legacy," to
"you are no longer the 'New Israel'—we are," to
"we are now YHWH's chosen."[33]

Whereas the descendants of the founding faction and the Pauline-Marcionites had distinct theological doctrines, the Pauline-Lukan faction championed a compromise—not an obvious recipe for fanaticism or militancy. Militancy, exclusivism, and triumphalism are puzzling characteristics for they do not fit the accommodating, consensus-building, and mid-ground positioning of a compromise creed. It seems intuitively sound to expect that ideological and religious militancy would emerge out of clear, distinct, and unequivocal formulations and tenets, not from a faction promoting a compromise. Furthermore, fashioning a compromise without the political power to impose it would seem to call for coalition building and accommodation—not extremism and militancy. How did the champions of compromise infuse their grassroots with the intensity and the zeal that came to characterize the proto-orthodox? Did extremism evolve as a defensive reaction by first- and second-century Pauline-Lukan believers who were chastised by their opponents for trying to be "all things to all people"? Can militancy be a dissonance reduction mechanism in situations of extreme uncertainty and chaos?

We have noted that the ascent of the Pauline-Lukan faction to preeminence lasted at least three hundred years. This protracted struggle reflects the fact that, until the fourth century, they did not have the tools, or the legitimacy, to impose their theological outlook and eradicate the traditions of their opponents. During this intermediate period, they had to limit themselves to the low efficiency and slow impact of verbal abuse, marginalizing, and disenfranchisement. This limited arsenal led to a protracted and inconclusive struggle where tempers often flared and resentment often reached the point of explosion. Lacking political or military power to attain theological ascendancy, the proto-orthodox used a peculiar mixture of militancy, exclusivism, "negative campaigning," coalition building, compromise, and accommodation. This seemingly counterintuitive "militant compromise" was successful by infusing the grassroots with enthusiasm and fervor, while at the same time creating an accommodating compromise that came to be rightfully known as the "Via Media." However, success came at the cost of an eclectic theology requiring substantial harmonizing. It is no surprise, therefore, that theologians have wrestled since the fourth century with the fault lines between diverse and differing, inherited and appropriated, theological traditions. The extent to which theological positions reflect the implied or stated interests of the protagonists is nothing short of remarkable. Regardless of one's position on whether theology is somewhat influenced, strongly influenced, or determined by socio-political circumstances, the apparent synchronization of these phenomena has accompanied us throughout. Socio-theological agendas and theological outlooks emerge as suspiciously symbiotic and interconnected. We cannot but marvel at the extent to which the Pauline-Lukan crusade for ascendancy seems to have promoted and nurtured the ever-growing tradition of emotional and theological anti-Judaism.

As we see the edifice of anti-Judaism grow before our eyes, it is difficult to restrain our outrage at the fact that vicious slander and defamation remained sacrosanct, authoritative, and influential for so long. Knowing their subsequent impact on attitudes toward Jews and toward Judaism, the polemical rampages of second and third century are hard to endure. Moreover, this derogatory and inflammatory hyperbole is abhorrent and unnecessary. It is abhorrent due to the fact that it contains the rationale for the future disenfranchisement and martyrdom of defenseless Jews. It is unnecessary due to the fact that integration of preceding lore does not need be derogatory, adversarial, or supersessionary.

Miscellaneous Disclaimers

A note of caution is appropriate: socio-theological processes are complex, protracted, interdependent, and elusive. The processes that we have attempted to identify and decipher are fog-like. "In real time," evolution and the trajectory ahead were unclear and uncertain. Long-term processes that are identifiable to us in hindsight were hidden from the protagonists. Only in retrospect can we sketch an outline for this rather intricate story. A complex reality where multiple protagonists and themes interact in a fluid and inconclusive manner for some three hundred years seems to be the best depiction of reality-on-the-ground as reflected in the textual corpus before us. During the early decades of the Jesus movement the internal divide between the Jewish followers of Jesus and mainstream Judaism looms large (i.e., the adversaries are specific groups within Judaism: the high priests, the Pharisees, the elders, and the scribes). During the last decades of the first century the epicenter shifts and points to growing opposition to the beliefs and traditions of the founding faction among Gentile believers. In the earlier layers the ordeal and the perspective of the Jewish followers of Jesus left footprints in the texts. As the movement becomes increasingly Gentile, the ordeal and the perspective of recent Gentile converts dominates the scene.

It is also possible that projection and externalization onto the inter-religious arena, and the emergence of the misperception about the existence of a "conflict between Judaism and Christianity," may have started earlier than implied by the trajectory suggested here. It is plausible and probable that the blurring, the fusion, and the confusion between "internal" and "external" Jews and between Judaism "within" and Judaism "without" may have started earlier than implied by my presentation. We can expect that in towns or regions where communities of Jews and of Jewish followers of Jesus coexisted, Gentile believers would maintain a clearer distinction of the two. In areas where Gentile believers would encounter only one type of "Jews" or none at all, the fusion, and the confusion would occur earlier and would be more pronounced.

Moreover, we should be hesitant to reconstruct a socio-theological reality by projecting a partial and posterior selection of texts onto the canvas of reality. In addition, the Lukan faction was not monolithic. We can distinguish moderate (Justin and Theophilous),[34] intermediate (Tertullian, Origen), and extreme (Melito, Chrysostom) anti-Judaism. Significantly, the Lukan leaders of the second and third century were defensive and abusive toward all their adversaries within, not just toward the "Ioudaioi." Indeed, their rampages against Pagans, Pauline-Marcionites, and Gnostics and against any and all adversaries and enemies thereafter, were also intense.

After Constantine

The New Testament is a canonical corpus that reflects significant underlying dissonances and differences that originate in the diversity of the early Jesus movement. The current canon first emerges in a list compiled by Athanasius, the bishop of Alexandria (*ca.* 367 CE). The later embrace of Athanasius's list and its eventual canonization embedded in the tradition

a large number of discrepancies, inconsistencies, and tensions that reverberate throughout the discourse to this day. Theological narratives require
centuries to evolve into coherent and harmonious discourses. Constantine's
patronage of Christianity catapulted a persecuted, militant, and exclusivist
religion-in-the-making to the center stage of the mightiest empire of the
era. More an agglomeration of incompatible, still evolving, and competing
versions of belief in Jesus than a mature theological worldview—the early
fourth-century strands of belief in Jesus were forced into a crucible that
demanded a compromise. At the Council of Nicea the divisions among the
different factions were deep. The leaders of the church had to be sequestered to force them to reach an agreement on a basic statement of belief.
Coerced by Constantine to present a united front and lured by the rapid
growth brought about by his patronage, Christian theologians and leaders
were pressured into crafting a clear and unanimous creed.

Only after Constantine's patronage and Theodosius's Christianizing of
the empire was "Orthodoxy" able to enforce its hegemony in more efficient
and expeditious ways. Only then will the orthodox yield real might and will
be able to persecute adversaries within more efficiently. As orthodoxy consolidated its ascendancy and its alliance with the mighty and the powerful,
a persecutory demeanor gradually matured. It progressed from the rancor of
peer infighting, to more efficient and emotionally detached mechanisms of
dissent control. This later phase, when "heresy" within and enemies without
are dealt with the sword and the power of empire, is beyond the scope of
this work.

History instructs us about the consequences of disenfranchising, delegitimating, or dehumanizing members of national, religious, or ethnic
communities. The anti-Jewish bias that we have tracked throughout was
the precursor, the enabler, and the facilitator of the endemic persecution
endured by the Jewish people since the fifth century. Spanning fifteen
hundred years, Jewish-Christian coexistence has had many highs and lows,
within an overall context of cyclical but ingrained anti-Judaism. From
Theodosius I (379–395 CE) onward, the Pauline-orthodox, now Orthodox
Christianity, imposed ever-increasing restrictions and burdens on the Jews:

- Jews were prohibited from proselytizing.
- Jews forced to convert to Christianity were not allowed to return to
  Judaism.
- Capital punishment was imposed for marrying a Jew.
- Jews were excluded from public office and the military.
- Special taxes were imposed on the Jewish population.
- Building of synagogues was forbidden.
- Jews were forced to celebrate Christian holy days.
- Jews were forced to listen to Christian evangelizing sermons.
- There were restrictions on any type of religious fraternizing.

Between 465 and 694, some 20 councils issued rulings regarding relations with Jews. Among their decrees[35]:

- Marriages between Jews and Christians were forbidden (Councils of Orleans, 533 and 538; Clermont, 535; Toledo, 589 and 633).
- Jews and Christians were forbidden to eat together (Councils of Vannes, 465; Agde, 506; Epaone, 517; Orleans, 538; Macon, 583; Clichy, 626–7).
- Jews were banned from public office (Councils of Clermont, 535; Toledo, 589; Paris, 614–5; Clichy, 626–7; Toledo, 633).
- Jews were prohibited from owning Christian slaves (Councils of Orleans, 538 and 541; Macon, 583; Toledo, 589, 633, and 656; Clichy, 626–7; Chalon-sur-Saone, *ca.* 650).
- Jews were forbidden from appearing in public during Easter (Councils of Orleans, 538; Macon, 583) and from working on Sunday (Council of Narbonne, 589).

From Theodosius onward, the coping mechanisms of European Jewry were, for the most part, defensive and escapist. Emigration, false conversion, and withdrawal from reality were commonplace. Jewish creativity and energy found release in the unlimited freedom of religious learning and in esoteric and mystical speculation. Submersion in religious learning and in the esoteric world of Kabbalah mysticism offered freedom from a world gone mad. By the seventh century, the anti-Jewish policies implemented from Theodosius onward brought about the almost complete de-Judaizing of Europe, a massive ethnic cleansing that has been largely erased from "history." The fate of the largest minority in the Roman Empire is largely unknown. Of the 5–6 million Jews living in the Roman Empire at the dawn of the Common Era, 2–3 million lived in Europe. By the seventh century, the Jewish population in the European lands of the Roman Empire plummeted to a meager remnant. How did they disappear? By what means was this "cleansing" achieved? The virulent anti-Jewish incitement pouring from all corners of European society does not leave much room for doubt as to the means. Most would have had to choose between forced conversion, expulsion, or worse. This cleansing and the trajectory below have been largely erased from Christendom's historical memory, creating a vacuum that has enabled the myth about the later origins of "modern anti-Semitism."

For the period after the seventh century, in addition to countless regional, local, and individual acts of disparagement, discrimination, and persecution, four large-scale cycles are identifiable beyond the initial de-Judaizing of Europe:

1. The French Carolingian and the British Anglo-Saxon monarchies, frozen in the Dark Ages, tried to emulate the economic success of the

Jewish-Muslim coexistence and invited Jews to settle in their midst. This cycle ended when, a few centuries later, the Jews were expelled and their property seized as the French (1182 and 1392) and British (1290) emerging elites started to see them as competitors.

2. Throughout Western Europe the era of the Crusades witnessed large-scale massacres of Jewish communities by mobs turned murderous by religious frenzy induced from the pulpits.

3. The Muslim conquest of Spain ushered a period of Jewish renaissance under Muslim patronage that lasted until the Christian conquest of Spain, resulting in the expulsion or forced conversion of all Jews (1492, from Portugal in 1497).

4. During the sixteenth and seventeenth centuries, Eastern European and German principalities, aware of the benefits that the Jews had brought to England, France, and Spain, invited them to dwell in their midst. This cycle ended a few centuries later with the Holocaust.

Summary

Throughout our journey we did encounter a variety of midway manifestations of the gravitation of the Lukan faction toward the theological strategy of appropriation-supersession. It seems that at first the tensions in the Jesus movement, between Jewish and Gentile believers, although present—did not take center stage. Initially, recent Gentile converts would be immersed in the excitement and enthusiasm that seems to have characterized the encounter with a universal faith based on individual belief. However, as time passed, new Gentile converts would have met the descendants of Jesus's disciples and first followers and their Gentile sympathizers in the public arena, and would become aware that they had been inducted into a faction at odds with the founding fathers of the movement, a volatile situation that required a dissonance-reducing narrative. In these circumstances, Pauline communities needed an account of the genesis of belief in Jesus that would bestow legitimacy to believers who embraced the Kerygma of the cross and resurrection, but rejected the beliefs and traditions embraced by Jesus and by those chosen by him to be the guardians of his legacy. Gentile believers yearned for legitimacy as rightful believers in Jesus and needed a reassuring foundational narrative and a description of their faith's origin that would address their continuity-discontinuity vis-à-vis the founding faction. The Gospel of Mark seems to have been crafted with these needs in mind. Disciples and family members that "do not understand," and disciples that "forsake Jesus," seem to have emerged to address the emotional needs of Gentile communities experiencing anxiety and doubt due to their estrangement from the Jewish founders. The implicit message: the ancestors of the Jewish followers of Jesus did not understand Jesus's legacy and betrayed him. All Jews, to the inclusion of the Jewish followers of Jesus, have forfeited God's favor. Therefore, they are not rightful custodians of Jesus legacy. Believers don't have to follow their beliefs and traditions to be rightful followers of Jesus. Gentiles are God's new chosen.

As time passed, tensions within the Jesus movement between Gentiles supporting the rejection of the beliefs and traditions of the founding fathers and Gentiles favoring a close affiliation with them, mounted to new highs. The schism erupted onto the surface. A more effective, comprehensive, and detailed response was required. Facing an uphill struggle for legitimacy vis-à-vis the descendants of Jesus's disciples and first followers, lacking a mature narrative, and standing on a still-evolving theology, Pauline-Lukan believers seem to have gradually gravitated toward a strategy built on the belittling of the disciples and on the denigration of the beliefs and traditions of their descendants. They also opted for the subversion-appropriation of elements, themes, and motifs quarried from their adversaries' lore. In need of a polemical arsenal to sever the influence that the descendants of the founding fathers had over some Gentiles, the de-Judaizing camp found in the lore of their opponents a throve of anti-Jewish-establishment stones that they could use to denigrate Judaism—the pillar on which the Jewish faction stood. By decontextualizing the Hebrew Scriptures and subverting-appropriating the founders' identity and anti-Jewish-establishment lore, and by subverting-appropriating the Jewish traditions of prophetic exhortation and self-criticism—Pauline leaders and intellectuals crafted a strategy that, although ultimately successful in de-Judaizing belief in Jesus, resulted in a protracted and rancorous struggle that lasted more than two centuries.

What began as the seemingly harmless denigration of the disciples aimed at defending the right of Gentiles to be rightful followers of Jesus without having to be Jews, gradually gravitated toward an exclusivist and supersessionary mindset. Expanding on Mark's deprecation of the disciples, and on the supersessionary foundation provided by Hebrews and Barnabas, Pauline-Lukan authors claimed that their opponents' understanding of Jesus's life and ministry, anchored in Judaism, was erroneous. The true meaning of Israelite history was to be understood and deciphered by non-Jews. Throughout the lore, authors obsessed with "the Jewish question" argued that "the Jews" are sinful, irredeemable, misunderstand their religious heritage, lost or never had the covenant, lost God's favor, and were no longer his chosen. The logic behind this strategy seems to be that if the Israelites were incompetent to properly interpret their own theological heritage, the Jewish faction could not understand Jesus's legacy either. The architects of the Pauline appropriation-supersession edifice maintained that Gentiles could not reinvent themselves outside the legitimacy inherent in the founding fathers, as Marcion and most Gnostics argued, and did set the markers of the theological construct that was to be the central anchor of "orthodoxy." This construct included three elements: (a) to accept the Jewish meta-narrative; (b) to gut out most of its institutions, beliefs, and traditions; and (c) to appropriate the remaining narrative to vest a non-Jewish edifice with legitimacy and antiquity. The tensions and ambiguities inherent in the Lukan appropriate-supersede answer to the continuity-discontinuity dilemma vis-à-vis the founding fathers triggered the emergence of the appropriation-supersession phenomenon, with horrific consequences. The anti-Jewish arguments, themes, motifs, sediments, and residues contained in the texts authored during this period are the building blocks of the anti-Jewish strand and the seeds of later anti-Semitism.

Afterthoughts

1. The term "anti-Semitic" should not be applied to the intent of authors, editors, and compilers of the New Testament texts due to the fact that these texts were authored within the relatively closed universe of the Jesus movement. Judaism was not a participant in these debates, nor was it the intended adversary. Moreover, the authors did not intend, nor anticipate, the consequences of their campaign to de-Judaize belief in Jesus and to appropriate the identity and lore of the descendants of Jesus's disciples and first followers. These early Gentile believers in Jesus must be exonerated of anti-Semitic intent despite the fact that the anti-Jewish strand embedded in the canonical and authoritative lore was the foundation, the precursor, and the enabler of what was to come. Furthermore, "anti-Semitism" is a nineteenth-century term associated with later socio-political realities, and should not be applied retroactively.[36] Therefore, and despite the heart's ambivalence, we must exonerate the writers and the early compilers and editors of the canonical and the authoritative texts from anti-Semitic intent. However, our exoneration of the authors' intent must be highly qualified due to the fact that these texts, permeated with the intense emotions that characterized the protracted effort to de-Judaize belief in Jesus, enabled and nurtured anti-Semitism.

2. Our focus on the unintended journey from polemic against the Jewish founders of the Jesus movement to anti-Semitism should not divert our attention from the generic and universal nature of the processes that underwrite human marches that culminate in ethical dead ends. This is a recurring danger in all human communities—amply attested by the dismaying persistence of this curse. The religions that tower over our world are idiosyncratic and carry in their lore the "debris" of particular trajectories, choices, and past conflicts—making them vulnerable to adversarial polemic.

3. Christianity is a religion of faith, love, grace, salvation, and redemption. The vast majority of believers in Jesus have no anti-Jewish or anti-Semitic inclinations. Furthermore, many of today's believers in Jesus consider Jews to be God's chosen people and have but the warmest attitudes toward them. Therefore, it is intriguing, perplexing, and noteworthy that most are unaware of the deep and pervasive presence of the anti-Jewish strand in their theology, culture, and lore. The implicit and explicit crescendo of anti-Jewish polemic that accompanies the tradition seems to elude the ears and hearts of most believers, despite lifetimes of exposure to the disparagement and to the vilification of Judaism, its customs, and traditions. For most, whose life in Christ is one of loving kindness and mercy, awakening to the anti-Jewish bent that permeates the canonical and authoritative lore is a troubling and disconcerting experience.[37] For Jews, the fact that disparagement, abuse, dismissal, and trespassing have been deemed appropriate for the exhortation, edification, and inspiration of the faithful is hard to accept or comprehend.

4. Although religions are self-referential discourses that do not require external validation, and Torah observance and the covenant between the Israelites and their God are not subject to validation by non-Jews, the anti-Jewish strand embedded in the Christian lore requires our attention and demands our concern. Sacred scriptures are the depositories of our collective engagement with the divine as understood through the fog of human imperfections and limitations. Imperfect hearts and minds can only produce imperfect vehicles of faith. Therefore, it is not surprising that believers were involved in religious debates, that tempers flared, and that the literature we surveyed was written. It is, however, deeply disappointing and troubling that religious leaders sanctified, exacerbated, and perpetuated the attitudes and emotions that accompanied the contentious evolution of belief in Jesus. For almost two millennia anti-Jewish attitudes were nurtured, deemed worthy, and edifying. The consequences of the unintended journey that ensued are sobering, their scope difficult to grasp.

During the last decades of the twentieth century, significant progress was made in the Christian march away from anti-Judaism. Although many scholars and theologians are engaged in the effort to define a positive Christian theology, free from the anti-Jewish scaffold, the great excitement of the first phase has subsided, while the most difficult tasks are still ahead. Replacing the "over and against" language of Christianity with a positive theology that would let go of the anti-Jewish prosthesis is no small task that has encountered a traditionalist backlash. The trend initiated by Vatican II has stalled after several decades of great expectations and significant achievements. It is not yet clear whether entrenched opposition to change or a wider acknowledgment of the validity of other paths to the divine will prevail.

In the past, believers could rightly claim innocent ignorance about the existence and the consequences of the anti-Jewish strand. However, twenty-first-century theologians, religious leaders, and believers seem to be poised to determine for all times, by action or by default, whether the anti-Jewish strand that lies dormant in their tradition reflects the spirit of God or the human shortcomings and imperfections of the authors and editors of the texts. My deep admiration for the sincere and awe-inspiring efforts of the last 40 years and my awareness of the excruciating difficulties ahead do not change the fact that Jewish lives, and the Christian soul, remain at risk. Although the anti-Jewish mindset has been weakened, the hosts of hate have not been eradicated, they have been partially subdued. This grave danger to the Christian soul and to Jewish lives dictates a decisive stand. Without it, the troublesome footprint of resentment toward adversaries that were Jews will continue to reverberate and point in the wrong direction. Regardless of whether the specific causal relationships suggested by this monograph do exist, the anti-Jewish strand remains intact in the texts. As long as the anti-Jewish narrative is available to nurture the fire, this ever-present danger may resurface, as exemplified by the four cycles of anti-Jewish recurrence surveyed earlier. The cyclical and recurring nature of the anti-Jewish phenomenon and the human propensity to fall prey to discourses of incitement must lead us to the somber assessment that despite great strides, recurrence is still the most probable outcome. History teaches us that when root causes are not eradicated, recurrence is the rule rather than the exception.

We must acknowledge that the "unintended journey" of early Gentile believers in Jesus will remain somewhat veiled and opaque. However, within the possible outcomes, the proposition that the anti-Jewish strand originated in a struggle between followers of Jesus with Jewish and Gentile inclinations and affiliations is deflationary. If explored further and found worthy, this meta-narrative may contribute to reduce the tragic and harmful impact that the anti-Jewish strand has had on the reading and understanding of the authoritative texts.

Reader comments, critiques, and reviews are welcome at:
anunintendedjourney@gmail.com

Appendix I : Paul in Modern Scholarship

The Traditional Paul

> Thus not only was he the first to lay down expressly and distinctly the principle of Christian universalism as a thing essentially opposed to Jewish particularism...We cannot call his conversion...anything but a miracle; and the miracle appears all the greater when we remember that in this revulsion of his consciousness he broke through the barriers of Judaism and rose out of the particularism of Judaism into the universal idea of Christianity.[1]

> In the epistle to the Romans Paul argued that the hardening and blinding of the Jews were included within God's purpose for the salvation of the world. It was a temporary divine dispensation to enable the Gentiles to hear and accept the gospel and so to stimulate the Jews, in their turn, to claim their rightful place within the true Israel of the Church.

> The obedience of faith abrogates the Law as a mediator for salvation, sees through the perversion of understanding it as a principle of achievement.[2]

> The alleged aim of the Law, that is has been given for life, and its alleged effect, that it creates sin and death.[3]

The Revised Paul

Paul's alleged anti-Judaism has been under intense scholarly scrutiny during the last three decades:

> It is the task of exegesis after Auschwitz precisely to expose the explicit or implicit anti-Judaism inherent in the tradition, including the New Testament itself. It is a task in which I have willingly participated, and when I began I expected to find anti-Judaism particularly present in Paul. That is not, however, the conclusion to which my own studies have led me.[4]

When his letters came to be read by Gentiles who little understood Judaism, the misinterpretation became almost inevitable.[5]

Why letters specifically addressed to Gentiles should have been understood as opposing Judaism is not hard to explain.[6]

Christian theologians have often in the past developed a theology of Judaism on the basis of Pauline epistles. Judaism was whatever Paul opposed or even the opposite of everything Paul said positively. Only in recent times have the scholarly maxim "ad fonts" and the religious injunction not to bear false witness been combined in the ideal of writing about Judaism solely from Jewish sources, read from the perspective of those sources. After the work especially of E. P. Sanders, it will never be possible to return to old habits. Whatever positions Paul was opposing, none of them could be called Judaism as such.

How, then, can twenty centuries of interpreters be so wrong? The answer is that the misreading is not only understandable but inevitable, given the framework within which Paul has been read in the time following his death. When people lost sight of the immediate circumstances of the letters and began to assume that his opponents were Jews outside the Jesus movement instead of other apostles within, when Paul was read through the lens of Acts and the New Testament, when Paul's intense eschatological worldview had to be abandoned, then the old traditional reading of Paul became inevitable. It is the result of reading Paul within a distant, alien framework, rather than the apostle's own, and of forgetting that Paul is the apostle to the Gentiles and is dealing with Gentiles and their new status in Christ.[7]

When we lose sight of the immediate settings of Paul's letters and assume-with all subsequent readers-that his audience and opponents were Jews rather than anti-Pauline apostles within the Jesus-movement. When we read Paul through the lens of the book of Acts and the New Testament canon. When we read back into Paul the rejection-replacement and triumphalist theology of early (and later) Christianity. When we ignore the intense eschatological framework of Paul's thought and action. When we read Paul with no eye or ear for his rhetorical strategies. When we come to Paul with a preconceived notion of Judaism that is an unrecognizable parody of historical reality. When we discard efforts to invent a "new" Paul due to the fact of their "fateful consequences for the whole of Christianity." In short, when we read Paul within alien frameworks, the old view becomes not just explicable but inevitable.[8]

In the end, we might decide to conclude that Paul was wrong, period. And put him aside altogether. But for many readers this is not an attractive option. He occupies more than one half of the Christian Bible. For some this has meant leaving Christianity altogether and moving into a post-Christian stance. For others, however, it has seemed impossible to shake the Pauline foundations of Christianity without destroying the faith completely.[9]

The loss of Paul's historical and cultural context and the concerns of later Christianity led to a different Paul.[10]

The supposed objection to Jewish self-righteousness is as absent from Paul's letters as self-righteousness itself is from Jewish literature.[11]

Paul writes to Gentile Christians, dealing with Gentile problems, foremost among which was the right for Gentiles qua Gentiles, without adopting the Torah of Israel, to full citizenship in the people of God. It is remarkable that in the endless discussion of Paul's understanding of the Law, few have asked what a first-century Jew would have thought of the Law as it relates to Gentiles.[12]

For Paul, Jesus was neither a new Moses nor the Messiah, nor the climax of the climax of the history of God's dealing with Israel, but the fulfillment of God's promises concerning the Gentiles, and this is what he accused the Jews of not recognizing. Paul never accused the Jews of lacking zeal for the Torah, and certainly not of legalism, but rather of disobedience to the new revelation he (Paul) had received.[13]

I will argue that Paul need not, indeed cannot, be read according to the contradictionists and that he is entirely innocent of all charges lodged against him by his critics:

1. He is not the father of anti-Judaism.
2. He was not the inventor of the rejection-replacement theory.
3. He did not repudiate the Law of Moses.
4. He did not argue that God had rejected Israel.
5. His enemies were not Jews outside the Jesus-movement but competing apostles within.
6. He did not expect Jews to find their salvation through Jesus Christ.[14]

"Paul thus speaks not to the exclusion of Judaism, but rather to the inclusion of Gentiles. Christ does not abrogate Torah. Rather, God has a double covenant with humanity, to the Jew first and also the Greek; through the Torah with Israel; and, now that the end of the ages is upon humankind, through Christ with the Gentiles...Scholars need neither endorse a caricature of Judaism nor invent reasons rooted in Paul's psyche to make sense of his hostile statements: he directs them against Judaizers, not Judaism per-se. Also, it accounts for his seeming contradictions...This interpretation allows Paul to be a first-century Jew rather than a misplaced fifth-century Augustinian, sixteenth-century Lutheran, or twentieth-century existentialist theologian. That is its great strength. Additionally—an advantage in this age of increased ecumenicalism—it clears Paul of the charge of Anti-Semitism and so makes him an attractive figure theologically. But can we responsibly "reinvent" an ecumenical Paul?"[15]

The question for Paul is not mainly the significance of the Torah for Jews but its significance for Jesus-believing Gentiles...The nasty things Paul says about the Law are intended to discourage Gentiles from embracing the Law and are thoroughly misunderstood if they are read as expressions of Paul's opinion about the value of the Law for Jews.[16]

for Paul, as for other Jews, the Law was and remained valid for Jews.[17]

Paul does not envision Israel's eschatological salvation as its absorption into the Gentile-Christian Church.[18]

Loss of Paul's historical and cultural context and concerns of later Christianity led to a different Paul.[19]

Paul Consistent or Erratic

His reaction to the possibility that his Galatian converts might accept the Law was so forceful that one expects him to have had a clear and decisive reason for responding as he did. And yet, to repeat, there is no agreement among scholars as to what that reason was, and still less is there agreement as to how to understand the relationship of his numerous statements about the Law to the position which he took in the Galatian controversy. What is interesting is how far Paul was from denying anything that he held deeply, even when he could not maintain all his convictions at once without both anguish and finally a lack of logic.[20]

Paul was a theologian in that he reflected on his gospel, but he was not a systematic theologian, not even when he wrote Romans. His theology is not his religion, but his own effort to express it in the circumstances which the various letters reflect. Further, I view Paul as a coherent thinker, despite the unsystematic nature of his thought and the variations in formulation.[21]

I happen to believe that there is, at least sometimes, a significant congruence between words and intentions, but I cannot prove this. In any case, dealing with the words alone is already a difficult task, as we shall see ... we need to be able to admit, in the end, that he was self-contradictory, inconsistent, unclear, irrelevant, and even wrong. But the words in the end are important.[22]

Charges of inconsistency and self contradiction have hounded Paul from antiquity to the present ... It is only fair to admit that Paul himself must bear partial responsibility for the problem.[23]

Paul's hermeneutic of the gospel is so determined by the contingent situations he addresses that the coherent and abiding elements of his gospel cannot be abstracted from their interplay with these various contingencies.[24]

The whole history of the interpretation of Paul ... is a single chain of misunderstandings.[25]

I can see only one way: contradictions and tensions have to be accepted as constant features of Paul's theology ... Paul's thought on the Law is full of difficulties and inconsistencies ... Paul the theologian is a less coherent and less convincing thinker than is commonly assumed.[26]

The Lutheran Paul has been replaced by an idiosyncratic Paul who in arbitrary and irrational manner turns his face against the glory and greatness of Judaism's covenant theology and abandons Judaism simply due to the fact it is not Christianity.[27]

If the choice lies between supposing that Paul was confused and contradictory and supposing that his text has been commented on and enlarged, I have no hesitation in choosing the second.[28]

Paul's thought is "so obscure, so complicated, so disjointed, that it is hard to see how Paul could have exerted such influence on his contemporaries."[29]

The man whose reputation was far from good in the Christian communities, who was considered a trouble-maker and someone whose views were vacillating and therefore unreliable had every reason to make clear his political position.[30]

Contradictions in Paul require an urgent solution.[31]

Nevertheless, I have come the conclusion that there is no single unity which adequately accounts for every statement about the Law. Against those who argue in favor of mere inconsistency, however, I would argue that Paul held a limited number of basic convictions which, when applied to different problems, led him to say different things about the Law.[32]

Notes

Personal Introduction

1. On the impact of this verse on Christian anti-Semitism, see Samuel Sandmel, *Anti-Semitism in The New Testament?* (1978), 66.
2. Christopher Leighton, in his introduction to N. Beck's *Mature Christianity, The Recognition and Repudiation of the Anti-Jewish Polemic of the New Testament* (1994).
3. "Those pages of history that Jews have committed to memory are the very ones that have been torn from Christian (and secular) history books." E. Flannery, *The Anguish of the Jews: Twenty-Three Centuries of Anti-Semitism* (1985).
4. "It is a fact well known in human history—and especially in the history of religions: that sayings which originally meant one thing later on were interpreted to mean something else, something which was felt to be more relevant to human conditions of later times." Stendahl Krister, *Paul among Jews and Gentiles* (1976), 94.

Preview

1. *Telos* (Greek)—end, result. History evolves in a purposeful (*telic*), rather than chaotic, manner.

The Protagonists

1. For detailed discussion, see p. 154.
2. For detailed discussion, see p. 157.
3. Stephen G. Wilson, ed., *Anti-Judaism in Early Christianity*, vol. 2 (1986), 48; and D. P. Efroymson, *Tertullian's Anti-Judaism and its Role in Theology* (1976), 112–146.
4. For detailed discussion, see p. 156.
5. The traditional kerygma, the basic Pauline formula of belief as reflected in I Cor. 15.3 and its variants in cf. Rom. 3.25; 5.9; Eph. 2.13; I Pet. 1.19; Rev. 1.5; 5.9; 7.14.
6. Clayton N. Jefford, *Reading the Apostolic Fathers* (1996), 55.

7. P. J. Donahue, *Jewish Christianity in the Letters of Ignatius* (1978), 87, identifies the "heretics" Ignatius is fighting against as Christian-Jews.
8. See Hans Jonas, *The Gnostic Religion* (1958), 31–46; B. Layton, *The Rediscovery of Gnosticism* (1980); Elaine Pagels, *The Gnostic Gospels* (1943); Kurt Rudolph, *Gnosis: The Nature & History of Gnosticism* (1987); and Bart Ehrman, *Lost Christianities: The Battle for Scripture and the Faiths We Never Knew* (2003).
9. Michael Williams, *Rethinking Gnosticism* (1996) for a general discussion of the topic. For detailed discussion, see p. 159.

1   The Anti-Jewish Strand in the New Testament

1. N. Beck, *Mature Christianity in the 21st Century* (1994).
2. Readers may want to keep these sources in mind, as a reference, as we decipher the anti-Jewish strand.
3. Selection of verses found in Ed Evans and Donald Hagner, *Anti-Semitism and Early Christianity* (1993), 1–3.
4. For a recent review of "Q research," see Darrell Bock, in *Rethinking the Synoptic Problem*, David Alan Black and David R. Beck, eds. (2001); Christopher Tuckett, *Q and the History of Early Christianity* (1996), Chapter 1, for a review of alternative views on the Synoptic problem. Also Helmut Koester, *Ancient Christian Gospels* (1990).

2   The Anti-Jewish Strand—The First Years

1. In John, Jesus's ministry seems to include three Passovers. See James D. G. Dunn, *Christianity in the Making—Vol 1—Jesus Remembered* (2003), 165–167.
2. On early diversity, see R. E. Brown, "Not Jewish Christianity and Gentile Christianity but Types of Jewish/Gentile Christianity," *CBQ 45*, January 1983.
3. In this monograph: anti-Judaic = the early stages of the emergence of anti-Jewish sentiment, the period before the rhetoric intensified and became ingrained in the cultural fabric of some communities of Gentile believers in Jesus. For further elaboration, see Chapters 4–8.
4. On the pre-Synoptic era, see J. S. Kloppenborg, *Excavating Q: The History and Setting of the Sayings Gospel* (2000), Chapter 1; Helmut Koester, *Ancient Christian Gospels* (1990), 128–171; John Dominic Crossan, *Four Other Gospels: Shadows on the Contours of Canon* (1986); Dunn, *Christianity in the Making—Vol 1—Jesus Remembered*, 60, 144, 147; and R. E. Brown, *The Death of the Messiah* (1994). Q is believed to be the earliest source, generally dated 40–50 CE.
5. George J. Brooke, *The Dead Sea Scrolls and the New Testament* (2005); George Nickelsburg, *Ancient Judaism and Christian Origins: Diversity* (2003), 48; and

James VanderKam and Peter Flint, *The Meaning of the Dead Sea Scrolls* (2002) are the best introductions to the subject.

6. "The sons of light," "the house of perfection and truth in Israel," the chosen ones, and so on (1QS 2.9; 3.25; 8.9; 11.7). Dunn *Christianity in the Making—Vol 1—Jesus Remembered*, 86.

7. Standing on George Nickelsburg, *Ancient Judaism and Christian Origins: Diversity* (2003), 48.

8. Standing on ibid. Similar presentation in Gerd Luedemannn, *The Unholy in Holy Scripture* (1997), 116. Also Dunn, *Christianity in the Making—Vol. 1—Jesus Remembered*, 86; and Anthony J. Saldarini, *Matthew's Christian-Jewish Community* (1994), 198–199.

9. Dunn, *Christianity in the Making—Vol. 1—Jesus Remembered*, 86.

10. See next segment and p. x and y for more on this topic and in G. W. Nickelsburg, *1 Enoch: A Commentary on the Book of 1 Enoch* (2001), 454–459.

11. Israel Knohl, *The Messiah before Jesus: The Suffering Servant of the Dead Sea Scrolls* (2000).

12. Nickelsburg, *Ancient Judaism and Christian Origins*, for comments on the impact of DSS scholarship on the Christian origins.

13. See David Flusser, *The Dead Sea Scrolls and Pre-Pauline Christianity* (1988, 23–25. At the other end of this side of the spectrum we encounter Robert Eisenman and Barbara Theiring, who believe that the Dead Sea Scrolls originated in the first century with distinct connections to the early, and pre-Gentile, Jesus movement.

14. The Pesher, Qumran's exegetical method, is unique to the community behind the Dead Sea Scrolls. Pesher (Hebrew for "meaning") is an exegetical method where biblical passages are seen as addressing present circumstances, not the original historical context.

15. Among the most important examples: Isaiah 42:52–53; Psalms 22, 69, 110, and 118:22- Daniel 7- Hosea 6:2- Zecharia 12:10- Matthew 1:23 (standing on Isaiah 7:14). Habakkuk 2:4 is used in Qumran (Pesher Habakkuk) and in Romans 1:17, Galatians 3:11, and Hebrews 10:37–380.

16. Knohl, *The Messiah before Jesus*.

17. Ibid.

18. Also in Daniel, 4 Ezra, 2 Baruch, and 1Enoch.

19. S. Lehne, *The New Covenant in Hebrews* (1990), 130–131; and W. D. Davies, "Torah in the Messianic Age and/or the Age to Come," *JBLMS* 7 (1952), 21–28.

20. The Teacher of Righteousness in Qumran texts. Jesus in the New Testament.

21. In the non-canonical texts of the period it is found in Barnabas and in the Didache. See Didache (chaps. 1–6) and Barnabas (2.10, 18.2). See also Nickelsburg, *1 Enoch*, 454–459.

22. For the John-Qumran connection see Mary L. Coloe and Tom Thatcher, eds., *John, Qumran, and the Dead Sea Scrolls: Sixty Years of Discovery and Debate* (2011).

23. G. Vermes, *The Dead Sea Scrolls in English* (1975), 265–268.

24. See detailed analysis in Harold W. Attridge, *The Epistle to the Hebrews* (1989), 192–195. See also Barnabas Lindars, *The Theology of the Letter to the Hebrews* (1991), 75.

25. See Mark 1:4–6 and Matthew 3:1–6.

26. During the second century Paulines split into Pauline-Lukan and Pauline-Marcionite strands.

27. "Thus Q cannot be seen as a teaching supplement for a community whose theology is represented by the Pauline kerygma. Q's theology and soteriology are fundamentally different." Helmut Koester, *Ancient Christian Gospels* (1990), 160.

28. The better known—L. Vaganay (Mark drew on proto-Mark), B. H. Streeter (proto-Luke first, second edition drew on Mark), and C. Lachmann and H. J. Holtzmann (Matt and Luke draw on proto-Mark). Other proposals include Koester's "dialogue Gospel" and Crossan's "Cross Gospel" whose existence as separate texts or textual traditions are hotly debated.

29. For an updated review on "the historical Jesus," see Amy-Jill Levine, Dale C. Allison Jr., and John Dominic Crossan, eds., *The Historical Jesus in Context* (2006).

3 THE ANTI-JUDAIC STRAND IN PAUL

1. For an updated, thorough, and comprehensive review of scholarship on the subject, see R. Bieringer and D. Pollefeyt, eds., *Paul and Judaism: Crosscurrents in Pauline Exegesis and the Study of Jewish-Christian Relations* (2012).

2. See analysis in Oskar Skarsaune and Reidar Hvalvik, eds., *Jewish Believers in Jesus* (2007), 151.

3. John G.Gager, *Reinventing Paul* (2000), 4–7.

4. My summary of E. P. Sanders, *Paul and Palestinian Judaism* (1977), 432.

5. Conversation with N. Beck (January 2008).

6. My interpretation of W. D. Davies, *Paul and Rabbinic Judaism* (1958), 324.

7. *Kerygma*—Greek for preaching. Bultmann distinguishes between two theological strata in the early Church: (i) the doctrine of the Mother-Church in Jerusalem, and (ii) "The Kerygma of the Hellenistic Community."

8. For an updated guide to the subject, see Hans-Josef Klauck, *The Religious Context of Early Christianity: A Guide to Graeco-Roman Religion* (2003). See also David Flusser, *The Dead Sea Scrolls and Pre-Pauline Christianity* (1988), 242. Further discussion of Gnosticism in p. 159.

9. The usefulness and relevancy of the term "Gnosticism" has recently been criticized as interest in Gnosticism has increased, due to its multiple meanings. See Michael Williams, *Rethinking Gnosticism* (1996).

10. My summary of Helmut Koester, *Ancient Christian Gospels* (1990), 125.

11. See ibid.; Bart Ehrman, *Lost Christianities: The Battle for Scripture and the Faiths We Never Knew* (2003); and Elaine Pagels, *The Gnostic Gospels* (1943).

12. For a detailed presentation of the Mystery Religions, see Hans-Josef Klaick, *The Religious Context of Early Christianity* (2003).

13. James D. G. Dunn, *Christianity in the Making—Vol. 1—Jesus Remembered* (2003), 181–184. "Paul in particular seems to show little interest in the ministry of Jesus and little knowledge of the Jesus tradition."

14. For Paul as integrator and redefiner, see Robin Scoggs, in *Pauline Conversations in Context*, J.C. Anderson, J. Capel, P. Sellew, and C. Seltzer, eds. (2002).

15. Hans Conzelmann, *An Outline of the Theology of the New Testament* (1969), 164, on the centrality of "by faith alone" in Paul's teaching.

16. Gerd Luedemann, *Paul—The Founder of Christianity* (2002), 16.

17. New English Bible version

18. See Appendix I: Paul in scholarship.

19. see also Stanley E. Porter and Dennis L. Stamps, eds., *The Rhetorical Interpretation of Scripture* (1999); Anthony J. Blasi, Jean Duhaime, and Paul-Andre' Turcotte, eds., *Handbook of Early Christianity* (2002), section 2, for a discussion of rhetorical techniques and their effectiveness. L. T. Johnson, *The New Testament's Anti-Jewish Slander and the Conventions of Ancient Polemic* (1989), 419–441; G. N. Stanton, *Aspects of Early Christian-Jewish Polemic and Apologetic* (1985); and Mary C. Boys, *Has God Only One Blessing?* (2000), 184–185.

20. Per Murray's research: F. C. Baur (1876); H. D. Betz (1979); F. F. Bruce (1982); E. D. Burton (1921); Gager (2000); G. Howard (1979); R. Jewett (1971); J. B. Lightfoot (1865); J. Murphy O'Connor (1996)—Michele Murray, *Playing a Jewish Game* (2004); David Flusser, "Paul's Jewish-Christian Opponents in the Didache," in Jonathan A. Draper, ed., *The Didache in Modern Research* (1996), 197; Gerd Luedemann, *Opposition to Paul in Jewish Christianity*, trans. E. Boring (1989), 1–34. H. J. Schoeps, *Jewish Christianity* (1969); A. F. J. Klijn, *The Study of Jewish-Christianity* (NTS 1973–74), 419–426. Updated views in Matt Jackson-Mccabe, ed., *Jewish Christianity Reconsidered* (2007).

21. Luedemann, *Paul—The Founder of Christianity*, 41, on the Jewish Christian ambivalence toward Paul.

22. On Paul's need and yearning for pre-eminence, see ibid., 187–191.

23. According to O. Skarsaune and R. Hvalvik, eds., *Jewish Believers in Jesus* (2007), the Gentiles he went to were the same as the ones he had already met in the synagogue (Acts 13:43; 18:7).

24. Douglas R. A. Hare, in A. T. Davies, *Anti-Semitism and the Foundations of Christianity* (1979), 30.

25. J. C. Becker, *Paul the Apostle—The Triumph of God in Life and Thought* (1980), 144. Non-Torah observance by Gentiles at the core of Paul's theology.

26. Magnus Zetterholm, *The Formation of Christianity in Antioch* (2003), 142, correctly identifies the lenient position of the early Jewish followers of Jesus toward the inclusion of gentiles. The argument was about Torah observance, not about inclusion.

27. Same position in Skarsaune and Hvalvik, *Jewish Believers in Jesus*, 151; and S. G. Wilson, *Luke and the Law* (2005), 68.

28. Similar views in John Gager, in A. H. Becker and A. Yoshiko, *The Ways That Never Parted* (2003), 146. For a balanced view of this relationship, see J. T. Sanders, *Schismatics, Sectarians, Dissidents, Deviants* (1993), 10–11.

29. For a similar view of the collapse of the Jerusalem compromise, see Philip Alexander, in James D. G. Dunn, ed., *Jews and Christians—the Parting of the Ways* (1989), 24.

30. G. Nickelsburg, *Ancient Judaism and Christian Origins: Diversity, Continuity and Transformation* (2003), Chapter 2; and E. P. Sanders, *Paul and Palestinian Judaism* (1977) for critiques of the traditional view of Judaism.
31. E. P. Sanders, *Paul and Palestinian Judaism* (1977). For a discussion of Sander's thesis, see E. Fabian, S. Heschel, M. Chancey, G. Tatum, eds., *Redefining First-Century Jewish and Christian Identities: Essays in Honor of Ed Parish Sanders* (2008).
32. See appendix I for further development of Paul in Modern Scholarship.
33. H. J. Schoeps, *Paul. The Theology of the Apostle in the Light of Jewish Religious History* (1961), 213–219, argues that Paul failed to see the connection between covenant and the Law.
34 See appendix I for a survey of modern scholarship on Paul.
35. Krister Stendahl, *Paul among Jews and Gentiles* (1976), 2.
36. Davies, *Paul and Rabbinic Judaism*, 70, pioneered the shift toward a Law observant Paul who opposed Law observance only as it regards Gentiles.
37. For the contrary view that Paul may be anti-Jewish, see J. C. Becker, *Paul the Apostle. The Triumph of God in Life and Thought* (1980), 75–90.
38. For an opposing view, see P. Richardson, *Israel in the Apostolic Church* (1969), 133–136.
39. Charlotte Klein, *Anti-Judaism in Christian Theology* (1978), 39–66. Luther's impact on later readings of the New Testament texts.
40. Sanders, *Paul and Palestinian Judaism*, 550–551.
41. See appendix I for a survey of modern scholarship on Paul.
42. See Magnus Zetterholm, *The Formation of Christianity in Antioch: A Social-Scientific Approach to the Separation between Judaism and Christianity* (2003), 156–166, for a consonant presentation of the Paul-James relationship.
43. For a somewhat different presentation, see P. J. Tomson, *If This Be from Heaven . . . : Jesus and the New Testament Authors in Their Relationship to Judaism* (2001), 400. Tomson sees a split within the Pauline tradition between the Lukean (non-anti-Jewish) tradition and the Ignatian interpretation that reads Paul as "anti-Jewish."
44. See Norman Beck's "The New Testament: A New Translation and Redaction."
45. An omnipotent, universal, and benevolent God.
46. Teleology is the philosophical study of purpose (from the Greek from telos, end, result).
47. Worldwide the earliest explorer of inner consciousness appears to be Siddhartha Gautama (The Buddha). There is no consensus on the date of the historical Buddha (estimates range from early fifth century to mid-fourth century BCE).
48. For a detailed discussion of Paul's "justification by faith alone" in the context of traditional versus new interpretations of Paul, see Westerholm Stephen *Understanding Paul: the early Christian worldview of the letter to the Romans* (2004, part 3 and 445).
49. 1 Cor. 1:23.
50. Similar views in Dunn, *Christianity in the Making—Vol. 1—Jesus Remembered*, 260.
51. Paul's Jewish grounding: W. D. Davies, *Paul and Rabbinic Judaism* (1958) pioneered the shift toward a Law-observant Paul who opposed Law observance

only as it regards Gentiles. Also E. P. Sanders, *Paul and Palestinian Judaism* (1977); Lloyd Gaston, *Paul and the Torah* (1987); John G. Gager, *Reinventing Paul* (2000); Luedemann, *Paul—The Founder of Christianity*, 136.

52. Standing on Paul M. Van Buren, *A Theology of the Jewish Christian Reality: Christ in Context* (1983), 274, but emphasizing the *intra-muros* nature of the debates (within the Jesus movement).

53. James D. G. Dunn, ed., Paul and the Mosaic Law: The Third Durham-Tübingen Research Symposium on Earliest Christianity and Judaism, Durham, September, 1994, 2001, 312.

54. Also Gaston, *Paul and the Torah*, 32.

55. Jacob Jervell, *The Theology of the Acts of the Apostles* (1996): Paul proselytizes in synagogues, creating friction and animosity; "we find nowhere in Acts Paul addressing audiences which consist of Gentiles only" (p. 85).

56. J. T. Sanders aims in the right direction when he states regarding Matthew: Nowhere does Matthew provide clues about the causes of this persecution, and the question of cause is the more puzzling due to the fact that, in the Jewish Christian source of Matthew, the Christian mission is clearly restricted to "Israel" (Mf 10.23). Therefore the synagogue flogging known to this Jewish Christian source cannot have been for the "crime" of admitting Gentiles to Christianity without converting them at the same time to Judaism. J. T. Sanders, in Blasi, Duhaime, and Turcotte, *Handbook of Early Christianity*, 362.

57. Traditionalist-universalist (Dunn), neo-traditionalist (Westerholm), Christological (E. P. Sanders), sociological (Watson), or revisionist (Stendahl, Gaston, Gager).

58. Similar views in Clark M. Williamson, *A Guest in the House of Israel* (1993), 87.

59. On Paul's need and drive for pre-eminence, see Luedemannn, *Paul—The Founder of Christianity*, 187–191.

60. My view on Paul is somewhat close to Räisänen's "probably not the dominant voice in early Christian theology," . . . not a "a theologian in the modern sense, and more a mix of charismatic enthusiast and pragmatic community organizer." Heikki Räisänen, *Paul and the Law* (1987), 200, 218.

61. On Jewish perspectives on Paul, see Daniel R. Langton, *The Apostle Paul in the Jewish Imagination: A Study in Modern Jewish-Christian Relations* (1999).

4   The Anti-Judaic Strand in Mark: The Need to Explain

1. On interdependence among the Synoptic Gospels, see Raymond E. Brown, *The Death of the Messiah* (1994), 40–46.

2. The minority view (that Mark is the latest of the Gospels) is presented by William Farmer in *Rethinking the Synoptic Problem,* David Alan Black and David R. Beck, eds. (2001).

3. Mark is the first Gospel (the "Perrin school"); Mark is the first written Gospel (W. Kelber); Mark and the redeemer myth (B. Mack); Mark is antiapostolic (T. J. Weeden, W. Kelber); Mark tames the original traditions (H. Koester;

M. Smith); Mark is in harmony with what went before (Brown, *The Death of the Messiah*, 47–49). See Craig Evans in *Reading the Gospels Today*, Porter Stanley, ed. (2004), 1–8, for an updated defense of Mark's priority.

4. On recent trends, see Janice Capel Anderson and Stephen D. Moore, eds., *Mark and Method: New Approaches in Biblical Studies* (2008).

5. Similar arguments in Kelber Werner, *The Oral and the Written Gospel* (1983), 130–131; and Lindsey P. Pherigo, *The Gospel According to Mark in the Interpreter's One Volume Commentary on the Bible* (1971), 644.

6. On this subject, see, e.g., T. J. Weeden, *Mark: Traditions in Conflict* (1971); J. B. Tyson, "The Blindness of the Disciples in Mark," *JBL* 80 (1961), 261–268.

7. See Robert A. Guelich (Mark 1:8–26, c1989, 361–362), R. P. Booth, "Jesus and the Laws of Purity: Tradition History and Legal History in Mark 7," *JSNT Sup* 13 (1986), 55–114; James G. D. Dunn, *Jesus, Paul and the Law* (1990), 37–60.

8. Oskar Skarsaune and Reidar Hvalvik, eds., *Jewish Believers in Jesus* (2007), 75.

9. For the historical Pilate, see Helen Bond, *Pontius Pilate in History and Interpretation* (1998); and Warren Carter, *Pontius Pilate: Portraits of a Roman Governor* (2003).

10. See Michael J. Cook, *Mark's Treatment of the Jewish Leaders* (1978), for a detailed discussion of this topic and for the peculiar exclusion of the Pharisees and Sadducees.

11. Israel Knohl, *The Messiah before Jesus: The Suffering Servant of the Dead Sea Scrolls* (2000).

12. B. Layton, *The Rediscovery of Gnosticism* (1980); Elaine Pagels, *The Gnostic Gospels* (1943). On cross-influence among Judaism, Christianity, and Gnosticism, see Alan F. Segal, in *Anti-Judaism in Early Christianity*, S. G. Wilson, ed. (1986), 133–162; Jonas Hans, *The Gnostic Religion* (1958).

13. Stephen G. Wilson, *Related Strangers: Jews and Christians* (1995), 216.

14. Indebted to ibid. and Judith M. Lieu, *Image and Reality* (1996), 264.

15. See Wilson, *Related Strangers*, 174–175. Similar views in James D. G. Dunn, *Christianity in the Making—Vol. 1—Jesus Remembered* (2003), 86 and 784; and Paul M. Van Buren, *A Christian Theology of the People of Israel* (1983), 244. Also J. D. Crossan, *Who Killed Jesus* (1957–59); Clark M. Williamson, *A Guest in the House of Israel* (1993), 60–61); Gerd Luedemannn, *The Unholy in Holy Scripture* (1997), 97–98.

16. Luedemannn, *The Unholy in Holy Scripture*, 86–91, 97–98.

17. Adiel Schremer, *Brothers Estranged: Heresy, Christianity, and Jewish Identity in Late Antiquity* (2010) and the discussion on "the parting of the ways" in p. x.

5   The Anti-Judaic Strand in Matthew: The Saga of the Jewish Followers of Jesus

1. Supportive of the origin of Matthew in a community of Torah-observant believers in Jesus of Jewish origin: J. A. Overman, *Matthew's Gospel and Formative Judaism* (1990); and A. J. Saldarini, *Matthew's Jewish Christian Community* (1994).

2. Probably written around 85–95 CE—Saldarini, *Matthew's Christian-Jewish Community*; and J. D. Crossan, *Who Killed Jesus?* (1995), 16.
3. Saldarini, *Matthew's Christian-Jewish Community*, 1.
4. Standing on Stephen G. Wilson, *Related Strangers: Jews and Christians* (1995), 50, 55. Further reading in W. D. Davies and Dale C. Allison, *A Critical and Exegetical Commentary on the Gospel According to Saint Matthew* (1991), vol. 1, 32.
5. R. E. Brown, *The Death of the Messiah* (1994), 388.
6. Ibid., 28–30.
7. For further reflection on Matthew's "anti-Jewish" inclinations, see Amy-Jill Levine, Philip Shiner, and Warren Carter, in *Anti Judaism and the Gospels*, William R. Farmer, ed. (1999).
8. For an updated review of scholarship on Matthew's author and socio-theological context, see David Sim and Boris Repschinski, eds., *Matthew and His Christian Contemporaries* (2008).
9. My interpretation of Wayne Meeks, ed., *Library of Early Christianity* (1986), 110.
10. "[T]he polemic corresponds to the established Jewish tradition of prophetic polemic against the political establishment in Jerusalem, and the people who had been misled by their leaders." Helmut Koester, *Ancient Christian Gospels* (1990), 230.
11. For Markan-Matthean divergences, see Jesper Svartvik in *Matthew and His Christian Contemporaries*, David Sim and Boris Repschinski, eds. (2008), Chapter 2.
12. On Matthew's authorship, see B. Przybylski in *Anti-Judaism in Early Christianity*, Peter Richardson and David Granskou, eds. (1986), vol. 1, 181– 200; W. D. Davies and D. C. Allison, *A Critical and Exegetical Commentary on the Gospel according to Saint Matthew* (1988), vol. 1, 7–58; G. N. Stanton, *A Gospel for a New People: Studies in Matthew* (1992), 131–139; Anthony J. Saldarini, *Matthew's Christian-Jewish Community* (1994), 7–10; and Wilson, *Related Strangers*, 46–56.
13. In this case from later to earlier, instead of the normal flow of authority from earlier to later traditions.
14. The term "proto-Matthean" includes Q and textual traditions originating in the Jewish followers of Jesus that may have been incorporated into Q and/or a proto-Matthean intermediate phase. See David Flusser, *The Dead Sea Scrolls and Pre-Pauline Christianity* (1988), 578–590; and Koester, *Ancient Christian Gospels*, 170–171. For a detailed presentation of the theory of a Proto-Matthew, see Malcom Lowe and David Flusser, "Evidence Corroborating a Modified Proto-Matthean Synoptic Theory," *NTS* 29 (1983), 25–47. Stendahl's work also supports a layered Matthew.
15. David Flusser and Malcom Lowe, "A Modified Proto-Matthean Synoptic Theory," *NTS* 29 (1983).
16. For the Qumran messiah, The Teacher of Righteousness, as a precursor of the Jesus story—Knohl Israel, *The Messiah before Jesus: The Suffering Servant of the Dead Sea Scrolls* (2000). For the impact of Psalms 2 on the Passion, see Crossan, *Who Killed Jesus?*

17. Raymond Brown, *The Birth of the Messiah* (1977), for the Jesus-Moses connection.
18. My elaboration of Saldarini, *Matthew's Christian-Jewish Community*, 196–197.
19. Ibid., 7–10. Implicit in Wilson, *Related Strangers*, 36–46. Amy-Jill Levine, *The Social and Ethnic Dimensions of Matthean Salvation History* (2003), 71–89, argued for authorship by a Jewish follower of Jesus.
20. Saldarini, *Matthew's Christian-Jewish Community*, 7–10.
21. See Wilson, *Related Strangers*, 36–46. Similar conclusions in E. P. Sanders and Margaret Davis, *Studying the Synoptic Gospels* (1989), 194.
22. Anthony J. Saldarini sees the Matthean text as a challenge to the Jewish establishment due to its refusal to embrace Jesus's ministry, not as a challenge to Judaism as such (*Matthew's Christian-Jewish Community*, 44). "The level of animosity, unprecedented in Matthew, let alone the other Gospels, strongly suggests that the scribes and Pharisees stand for contemporaries with whom the author is in conflict." Wilson, *Related Strangers*, 50.
23. R. E. Brown, *The Death of the Messiah* (1994), 62.
24. Saldarini comments on Matthew's views on the Gentiles: "Matthew may be implying that they have the potential to be members of his group of believers in Jesus, but they are not yet members, nor does the narrative indicate that they will become so. Matthew may have in mind the phenomenon of the gentiles sympathetic to the synagogue who were not Jews, but who were nevertheless not totally other. Within the narrative, the gentile characters are secondary to members of Israel, and their story is partial and unfinished." Saldarini, *Matthew's Christian-Jewish Community*, 82.
25. "The very fact that in Matt (14:33) all the disciples once confessed Jesus as God's Son makes their flight from Gethsemane more reprehensible. Similarly, that in his personal confession Peter, the rock of faith, had hailed Jesus as 'the Messiah, the Son of the living God' (16:16–18) heightens the irony of his denying Jesus at the very moment the high priest is adjuring Jesus by 'the living God' to say if he is 'the Messiah, the Son of God.'" See Brown, *The Death of the Messiah*, 28–30. On the other hand, the Markan denigration of the Torah-observant faction is also somewhat mitigated by the high praise of Peter (Matt. 16:17–19) and by the correction of the slander that Jesus's family thought he was insane. (See Mark 3:10.35 and 6:1.4 versus Matt. 13:53.58.)
26. Denigration of ancestors was a biblical staple (see p. 194). See the denigration of Aaron by the Deuteronomist writer (most probably member of the contending Mushite priestly clan) and of the ancestors of most of the Judean enemies (Moab, Edom, etc.). Also N. A. Beck, *Mature Christianity, The Recognition and Repudiation of the Anti-Jewish Polemic of the New Testament* (1994), 57–59. See also Robert Goldenberg, *The Nations That Know Thee Not: Ancient Jewish Attitudes toward Other Religions* (1997).
27. The increased inclination to exonerate the Romans is showcased in the heightened emphasis on the "Jewish culpability," and in the additions to the Markan story (Pilate's wife[27:19] and the hand-washing scene of Pilate [27:24–25]).
28. In harmony with Koester, *Ancient Christian Gospels*, 170–171.

29. Saldarini, *Matthew's Christian-Jewish Community*, 7–10; and Wilson, *Related Strangers*, 46–56, support continuity. J. P. Meier, *The Vision of Matthew* (1979), 229–235; R. A. Guelich, *The Sermon on the Mount* (1982), 134–174; L. Gaston, "The Messiah of Israel and the Teacher of the Gentiles," *Int.* 29 (1975), 24–40; and Davies and Allison, *A Critical and Exegetical Commentary on the Gospel according to Saint Matthew 1988*, 481–503, support discontinuity.

30. On the continued Torah observance of Jewish Christians, see Saldarini, *Matthew's Christian-Jewish Community*, 114–174.

6 THE ANTI-JUDAIC STRAND IN LUKE/ACTS: YEARNING FOR RESPECTABILITY

1. A more complete engagement with the Knox-Tyson-Townsend view in p. 61.
2. For a review of unconventional approaches to Luke interpretation, see Joel B. Green, ed., *Methods for Luke Methods in Biblical Interpretation* (2010).
3. See R. E. Brown, *The Death of the Messiah* (1994), 30–31; and Peter Tomson, *Jesus and the New Testament Authors in their Relationship to Judaism* (2001), 24, 223.
4. D. Tiede, in J. B. Tyson, *Luke-Acts and the Jewish People* (1988), 21–34; Dunn, *Jews and Christians: The Parting of the Ways, A. D. 70 to 135* (1989), 149–151; Israel R. Tannehill, *The Narrative Unity of Luke-Acts* (1990); Brown, *The Death of the Messiah*, 389–390; Tomson, *Jesus and the New Testament Authors*, 214.
5. J. T. Sanders, *The Jews in Luke-Acts* (1987), 39–42 and 296–299; Jacob Jervell, *Luke and the People of God. A New look at Luke-Acts* (1972), 62–64; J. B. Tyson, *Images of Judaism in Luke-Acts* (1992), 158–180; Stephen G. Wilson, *Related Strangers: Jews and Christians* (1995), 57–58.
6. See Tyson, *Luke-Acts and the Jewish People*, 130.
7. Ibid., 129.
8. Somewhat similar view in Samuel Sandmel, *Anti-Semitism in The New Testament?* (1978), 73.
9. The scribes and the Pharisees are the main Matthean enemies. Peter Tomson, *Jews and the New Testament Authors* (2001), 276. Michael J. Cook, *Mark's Treatment of the Jewish Leaders* (1978), claims that the "scribes" originate from Mark and that neither know who they truly are.
10. Stephen G. Wilson, ed., *Anti-Judaism in Early Christianity, Vol. 2* (1986), 48; and D. P. Efroymson, *Tertullian's Anti-Judaism and Its Role in Theology* (1976), 112–146.
11. John Knox, *Marcion and the New Testament* (1942); and "Marcion and the Synoptic Problem," in *Jesus, the Gospels and the Church*, E. P. Sanders, ed. (1987), 25–31; Joseph Tyson, *Marcion and Luke-Acts* (2006).
12. John Knox, *Marcion and the New Testament: An Essay in the Early History of the Canon* (1942).
13. Standing on Tyson, *Marcion and Luke-Acts*, 78–79; and Knox, *Marcion and the New Testament*, 117–119.

14. Standing on Tyson, *Marcion and Luke-Acts*, 48–49.
15. Townsend, "The Date of Luke-Acts," in *Luke-Acts: New Perspectives from the Society of Biblical Literature Seminar*, Charles H. Talbert, ed. (1984), 47–62; Andrew Gregory, "The Reception of Luke and Acts in the Period before Irenaeus: Looking for Luke in the Second Century," *WUNT* 2:169 (2003); Tyson, *Marcion and Luke-Acts*, 11.
16. See p. 157.
17. "Luke-Acts is one of the most pro-Jewish and one of the most anti-Jewish writings in the New Testament." L. Gaston in *Anti-Judaism in Early Christianity*, Peter Richardson and David Granskou, eds. (1986), vol. 1, 127–153; and Wilson, *Related Strangers*, 64–65. For discussions of this range: Wilson, *Related Strangers*, 56–71, esp. 57; and Brown, *The Death of the Messiah*, 389–390. Also Sandmel, *Anti-Semitism in The New Testament?*, 73); and N. A. Beck, *Mature Christianity, The Recognition and Repudiation of the Anti-Jewish Polemic of the New Testament* (1994), 207.
18. Mary C. Boys, *Has God Only One Blessing?* (2000), 85.
19. Standing on Wilson, *Related Strangers*, 64–65.
20. On the origins of the genre, see A. Portier-Young, *Apocalypse against Empire: Theologies of Resistance in Early Judaism* (2011).
21. Acts 16:1–3; 21:18–28; 23:5; 24:14–15, 17–18; 25:8, 10; 26:4–8, 22.
22. Similar view in Patrick J. Hartin, *James of Jerusalem: Heir to Jesus of Nazareth* (2004), 135–140.

7   THE ANTI-JUDAIC STRAND IN JOHN: ESTRANGEMENT

1. J. D. Crossan, *Who Killed Jesus* (1995), 20–25.
2. Joseph Stiassny, *Development of the Christians' Self-understanding in the Second Part of the First Century, Immanuel 1* (1972), 32–34; Rosemary R. R., *Faith and Fratricide* (1974), 16; Eldon J. Epp, *Anti-Semitism and the Popularity of the Fourth Gospel in Christianity* (1975), 35–57; Reginald Fuller, "The Jews' in the Fourth Gospel," *Dialog* 16 (1977), 31–37; S. Sandmel, *Anti-Semitism in the New Testament?* (1978), 119; J. Townsend, "The Gospel of John and the Jews," in *Anti-Semitism and the Foundations of Christianity*, A. Davies, ed. (1979), 60, 72–97; John Koenig, *Jews and Christians in Dialogue: New Testament Foundations* (1979), 131, 137; J. E. Leibig, "John and The Jews: Theological Anti-Semitism in the Fourth Gospel," *JES* (1983), 224; Clark M. Williamson and R. J. Allen, *Interpreting Difficult Texts* (1989), 48–55; Peter Tomson, *Jews and the New Testament Authors* (2001), 401–404; N. A. Beck, *Mature Christianity, The Recognition and Repudiation of the Anti-Jewish Polemic of the New Testament* (1994), 199–241; Reimund Bieringer, Didier Pollefeyt, and Frederique Vandecasteele-Vanneuville, eds., *Anti-Judaism and the Fourth Gospel* (2001), 42, 109; Lars Kierspel, *The Jews and the World in the Fourth Gospel* (2006); R. Alan Culpepper, in *Anti-Judaism and the Fourth Gospel*, Bieringer, Pollefeyt, and Vandecasteele-Vanneuville, 81; C. K. Barrett, *The Gospel of John*

and Judaism (1975), 71; W. Meeks, "Am I a Jew? Johannine Christianity and Judaism," in *Christianity, Judaism and Other Graeco-Roman Cults*, J. Neusner, ed. (1975), 172; Bieringer, Pollefeyt, and Vandecasteele-Vanneuville, *Anti-Judaism and the Fourth Gospel*, 4.

3. J. L. Martyn, *History and Theology in the Fourth Gospel* (1979).

4. The Descendants of Jesus's disciples and followers considered Jesus an exalted human, not a divine being.

5. Standing on N. Beck's presentation of the issue (*Mature Christianity*, 296–297, 304–305, 309).

6. U. C. von Wahlde, "The Johannine 'Jews': A Critical Survey," *NTS* 28 (1982), 33–60.

7. Tomson, in *Anti-Judaism and the Fourth Gospel*, Bieringer, Pollefeyt, and Vandecasteele-Vanneuville, 198.

8. James H. Charlesworth, in *Anti-Judaism and the Fourth Gospel*, Bieringer, Pollefeyt, and Vandecasteele-Vanneuville, 257–259, advocates "some Judean leaders" for 5:1, 16; 7:1; 9:22; 11:54; 18:36; 19:38; 20:19. Others on the multivalency of the term: von Wahlde, "The Johannine 'Jews,'" 33–60; M. Lowe, "Who Were the 'Ioudaioi,'" *NovTIS* (1976), 101–130, 106–107); J. Ashton, "The Identity and Function of the 'Ioudaioi' in the Fourth Gospel," *NovT 27* (1983), 40–75, 55–57; R. A. Culpepper, "The Gospel of John as a Threat to Jewish-Christian Relations," in *Overcoming Fear between Jews and Christians -Shared Ground among Jews and Christians 3*, J. H. Charlesworth with F. X. Blisard and J. L. Gorham, eds. (1993), 21–43, 27; J. C. O'Neill, "'The Jews' in the Fourth Gospel," *IBS* 18 (1996), 58–74, for an overview of the subject. U. C. von Wahlde, *The Jews' in the Gospel of John: Fifteen Years of Research* (2000), 30–55; Charlesworth, in *Anti-Judaism and the Fourth Gospel*, Bieringer, Pollefeyt, and Vandecasteele-Vanneuville, 254–255.

9. See Stephen G. Wilson, *Related Strangers: Jews and Christians* 1995), 147–163.

10. Gill Christopher, ed., *The Discourses of Epictetus* (1995).

11. S. J. D. Cohen, *The Beginnings of Jewishness: Boundaries, Varieties, Uncertainties*, c1999 70–73.. Similar views in D. Rensberger, in *Anti Judaism and the Gospels*, William R. Farmer, ed. (1999), 123.

12. De Jounge, in *Anti-Judaism and the Fourth Gospel*, Bieringer, Pollefeyt, and Vandecasteele-Vanneuville, 121 and Chapter 6, standing on B. W. J. de Ruyter.

13. Besides Brown and Martyn, I would point the following influential works that touch on the socio-historical context of Carroll K. L. John, "The Fourth Gospel and the Exclusion of Christians from the Synagogue," *BJRL* 40 (1957); W. A. Meek, "The Man from Heaven in Johannine Sectarianism," *JBL* 91 (1972); and B. J. Malina, "The Gospel of John in Sociolinguistic Perspective," Center for Hermeneutical Studies in Hellenistic and Modern Culture, Colloquy 48; R. A. Culpepper and C. Clifton Black, *Exploring the Gospel of John* (1996); and Paul N. Anderson, *The Riddles of the Fourth Gospel: An Introduction to John* (2011).

14. James R. Mueller, in *Anti-Semitism and Early Christianity*, Evans Ed and Hagner, eds. (1993), 257, who points to W. Bauer (*Orthodoxy and Heresy in Earliest*

Christianity, ed. R. Kraft and G. Krodel [1971], H. Koester, *Introduction to the New Testament, vol. 2: History and Literature of Early Christianity* [1982], and Hennecke-Schneemelcher-Wilson, *New Testament Apocrypha*, 1.134–78), the earliest to identify this phenomenon.

15. John makes "a connection between 'the Jews' who condemned Jesus and Jews known to the Christian community at a later time. By means of this transfer of hostility, effected by the two levels of meaning Martyn found in the Gospel, the Gospel creates a dangerous potential for anti-Semitism." Culpepper, in *Anti-Judaism and the Fourth Gospel*, Bieringer, Pollefeyt, and Vandecasteele-Vanneuville, 66.

16. Peter Tomson, *Jesus and the New Testament Authors in their Relationship to Judaism* (2001), 401–404.

17. J. L. Martyn, *History and Theology in the Fourth Gospel* (1968), 90–121; J. T. Sanders, *Schismatics, Sectarians, Dissidents, Deviants* (1993), 44–48; Raymond E. Brown, *The Community of the Beloved Disciple* (1979), 292–316; Tomson, *Jesus and the New Testament Authors*, 401–404; Tomson, in *Anti-Judaism and the Fourth Gospel*, Bieringer, Pollefeyt, and Vandecasteele-Vanneuville, 198– 199. For a theological, historical, and literary analysis of John's riddles, see Anderson, *The Riddles of the Fourth Gospel*.

18. Raymond E. Brown, *The Death of the Messiah* (1994), 83–85. A three-stage transition is also supported by others including J. T. Sanders, *Schismatics, Sectarians, Dissidents, Deviants* (1993), 44–48; and Tomson, *Jesus and the New Testament Authors*, 401–404.

19. Seven groups of protagonists have been identified by Brown, *The Community of the Beloved Disciple*, 59–91: the world, the Jews, the adherents of John the Baptist, Crypto-Christians, the Jewish Christian Churches of inadequate faith, the apostolic churches, and the Johannines.

20. Carroll, "The Fourth Gospel.",

21. Follows my summary of R. E. Brown, *The Gospel according to John* (1966) *The Community of the Beloved Disciple*, 22–25.

22. Brown, *The Community of the Beloved Disciple*, 13.

23. Ibid., 23.

24. Docetism: Jesus was only divine; his physical appearance was an illusion. See James D. G. Dunn, *Unity and Diversity in the New Testament* (1990), 296–305.

25. Similar argument in Sanders, *Schismatics, Sectarians, Dissidents, Deviants*, 44–48; and H. J. De Jonge, in *Anti-Judaism and the Fourth Gospel*, Bieringer, Pollefeyt, and Vandecasteele-Vanneuville, 121–122, 139–140.

26. Tomson, *Jesus and the New Testament Authors*, 329, 401–404); similar transitions in Brown, *The Death of the Messiah*, 83–85; and Sanders, *Schismatics, Sectarians, Dissidents, Deviants*, 44–48.

27. R. T. Fortna, *The Gospel of Signs* (1970), 32 note 6. See the next segment for more on the evolution of the text.

28. A. Reinhartz, in *Anti-Judaism and the Fourth Gospel*, Bieringer, Pollefeyt, and Vandecasteele-Vanneuville, 220.

29. Martyn, *History and Theology in the Fourth Gospel*.

30. Urban C. von Wahlde, *The Earliest Version of John's Gospel: Recovering the Gospel of Signs* (1989), 34–43, 162–164; Sanders, *Schismatics, Sectarians, Dissidents, Deviants*.

31. Martyn, *History and Theology in the Fourth Gospel.*

32. The intra-Gentile debate surfaced a bit later and is a main subject of the Johannine Epistles. Docetic: Jesus was only divine; his human presence was an illusion.

33. David Rensberger, in *What Is John? Readers and Readings of the Fourth Gospel*, F. F. Segovia, ed. (1996), 146.

34. See chapter on supersession theology (p. 103).

35. A. J. Mattill, "Johannine Communities behind the 'Fourth Gospel: Georg Richter's Analysis,'" *TS* 38 (1977), 294–315.

36. Standing on Beck, *Mature Christianity*, 310.

37. Same argument in Rensberger, in *What Is John?*, Segovia, 141–142.

38. Support for this assessment in H. Koester and J. M. Robinson, *Trajectories through Early Christianity* (1971), 115; W. D. Davies, "Paul and the People of Israel," *NTS* 24 (1977), 4–39; G. Strecker, "On the Problem of Jewish Christianity," appendix to Bauer, *Orthodoxy and Heresy in Earliest Christianity*, 241–245.

39. Brown, *The Community of the Beloved Disciple*, 82–83.

40. My summary of Beck, *Mature Christianity*, 311.

41. Standing on ibid., 297.

42. Rensberger's sources: D. Rensberger, *Johannine Faith and Liberating Community* (1988), 27–28; Meeks, "The Man from Heaven in Johannine Sectarianism," 44–72; B. J. Malina, *The Gospel of John in Sodolinguistic Perspective* (1985); J. Neusner, ed., *Christianity, Judaism, and Other Graeco-Roman Cults* (1975), 2:1–23; J. H. Elliot, *A Home for the Homeless: A Sociological Exegesis of 1 Peter* (1981), 73–78. Strands of early Christianity as sectarians: R. Scroggs, *The Earliest Christian Communities as Sectarian Movement*. Studies for Morton Smith at Sixty, 4 vols., *SJLA* 12.

43. Rensberger, in *What Is John?*, Segovia, 139–142; and Rensberger, in *Anti Judaism and the Gospels*, Farmer, 150, 152, 154, concludes that John reflects a dissident and marginalized community confronting an orthodoxy or a majority view.

44. Rensberger, in *What Is John?*, Segovia, 139–142.

45. Martyn, *History and Theology in the Fourth Gospel*; Brown, *The Community of the Beloved Disciple*; R. Kysar, "The Gospel of John in Current Research," *RSR9* (1983), 316; W. A. Meeks, in *'To See Ourselves as Others See Us': Christians, Jews, 'Others' in Late Antiquity*, J. Neusner and E. S. Frerichs, eds. (1985), 94; G. M. Smiga, *Pain and Polemic: Anti-Judaism in the Gospels* (1992), 137; Beck, *Mature Christianity*, 288; David Rensberger and Adele Reinhartz, in *What Is John?*, Segovia. Sanders, *Schismatics, Sectarians, Dissidents, Deviants*, 44–48.

46. For a survey of these issues, see Bieringer and Vandecasteele-Vanneuville, *Anti-Judaism and the Fourth Gospel*, 63.

47. Bieringer, Pollefeyt, and Vandecasteele-Vanneuville, in *Anti-Judaism and the Fourth Gospel*, 29.

48. Culpepper, in *Anti-Judaism and the Fourth Gospel*, Bieringer, Pollefeyt, and Vandecasteele-Vanneuville, 67.
49. Gerd Luedemannn, *The Unholy in Holy Scripture* (1997), 110–120.
50. Martyn, *History and Theology in the Fourth Gospel*, 2d ed.; and R. Kysar, "The Gospel of John in Current Research," *RSR9* (1983), 316.
51. Martyn, *History and Theology in the Fourth Gospel*, 2d ed., 50–62. Since, Martyn has modified his views in harmony with the emerging consensus.
52. A. Reinhartz, "The Johannine Community: A Reappraisal," in *What Is John?* vol. 2, Segovia.
53. J. Townsend, "The Gospel of John—Jews: The Story of a Religious Divorce," in *Anti-Semitism and the Foundations Christianity*, A. Davies, ed. (1979), 72–97, 87; C. K. Barnett, *The Gospel According to St. John*, 2nd ed. (1978), 361; John Painter, *John 9, John, Witness and Theologian* (1975), 38; R. Culpepper, *Exploring the Gospel of John* (1996), 280–282.
54. Reuven Kimelman, in *Jewish and Christian Self Definition*, E. P. Sanders ed., with A. I. Baumgarten and Alan Mendelson (1981), 226–244, 391–403; P. van der Horst, "The Birkat Ha-Minim in Recent Research," *ExpTim* 105 (1994); S. T. Katz, "Issues in the Separation of Judaism and Christianity after 70 C. E.: A Reconsideration," *JBL* 103 (1984), 43–76, 74.
55. See H. J. De Jonge, in *Anti-Judaism and the Fourth Gospel*, Bieringer, Pollefeyt, and Vandecasteele-Vanneuville, 121–140.
56. Brown, *The Community of the Beloved Disciple*, 41–42.
57. Bieringer, Pollefeyt, and Vandecasteele-Vanneuville, eds, *Anti-Judaism and the Fourth Gospel*, 200, 32–33.
58. Culpepper, in *Anti-Judaism and the Fourth Gospel*, Bieringer, Pollefeyt, and Vandecasteele-Vanneuville, 82.
59. Similar views in Brown, *The Community of the Beloved Disciple*, 41.
60. Standing on De Jounge, in *Anti-Judaism and the Fourth Gospel*, Bieringer, Pollefeyt, and Frederique Vandecasteele-Vanneuville, 134 and Chapter 6.
61. These differing Gentile believers in Jesus may be De Jonge's "Christian contemporaries who did not accept all, or perhaps only a portion, of John's Christology." De Jonge, in *Anti-Judaism and the Fourth Gospel*, Bieringer, Pollefeyt, and Vandecasteele-Vanneuville, 134.
62. Tomson, *Jesus and the New Testament Authors*, 407.
63. Townsend, "The Gospel of John," in *Anti-Semitism and the Foundations Christianity*, Davies,, 72–97, 87. Similar views in Tomson, in *Anti-Judaism and the Fourth Gospel*, Bieringer, Pollefeyt, and Vandecasteele-Vanneuville, 198–199; and Beck, *Mature Christianity*, 296.
64. G. Vermes, *The Changing Faces of Jesus* (2000), 11.
65. For a more detailed analysis and comparison of missionary and secessionist communities, see p. 93.
66. See Kierspel, *The Jews and the World in the Fourth Gospel*; E. J. Epp, "Anti-Semitism and the Popularity of the Fourth Gospel in Christianity," *CCARJ/22* (1975), 35–57; Culpepper, in *Anti-Judaism and the Fourth Gospel*, Bieringer, Pollefeyt, and Vandecasteele-Vanneuville, 81; Barrett, *The Gospel of John and Judaism*, 71; Meeks, "Am I a Jew?" Neusner, 172; Bieringer,

Pollefeyt, and Vandecasteele-Vanneuville, *Anti-Judaism and the Fourth Gospel*, 4.

67. Charlesworth, in *Anti-Judaism and the Fourth Gospel*, Bieringer, Pollefeyt, and Vandecasteele-Vanneuville, 248; and Luedemannn, *The Unholy in Holy Scripture*, 94–95, 110.

68. Standing on Beck, *Mature Christianity*, 306–307.

8 THE ANTI-JUDAIC STRAND IN REVELATION: JUDAISM WITHIN

1. Consonant views in Peter J. Tomson, *If This Be from Heaven: Jesus and the New Testament Authors in Their Relationship to Judaism* (2001), 362, 365, 366.

2. The earliest were B. M. Newman Jr., *Rediscovering the Book of Revelation* (1968), 30; and J. M. Robinson and H. Koester, *Trajectories through Early Christianity* (1971), 114–157. See more updated views in John Gager, *The Origins of Anti-Semitism* (1985), 131; Lloyd Gaston, *Studies in Christianity and Judaism*, S. G. Wilson, ed. (1986), 42–43; Stephen G. Wilson, *Related Strangers: Jews and Christians* (1995), 163; Murray Michele, *Playing a Jewish Game* (2004), 78.

3. For the view that the adversaries are mainstream Jews, see D. M. Smith, "Judaism and the Gospel of John," in *Jews and Christians: Exploring the Past, Present, and Future*, J. H. Charlesworth, ed. (1990), 88–89; and Yarbro A. Collins, *Crisis and Catharsis: The Power of the Apocalypse* (1984), 85–87.

4. Standing on Wilson Stephen G. (Related Strangers: Jews and Christians, 1995, 147, 162–3)

5. Gal. 2:14, 3; 5:2–12; 6:12, 15; and Magn. 8:1–2; 9:1; 10:3, and Phld. 6:1. Segment stands on Murray, *Playing a Jewish Game*, 78–79.

6. See Gager, *The Origins of Anti-Semitism*, 131; Gaston, *Studies in Christianity and Judaism*, 42–43; Wilson, *Related Strangers*, 163; Murray, *Playing a Jewish Game*, 78.

7. Indebted to Wilson, *Related Strangers*, 147–163; Murray, *Playing a Jewish Game*, 78.

8. Similar to those proselytes Justin refers to others as being more active in persecution of Gentile believers in Jesus than the Jews (Dial. 122). Wilson, *Related Strangers*, 163.

9. For differing views, see Gager, *The Origins of Anti-Semitism*, 131; Gaston, *Studies in Christianity and Judaism*, 42–43; Wilson, *Related Strangers*, 163; Murray, *Playing a Jewish Game*, 78.

10. The beast (Nero), the seven hills that surround Rome, and 666 or 676 (the numerological equivalents of the two ways Nero's name is written in Hebrew).

11. About Gentile Judaizers (Gentile sympathizers with the Jewish followers of Jesus), see Gager, *The Origins of Anti-Semitism*, 131; Gaston, *Studies in Christianity and Judaism*, 42–43; Wilson, *Related Strangers*, 163; and Murray, *Playing a Jewish Game*, 78–79—although most of these analyses cast the context as inter-religious.

9   THE ANTI-JEWISH STRAND—
THE EMBRYONIC STAGE SUMMARY

1. On early diversity, see R. E. Brown, "Not Jewish Christianity and Gentile Christianity but Types of Jewish/Gentile Christianity," *CBQ 45* (January 1983).
2. I present these two types of communities as a conceptual model, see Magnus Zetterholm, *The Formation of Christianity in Antioch: A Social-Scientific Approach to the Separation between Judaism and Christianity* (2003), who advocates a secession of Gentile believers in Jesus from a synagogue of Jewish followers of Jesus as the pivot for the separation of the two communities in Antioch.
3. James R. Mueller, in *Anti-Semitism and Early Christianity*, Craig Evans and Donald Hagner, eds. (1993), 257, who points to Walter Bauer, *Orthodoxy and Heresy in Earliest Christianity*, R. Kraft and G. Krodel, eds. (1971); H. Koester, *Introduction to the New Testament, vol. 2: History and Literature of Early Christianity* (1982); and Hennecke-Schneemelcher-Wilson, *New Testament Apocrypha*, 1.134–78, the earliest to identify this phenomenon.
4. As far as I can tell, the argument that Christian orthodoxy became dominant following a confrontation with other forms of belief in Jesus originates with Bauer, *Orthodoxy and Heresy in Earliest Christianity*. For insight into this period I am indebted to Bart Ehrman, *Lost Christianities: The Battle for Scripture and the Faiths We Never Knew* (2003); and Stephen G. Wilson, *Related Strangers: Jews and Christians* (1995).
5. On the cross-influence among Judaism, Christianity, and Gnosticism, see Alan F. Segal in *Anti-Judaism in Early Christianity*, vol. 2, Stephen G. Wilson, ed. (1986), 133–162.
6. Both sides of the debate among Jews considered Jesus an exalted human, not a divine being.
7. D. R. A. Hare, "The Rejection of the Jews in the Synoptic Gospels and Acts," in *Anti-Semitism and the Foundations of Christianity*, A. T. Davis, ed. (1979), 28–32.
8. Instead of Hare's problematic "prophetic anti-Judaism."
9. Instead of Hare's problematic "Jewish-Christian anti-Judaism."
10. Standing on Michele Murray, *Playing a Jewish Game* (2004), 147, 150.

10   SUPERSESSION

1. There are traces and insinuations of the term "New Israel" in Matthew, Hebrews, and in the Pauline letters but the unequivocal and overt claim to the designation "New Israel" does not occur in any of the New Testament documents.
2. The prophet Nahum being the most extreme.
3. More on this subject in Richard A. Horsley and John S. Hanson, *Bandits Prophets and Messiahs: Popular Movements at the Time of Jesus* (1985), Chapter 1.

4. For an introduction to the popular movements of early Christianity, see Horsley and Hanson, *Bandits, Prophets and Messiahs*.

5. R. R. Ruether, *Faith and Fratricide: The Theological Roots of Anti-Semitism* (1974), 90–91.

6. Standing on Craig A. Evans and Donald A. Hagner, *Anti-Semitism and Early Christianity* (1993), 9–17.

7. N. A. Beck, *Mature Christianity: The Recognition and Repudiation of the Anti-Jewish Polemic of the New Testament* (1985), 11–13.

8. Standing on Robert Wilken, *John Chrysostom and the Jews* (1983), 133.

9. The supremacy of one God—during the last two thousand years Judaism has evolved away from its tribal crucible toward a universalistic and monotheistic outlook, while still partially anchored in its ancestral (henotheistic) tribal origins.

10. Monotheism—belief in an omnipotent, omnipresent, and omniscient deity.

11. For a summary evaluation of the impact of 70 and 135 CE, see Stephen G. Wilson, *Related Strangers: Jews and Christians* (1995), 3–5.

12. G. Alon, *The Jews in Their Land in the Talmudic Age* (1989), vol. 1, esp. 1–17. See also B. Isaac, *Judaea after A. D. 70* (1984); E. M. Smallwood, *The Jews under Roman Rule* (1976), 327–371.

13. See P. Richardson, *Israel in the Apostolic Church* (1969), 33–38; L. H. Schiffman, *Who Was a Jew?* (1985), 75–78; M. Simon, *Versus Israel* (1986), 3–65; J. Dunn, *The Partings of the Ways* (1991), 230, 245; Wilken, *John Chrysostom and the Jews*, 150–151, 163; and Wilson, *Related Strangers*, 4–5, 8–11, and 285–288. Subject also covered on p. 111, 154.

14. Wilson, *Related Strangers*, 4–5.

15. Standing on Wilken, *John Chrysostom and the Jews*, 150–151.

16. George Nickelsburg, *Ancient Judaism and Christian Origins: Diversity, Continuity and Transformation* (2003), 59, 116–117.

17. Doron Mendels, *The Rise and Fall of Jewish Nationalism* (1992), 55–80.

18. Nickelsburg, *Ancient Judaism and Christian Origins*, 59.

19. John T. Pawlikowski, *Jesus and the Theology of Israel* (1989), 66.

20. E. P. Sanders, *Jesus and Judaism* (1985), 61–76.

21. In James H. Charlesworth, *Jesus and the Dead Sea Scrolls* (1992), 235–253.

22. James D. G. Dunn, *Christianity in the Making—Vol. 1—Jesus Remembered* (2003), 785.

23. Wilson, *Related Strangers*, 287.

24. Houses of prayer are attested in the Diaspora since the third century BC. Synagogues, gathering places where the Torah was read, are widely attested in Judea from the late second century BC onward.

25. Ibid.

26. The disciples that "did not understand," "abandoned," and "denied" and the "hidden Messiah motif."

27. On two covenant theologies, see Reinhold Niebuhr and Paul Tillich, in *Christ in the Light of the Christian-Jewish dialog*, John T. Pawlikowski, eds. (1982), 122; and J. C. Rylaarsdam, *Jewish-Christian Relationships: The Two Covenants and the Dilemmas of Christology in Grace upon Grace*, J. I. Cook, ed. (1975), 72. Donald G. Bloesch, "All Israel Will Be Saved: Supersessionism and the Biblical

Witness," *Int* 43 (1989), 131; and Thomas Breidenthal, *Neighbor-Christology: Reconstructing Christianity before Supersessionism* (1999), 319, reject the view that the church surpasses or supersedes Israel.

11   The Anti-Jewish Strand in Hebrews

1. D. A. Hagner, *Hebrews* (1983), 9.
2. Stephen G. Wilson, *Related Strangers: Jews and Christians* (1995).
3. Hebrews' scholarship (not an exhaustive list): B. P. W. S Hunt, "The Epistle to the Hebrews or against the Hebrews?" *SE* 2 (1964), 408; Samuel Sandmel, *Anti-Semitism in the New Testament?* (1978), 121; N. A. Beck, *Mature Christianity in the 21st Century: The Recognition and Repudiation of the Anti-Jewish Polemic of the New Testament*, 2d ed. (1994); Barnabas Lindars, "The Rhetorical Structure of Hebrews," *NTS* 35 (1989), 392 n. 2; Robert W. Wall and William Lane, in *Anti-Semitism and Early Christianity*, Craig Evans and Donald Hagner, eds. (2002), 199, 173; William Lane, *Hebrews 1–8, WBC 47a* (1991); Marie E. Isaacs, "Hebrews," in *Early Christian Thought in Its Jewish Context*, J. Barclay and J. Sweet, eds. (1996), 158; Harold W. Attridge, *The Epistle to the Hebrews* (1989), 9; Donald Hagner, *Encountering the Book of Hebrews* (2002), 35–36; Luke Timothy Johnson, "The New Testament's Anti-Jewish Slander and the Conventions of Ancient Polemic," *JBL* 108 (1989), 423–424; David A. deSilva, *Perseverance in Gratitude: A Socio-Rhetorical Commentary on the Epistle "to the Hebrews"* (2000), 263; Craig R. Koester, *Hebrews* (2001), 54; Clark M. Williamson, "Anti-Judaism in Hebrews?" *Int* 57 (2003), 266–279.
4. R. Alan Culpepper, "Mapping the Textures of the New Testament Criticism: A Response to Socio-Rhetorical Criticism," *JSNT* 70 (1998), 73; and David A. deSilva, "Heb 6:4–8: A Socio-Rhetorical Investigation," *TynBul* 50 (1999), 33–57, 225–236.
5. Victor Turner, *The Forest of Symbols* (Ithaca, NY: Cornell University Press, 1967).
6. Perdue juxtaposes Judaism to "Christianity," an anachronistic application.
7. Simon Tugwell, *The Apostolic Fathers* (1986), 24–25.
8. Wilson, *Related Strangers*, 110; Barnabas Lindars, *The Theology of the Letter to the Hebrews* (1991), 1.
9. F. F. Bruce, *The Epistle to the Hebrews* (1964), xliii; Harold W. Attridge, *The Epistle to the Hebrews* (1989); Lane, *Hebrews 1–8, WBC 47a*, lxvi; Lindars, *The Theology of the Letter to the Hebrews*, 21; Paul Ellingworth, *The Epistle to the Hebrews* (1993), 33; Craig R. Koester, *Hebrews* (2001), 54.
10. L. Salevao, *Legitimation in the Letter to the Hebrews: The Construction and Maintenance of a Symbolic Universe* (2002), 340.
11. Wilson, *Related Strangers*, 117; and S. Lehne, *The New Covenant in Hebrews* (1990), 103–104, 115, acknowledge them as part of the influences on the addressees.
12. Lehne, *The New Covenant in Hebrews*, 94.
13. Ibid., 120–121.

14. This is the majority view among scholars. See Philip E. Hughes, *A Commentary on the Epistle to the Hebrews* (1977), 260; Attridge, *The Epistle to the Hebrews*, 10–13; Bruce, *The Epistle to the Hebrews*, rev ed. (1990), 155; James D. G. Dunn, *The Partings of the Ways Between Christianity and Judaism* (1990); Lindars, *The Theology of the Letter to the Hebrews*, 10–11; Ellingworth, *The Epistle to the Hebrews*, 80; Wilson, *Related Strangers*, 127; Koester, *Hebrews*, 7.
15. Similar view in Lehne, *The New Covenant in Hebrews*, 15.
16. Similar views in ibid., 94.
17. See p. 93.
18. Most scholars argue that the community in Hebrews had separated itself from establishment Judaism. See Johnson, "The New Testament's Anti-Jewish Slander," 423–424; Lindars, *The Theology of the Letter to the Hebrews*, 11; Pamela M. Eisenbaum, "The Jewish Heroes of Christian History: Hebrews 11 in Literary Context," *SBLDS* 156 (1997), 10; and Salevao, *Legitimation in the Letter to the Hebrews*, 192–195. For a differing view, see Lane, *Hebrews 1–8*, *WBC 47a*, cxxvii.
19. Standing on Attridge, *The Epistle to the Hebrews*, 227.
20. Standing on Koester, *Hebrews*, 385.
21. See Hagner, *Hebrews*, 9.
22. See discussion in p. 32, 33, 225.
23. For the "revised Paul," see p. 32, 33, 225.
24. Standing on Wilson, *Related Strangers*, 17–118.
25. Exodus 28:1; Leviticus 21:10.
26. Exodus 28:1; Leviticus 1:5–7, 8:1–3; 21:1; Numbers 1:47–51; 3:5–9.
27. Malachi (1:6–2:9); Testament of Levi (T. Levi 14:5–8, 15:1–2; 16:1; 17:1, 18:1–3); 1 and 2 Maccabees (1 Macc. 2:23–27; 2 Macc. 4:24–25); Psalms of Salomon (Pss. Sol. 1:8, 2:3–4); Dead Sea Scrolls (CD 2.12–20, CD 4.18–19, and 5.6–8); IQpHab 8.8–13, IQpHab 9.4–5, 1QS 4.25.
28. Some Melchizedek speculation appears in the Qumran texts and in 2 Enoch and may have originated there. There is an equally enigmatic resurfacing of Melchizedek in Psalm 110:4.
29. See detailed analysis in Attridge, *The Epistle to the Hebrews*, 192–195.
30. G. Vermes, *The Dead Sea Scrolls in English* (1975), 265–268.
31. Lindars, *The Theology of the Letter to the Hebrews*, 75.
32. We already discussed the general Qumran/New Testament connection in p. 13.
33. Attridge, *The Epistle to the Hebrews*, 192–195.
34. Wilson, *Related Strangers*, 119.
35. Ibid.
36. Segment indebted to Lindars, *The Theology of the Letter to the Hebrews*, 75.
37. Ibid., 137.
38. See Lane, *Hebrews 1–8*, *WBC 47a*, 258; and Koester, *Hebrews*, 436.
39. Lehne, *The New Covenant in Hebrews*, 22.
40. Ibid., 36.
41. That is, Psalm 110:4; Jeremiah 31:31–35.
42. Lehne, *The New Covenant in Hebrews*, 94; and C. Spicq, *L'Epitre aux Hebreux* (1952), 13.

43. Hebrews uses the Septuagint version of Jeremiah 31:31–34.
44. Lehne, *The New Covenant in Hebrews*, 130–131; and W. D. Davies, "Torah in the Messianic Age and/or the Age to Come," *JBLMS* 7 (1952), 21–28.
45. On the supersessionary message of Hebrews, see David A. deSilva, *Perseverance in Gratitude: A Socio-Rhetorical Commentary on the Epistle "to the Hebrews"* (2000), 287. See also Attridge, *The Epistle to the Hebrews*, 228; Hughes, *A Commentary on the Epistle to the Hebrews*, 302; Ellingworth, *The Epistle to the Hebrews*, 413, 417; Johnson, "The New Testament's Anti-Jewish Slander," 423–424; Lindars, *The Theology of the Letter to the Hebrews*, 11; Eisenbaum, "The Jewish Heroes of Christian History," 10; Salevao, *Legitimation in the Letter to the Hebrews*, 192–195). See also Bruce, *The Epistle to the Hebrews*, 179; Hagner, *Hebrews*, 124; H. W. Montefiore, *The Epistle to the Hebrews* (Harper & Row, 1964), 142; Homer A. Kent, "The New Covenant and the Church," *GTJ* 6 (1985), 295; J. R. Walters, "The Rhetorical Arrangement of Hebrews," *As* 7/51 (1996), 59–70. For differing views, see Lane, *Hebrews 1–8, WBC 47a*, 210..
46. Psalms 26:6–7; 50:8–14; 51; 69:32; 107:22; 116:17; 119:108. See also Lindars, *The Theology of the Letter to the Hebrews*, 88–89; W. Thompson, "Hebrews 9 and Hellenistic Concepts of Sacrifice," *JBL* 98 (1979); and H. J. Kraus, *Worship in Israel* (1966); V. Nikiprowetzky, "La spiritualisation des sacrifices et le culte sacrificiel au temple de Jerusalem chez Philon d'Alexandrie," *Sem* 17 (1967), 79.
47. Samuel 15:22; Amos 4:4; 5:21–27; Hosea 6:6; 8:11–13; 13:2; Isaiah 1:10–15; 43:23–25; 65:3–11; 66:2–4, 17; Jeremiah 6:20; 7:21–24; 11:15; 19:5; 32:25; Habakkuk 1:16; Ezekiel 16:15–21; 23:36–39; Malachi 1:7–8; 3:8–9, Psalms 50:8–10; 51:16–17.
48. Thompson, "Hebrews 9 and Hellenistic Concepts of Sacrifice," 567.
49. Robert A. Kugler, *Religion in the Dead Sea Scrolls*, eds. John J. Collins and Robert A. Kugler (2000), 90.
50. Lindars, *The Theology of the Letter to the Hebrews*, 10.
51. See Aharon R. E. Agus, *The Binding of Isaac and Messiah: Law, Martyrdom, and Deliverance in Early Rabbinic Religiosity* (1988).
52. See p. 13.
53. Segment stands on Hagner, *Hebrews*, 14–15.
54. See p. 200.
55. Wilson, *Related Strangers*, 120. Similar views in Lehne, *The New Covenant in Hebrews*, 117.
56. Standing on Lindars, *The Theology of the Letter to the Hebrews*, 1. See more on this subject on p. 120.
57. D. A. Hagner, "A Positive Theology of Judaism from the New Testament," *SEA* 69 (2004), 14; Donald G. Bloesch, *"All Israel Will Be Saved": Supersessionism and the Biblical Witness* (1989), 139, 140.
58. The Roman positive view of Greek culture, and the Buddhist positive relationship vis-à-vis Hinduism might be the most notable.
59. See John Fischer, "Covenant Fulfillment and Judaism in Hebrews," *ERT* 13 (1989), 1–6; Robert W. Wall and William Lane, in *Anti-Semitism and*

Early Christianity, eds. Craig Evans and Donald Hagner (1993), 180–181; Steven McKenzie, *Covenant* (2000), 118–121; Williamson, "Anti-Judaism in Hebrews?" 266–279; Hagner, "A Positive Theology of Judaism from the New Testament," 14–18. Critical views of the Epistle: Beck, *Mature Christianity*; Wilson, *Related Strangers*; Williamson, "Anti-Judaism in Hebrews?" 270.

60. Donald G. Bloesch, describing this worldview, writes, "Christianity represents not the annulment of the heritage of Israel but its fulfillment even in the midst of negation" (*"All Israel Will Be Saved"* 139).

61. Hagner, *Hebrews*, 109. See also Ellingworth, *The Epistle to the Hebrews*, 381–382; Gordon, *Hebrews*, 27–28; Hughes, *A Commentary on the Epistle to the Hebrews*, 258; Spicq, *L'Epitre aux Hebreux*, 125; Johnson, "The New Testament's Anti-Jewish Slander," 423–424; Lindars, *The Theology of the Letter to the Hebrews*, 11; Eisenbaum, "The Jewish Heroes of Christian History," 10; Salevao, *Legitimation in the Letter to the Hebrews*, 192–195. Contrary views in Lane, *Hebrews 1–8, WBC 47a*, 185.

62. Wilson, *Related Strangers*, 121.

12 THE ANTI-JEWISH STRAND IN BARNABAS

1. 96–98 CE.
2. J. C. Paget, *The Epistle of Barnabas* (1994), 2; and Stephen G. Wilson, *Related Strangers: Jews and Christians* (1995), 110–142, among many.
3. Simon Tugwell, *The Apostolic Fathers* (1986), 23.
4. For full discussion, see P. Richardson and M. B. Shukster, "Barnabas, Nerva, and the Yavnean Rabbis," *JTS* n. S. 34 (1983), 32–55; Paget, *The Epistle of Barnabas*, 51; Wilson, *Related Strangers*, 34–37 and 132–133.
5. My rewording of Wilson, *Related Strangers*, 139.
6. My summary of Paget, *The Epistle of Barnabas*, 2, 248, and 256.
7. See his "explanations" on the origins of Jewish food laws and customs 10.1–12. Also Paget, *The Epistle of Barnabas*, 2, 72.
8. G. Alon, "Halacha in the Epistle of Barnabas," *Tarbiz* 12 (1940), 20–41.
9. Jewish numerology, i.e., the use of numbers as a mystical vehicle.
10. Standing on Paget, *The Epistle of Barnabas*, 2, 260–262.
11. Wilson, *Related Strangers*, 139.
12. Follows my condensation of Wilson, *Related Strangers*, 128–129; Paget, *The Epistle of Barnabas*, 56; Clayton N. Jefford, *Reading the Apostolic Fathers* (1996), 20; and Tugwell, *The Apostolic Fathers*, 23.
13. Wilson, *Related Strangers*, 137; and Paget, *The Epistle of Barnabas*, 9.
14. James R. Mueller, in *Anti-Semitism and Early Christianity*, Evans Ed and Hagner (1993), 257, points to W. Bauer, *Orthodoxy and Heresy in Earliest Christianity*, R. Kraft and G. Krodel, eds. (1971); H. Koester, *Introduction to the New Testament, vol. 2: History and Literature of Early Christianity* (1982); and Hennecke-Schneemelcher-Wilson, *New Testament Apocrypha*, 1.134–78, as the earliest to identify this phenomenon.

15. See discussion on missionary and secessionist communities on p. 93.
16. Wilson, *Related Strangers*, 137; and Michele Murray, *Playing a Jewish Game* (2004), 54.
17. Murray, *Playing a Jewish Game*, 51.
18. Per Wilson, *Related Strangers*, 136.
19. My elaboration of Paget, *The Epistle of Barnabas*, 59; and Murray, *Playing a Jewish Game*, 58.
20. My summary of Tugwell, *The Apostolic Fathers*, 28–33.
21. Wilson, *Related Strangers*, 137–138); Reidar Hvalvik, *The Struggle for Scripture and Covenant* (1996), 147–148); and Murray, *Playing a Jewish Game*, 52.
22. For further reading, see Richardson and Shukste, "Barnabas, Nerva, and the Yavnean Rabbis," 37; Paget, *The Epistle of Barnabas*, 69–70; Wilson, *Related Strangers*, 9–10; Murray, *Playing a Jewish Game*, 47.
23. My rewording of Wilson, *Related Strangers*, 9–10.
24 See further discussion in chapter 10.
25. Ibid.
26. Tugwell, *The Apostolic Fathers*, 40–41.
27. Standing on Murray, *Playing a Jewish Game*, 58.
28. Ibid., 57.
29. My elaboration of Murray, *Playing a Jewish Game*, 57; and Wilson, *Related Strangers*, 130.
30. See Murray, *Playing a Jewish Game*, 57.
31. Summary of Wilson, *Related Strangers*, 130.
32. Same argument in Hvalvik, *The Struggle for Scripture and Covenant*, 99; and Murray, *Playing a Jewish Game*, 56, regarding Judaism, not the Jewish followers of Jesus.
33. Tugwell, *The Apostolic Fathers*, 36.
34. My condensation of Wilson's thematic introduction (*Related Strangers*, 128 and 130). In parenthesis: my modification.
35. J. B. Lightfoot, trans., *The Epistle of Barnabas*: http://www.earlychristian writings.com.
36. On the Pesher exegetical method, see p. 15.
37. Summary stands on Paget, *The Epistle of Barnabas*.
38. See pp. 14–15 and 146 for more on this topic and in G. W. Nickelsburg, *1 Enoch: A Commentary on the Book of 1 Enoch* (2001), 454–459.
39. On secessionary communities, see p. 93.
40. Evil is "everywhere" (2:1; 4:1; 9:4, 13).
41. My condensation of Paget, *The Epistle of Barnabas*, 197–199.
42. Standing on Murray, *Playing a Jewish Game*, 54.
43. My fusion of Tugwell, *The Apostolic Fathers*, 38; and Paget, *The Epistle of Barnabas*, 52, 69–70.
44. Paget, *The Epistle of Barnabas*, 69–70.
45. Nicholas R. M. De Lange, *Origen and the Jews: Studies in Jewish-Christian Relations in Third Century Palestine* (1976); Wayne A. Meeks and Robert L. Wilken, *Jews and Christians in Anlioch in the First Four Centuries of the Common Era* (1978), 27; J. R. Donahue, *Jewish-Christian Controversy in the*

Second Century: Justin Martyr (1973), 254; M. Simon, *Versus Israel-Jews and Christians in the Roman Empire* (1986), xii; Miriam S. Taylor, *Anti-Judaism and Early Christian Identity: A Critique of the Scholarly Consensus* (1997).

46. G. Strecker, in W. Bauer, *Orthodoxy and Heresy in Earliest Christianity*, R. Kraft and G. Krodel, eds. (1971), 262; John Gager, *The Origins of Anti-Semitism* (1985), 115 and 132; Wilken, *John Chrisostom and the Jews* (1983); Lloyd Gaston, "Retrospect," in *Anti-Judaism in Early Christianity*, vol. 2, Stephen G. Wilson, ed. (1986), 166; *Studies in Christianity and Judaism,* S. G. Wilson, ed. (1986), 33–44; Judith M. Lieu, *Neither Jew nor Greek? Constructing Early Christianity* (2003); Murray, *Playing a Jewish Game*, 2.

47. Murray, *Playing a Jewish Game*.

48. Standing on Murray, *Playing a Jewish Game*, 52–53.

49. Paget, *The Epistle of Barnabas*, 185.

50. A sample would include 2:10; 3:6; 4:6b, 7; 8:1; 9:4; 10:2; 12:10f; 14:1–4; 15:8; 16:2f.

51. Standing on Wilson, *Related Strangers*, 128–129.

13   THE SECOND-CENTURY PROTAGONISTS

1. See more details in W. Bauer, *Orthodoxy and Heresy in Earliest Christianity*, ed. R. Kraft and G. Krodel (1971).

2. The Synoptic Sayings Source.

3. See Helmut Koester, *Ancient Christian Gospels* (1990), 165; and Bart Ehrman, *Lost Christianities: The Battle for Scripture and the Faiths We Never Knew* (2003) on this subject.

4. Summary of Koester, *Ancient Christian Gospels*, introduction.

5. See R. E. Brown, "Not Jewish Christianity and Gentile Christianity but Types of Jewish/Gentile Christianity," *CBQ* 45 (January 1983) for early diversity.

6. It was in Antioch that the followers of Christ were first called "Christians" (Acts 11:26).

7. I first encountered the term in Bart Ehrman's *Lost Christianities*.

8. I build on B. J. Malina, *Jewish-Christianity or Christian-Judaism: Toward a Hypothetical Definition* (1976), 46–47. On "Jewish Christianity," see H. J. Schoeps, *Jewish Christianity* (1969); G. Strecker, "On the Problem of Jewish Christianity," in *Orthodoxy and Heresy in Earliest Christianity*, by W. Bauer, trans. R. A. Kraft and G. Kroedel, eds. (1971), 241–285; A. Kraft, "In Search of 'Jewish Christianity' and its Theology: Problems of Definition and Methodology," *Recherches de Sciences Religieuse* 60 (1972), 81–96; A. F. J. Klijn and G. J. Reinink, *Patristic Evidence for Jewish-Christian Sects* (1973); A. F. J. Klijn, "The Study of Jewish-Christianity," *NTS* (1973–74), 419–426; J. D. G. Dunn, *Unity and Diversity in the New Testament* (1977), 239–266; S. K. Riegel, "Jewish Christianity: Definitions and Terminology," *NTS* 24 (1978), 411; R A. Fritz, *Nazarene Jewish Christianity: From the End of the First Century Until Its Disappearance in the Fourth Century* (1988); R. E. Van Voorst, *The Ascents of James: History and Theology of a Jewish-Christian Community* (1989);

Gerd Ludemann, *Opposition to Paul in Jewish Christianity*, trans. E. Boring (1989), 1–34. Updated views in O. Skarsaune and R. Hvalvik, eds., *Jewish Believers in Jesus* (2007); and Matt Jackson-Mccabe, ed., *Jewish Christianity Reconsidered* (2007). See also Shaye J. D. Cohen, *From the Maccabees to the Mishnah* (1987), 168; and J. T. Sanders, *Schismatics, Sectarians, Dissidents, Deviants* (1993), 58.

9. Lawrence Schiffman, *Who was a Jew?* (1985); and Adiel Schremer, *Brothers Estranged: Heresy, Christianity, and Jewish Identity in Late Antiquity* (2010).

10. Justin Martyr, Irenaeus, Tertullian, and Jerome are considered by most to be the earliest Christian apologists (Christian apologetics is a field of Christian theology that aims to present a rational basis for the Christian faith, defend the faith against objections, and expose the perceived flaws of other worldviews).

11. Skarsaune and Hvalvik, *Jewish Believers in Jesus*.

12. See table 13.1 for a summary of the theology of the Jewish followers of Jesus

13. T. Stylianopoulos, *Justin Martyr and the Mosaic Law* (1975), 26; D. P. Efroymson, in *Anti-Semitism and the Foundations Christianity*, A. T. Davies, ed. (1979), 105. A minority view (Knox, Tyson, and Townsend) sees Luke/Acts as addressing Marcion's challenge.

14. For an updated guide to the subject, see Hans-Josef Klauck, *The Religious Context of Early Christianity: A Guide to Graeco-Roman Religion* (2003).

15. Scholarship abounds with references to the contribution of Christian self-definition to anti-Judaism. See detailed discussions in R. R. Ruether, *Faith and Fratricide: The Theological Roots of Anti-Semitism* (1974), 181; and in Lloyd Gaston, in *Anti-Judaism in Early Christianity*, vol. 2, Stephen G. Wilson, ed. (1986), 164.

16. Joseph Tyson, *Marcion and Luke-Acts* (2006), 26–31.

17. Standing Stephen G. Wilson, *Related Strangers: Jews and Christians* (1995), 208.

18. Wilson, *Anti-Judaism in Early Christianity*, vol. 2, 48; and D. P. Efroymson, *Tertullian's Anti-Judaism and Its Role in Theology* (1976), 112–146.

19. Similar view in Wilson, *Related Strangers*, 214–215.

20. According to Tertullian, Marcion was "forced to form an alliance with the Jewish error and construct for himself an argument from it" (*Adv. Marc.* 6.2; cf. 23.1) also Judith M. Lieu, *Image and Reality* (1996), 264.

21. See discussion in Lieu, *Image and Reality*, 269–270.

22. Indebted to Wilson, *Related Strangers*, 216; and Lieu, *Image and Reality*, 264.

23. See Wilson, *Related Strangers*, 216. Also Michele Murray, *Playing a Jewish Game* (2004), 102; and Miriam Taylor, *Anti-Judaism and Early Christian Identity* (1995), 171.

24. This segment feeds on Taylor, *Anti-Judaism and Early Christian Identity*, 171.

25. See Michael Williams, *Rethinking Gnosticism* (1996), for a general discussion of the topic. For detailed discussion, see p. x.

26. Hans Jonas, *The Gnostic Religion* (1958), 31–46. Gnosticism impacted Judaism too. Kabbalah was to G. Sholem "Jewish Gnosticism." Others support the Jewish origins of Gnosticism. B. Layton, *The Rediscovery of Gnosticism* (1980); Elaine Pagels, *The Gnostic Gospels* (1943); and Kurt Rudolph, *Gnosis: The Nature & History of Gnosticism* (1987).

27. Wilson, *Related Strangers*, 204. See also G. A. Strousma, *Another Seed: Studies in Gnostic Mythology*, Nag Hammadi Studies, No. 24 (1997).

28. On the Gnostic impact on early Christianity, see Klaick Hans-Josef, *The Religious Context of Early Christianity* (2000), part VI. On cross-influence between Judaism, Christianity, and Gnosticism, see Alan F. Segal, in *Anti-Judaism in Early Christianity*, vol. 2, Wilson, 133–162.

29. See Jonas, *The Gnostic Religion*, 31–46; Layton, *The Rediscovery of Gnosticism*; Pagels, *The Gnostic Gospels*; and Kurt, *Gnosis*.

30. See Origen, Evagrius of Pontus, and others. Mystical and Gnostic affinities brought about Origen's condemnation as a heretic by the second council of Constantinople (CE 553).

31. A self-standing chapter is dedicated to the Gentile sympathizers with the Jewish followers of Jesus.

32. Similar views in David Sim and Boris Repschinski, eds., *Matthew and His Christian Contemporaries* (2008), 7.

33. Lieu, *Image and Reality*, 264–265.

34. Bart Ehrman, *The New Testament: Historical Introduction* (2007).

35. Supersession theology is sometimes referred to as substitution or replacement theology (see chapter 10).

36. See John Gager, *The Origins of Anti-Semitism* (1985), 189.

37. As highlighted in table 13.1.

38. For the opposite view, which argues for high literacy levels in the Roman world, see J. T. Townsend, "Ancient Education in the Time of the Early Roman Empire," in *The Catacombs and the Colesseum*, S. Benko and J. J. O'Rourke, eds. (1971), 139–163.

14 THE ANTI-JEWISH STRAND IN IGNATIUS

1. Clayton N. Jefford, *Reading the Apostolic Fathers* (1996), 54. Eusebius places the martyrdom of Ignatius in the reign of Trajan (98–117).

2. Simon Tugwell, *The Apostolic Fathers* (1986), 105.

3. Interesting analysis of the de-Judaizing thrust of Ignatius's ministry in David Sim and Boris Repschinski, eds., *Matthew and His Christian Contemporaries* (2008), Chapter 8.

4. Jefford, *Reading the Apostolic Fathers*, 55.

5. P. J. Donahue, *Jewish Christianity in the Letters of Ignatius* (1978), 87, identifies the "heretics" Ignatius is fighting against as Christian Jews.

6. My elaboration of Tugwell, *The Apostolic Fathers*, 105.

7. My rewording Michele Murray's presentation in *Playing a Jewish Game* (2004).

8. Stephen G. Wilson, *Related Strangers: Jews and Christians* (1995), 147–165.

9. J. B. Lightfoot, trans., *Ignatius, the Epistle to the Philadelphians*, http://www .earlychristianwritings.com.

10. Ibid.

11. Similar views in Murray, *Playing a Jewish Game*, 90–91.

12. Ignatius here resonates with Barnabas who took similar positions.
13. J. T. Sanders, *Schismatics, Sectarians, Dissidents, Deviants* (1993), 197.
14. Standing on Wilson, *Related Strangers*, 219–220; and Tugwell, *The Apostolic Fathers*, 104–106.
15. Michael Isacson, *To Each Their Own Letter: Structure, Themes, & Rhetorical Strategies in the Letters of Ignatius of Antioch* (2004), 888.
16. Tugwell, *The Apostolic Fathers*, 110.
17. Wilson, *Related Strangers*, 117.
18. Tugwell, *The Apostolic Fathers*, 106–107, 114–115; Wilson, *Related Strangers*, 117; Jefford, *Reading the Apostolic Fathers*, 64–66.

15   THE ANTI-JEWISH STRAND IN JUSTIN: THE DIALOGUE WITH TRYPHO THE JEW

1. J. D. Crossan, *The Cross That Spoke* (1988), 66.
2. My elaboration of Murray Michele's summary, *Playing a Jewish Game* (2004), 96.
3. A Jewish audience is suggested by T. Stylianopoulos, *Justin Martyr and the Mosaic Law* (1975), 35–44.
4. See Stephen G. Wilson, *Related Strangers: Jews and Christians* (1995), 165–167; and Murray, *Playing a Jewish Game*, 96.
5. Wilson, *Related Strangers*, 165–167.
6. The embryonic stages of the doctrines that will eventually be known as "Christian Orthodoxy." Similar views in P. Richardson, *Israel in the Apostolic Church* (1969), 9–13; and Wilson, *Related Strangers*, 269–270.
7. Citations per Anthony J. Saldarini, *Matthew's Christian-Jewish Community* (1994), 22–23.
8. Murray, *Playing a Jewish Game*, 95–96.
9. Somewhat similar in ibid., 98–99.
10. Wilson, *Related Strangers*, 277.
11. Similar argument in ibid., 269–270.
12. See Miriam Taylor, *Anti-Judaism and Early Christian Identity* (1995), 170–172.
13. For discussion of the anti-Judaism of the *Dialogue,* see Wilson, *Related Strangers*, 265–274; and H. Remus, in *Anti-Judaism in Early Christianity*, S. G. Wilson, ed. (1986), vol. 2, 74–80.
14. For a recent survey of scholarship on this subject, see Murray, *Playing a Jewish Game*, 141–148. See G. Strecker, in W. Bauer, *Orthodoxy and Heresy in Earliest Christianity*, R. Kraft and G. Krodel, eds. (1971), 262; John G. Gager, *The Origins of Anti-Semitism* (1983), 115 and 132; Robert Wilken, *John Chrisostom and the Jews* (1983); Lloyd Gaston, "Retrospect," in *Anti-Judaism in Early Christianity, Vol. 2*, Wilson, ed. (1986), 166; L *Studies in Christianity and Judaism*, Wilson, ed. (1986), 33–44; Judith M. Lieu, *Neither Jew Nor Greek? Constructing Early Christianity*, (2003); Murray, *Playing a Jewish Game*, 2. See p. 199 on the subject.

15. Murray, *Playing a Jewish Game*, 98–99.
16. Same conclusion in ibid.
17. Irenaeus tells us that Justin Martyr wrote a work against Marcion, which is now lost. See also Wilson, *Related Strangers*, 268 and 274–278; Stylianopoulos, *Justin Martyr and the Mosaic Law*, 20–32; Taylor, *Anti-Judaism and Early Christian Identity*, 171; and D. P. Efroymson, in *Anti-Semitism and the Foundations Christianity*, A. T. Davies and A. T. Ed, eds. (1979), 105.
18. Just to name the latest: H. Remus, in *Anti-Judaism in Early Christianity, Vol. 2*, Wilson, 69–80; W. Horbury, in *Jews and Christians: The Parting of the Ways A. D. 70 to 135*, James D. G. Dunn, ed. (1992), 326–345; and J. T. Sanders, *Schismatics, Sectarians, Dissidents, Deviants* (1993), 50–55; Murray, *Playing a Jewish Game*, 91.
19. Wilson, *Related Strangers*, 260.

16   The Anti-Jewish Strand in Melito

1. Standing on Stephen G. Wilson, *Related Strangers: Jews and Christians* (1995), 248; and Michele Murray, *Playing a Jewish Game* (2004), 113.
2. Stephen Wilson, ed., *Anti-Judaism in Early Christianity* (1986), vol. 2, 98; A. T. Kraabel, *Judaism in Western Asia Minor* (1968), 216–217.
3. "Quartodecimanism" refers to the practice of fixing the celebration of Passover for Christians on the fourteenth day of Nisan in the Old Testament's Hebrew Calendar. A controversy arose concerning whether it should instead be celebrated on one particular Sunday each year, which is now the floating holiday that is commonly called Easter Sunday.
4. Standing on Murray, *Playing a Jewish Game*, 106–107.
5. Further reading in Wilson, ed., *Anti-Judaism in Early Christianity*, vol. 2, 97; Miriam Taylor, *Anti-Judaism and Early Christian Identity* (1995), 58; Murray, *Playing a Jewish Game*, 114.
6. A. Hansen, *The Sitz im Leben of the Paschal Homily of Melito of Sardis* (1968) 180; K. W. Noakes, *Melito of Sardis and the Jews* (1975), 246; S. G. Wilson, ed., *Anti-Judaism in Early Christianity*, vol. 2, 95–100; and David Satran in *Contra Iudaeos*, Ora Limor, Maurice R. Hayoun, and Guy G. Stroumsa, eds., (1996), 49–58; Diss. Abstracts 29 (1969) 2343 A.
7. Wilson, *Related Strangers*, 257.
8. Stroumsa Guy G. (*Contra Iudaeos*, 1996, 8–10). Ora Limor, Maurice R. Hayoun, Guy G. Stroumsa eds., *Contra Iudaeos*. 1996.
9. http://www.kerux.com/documents/KeruxV4N1A1.asp
10. We may point out that the virulence of this disturbing text is somewhat similar to the viciousness of protestant anti-Catholic and of catholic anti-protestant polemic during the sixteenth century.
11. See Wilson, *Related Strangers*, 257.
12. Paraphrasing Murray, *Playing a Jewish Game*, 116.
13. More in Wilson, *Related Strangers*, 254.

17   THE ANTI-JEWISH STRAND
IN CHRYSOSTOM

1. Chrysostom: Golden-mouth.
2. This segment is my condensation and interpretation of Robert Wilken, *John Chrysostom and the Jews* (1983), xv, 29–30, and 32.
3. Paul W. Harkins, *Discourses against Judaizing Christians* (1979), v.
4. Wilken, *John Chrysostom and the Jews*, 124, 148–149; and Pieter W. Van Der Horst, in *Christian-Jewish Relations through the Centuries*, Stanle E. Porter and Brook W. R. Pearson, eds. (2000), 228–229.
5. Segments from John Chrysostom, *Discourses against Judaizing Christians*, vol. 68 of Fathers of the Church, trans. Paul W. Harkins (1979). See commentary on Antioch's Gentile Judaizers in M. Simon, *Versus Israel—Jews and Christians in the Roman Empire* (1986), 374.
6. John Chrysostom, *Eight Homilies against the Jews, Patrologia Greaca*, vol. 98. Internet History Sourcebooks Project, ed. Paul Halsall, Fordham University: http://www.fordham.edu/Halsall/index.asp.
7. Wilken, *John Chrysostom and the Jews*, 118.
8. Chrysostom, *Eight Homilies against the Jews*.
9. James Parkes, *Anti-Semitism* (1969), 153.
10. Simon, *Versus Israel*, 145.
11. My summary of Stephen G. Wilson, *Related Strangers: Jews and Christians* (1995), 128; and Simon Tugwell, *The Apostolic Fathers*,(1986), 23.
12. Chrysostom, *Eight Homilies against the Jews*.
13. On this subject, see Wilken, *John Chrysostom and the Jews*, 68.
14. On the Jews of ancient Antioch, see C. H. Kraeling, "The Jewish Community at Antioch," *JBL* 51 (1932), 130–160; G. Downey, *A History of Antioch in Syria, from Seleucus to the Arab Conquest* (1961), 447–449.
15. Van Der Horst, in *Christian-Jewish Relations through the Centuries*, Porter and Brook, 233.
16. See the notes on the book's cover; a unique fifth-century presentation of the Gentile and Jewish Churches, depicted side by side and of apparent equal standing.
17. Similar views in Wilken, *John Chrysostom and the Jews*, 67.
18. Jaclyn L. Maxwell, *Christianization and Communication in Late Antiquity: John Chrysostom and His Congregation in Antioch* (2006).
19. For a survey, see Edward Kessler, *An Introduction to Jewish-Christian Relations* (2010), Chapter 3.
20. Standing on Wilken, *John Chrysostom and the Jews*, 163–164.

18   RECAPITULATION

1. My wording of the grievances of Gentile followers of Paul against Gentile sympathizers with the Jewish followers of Jesus.

2. Gentile sympathizers with the Jewish faction responding to the proto-orthodox (my wording).

3. In this summary subsection we will concentrate on Mark, John, Barnabas, and Justin despite the fact that this theme reverberated throughout the lore. Mark, acknowledged by most as the Gospel on which the anti-Jewish strand stands, is of special interest to us.

4. See N. A. Beck, *Mature Christianity: The Recognition and Repudiation of the Anti-Jewish Polemic of the New Testament* (1994), 57–59.

5. The struggle between the Mushite and Aaronid priestly clans, the tensions between the tribal and monarchical power structures and between the monarchy and the religious establishment.

6. Philistines, Amalek, Edom, Moab.

7. Similar arguments in Kelber Werner, *The Oral and the Written Gospel* (1983), 130–131; and Lindsey P. Pherigo, "The Gospel According to Mark," in *The Interpreter's One Volume Commentary on the Bible* (1971), 644..

8. In the context of the motifs enumerated later, the choice of Judas as the disciple that would betray Jesus, and the convenient fact that his name resonates with Iudaeos ("Jews") cease to be a coincidence and are suspect of being another of many hints at the tendentious nature of the narrative.

9. See p. 199.

10. Eusebius's penchant for pandering was identified early and was accused of "being more intent on the rhetorical finish of his composition and the praises of the emperor, than on an accurate statement of facts." See Socrates Scholasticus's *Historia Ecclesiastica*.

11. James R. Mueller, in *Anti-Semitism and Early Christianity*, Evans Ed and Hagner (1993), 257, who points to W. Bauer, *Orthodoxy and Heresy in Earliest Christianity*, eds. R. Kraft and G. Krodel (1971); H. Koester, *Introduction to the New Testament, vol. 2: History and Literature of Early Christianity, 1982*; and Hennecke-Schneemelcher-Wilson, *New Testament Apocrypha*, 1.134–78, as the earliest to identify this phenomenon.

12. Similar to the Jewish use of "Hellenists" to denigrate Jews with Greek inclinations and affiliations.

13. L. T. Johnson, *The New Testament's Anti-Jewish Slander and the Conventions of Ancient Polemic* (1989), 419–441. Also See Anthony J. Blasi, Jean Duhaime, and Paul-Andre' Turcotte, eds., *Hanbook of Early Christianity* (2002), section 2, for a discussion of rhetorical techniques and their effectiveness. Also: Stanley E. Porter and Dennis L. Stamps, eds., *The Rhetorical Interpretation of Scripture* (1999); G. N. Stanton, *Aspects of Early Christian-Jewish Polemic and Apologetic* (1985).

14. See Michele Murray's *Playing a Jewish Game* (2004) for an updated and detailed study on Gentile Judaizing.

15. Ibid., 40–41.

16. Ibid., 118–119.

17. For a recent survey of scholarship on this subject, see ibid., 141–148. See G. Strecker, in Bauer, *Orthodoxy and Heresy in Earliest Christianity*, Kraft and Krodel, 262; John G. Gager, *The Origins of Anti-Semitism* (1983), 115 and 132; Robert Wilken, *John Chrisostom and the Jews* (1983); Lloyd Gaston,

"Retrospect," in *Anti-Judaism in Early Christianity*, vol. 2, Stephen G. Wilson, ed. (1986), 166; *Studies in Christianity and Judaism*, S. G. Wilson, ed., (1986), 33–44; Judith M. Lieu, *Neither Jew nor Greek? Constructing Early Christianity* (2003); Murray, *Playing a Jewish Game*, 2.

18. From the perspective of non-Jewish believers in Jesus it may be said that Paul is defending his mission to the Gentiles. However, from a Jewish perspective Paul's ministry was aimed at de-Judaizing Gentile Belief in Jesus.

19. On the meager evidence for Jewish proselytizing: "What Parting of the Ways?" In *The Ways that Never Parted*, Paula Fredriksen, ed. (2003), 48–56; Miriam S. Taylor, *Anti-Judaism and Early Christian Identity: A Critique of the Scholarly Consensus* (1995); Murray, *Playing a Jewish Game*, 118–119; Martin Goodman, *The Jews among Pagans and Christians: In the Roman Empire* (1992), 53, 55, 70–71; T. Kraabel, *The Roman Diaspora: Six questionable assumptions* (1982), 451–452; David Rokeah, *Jews, Pagans and Christians in Conflict* (1982), 32–44; and I. Levinskaya, *The Book of Acts in its First Century Setting. V. Diaspora Setting* (1996), 21–47. For the opposite position: D. Georgi, *The Opponents of Paul in Second Corinthians* (1986), 83–228; L. H. Feldman, *Jew and Gentile in the Ancient World* (1993), 288–415. Standing on Murray, *Playing a Jewish Game*, 118–119.

20. One of the earlies was M. Simon, *Versus Israel-Jews and Christians in the Roman Empire*, French ed. (1964), 356–393 esp. 383.

21. For support to the conclusion that Gentile believers in Jesus underwent a process of individuation-estrangement vis-à-vis the descendants of Jesus's disciples and followers, and not "Judaism," see chapter 7 in this volume.

22. On the absence of anti-Christian polemic in the foundational texts of Rabbinic Judaism, see Eugene Fisher and L. Klenicki, eds., *Root and Branches: Biblical Judaism, Rabbinical Judaism and Early Christianity* (1987).

23. J. Lighthouse, in *Anti-Judaism in Early Christianity*, vol. 2, Wilson, 106.

24. Wilson, *Related Strangers*, 47; D. A. Hagner, "The Sitz im Leben of the Gospel of Matthew," in *Society of Biblical Literature 1985*, Seminar Papers, K. H. Richards, ed. (1985), 244–270; Reuven Kimelman, in *Jewish and Christian Self-Definition*, E. P. Sanders, ed., with A. I. Baumgarten and Alan Mendelson (1981), 226–244, 391–403; P. van der Horst, "The Birkat Ha-Minim in Recent Research," *ExpTim* 105 (1994); S. T. Katz, "Issues in the Separation of Judaism and Christianity after 70 C. E.: A Reconsideration," *JBL* 103 (1984), 43–76, 74; Lawrence Schiffman, *Who was a Jew?* (1985), 61; J. A. Overmann, *Matthew's Gospel and Formative Judaism* (1990), 48–56; and Adiel Schremer, *Brothers Estranged: Heresy, Christianity, and Jewish Identity in Late Antiquity* (2010). See also discussions on p. 80.

25. Jewish followers of Jesus were often labeled as "Jews" by Gentile opponents within the Jesus movement. See Bauer, *Orthodoxy and Heresy in Earliest Christianity*, Kraft and Krodel; Koester, *Introduction to the New Testament, vol. 2: History and Literature of Early Christianity*; and Hennecke-Schneemelcher-Wilson, *New Testament Apocrypha*, 1.134–78, 5, as the earliest to identify this phenomenon.

26. Justin, Dial. 16, 17, 32, 34, 117, 131, 133, 136, 137, Irenaeus, Adv. Haer. 4.21.3, Cf. Mart. Pol. 13.2, 17.2, and 18.1, which tells of the Jews' complicity in the death of Polycarp, Origen, Gen. Horn. 13.3.
27. Wilson, *Related Strangers*, 181.
28. For traces in the pseudo-Clementine literature of a "Jewish-Christian" response, see Bart Ehrman, *Lost Christianities: The Battle for Scripture and the Faiths We Never Knew* (2003), 182–185.
29. See Bart Ehrman's insightful development of this theme as it applies to our subjects (ibid.).
30. Joseph Tyson, *Marcion and Luke-Acts* (2006), 131.
31. See Wilson, *Related Strangers*, 219–220.
32. Similar views in Tyson, *Marcion and Luke-Acts*, 131.
33. This sequence is my modification of R. Hilberg, *The Destruction of the European Jews* (1979).
34. Taylor, *Anti-Judaism and Early Christian Identity*, 62–63.
35. Mary C. Boys, *Has God Only One Blessing?* (2000), 58.
36. Clark M. Williamson, "Anti-Judaism in Hebrews?" *Int* 57 (2003), 266–279.
37. "Those pages of history that Jews have committed to memory are the very ones that have been torn from Christian (and secular) history books." E. Flannery, *The Anguish of the Jews: Twenty-Three Centuries of Anti-Semitism* (1985).

Appendix I: Paul in Modern Scholarship

1. F. C. Baur, *The Church History of the First Three Centuries* (1875).
2. Ernst Kasemann, *Commentary on Romans* (1980), 94.
3. Hans Conzelmann, *An Outline of the Theology of the New Testament* (1969), 226.
4. Lloyd Gaston, *Paul and the Torah* (1987), 2.
5. W. D. Davies, *People of Israel* (1977), 22.
6. Gaston, *Paul and the Torah*, 8.
7. Ibid., 135.
8. John Gager, in *The Ways That Never Parted*, A. H.Becker and A. Yoshiko (2003), 75.
9. Ibid., 151.
10. Stanley Stowers, *A Rereading of Romans* (1994), 326.
11. E. P. Sanders, *Paul, the Law, and the Jewish People* (1983), 156.
12. Gaston, *Paul and the Torah*, 23.
13. John Gager, *The Origins of Anti-Semitism* (1983), 195.
14. John G. Gager, *Reinventing Paul* (2000), 9–10.
15. Paula Fredricksen, *From Jesus to Christ* (1988), 161–162.
16. Michael Wyschogrod, *The Impact of Dialogue* (1990), 731–733.
17. Peter Tomson, *Paul and the Jewish Law* (1990), 238.
18. J. C. Becker, *Paul the Apostle. The Triumph of God in Life and Thought* (1980), 334.

19. Stowers, *A Rereading Romans*, 326.
20. E. P. Sanders, *Paul, the Law, and the Jewish People* (1983), 14, 132, 199.
21. E. P. Sanders, *Paul and Palestinian Judaism* (1977), 433.
22. Gager, *Reinventing Paul*, 9–10.
23. Ibid., 147.
24. Becker, *Paul the Apostle*, 20.
25. H. J. Schoeps, *Paul. The Theology of the Apostle in the Light of Jewish Religious History,* 262.
26. Räisänen, *Paul and the Law*, 10f, 201f, 264.
27. James D. G. Dunn, *Christology in the Making* (1990) for a critique of the "revised" Paul.
28. J. C. O'Neill, *The Recovery of Paul's Letter to the Galatians* (1972), 86.
29. J. C. O'Neill, *Paul's Letter to the Romans* (1975), 16.
30. E. Bammel and C. F. D. Moule, *Jesus in the Politics of His Day* (1984), 370.
31. Hans Hubner, *Law in Paul's Thought* (1983).
32. Sanders, *Paul, the Law, and the Jewish People*, 147–148 and 154.

Bibliography

Modern abbreviations: http://www.Continuumbooks.com/download/Bibliographical .pdf.

Ancient abbreviations: http://www.Continuumbooks.com/download/AncientSources .pdf.

Agus, Aharon R. E. *The Binding of Isaac and Messiah: Law, Martyrdom, and Deliverance in Early Rabbinic Religiosity.* Albany: SUNY Press, 1988.

Alon, Gedaliah. *The Jews in Their Land in the Talmudic Age (70–640 C E.).* Cambridge, MA: Harvard University Press, 1989.

Anderson, Janice Capel, and Stephen D. Moore, eds. *Mark and Method: New Approaches in Biblical Studies.* Minneapolis: Fortress Press, c2008.

Anderson, Paul N. *The Riddles of the Fourth Gospel: An Introduction to John.* New Haven: Yale University Press, 2011.

Attridge, Harold W. *The Epistle to the Hebrews.* Philadelphia: Fortress Press, 1989.

Audet, Jean-Paul. "Affinites litteraires et doctrinales du 'Manuel de Discipline.'" *Revue biblique* 59 (1952): 219–238.

Aune, David E. *Prophecy in Early Christianity and the Ancient Mediterranean World.* Grand Rapids, MI: Eerdmans, 1983.

Bammel, Ernst, and C. F. D. Moule, eds. *Jesus and the Politics of His Day.* Cambridge: Cambridge University Press, 1984.

Barrett, C. K. *The Gospel according to St. John.* London: SPCK, 1978.

———. *The Gospel of John and Judaism.* Philadelphia: Westminster Press, 1978.

Bauer, Walter. *Orthodoxy and Heresy in Earliest Christianity.* Philadelphia: Fortress Press, 1971.

Baur, F. C. *The Church History of the First Three Centuries.* BiblioLife, 1875.

Beck, Norman A. *Mature Christianity in the 21st Century: The Recognition and Repudiation of the Anti-Jewish Polemic of the New Testament.* Philadelphia: American Interfaith Institute, 1994.

Beker, J. Christaan. *Paul the Apostle: The Triumph of God in Life and Thought.* Edinburgh: Clark, 1980.

Bieringer, R., and D. Pollefeyt, eds. *Paul and Judaism: Crosscurrents in Pauline Exegesis and the Study of Jewish-Christian Relations.* London: T&T Clark International, 2012.

Black, David Alan, and David R. Beck. *Rethinking the Synoptic Problem.* Grand Rapids: Baker Academic, 2001.

Blasi, Anthony J., Jean Duhaime, and Paul-André Turcotte, eds. *Handbook of Early Christianity: Social Science Approaches.* Walnut Creek: AltaMira Press, 2002.

Bloesch, Donald G. "All Israel Will Be Saved: Supersessionism and the Biblical Witness." *Int* 43 (1989): 131, 139.

Bock, Darrell. In *Rethinking the Synoptic Problem*, edited by David Alan Black and David R. Beck. Grand Rapids, MI: Baker Academic, 2001.

Bonhoffer, D. *No Rusty Swords—Letters, Lectures and Notes S 1928–1936*. New York: Collins, 1947.

Booth, R. P. "Jesus and the Laws of Purity: Tradition History and Legal History in Mark 7." *JSNT* (1986): Suppl. 13, 55–114.

Borg, Marcus J., ed. *Jesus at 2000*. Boulder, CO: Westview Press, 1997.

Borgen, Peder. In *Anti-semitism and Early Christianity: Issues of Polemic and Faith*, edited by Craig A. Evans and Donald A. Hagner. Minneapolis: Fortress Press, 1993.

Borgen, Peder. *Early Christianity and Hellenistic Judaism*. Edinburgh: T&T Clark International, 1996.

Boyarin, Daniel. *A Radical Jew: Paul and the Politics of Identity*. London: University of California Press, 1994.

Boys, Mary C. *Has God Only One Blessing?: Judaism as a Source of Christian Self-Understanding*. New York: Paulist Press, 2000.

Brandon, S. G. F. *The Fall of Jerusalem and the Christian Church: A Study of the Effects of the Jewish Overthrow of AD 70 on Christianity*. London: SPCK, 1951.

———. *Jesus and the Zealots*. Charles Scribner, 1967.

Bratton, F. *The Crime of Christendom: The Theological Sources of Christian Antisemitism*. Santa Barbara, CA: Fithian Press, 1969.

Breidenthal, Thomas. "Neighbor-Christology: Reconstructing Christianity Before Supersessionism." *Cross Currents* 49 (1999): 319.

Brooke, George. *The Dead Sea Scrolls and the New Testament*. London: Augsburg Fortress Publishers, 2005.

Brown, R. E. *The Birth of the Messiah: A Commentary on the Infancy Narratives in Matthew and Luke*. Garden City: Image Books, 1979, c1977.

———. *The Community of the Beloved Disciple*. London: G. Chapman, 1979.

———. *The Death of the Messiah: From Gethsemane to the Grave: A Commentary on the Passion Narratives in the Four Gospels*. New York: Doubleday, 1994.

———. "The Johannine Perspective on Christian Diversity in the Late First Century." *JBL* (1978).

———. "Not Jewish Christianity and Gentile Christianity but Types of Jewish/Gentile Christianity." *CBQ* 45 (1983): 74–79.

Bruce, F. F. "The Epistle to the Hebrews." In *New London Commentary*, xxiii–xxx. London, 1965.

———. "To the Hebrews or to the Essenes?" *NTS* 9 (1963): 217–232.

Bultmann, R. *The Gospel according to John*. Blackwell, 1971.

———. *Theology of the New Testament*. London: SCM, 1971.

Carroll, K. L. "The Fourth Gospel and the Exclusion of Christians from the Synagogue." *BJRL* 40 (1957).

Charlesworth, J. H. In *Judaisms and Their Messiahs at the Turn of the Christian Era*, edited by William S. Green, Ernest Frerichs, and Jacob Neusner. Cambridge: Cambridge University Press, 1987.

Charlesworth, J. H., H. Lichtenberger, and G. S. Oegerna, eds. *Qumran-Messianism*. Tübingen: Paul Mohr Verlag, 1998.

Charlesworth, James H. In *Anti-Judaism and the Fourth Gospel: Papers of the Leuven Colloquium, 2000*, edited by Reimund Bieringer, Didier Pollefeyt, and Frederique Vandecasteele-Vanneuville. Boston: Brill Academic Publishers, 2001.

———. *Jesus and the Dead Sea Scrolls (The Anchor Yale Bible Reference Library)*. Yale: Yale University Press, 1992.

Charlesworth, James H., et al., eds. *The Messiah: Developments in Early Judaism Find Christianity*. Minneapolis: Fortress Press, 1992.

Chilton, Bruce, and Craig A. Evans, eds. *James the Just and Christian Origins*. Boston: Brill Academic Publishers, 1999.

Chrysostom, John. *Discourses against Judaizing Christians*, translated by Paul W. Harkins. Washington: Catholic University of America Press, c1979.

Clayton, N. Jefford, Kenneth J. Harder, and Louis D. Amezaga. *Reading the Apostolic Fathers: An Introduction*. Peabody, MA: Hendrickson Publishers, 1996.

Cohen, Arthur A. *The Myth of the Judeo-Christian Tradition, and Other Dissenting Essays*. New York: Schocken Books, 1969.

Cohen, Shaye J. D. *The Beginnings of Jewishness: Boundaries, Varieties, Uncertainties*. Berkeley: University of California Press, 1999.

———. *From the Maccabees to the Mishnah*. Philadelphia: Westminster Press, 1987.

Cohn-Sherbok, Dan, and John M. Court, eds. *Religious Diversity in the Graeco-Roman World: A Survey of Recent Scholarship (Biblical Seminar)*. London: T & T Clark Publishers, 2001.

Collins, John J., and Gregory E. Sterling, eds. *Hellenism in the Land of Israel*. Notre Dame: University of Notre Dame, 2001.

Collins, A. Yarbro. *Crisis and Catharsis: The Power of the Apocalypse, 1984*. Philadelphia: Westminster Press, c1984.

———. "Vilification and Self-Definition in the Book of Revelation." *HTR* 79, 1 (1986): 308–320.

Collins, John J. *The Scepter and the Star: The Messiahs of the Dead Sea Scrolls and Other Ancient Literature*. New York: Doubleday, 1995.

Coloe, Mary L., and Tom Thatcher, eds. *John, Qumran, and the Dead Sea Scrolls: Sixty Years of Discovery and Debate*. Atlanta, GA: Society of Biblical Literature, 2011.

Conzelmann, Hans. *An Outline of the Theology of the New Testament*. London: SCM Press, 1969.

Cook, M. J. "Mark's Treatment of the Jewish Leaders." *Novum Testamentum* (1978): Suppl. 51.

Cross, Frank. *The Ancient Library of Qumran*. London: Sheffield Academic Press, 1995.

Crossan, John Dominic. *The Cross That Spoke: The Origins of the Passion Narrative*. Eugene, OR: Wipf & Stock Publishers, 1998.

———. *Four Other Gospels: Shadows on the Contours of Canon*. Sonoma: Polebridge Press, 1986.

———. *The Historical Jesus*. New York: HarperCollins, 1992.

———. *Jesus: A Revolutionary Biography*. San Francisco: HarperOne, 1994.

———. *Who Killed Jesus? Exposing the Roots of Anti-Semitism in the Gospel Story of the Death of Jesus*. San Francisco: Harper, 1995.

Crowley, Paul, ed. *Proceedings of the Catholic Theological Society of America*. 1998.

Culpepper, R. A. In *Anti-Judaism and the Fourth Gospel: Papers of the Leuven Colloquium, 2000*, edited by Reimund Bieringer, Didier Pollefeyt, and Frederique Vandecasteele-Vanneuville. Boston: Brill Academic Publishers, 2001.

Culpepper, R. A. In *What Is John?* edited by Segovia Fernando F. Atlanta: Scholars Press, 1996–8.

———. "Mapping the Textures of the New Testament Criticism: A Response to Socio-Rhetorical Criticism." *Journal for the Study of the New Testament* 70 (1998): 73. In *Essays on Jewish and Christian Literature and History*, edited by Richard T. White and Philip R. Davies. London: Sheffield Academic Press, 1990.

Culpepper, R. A., and C. Clifton Black, eds. *Exploring the Gospel of John.* Louisville: Westminster John Knox Press, 1996.

Davies, Alan T., ed. *Antisemitism and the Foundations of Christianity.* New York: Paulist Press, c1979.

Davies, W. D. *Paul and Rabbinic Judaism—Some Rabbinic Elements in Pauline Theology.* London: SPCK, 1958.

———. "Paul and the People of Israel." *NTS* 24 (1977).

———. "Torah in the Messianic Age and/or the Age to Come." *JBLMS* 7 (1952): 21–30.

Davies, W. D., and Dale C. Allison, Jr. *A Critical and Exegetical Commentary on the Gospel according to Saint Matthew.* London: T&T Clark International, 2004.

De Jonge, H. J. In *Anti-Judaism and the Fourth Gospel: Papers of the Leuven Colloquium, 2000*, edited by Reimund Bieringer, Didier Pollefeyt, and Frederique Vandecasteele-Vanneuville. Boston: Brill Academic Publishers, 2001.

deSilva, David A. "Heb 6:4–8: A Socio-Rhetorical Investigation." *TynBul* 50 (1999): 50, 225–236.

———. *Perseverance in Gratitude: A Socio-Rhetorical Commentary on the Epistle "to the Hebrews."* Grand Rapids: Eerdmans, 2000.

Donahue, J. R. *Jewish-Christian Controversy in the Second Century: Justin Martyr.* 1973.

Donahue, P. J. "Jewish Christianity in the Letters of Ignatius, 1978." *Vigilae Christianae* 32 (1978): 81–93.

Downey, G. *A History of Antioch in Syria, from Seleucus to the Arab Conquest.* Princeton, NJ: Princeton University Press, 1961.

Draper, J. A. "Torah and Troublesome Apostles in the Didache Community." *Novum Testamentum* 33, 4 (1991): 347–372.

Dunn, James D. G. *Christology in the Making.* London: SCM Press, 1990.

———. *Did the First Christians Worship Jesus?* Westminster: John Knox Press, 2010.

———. In *Anti-Judaism and the Fourth Gospel: Papers of the Leuven Colloquium, 2000*, edited by Reimund Bieringer, Didier Pollefeyt, and Frederique Vandecasteele-Vanneuville. Boston: Brill Academic Publishers, 2001.

———. *Jesus, Paul, and the Law: Studies in Mark and Galatians.* Louisville, KY: Westminster/John Knox Press, c1990.

———. *The Partings of the Ways: Between Christianity and Judaism and Their Significance for the Character of Christianity.* London: SCM, 1992.

———. *Unity and Diversity in the New Testament.* London: SCM Press, 1990.

———, ed. *Jews and Christians: The Parting of the Ways, A. D. 70 to 135: The Second Durham-Tübingen Research Symposium on Earliest Christianity and Judaism (Durham, September 1989).* Grand Rapids: Eerdmans, 1989.

———. *Paul and the Mosaic Law: The Third Durham-Tubingen Research Symposium on Earliest Christianity & Judaism.* University of Durham: Coronet Books Inc, 2001.

Dweet, J. *Revelation.* London: SCM Press, 1979.

Eckardt, A. Roy. *Jews and Christians, the Contemporary Meeting*. New York: Association Press, 1979.

———. *Reclaiming the Jesus of History: Christology Today*. Minneapolis: Fortress Press, 1992.

Edwards, R. B. "John and the Johannines." *The Bible Translator*, 43, no. 1 (1992): 140.

Efroymson, D. P. In *Antisemitism and the Foundations of Christianity*, edited by Davies Alan. New York: Paulist Press, 1979.

———. *Tertullian's Anti-Judaism and Its Role in Theology*. Philadelphia, PA: Temple University, 1976.

Ehrman, Bart D. *After the New Testament: A Reader in Early Christianity*. New York: Oxford University Press, 1999.

———. *Lost Christianities: The Battle for Scripture and the Faiths We Never Knew*. New York: Oxford University Press, 2003.

———. *The New Testament: Historical Introduction*. New York: Oxford University Press, 2007.

———. *The Orthodox Corruption of Scripture: The Effect of Early Christological Controversies on the Text of the New Testament*. New York: Oxford University Press, 1993.

Eisenbaum, Pamela M. "The Jewish Heroes of Christian History: Hebrews 11 in Literary Context." *SBLDS* 156 (1997): 10.

Eisenman, Robert H. *James, the Brother of Jesus*. New York: Viking, 1997.

Ellingworth, Paul. *The Epistle to the Hebrews*. Grand Rapids: Eerdmans, 1993.

Elliot, J. H. *A Home for the Homeless: A Sociological Exegesis of 1 Peter*. Philadelphia: Fortress Press, c1981.

Epictetus. *The Discourses of Epictetus*, edited by Gill Christopher. London: J.M. Dent, 1995.

Epp, Eldon J. "Antisemitism and the Popularity of the Fourth Gospel in Christianity." *CCARJ* 22 (1975).

Fabian E., S. Heschel, M. Chancey, and G. Tatum, eds. *Redefining First-Century Jewish and Christian Identities: Essays in Honor of Ed Parish Sanders*. Notre Dame, IN: University of Notre Dame Press, c2008.

Farmer, W. In *Rethinking the Synoptic Problem*, edited by David Alan Black and David R. Beck. Grand Rapids, MI: Baker Academic, c2001.

Farmer, William R., ed. *Anti-Judaism and the Gospels*. Harrisburg: Trinity Press International, 1999.

Fiorenza, Elisabeth Schussler. "Cultic Language in Qumran and in the NT." *CfiQ* 38 (1976): 159–177.

Fischer, John. "Covenant Fulfillment and Judaism in Hebrews." *ERT13* (1989): 1–6.

Fisher, Eugene J. "The Church's Teaching on Supersessionism." *BAR* 17 (1991): 58.

———. *Faith without Prejudice: Rebuilding Christian Attitudes toward Judaism*. New York: Crossroad, 1993.

———. *Interwoven Destinies: Jews and Christians through the Ages*. New York: Paulist Press, 1987.

Fisher, Eugene J., A. James Rudin, and Marc H. Tanenbaum, eds. *Twenty Years of Jewish-Catholic Relations*. New York: Paulist Press, c1986.

Flannery, Austin P. *Documents of Vatican II*. Grand Rapids: Eerdmans, 1975.

Flannery, Edward H. *The Anguish of the Jews: Twenty-Three Centuries of Antisemitism*. New York: Paulist Press, c1985.

Flusser, D. "The Dead Sea Scrolls and Pre-Pauline Christianity." In *Judaism and the Origins of Christianity*. New York: Gefen Books, 1988.

———. In *The Didache in Modern Research*, edited by Jonathan A. Draper. Peabody, MA: Brill Academic Publishers, 1996.

———. "The Jewish-Christian Schism (Part II)." *Immanuel* 17 (Winter 1983–84): 35–37.

———. *Jewish Sources in Early Christianity*. New York: Adama Books, 1987.

Flusser, D., and M. Lowe. "A Modified Proto-Matthean Synoptic Theory." *NTS* 29 (1983).

Fortna, R. T. *The Gospel of Signs: A Reconstruction of the Narrative Source Underlying the Fourth Gospel*. London: Cambridge University Press, 1970.

Franklin, Sherman, trans. *Luther's Works*. Philadelphia: Fortress, 1971.

Frazer, Sir James. *The Golden Bough*. New York: New American Library, 1987.

Fredriksen, Paula. *From Jesus to Christ: The Origins of the New Testament Images of Jesus*. New Haven: Yale University Press, c1988.

———. *Jesus of Nazareth, King of the Jews: A Jewish Life and the Emergence of Christianity*. New York: Vintage Books, 1998.

Frend, William H. C. *Martyrdom and Persecution in the Early Church*. Grand Rapids, MI: Baker Book House, 1981.

Fritz, R. A. *Nazarene Jewish Christianity: From the End of the First Century Until Its Disappearance in the Fourth Century*. Jerusalem: Magnes Press, Hebrew University, 1988.

Fuller, Reginald. "The Jews in the Fourth Gospel." *Dialog* 16 (1977): 16.

Funk, Robert W. *Honest to Jesus: Jesus for a New Millennium*. San Francisco: HarperSanFrancisco, c1996.

Gager, John G. In *The Ways That Never Parted: Jews and Christians in Late Antiquity and the Early Middle Ages*, edited by Annette Yoshiko Reed and Adam H. Becker. Tübingen: Paul Mohr Verlag, 2003.

———. *The Origins of Anti-Semitism: Attitudes toward Judaism in Pagan and Christian Antiquity*. New York: Oxford University Press, 1983.

———. *Reinventing Paul*. New York: Oxford University Press, 2000.

Gaston, Lloyd. *Anti-Judaism in Early Christianity*. Vol. 2. *Separation and Polemic*." Studies in Christianity and Judaism. 1096. Published for the Canadian Corp. for Studies in Religion/Corporation canadienne des sciences religieuses. Waterloo: Wilfrid Laurier University Press, 1986.

———. "The Messiah of Israel and the Teacher of the Gentiles." *Int*. 29 (1975).

———. "On M. T. Melakhim 8,11 (Lloyd Gaston, 1987–13)." 1087.

———. *Paul and the Torah*. Vancouver: University of British Columbia Press, 1987.

Gershon, Sholem. *Major Trends in Jewish Mysticism*. New York: Schocken, 1961.

Goldenberg, Robert. *The Nations That Know Thee Not: Ancient Jewish Attitudes towards Other Religions*. New York: New York University Press, c1997.

Goodman, Martin. In *The Jews Among Pagans and Christians: In the Roman Empire*, edited by Judith Lieu, John North, and Tessa Rajak. London: Routledge, 1992.

———. "Proselytizing in Rabbinic Judaism." *Journal of Jewish Studies* 38 (1989).

Goppelt, Leonhard. *Jesus, Paul and Judaism*. Nashville: T. Nelson, 1964.

Gould, Allan, ed. *What Did They Think of the Jews?* Northvale: J. Aronson, c1991.

Green, Joel B., ed. *Methods for Luke Methods in Biblical Interpretation*. Cambridge: Cambridge University Press, 2010.

Green, Martin. *The Origins of Nonviolence: Tolstoy and Gandhi in Their Historical Settings.* University Park, PA: Pennsylvania State University Press, c1986.

Green, William Scott. *Approaches to Ancient Judaism: Theory and Practice.* Missoula: Scholars Press for Brown University, c1980.

Greenspoon, Leonard J., Dennis Hamm, and Bryan F. LeBeau, eds. *The Historical Jesus through Catholic and Jewish Eyes.* Harrisburg: Trinity Press International, c2001.

Gregory, Andrew. "The Reception of Luke and Acts in the Period before Irenaeus: Looking for Luke in the Second Century." *WUNT* 2:169 (2003).

Guelich, Robert A. *Mark 1–8: 26.* Waco, TX: Word Books, c1989.

———. *Sermon on the Mount: A Foundation for Understanding.* Nashville, TN: W Publishing Group, 1982.

Hagner, D. A. *Encountering the Book of Hebrews.* Grand Rapids: Baker Academic, c2002.

———. *Hebrews.* San Francisco: Harper & Row, 1983.

———. *The Jewish Reclamation of Jesus.* Eugene, OR: Wipf & Stock Publishers, 1984.

———. "A Positive Theology of Judaism from the New Testament." *SEA* 69 (2004): 14–18.

———. "The Sitz im Leben of the Gospel of Matthew." In *Society of Biblical Literature 1985 Seminar Papers*, edited by K. H. Richards. Atlanta: Scholars Press, 1985.

Hall, Stuart George. *On Pascha and Fragments—Melito of Sardis; Texts and Translations.* Oxford: Clarendon Press, 1979.

Hansen, Adolph. "The Sitz im Leben of the Paschal Homily of Melito of Sardis." Unpublished PhD dissertation, Northwestern University—Diss. Abstracts 29 (1969), 1968.

Hare, D. R. A. In *Antisemitism and the Foundations of Christianity*, edited by Alan Davies. New York: Paulist Press, c1979.

———. *Jewish Persecution of Christians in the Gospel according to Saint Matthew.* Grand Rapids, MI: Academie Books, c1984.

———. "The Rejection of the Jews in the Synoptic Gospels and Acts." In *Anti-Semitism and the Foundations of Christianity*, edited by Alan Davies, 28–32. New York: Paulist Press, c1979.

———. "The Relationship between Jewish and Gentile Persecution of Christians." *JES* IV.

Harnack, Von Adolf. *Expansion of Christianity in the First Three Centuries.* Freeport, NY: Books for Libraries Press, 1972.

Hengel, Martin. *Acts and the History of Earliest Christianity.* Philadelphia: Fortress Press, 1979.

———. *Judaism and Hellenism: Studies in Their Encounter in Palestine during the Early Hellenistic Period.* London: SCM Press, 1974.

Herford, R. Travers. *Christianity in Talmud and Midrash.* New York: Ktav Pub. House, 1975.

Hess, Richard S., and Carroll R. M. Daniel, eds. *Israel's Messiah in the Bible and the Dead Sea Scrolls.* Grand Rapids: Baker Academic, c2003.

Hilberg, R. *The Destruction of the European Jews.* New York: Harper Colophon, 1979.

Horbury, William. In *Jews and Christians: The Parting of the Ways, A. D. 70 to 135: The Second Durham-Tübingen Research Symposium on Earliest Christianity and*

Judaism (Durham, September 1989), edited by J. D. G. Dunn. Grand Rapids: Eerdmans, 1992.

———. *Jewish Messianism and the Cult of Christ*. London: SCM Press, 1998.

Horsley, Richard A. *Jesus and the Spiral of Violence*. San Francisco: Harper & Row, 1967.

———. *Sociology and the Jesus Movement*. New York: Crossroad, 1989.

Horsley, Richard A., and John S. Hanson. *Bandits, Prophets, and Messiahs*. Minneapolis: Winston Press, 1985.

Horst, P. van der. "The Birkat Ha-Minim in Recent Research." *ExpTim* 105 (1994).

Horton, Fred L. "Melchizedek Tradition through the First Five Centuries C.E." *SNTSMS* 30 (1976).

Hubner, Hans. *Law in Paul's Thought*. London: T & T Clark Publishers, 1983.

Hughes, Philip E. *A Commentary on the Epistle to the Hebrews*. Grand Rapids: Eerdmans, 1977.

Hunt, B. P. W. S. "The Epistle to the Hebrews or against the Hebrews? Anti-Judaic Treatise?" *SE* (1964): 408.

Hurtado, Larry W. *At the Origins of Christian Worship: The Context and Character of Earliest Christian Devotion*. Grand Rapids: W.B. Eerdmans Pub. Co., 2001.

———. *One God, One Lord: Early Christian Devotion and Ancient Jewish Monotheism*. Philadelphia: Fortress Press, c1998.

Hvalvik, Reidar. *The Struggle for Scripture and Covenant: The Purpose of the Epistle of Barnabas and Jewish-Christian Competition in the Second Century*. Tübingen: J.C.B. Mohr (Paul Siebeck), 1996.

Idel, M. *Messianic Mystics*. New Haven: Yale University Press, c1998.

Indinopulos, T. A., and R. B. Ward. "Is Christology Inherently Anti-Semitic?" *Journal of the American Academy of Religion* 45 (1977).

Isaac, B. "Judea after AD 70." *JJS* 35 (1984).

Isaac, B., and A. Oppenheimer. "The Revolt of Bar Kochba." *JJS* 36 (1985).

Isaacs, Marie E. "Hebrews." In *Early Christian Thought in Its Jewish Context*, edited by J. Barclay and J. Sweet, 158. Cambridge: Cambridge University Press, 1996.

Isacson, Michael. *To Each Their Own Letter: Structure, Themes, & Rhetorical Strategies in the Letters of Ignatius of Antioch*. Stockholm: Almquiest & Wiksell Intl, 2004.

Jefford, C. N., K. J. Harder, and Louis D. Amezaga, Jr. *Reading the Apostolic Fathers*. Peabody, MA: Hendrickson Publishers, 1996.

Jefford, C. N. *The Sayings of Jesus in the Teaching of the Twelve Apostles*. Boston: Brill Academic Publishers, 1989.

Jervell, Jacob. *Luke and the People of God*. Eugene, OR: Wipf & Stock Publishers, 1972.

———. *The Theology of the Acts of the Apostles*. New York: Cambridge University Press, 1996.

Johnson, L. T. "The New Testament's Anti-Jewish Slander and the Conventions of Ancient Polemic." *Journal of Biblical Literature* 108, no. 3 (Autumn 1989).

Johnsson, W. G. "The Cultus of Hebrews in Twentieth-Century Scholarship." *ExpTim* 89 (1977–8): 104–108.

Jones, F. Stanley. *An Ancient Jewish Christian Source on the History of Christianity: Pseudo-Clementine Recognitions 1. 27–71*. Atlanta: Scholars Press, 1995.

Jonas, Hans. *The Gnostic Religion: The Message of the Alien God and the Beginnings of Christianity.* Boston: Beacon Press, 1958.

Juel, Donald. *Messianic Exegesis: Christological Interpretation of the Old Testament in Early Christianity.* Philadelphia: Fortress Press, c1988.

Justin. *Dialogue with Trypho.* Washington, DC: Catholic University of America Press, c2003.

Kasemann, Ernst. *Commentary on Romans.* Grand Rapids, MI: Eerdmans, c1980.

Katz, S. T. "Issues in the Separation of Judaism and Christianity after 70 C.E." *JBL* 103 (1984).

Kee, Howard Clark. *Knowing the Truth: A Sociological Approach to New Testament Interpretation.* Minneapolis: Fortress Press, c1989.

Kent, Homer A. "The New Covenant and the Church." *GTJ* 6 (1985): 295.

Kessler, Edward. *An Introduction to Jewish-Christian Relations.* Cambridge: Cambridge University Press, 2010.

Kierspel, Lars. *The Jews and the World in the Fourth Gospel: Parallelism, Function, and Context* (Wissenschaftliche Untersuchingen Zum Neuen Testament). Tübingen: Mohr Sieback, 2006.

Klassen, Lars. In *Anti-Judaism in Early Christianity*, edited by Peter Richardson with David Granskou. Waterloo: Wilfrid Laurier University Press, 1986.

Klauck, Hans-Josef. *The Religious Context of Early Christianity: A Guide to Graeco-Roman religions.* Minneapolis: Fortress Press, c2003.

Klein, Charlotte. *Anti-Judaism in Christian theology.* London: SPCK, c1978.

Klenicki, Leon, and Eugene J. Fisher. *Root and Branches: Biblical Judaism, Rabbinic Judaism and Early Christianity.* Winona: Saint Mary's Press, 1987.

Klijn, A. F. J. "The Study of Jewish-Christianity." *NTS* (1973–74): 491–426.

Klijn, A. F. J., and G. J. Reinink. *Patristic Evidence for Jewish-Christian Sects.* Leiden: Brill, 1973.

Kloppenborg, J. *Excavating Q: The History and Setting of the Sayings Gospel.* Minneapolis: Fortress Press, 2000.

———. "The Transformation of Moral Exhortation in Didache 1–5 in 'The Didache in Context: Essays on Its Text, History and Transmission.'" *NovTSup* 77 (1995): 88–109.

Kloppenborg, John S. *Q Parallels: Synopsis, Critical Notes & Concordance.* Sonoma: Polebridge Press, c1988.

———, ed. *Conflict and Invention: Literary, Rhetorical, and Social Studies on the Sayings Gospel Q.* Trinity Pr Intl, 1995.

Knohl, Israel. *The Messiah before Jesus: The Suffering Servant of the Dead Sea Scrolls.* Berkeley: University of California Press, 2000.

Knox, John. *Marcion and the New Testament.* New York: AMS Press, c1942.

Kobelski, Paul J. "Melchizedek and Melchiresha." *Catholic Biblical Quarterly Monograph Series* 10 (1981).

Koenig, John. *Jews and Christians in Dialogue: New Testament Foundations.* Philadelphia: Westminster Press, c1979.

Koester, Craig R. *Hebrews.* New York: Doubleday, 2001.

Koester, Helmut. *Ancient Christian Gospels: Their History and Development.* London: SCM Press, 1990.

Koester, Helmut, and J. M. Robinson. *Trajectories through Early Christianity.* Philadelphia: Fortress Press, 1971.

Kraabel, A. "Melito the Bishop and the Synagogue at Sardis: Text and Context." In *Studies Presented to George MA Hanfmann*, edited by J. G. Pedley, J. A. Scott, and D. G. Mitten. Fogg Art Museum, Harvard University, *Monographs in Art and Archaeology* 2. Cambridge: Fogg Art Museum, 1971. 81, n. 25. 1971.

Kraabel, A. T. "Judaism in Western Asia Minor under the Roman Empire." PhD diss., Cambridge: Harvard University, 1968.

Kraabel, T. "The Roman Diaspora: Six Questionable Assumptions." *JJS* 33 (1982): 455.

Kraeling, C. H. "The Jewish Community at Antioch." *JBL* 51 (1932): 130–160.

Kraft, A. "In Search of 'Jewish Christianity' and Its Theology: Problems of Definition and Methodology." *Recherches de Sciences Religieuse* 60 (1972): 81–86.

Kugel, James L., and Rowan A. Greer. *Early Biblical Interpretation*. Philadelphia: Westminster Press, c1986.

Kugler, Robert A. "Rewriting Rubrics: Sacrifice and the Religion of Qumran." In *Religion in the Dead Sea Scrolls*, edited by John J. Collins and Robert A. Kugler, 90. Grand Rapids: Eerdmans, 2000.

Kuhn, Thomas S. *The Structure of Scientific Revolutions*. Chicago: University of Chicago Press, 1970.

Kysar, R. "The Gospel of John in Current Research." *RSR9* (1983).

———. "The Promises and Perils of Preaching on the Gospel of John." *JBL* 99, Issue 1 (1980): 148.

Lane, William. "Hebrews 1–8." *Word Biblical Commentary* 47a (1991).

Lange de, N. R. M. *Origen and the Jews: Studies in Jewish-Christian Relations in Third-Century Palestine*. Cambridge: Cambridge University Press, 1976.

Langton, Daniel R. *The Apostle Paul in the Jewish Imagination: A Study in Modern Jewish-Christian Relations*. Cambridge: Cambridge University Press, 1999.

Layton, Bentley, ed. *The Rediscovery of Gnosticism*. London: E.J. Brill, c1980.

Lehne, S. *The New Covenant in Hebrews*. Sheffield: JSOT, 1990.

Leibig, J. E. "John and the Jews: Theological Anti-Semitism in the Fourth Gospel." *JES* 20 (1983): 209–35.

Levine, Amy-Jill. *The Misunderstood Jew*. San Francisco: HarperSanFrancisco, c2006.

———. *The Social and Ethnic Dimensions of Matthean Salvation History*. Collegeville, Minnesota: Liturgical Press, 2003.

Levine, Amy-Jill, Dale C. Allison Jr., and John Dominic Crossan, eds. *The Historical Jesus in Context*. Princeton, NJ: Princeton University Press, c2006.

Lieu, Judith M. *Image and Reality: The Jews in the World of the Christians in the Second Century*. Edinburgh: T & T Clark Publishers, 1992.

———. *Neither Jew Nor Greek?: Constructing Early Christianity*. Edinburgh: T & T Clark Publishers, 2003.

Limor, Ora Hayoun, Maurice R. Stroumsa, and Guy G. eds. *Contra Iudaeos*. Tübingen: Mohr Siebeck 1996.

Lindars, Barnabas. "The Rhetorical Structure of Hebrews." *New Testament Studies* 35 (1989): 392 n. 2.

———. *The Theology of the Letter to the Hebrews*. Cambridge: Cambridge University Press, 1991.

Littell, Franklin H. *The Crucifixion of the Jews*. Macon: Mercer University Press, 1975, c1986.

Louth, A. *Early Christian Writings.* London: Penguin, 1987.

Ludemann, Gerd. *Heretics: The Other Side of Early Christianity.* Louisville, KY: Presbyterian Publishing Corporation, 1996.

————. *Opposition to Paul in Jewish Christianity,* trans lated by E. Boring. Minneapolis: Fortress Press, c1989.

————. *Paul: The Founder of Christianity.* Amherst, NY: Prometheus Books, 2002.

————. *The Unholy in Holy Scripture: The Dark Side of the Bible.* London: SCM Press, 1997.

Luther, Martin. *The Jews and Their Lies.* Reedy, WV: Liberty Bell Publications, 1543.

Maccoby, Hyam. *Jesus the Pharisee.* London: SCM Press, 2003.

Mack, Burton L. *A Myth of Innocence: Mark and Christian Origins.* Philadelphia: Fortress Press, c1988.

Malina, B. J. "The Gospel of John in Sociolinguistic Perspective." In *Colloquy 48.* Berkeley: Center for Hermeneutical Studies in Hellenistic and Modern Culture, 1985.

————. "Jewish Christianity or Christian Judaism: Toward a Hypothetical Definition." *Journal for the Study of Judaism* (1976).

Malina, B. J., and H. C. Waetjen, eds. *The Gospel of John in Sociolinguistic Perspective.* Berkeley: Center for Hermeneutical Studies in Hellenistic and Modern Culture, c1985.

Marcus, Joel. *Mark 1–8. A New Translation with Introduction and Commentary—Anchor Bible 27.* New York: Doubleday, 2000.

Martyn, J. L. *The Gospel of John in Christian History.* Mahwah, NJ: Paulist Press, 1978.

Martyn, J. Louis. *History & Theology in the Fourth Gospel.* Nashville: Abingdon, c1968.

Matt, Jackson-Mccabe ed. *Jewish Christianity Reconsidered.* Minneapolis: Fortress Press, c2007.

Mattillm, A. J. "Johannine Communities behind the 'Fourth Gospel': Georg Richter's Analysis." *TS* 38 (1977).

Maxwell, Jaclyn L. *Christianization and Communication in Late Antiquity: John Chrysostom and His Congregation in Antioch.* Cambridge: Cambridge University Press, 2006.

McKnight, Scot. *A Light among the Gentiles: Jewish Missionary Activity in the Second Temple Period.* Minneapolis: Fortress Press, c1991.

Meeks, W. A. "Am I a Jew?" In *Christianity, Judaism and other Greco-Roman Cults,* edited by Jacob Neusner. Leiden: Brill, 1975.

————. "The Man from Heaven in Johannine Sectarianism." *JBL* 91 (1972).

Meeks, W. A., and Robert L. Wilken. *Jews and Christians in Antioch in the First Four Centuries of the Common Era.* New Haven: Scholars Press, c1978.

Meier, John P. *The Vison of Matthew: Christ, Church, and Morality in the First Gospel.* Eugene, OR: Wipf & Stock Publishers, 1979.

Mendels, Doron. *The Rise and Fall of Jewish Nationalism.* New York: Doubleday, 1992.

Montefiore, W. *The Epistle to the Hebrews.* New York: Harper & Row, 1964.

Moore, George F. "Christian Writers on Judaism." *Harvard Theological Review* 14 (1921).

Moore Cross, Frank. *Ancient Library of Qumran.* Sheffield, England: Sheffield Academic Press, 1995.

Munck, Johannes. *Paul and the Salvation of Mankind.* Atlanta: John Knox Press, c1959.

Murphy-O' Connor, J. *Paul: A Critical Life.* Oxford: Oxford University Press, 1996.

Murray, Michele. *Playing a Jewish Game: Gentile Christian Judaizing in the First and Second Centuries CE.* Waterloo: Wilfrid Laurier University Press, 2004.

Neusner, Jacob. *From Politics to Piety: The Emergence of Pharisaic Judaism.* Englewood Cliffs: Prentice-Hall, c1973.

Neusner, Jacob. *Jews and Christians: The Myth of a Common Tradition.* London: SCM Press, 1991.

———. *Judaism When Christianity Began: A Survey of Belief and Practice.* Louisville: Westminster John Knox Press, c2003.

Neusner, Jacob, and Ernest S. Frerichs, eds. *"To See Ourselves as Others See Us": Christians, Jews, "Others" in Late Antiquity.* Chico: Scholars Press, c1985.

Neusner, Jacob, William S. Green, and Ernest Frerichs, eds. *Judaisms and Their Messiahs at the Turn of the Christian Era.* Cambridge: Cambridge University Press, 1987.

Nickelsburg, George W. *Ancient Judaism and Christian Origins: Diversity, Continuity, and Transformation.* Minneapolis: Fortress Press, c2003.

Nickelsburg, George W, and Baltzer, Klaus. *1 Enoch 1: A Commentary on the Book of 1 Enoch: Chapters 1–36; 81–108.* Minneapolis: Fortress, 2001.

Nickelsburg, George W. E., and George W. MacRae, eds. *Christians among Jews and Gentiles.* Philadelphia: Fortress Press, c1986.

Niebuhr, Reinhold. *Moral Man and Immoral Society: A Study in Ethics and Politics.* Whitefish, MT: Kessinger Publishing, 1932.

Noakes, K. W. "Melito of Sardis and the Jews." *Studia Patristica* 13 (1975): 244–249.

North, John. "Religious Toleration in Republican Rome." *Cambridge Philological Society* n.s. 25 (1979): 96–97.

O' Neill, J. C. *Paul's Letter to the Romans.* London: Penguin Books, 1975.

———. *The Recovery of Paul's Letter to the Galatians.* London: SPCK, 1972.

Oakes, Robert. "Union with God: A Theory." *Faith and Philosophy* VII (1990): 165–176.

Omanson, Roger L. "A Superior Covenant: Hebrews 8:1–10:18." *RevExp* 82 (1985): 370.

Origen. "On First Pinciples." 4.1.3–4; 4.2.2.

Overman, J. Andrew. *Matthew's Gospel and Formative Judaism.* Minneapolis: Fortress Press, 1990.

Pagels, Elaine. *The Gnostic Gospels.* New York: Phoenix Press, 1943.

Paget, J. C. *The Epistle of Barnabas.* Tubingen: J.C.B. Mohr, 1994.

Painter, John. *John, Witness and Theologian.* London: SPCK, 1975.

Parkes, James. *Antisemitism.* London: Mitchell, 1969.

———. *The Conflict of the Church and the Synagogue: A Study in the Origins of Antisemitism.* London: Vallentine Mitchell, 1961, 1969, 1974.

———. *Prelude to Dialogue: Jewish-Christian Relationships.* London: Vallentine Mitchell, 1969.

Parrinder, Geoffrey. *Mysticism in the World Religions.* London: Sheldon Press, 1976.

Pawlikowski, John T. In *Christ in the Light of the Christian-Jewish Dialog*, 59–75. New York: Paulist: Paulist Press, 1982.

———. *Jesus and the Theology of Israel*. Wilmington, DE: Michael Glazier Books, 1989.

Pearson, Birger A. *Gnosticism, Judaism, and Egyptian Christianity*. Minneapolis: Fortress Press, c1990,.

Pherigo, Lindsey P. "The Gospel According to Mark." In *The Interpreter's One Volume Commentary on the Bible*, edited by Charles M. Laymon. Nashville: Abingdon Press, 1971.

Pomykala, K. E. *The Davidic Dynasty Tradition in Early Judaism: Its History and Significance for Messianism*. London: Scholars Press, c1995.

Porter, Stanley E. *Reading the Gospels Today*. Grand Rapids: Wm. B. Eerdmans, 2004.

———. *The Rhetorical Interpretation of Scripture*. Sheffield: Sheffield Academic, 1999.

Porter, Stanley E., and W. R. Pearson Brook, eds. *Christian-Jewish Relations through the Centuries*. Louisville, KY: T & T Clark International, 2004.

Powell, Mark Allan. *Jesus as a Figure in History*. Louisville: Westminster John Knox Press, 1998.

Portier-Young, A. *Apocalypse against Empire: Theologies of Resistance in Early Judaism*. Grand Rapids: Wm. B. Eerdmans Publishing Company, 2011.

Quispel, G. *Gnostic Studies*. Boston: Brill Academic Publishers, 1974: vol.1, part 2.

Rahner, Karl. *Spiritual Exercises*. New York: Herder and Herder, 1965.

Räisänen, Heikki. *Paul and the Law*. Philadelphia: Fortress Press, 1987.

Reinhartz, A. In *Anti-Judaism and the Fourth Gospel: Papers of the Leuven Colloquium, 2000*, edited by Reimund Bieringer, Didier Pollefeyt, and Frederique Vandecasteele-Vanneuville. Boston: Brill Academic Publishers, 2001.

———. In *"What Is John?"* edited by Fernando F. Segovia. Atlanta: Scholars Press, 1996–1998.

Remus, Harold. "Justin Martyr's Argument with Judaism." In *Anti-Judaism in early Christianity*, by Peter Granskou and David Richardson. Waterloo: Wilfrid Laurier University Press, 1986.

Rensberger, David. In *What Is John?* edited by Fernando F. Segovia. Atlanta: Scholars Press, 1996–1998.

———. *Johannine Faith and Liberating Community*. Philadelphia: Westminster Press, c1988.

Richardson, P., and M. B. Shukster. "Barnabas, Nerva, and the Yavnean Rabbis." *JTS* (1983): n.s. 34.

Richardson, Peter. *Israel in the Apostolic Church*. London: Cambridge University Press, 1969.

Richardson, Peter, and David Granskou, eds. *Anti-Judaism in Early Christianity Vol 1—Paul and the Gospels*. Waterloo: Wilfrid Laurier University Press, 1986.

Riegel, S. K. "Jewish Christianity: Definitions and Terminology." *NTS* 24 (1978): 411.

Roetzel, Calvin J., Philip Sellew, Claudia Setzer, and Janice Capel Anderson. *Pauline Conversations in Context: Essays in Honor of Calvin J. Roetzel*. New York: Mayflower Books, 2002.

Rokeah, David. *Jews, Pagans, and Christians in Conflict*. Jerusalem: Magnes Press, Hebrew University, 1982.

Rowland, Christopher. *The Open Heaven: A Study of Apocalyptic in Judaism and Early Christianity.* London: SPCK, 1982.

Ruether, R. R. *Faith and Fratricide: The Theological Roots of Anti-Semitism.* New York: Seabury Press, 1974.

———. In *Antisemitism and the Foundations of Christianity*, edited by Alan Davies. New York: Paulist Press, 1979.

Rylaarsdam, J. Coert. "Jewish-Christian Relationships: The Two Covenants and the Dilemmas of Christology." In *Grace upon Grace*, edited by J. I. Cook, 72. Grand Rapids: Eerdmans, 1975.

Saldarini, Anthony J. *Matthew's Christian-Jewish Community.* Chicago: University of Chicago Press, 1994.

———. *Pharisees, Scribes and Sadducees in Palestinian Society: A Sociological Approach.* Wilmington: M. Glazier, 1988.

Salevao, L. *Legitimation in the Letter to the Hebrews: The Construction and Maintenance of a Symbolic Universe.* London: Sheffield Academic Press, 2002.

Sanders, E. P. *The Historical Figure of Jesus.* London: Allen Lane, 1993.

———. *Paul and Palestinian Judaism: A Comparison of Patterns of Religion.* Philadelphia: Fortress Press, 1977.

———. *Paul, the Law, and the Jewish People.* Philadelphia: Fortress Press, c1983.

———. *Studying the Synoptic Gospels.* London: SCM Press, 1989.

Sanders, E. P., ed. *Jesus, the Gospels and the Church.* Macon, GA: Mercer University Press, 1987.

———, E.P. Sanders with A.I. Baumgarten and Alan Mendelson. *Jewish and Christian Self-Definition.* London: SCM Press, 1980.

Sanders, Jack T. *The Jews in Luke—Acts.* London: SCM, 1987.

———. *Schismatics, Sectarians, Dissidents, Deviants: The First One Hundred Years of Jewish-Christian Relations.* London: SCM Press, 1993.

Sandmel, Samuel. *Anti-Semitism in the New Testament?* Philadelphia: Fortress Press, c1978.

———. *Judaism and Christian Beginnings.* New York: Oxford University Press, 1978.

Satran, David. In *Contra Iudaeos*, edited by G. G. Limor and O. Stroumsa, 49–58. Tübingen: J.C.B. Mohr (Paul Siebeck), 1996.

Schiffman, Lawrence H. *Who Was a Jew?: Rabbinic and Halakhic Perspectives on the Jewish Christian Schism.* Hoboken: Ktav Pub. House, 1985.

Schimmel, A., and A. Falaturi, eds. *We Believe in One God: The Experience of God in Christianity and Islam.* London: Burns and Oates, 1979.

Schnackenburg, Rudolf. *The Gospel According to St. John.* London: Burns & Oates, 1968–1982.

Schneemelcher, Wilhelm and R. McL. Wilson, eds. *New Testament Apocrypha*, English translation edited by R. McL. Wilson. Louisville, KY: Westminster Press, 1963.

Schoeps, H. J. *Jewish Christianity.* Philadelphia: Fortress Press, 1969.

———. *Paul. The Theology of the Apostle in the Light of Jewish Religious History.* London: Westminster, 1961.

Scholem, Gershon. *The Messianic Idea in Judaism.* New York: Schocken, 1971.

Schremer, Adiel. *Brothers Estranged: Heresy, Christianity, and Jewish Identity in Late Antiquity.* New York: Oxford University Press, 2010.

Schurer, Emil. *A History of the Jewish People in the Time of Jesus Christ.* Peabody, MA: Hendrickson Publishers, 1994.

Segovia, F. F., ed. *What Is John?* Atlanta: Scholars Press, 1996–1998.

Setzer, Claudia J. *Jewish Responses to Early Christians: History and Polemics, 30–150 C. E.* Minneapolis: Fortress Press, 1994.

Sevenster, J. N. *The Roots of Pagan Anti-Semitism in the Ancient World.* Leiden: Brill, 1975.

Sim, David, and Boris Repschinski, eds. *Matthew and His Christian Contemporaries.* London, New York: T&T Clark International, 2008.

Simon, M. *Jerry Falwell and the Jews.* Middle Village: Jonathan David Publishers, 1984.

Simon, Marcel. *Verus Israel: A Study of the Relations between Christians and Jews in the Roman Empire, 135–425.* New York: Oxford University Press, 1986.

Skarsaune, Oskar. *Proof from Prophecy: A Study in Justin Martyr's Proof Text Tradition.* Boston: Brill Academic Publishers, 1987.

Skarsaune, Oskar, and Reidar Hvalvik, eds. *Jewish Believers in Jesus: The Early Centuries.* Peabody, MA: Hendrickson Publishers, 2007.

Smallwood, E. Mary. *The Jews under Roman Rule: From Pompey to Diocletian: A Study in Political Relations.* Boston: Brill Academic Publishers, 1976.

Smiga, G. M. *Pain and Polemic: Anti-Judaism in the Gospels.* New York: Paulist Press, c1992.

Smith, D. M. "Judaism and the Gospel of John." In *Jews and Christians: Exploring the Past, Present, and Future,* edited by J. H. Charlesworth. New York: Crossroad, 1990.

Smith, Morton. *Palestinian Parties and Politics That Shaped the Old Testament.* New York: Columbia University Press, 1971.

Spicq, C. *L'Epitre aux Hebreux.* Paris: Gabalda, 1952.

Stanton, G. N. "Aspects of Early Christian-Jewish Polemic and Apologetic." *New Testament Studies* 31 (1985): 377–392.

Stanton, Graham N. *A Gospel for a New People: Studies in Matthew.* Edinburgh: T & T Clark, 1992.

Stendahl, Krister. "The Harvard Theological Review." *The Harvard Theological Review* 56, no. 3 (July 1963): 199–215.

———. *Paul among the Jews and Gentiles.* Philadelphia: Fortress Press, c1976.

———. *The School of St. Matthew, and Its Use of the Old Testament.* Philadelphia: Fortress Press, 1968.

Stern, Menahem. *Greek & Latin Authors on Jews & Judaism.* Port Jervis, NY: Lubrecht & Cramer Ltd, 1981.

Stiassny, J. "Development of the Christians' Self-Understanding." *Immanuel* 1 (1972).

Stowers, Stanley K. *A Rereading of Romans: Justice, Jews, and Gentiles.* New Haven: Yale University Press, c1994.

Strecker, G. In *Orthodoxy and Heresy in Earliest Christianity,* edited by Walter Bauer. Philadelphia: Fortress Press, 1971.

Strecker, Georg. "An Ancient Jewish Christian Source on the History of Christianity." *Pseudo-Clementine Recognitions* (1995): 1.27–71.

Stroumsa, Gedaliahu A. G. "Another Seed: Studies in Gnostic Mythology." *Nag Hammadi Studies* no. 24 (Brill Academic Publishers), 1997.

Stuart, George Hall, ed. *On Pascha and Fragments.* Oxford: Clarendon Press, 1979.

Stuckenbruck, Loren T., and Wendy E. S. North, eds. *Early Jewish and Christian Monotheism.* London: T & T Clark International, 2004.

Stylianopoulos, Theodore. *Justin Martyr and the Mosaic Law.* Cambridge: Society of Biblical Literature, 1975.

Tannehil, Robert C. *The Narrative Unity of Luke-Acts: A Literary Interpretation.* Philadelphia: Fortress Press, c1986–c1990.

Taylor, Miriam S. *Anti-Judaism and Early Christian Identity: A Critique of the Scholarly Consensus.* Boston: Brill Academic Publishers, 1997.

Tcherikover, Victor. *Hellenistic Civilization and the Jews.* Philadelphia: Jewish Publication Society of America, 1971.

Theissen, Gerd, and Annette Merz. *The Historical Jesus: A Comprehensive Guide.* Minneapolis: Fortress Press, 1998.

Thompson, James W. "Hebrews 9 and Hellenistic Concepts of Sacrifice." *JBL* (1979): 568.

Tomson, P. J. *Anti-Judaism and the Fourth Gospel: Papers of the Leuven Colloquium, 2000,* edited by Reimund Bieringer, Didier Pollefeyt, and Frederique Vandecasteele-Vanneuville. Boston: Brill Academic Publishers, 2001.

Tomson, Peter. *If This Be from Heaven . . . : Jesus and the New Testament Authors in Their Relationship to Judaism.* London: Sheffield Academic Press, 2001.

Tomson, Peter J. *Paul and the Jewish Law.* Assen: Van Gorcum, 1990.

Townsend, J. In *Antisemitism and the Foundations of Christianity,* edited by Alan Davies. New York: Paulist Press, c1979.

Townsend, J. T. "The Date of Luke-Acts." In *Luke-Acts: New Perspectives from the Society of Biblical Literature Seminar,* edited by Charles H. Talbert. New York: Crossroad, 1984.

Tuckett, Christopher M. *Q and the History of Early Christianity.* Edinburgh: T&T Clark, 1996.

Tugwell, Simon. *The Apostolic Fathers.* London: Geoffrey Chapman, 1989.

Turner, Victor. *The Forest of Symbols.* Ithaca, NY: Cornell University Press, 1967.

Tyson, J. B. "The Blindness of the Disciples in Mark." *JBL* 80 (1961): 261–268.

———. *Images of Judaism in Luke-Acts.* Columbia: University of South Carolina Press, c1992.

———. *Luke-Acts and the Jewish People: Eight Critical Perspectives.* Minneapolis: Augsburg Publishing House, c1988.

———. *Marcion and Luke-Acts: A Defining Struggle.* Columbia: University of South Carolina Press, c2006.

Van Buren, Paul M. *According to the Scriptures: The Origins of the Gospel and of the Church's Old Testament.* Grand Rapids: W. B. Eerdmans, c1998.

———. *A Theology of the Jewish-Christian Reality, Part 3: Christ in Context.* New York: Seabury Press, 1980–1983.

———. *Discerning the Way: A Theology of the Jewish-Christian Reality.* New York: Harper & Row, 1980.

———. *A Theology of the Jewish-Christian Reality, Part II: A Christian Theology of the People Israel.* London: T & T Clark Publishers, 1987.

VanderKam, James, and Peter Flint. *The Meaning of the Dead Sea Scrolls.* San Francisco: HarperSanFrancisco, c2002.

Vermes, Geza. *The Changing Faces of Jesus.* London: Allen Lane, 2000.

———. *The Dead Sea Scrolls in English.* Harmondsworth: Penguin, 1975.

———. *The Gospel of Jesus the Jew.* Newcastle upon Tyne: Pennsylvania State University Press, 1981.

Voorst, R. E. Van. *The Ascents of James: History and Theology of a Jewish-Christian Community.* Atlanta, GA: Society of Biblical Literature, 1989.

Wahlde von, Urban C. *The Earliest Version of John's Gospel: Recovering the Gospel of Signs.* Wilmington: Michael Glazier, 1989.

———. "The Jews in the Gospel of John: Fifteen Years of Research." *Ephemerides Theologicae Lovanienses* 76, no. 1 (2000): 30–55.

———. "The Johannine 'Jews': A Critical Survey." *NTS* 28 (1982).

Walters, J. R. "The Rhetorical Arrangement of Hebrews." *As* 7/51 (1996): 59–70.

Watson, Francis. *Paul, Judaism, and the Gentiles: A Sociological Approach.* Cambridge: Cambridge University Press, 1986.

Weeden, Theodore J. *Mark: Traditions in Conflict.* Philadelphia: Fortress Press, 1971.

Werner, Kelber. *The Oral and the Written Gospel.* Philadelphia: Fortress Press, c1983.

Westerholm, Stephen. *Perspectives Old and New on Paul: The "Lutheran" Paul and His Critics.* Grand Rapids: Eerdmans, c2004.

Wilken, Robert. *The Christians as the Romans Saw Them.* New Haven: Yale University Press, c1984.

———. *John Chrysostom and the Jews: Rhetoric and Reality in the Late 4th Century.* Berkeley: University of California Press, c1983.

———. *Judaism and the Early Christian Mind: A Study of Cyril of Alexandria's Exegesis and Theology.* New Haven: Yale University Press, 1971.

———. "Judaism in Roman and Christian Society." *The Journal of Religion—JSTOR* (1967): 313–330.

Williams, Michael Allen. *Rethinking "Gnosticism": An Argument for Dismantling a Dubious Category.* Princeton: Princeton University Press, c1996.

Williamson, Clark M. *A Guest in the House of Israel: Post-Holocaust Church Theology.* Louisville: Westminster/John Knox Press, 1993.

———. *Has God Rejected His People?: Anti-Judaism in the Christian Church.* Nashville: Abingdon, c1982.

———. *Preaching the Gospels without Blaming the Jews: A Lectionary Commentary.* Louisville: Westminster John Knox Press, c2004.

Williamson, Clark M., and Ronald J. Allen. *Interpreting Difficult Texts: Anti-Judaism and Christian Preaching.* London: SCM Press, 1989.

Wilson Trigg, Joseph. *Origen: The Bible and Philosophy in the Third-Century Church.* London: SCM Press, 1985.

Wilson, Stephen G. *Luke and the Law.* Cambridge: Cambridge University Press, 2005.

———. *Related Strangers: Jews and Christians, 70–170 C. E.* Minneapolis: Fortress Press, 1995.

Wilson, Stephen G., ed. *"Anti-Judaism in Early Christianity.* Vol. 2. *Separation and Polemic."* Studies in Christianity and Judaism. 1096. Published for the Canadian Corp. for Studies in Religion/Corporation canadienne des sciences religieuses. Waterloo, Ontario: Wilfrid Laurier University Press, 1986.

Winter, Paul Burkill, T. Alec, and Geza Vermes. *On the Trial of Jesus.* Berlin: De Gruyter, 1974.

Wyschogrod, Michael. *Abraham's Promise: Judaism and Jewish-Christian Relations.* Grand Rapids: Eerdmans Press, 1990.

Yavetz, Z. "Judeophobia in Classical Antiquity. A Different Approach." *JJS* 44 (1993).

Zetterholm, Magnus. *The Formation of Christianity in Antioch: A Social-Scientific Approach to the Separation between Judaism and Christianity.* London: Routledge, 2003.

Thematic Index

The index covers themes, not keywords. The most important occurrences appear first. Secondary occurrences follow.

Acts
  anti-Jewish bias, 8
  see also Luke-Acts
anti-Jewish strand, 1–11, 206–10
  Acts, 8
  escalation, 95–9, 79–80
  Hebrews, 9
  John, 9
  Mark, 4
  Matthew, 5
  Paul, 9
  Revelation, 10
anti-Jewish-establishment rhetoric,
    12–13, 20, 44, 53–5, 83, 95–8,
    112, 121, 146, 199, 207–8, 220
anti-Semitism, 221, 84, 99, 100, 129,
    149, 198, 209, 210, 218
appropriation, 1, 129, 175–80, 201,
    207, 213–14, 35, 52, 57, 73,
    83, 95, 104, 112, 121, 124,
    126, 128
  John, 83
  Justin, 175–6
  see also de-contextualization
author's synopsis
  Barnabas, 147–150
  Chrysostom, 189–92
  Hebrews, 131–7
  John, 82–5
  Justin, 177–8
  Luke/Acts, 64–6
  Mark, 46–8
  Matthew, 56–8
  Paul, 35–8

Barnabas
  adversaries, 141–3
  author's synopsis, 147–150
  background, 139–41
  covenant, Barnabas, 142–3
  dietary law, 144
  disciples, 195
  Sabbath, 145
  the Temple, 143–4
  Torah observance, 144
benediction against the heretics, 80, 205
Birkhat Haminim, 80, 205

Chrysostom
  author's synopsis, 188–192
  background, 185, 188–9
  sermons, 185–8
circumcision
  Barnabas, 145
Constantine, after, 216–19
continuity-discontinuity, 63–5, 96,
    119, 133–6, 142, 219
covenant
  Barnabas, 142–3
  Hebrews, 123–5

de-contextualization, 2, 127, 126,
    134, 220, 19, 42, 98, 112
  see also Pesher
deicide
  Melito, 180–2
de-Judaizing belief in Jesus, 196–7,
    202–4, 38, 46–7, 58, 61,
    99, 103–104, 134, 149, 172

destruction of the Temple, 108–12
  supersession, 108–12
dialogue with Trypho the Jew
  see Justin
dietary law
  Barnabas, 144
  Mark, 41–3
disciples
  Barnabas, 195
  challenging of, 196–7
  denigration of, 40–2
  Hebrews, 195
  John, 195
  Mark, 40–2
  Synoptics, 193–5

estrangement, 39–40, 75–9, 195–8,
  206, 219, 48, 65, 72, 84, 91,
  96, 99, 118, 132, 164,
  191, 208
  John, 71–74, 75–79
ethical monotheism, 108
  sin, 108
exclusivism, 213–15

first century, summary, 93–104
forfeiture of God's favor
  supersession, 105
founding fathers
  Revelation, 89–90
  see also Jewish followers of Jesus

Gentile sympathizers with Judaism,
  199–204, 88, 89, 148, 178,
  179, 188
  Qumran, 145–7
Gentile sympathizers with the Jewish
  followers of Jesus, xxiv, 160–1,
  202–4, 36–7, 69, 31, 40, 57,
  72, 79, 82, 88, 89, 94, 97, 119,
  132, 148, 168, 176,
  178, 188–90, 219
  Revelation, 89
Gnostic believers in Jesus, xxiv,
  159–60, 155, 158, 163, 212
Gnosticism
  see Gnostic believers in Jesus

God's retribution
  supersession, 107

Hebrews
  addressees, 117–20
  anti-Jewish bias, 9
  author's synopsis, 131–7
  background, 127–8
  context, 117–20
  covenant, 123–5
  disciples, 195
  introduction, 115–1117
  priesthood, 121–3
  Qumran, 127–8, 122, 125, 126
  sacrifices, 125–6
  scholarship, 129–30
  supersession, 128–9
  theology, 120–1

Ignatius
  adversaries, 168–9
  background, 167–8
  Magnesians, 170–1
  Philadelphians, 169–70
Ioudaioi, 68–70
  John, 68–70

Jesus's death, responsibility for,
  43–6, 19, 50, 58, 80,
  158, 183
Jewish followers of Jesus, xxiii,
  154–6, 79–80, 95–9, 63–5,
  39–46, 75–9, 195–8
  challenge to, 196–207
  John, 76
  Justin, 173–7
  Luke/Acts, 60–1
  Paul, 26–9
  Revelation, 90
  see also disciples
Jewish-Christian
  conflict, 199–202, 204–6, 99
  see also Jewish followers of Jesus
John
  anti-Jewish bias, 9
  appropriation, 83
  author's synopsis, 82–5

current dilemmas, 79–82
disciples, 195
estrangement, 75–9, 71–4
evolution of the text, 71–5
Ioudaioi, 68–70
scholarship, 80–82
supersession, 74
Judaism, 216–19, 199–202, 204–6,
    221–4, 51–3
Judaizing, 202–4
Judean self-criticism, 105–7, 2,
    13, 149, 189, 197, 220
Justin
    addresses, 173–5
    adversaries, 176–7
    appropriation, 175–6
    author's synopsis, 177–8
    Jewish followers of Jesus, 173–7
    protagonists, 173–5
    supersession, 175–6

law, the
    in Paul, 29–30
    see also Torah observance
legitimacy, 196–7
    Luke/Acts, 63–5
Luke/Acts
    anti-Jewish bias, 6
    author's synopsis, 64–6
    Jewish followers of Jesus, 60–1
    legitimacy, 63–5
    Marcion, 61–3

Magnesians
    Ignatius, 170–1
Marcion
    Luke-Acts, 61–3
    opposition to, 61–3
    see also Pauline-Marcionite
        believers in Jesus
Mark
    anti-Jewish bias, 4
    author's synopsis, 46–8
    disciples, 40–2
Matthew
    anti-Jewish bias, 5
    anti-Jewish rhetoric, 53–4

author's synopsis, 56–8
authorship and setting, 51–2
Judaism, 51–3
Melito
    the author, 183–4
    background, 179–80
    deicide, 180–2
    Peri Pascha, 180–2
    theology, 182–3
missionary and secessionist
    communities, 93–5
mysteries, 162–3

New Testament
    anti-Jewish strand, 1–11
    canonization, 216–17
    and Qumran, 13–18

Paul
    Acts, 33–4
    anti-Jewish bias, 9
    author's synopsis, 35–8
    controversial, 25
    Jewish followers of Jesus, 26–9
    Judaism, 21–3
    the Law, 29–30
    scholarship, 30, 225–31
    subservient to James, 26, 60–4
    theology, 24–25
Pauline
    see Pauline-Lukan believers
        in Jesus
Pauline-Lukan believers in Jesus, xxiv,
    156–7, 211–15
Pauline-Marcionite believers in Jesus,
    xxiii, 157–9, 211–13
Peri Pascha
    Melito, 180–2
Pesher, 15, 17, 126, 127, 146
Philadelphians
    Ignatius, 169–70
Pilate, 44, 80
postcanonical era, 197–9
pre-Synoptic era, 11–20
priesthood
    Hebrews, 121–3
projection onto Judaism, 199–202

Qumran
   Barnabas, 145–7
   Hebrews, 127–8, 122, 125, 126
   and the New Testament, 13–18

Revelation
   anti-Jewish bias, 10
   Gentile sympathizers with
      Judaism, 89
   Gentile sympathizers with the Jewish
      followers of Jesus, 89
   Judaism, 88
rhetoric
   anti-Jewish-establishment, 12–13
Roman persecution, 63–4

Sabbath, 40–2, 176
sacrifices
   Hebrews, 125–6
scholarship
   Hebrews, 129–30
   John, 80–82
   Paul, 30, 225–31
secessionist and missionary
      communities, 93–5
second century summary, 163–5
self-criticism, Judean, 105–7, 2, 13,
      149, 189, 197, 220
sermons
   Chrysostom, 185–8
sin, 108, 105–7, 149, 189, 197, 220
supersession
   destruction of the Temple, 108–12

forfeiture of God's favor, 105
God's retribution, 107
Hebrews, 128–9
introduction, 103–5
John, 74
Judean self-criticism, 105–7
Justin, 175–6
sin, 108
Synoptic
   disciples, 193–5
   pre-Synoptic era, 11–20

Temple, the
   Barnabas, 143–4
   destruction of, 108–12
   supersession, 108–12
theology
   Hebrews, 120–1
   Melito, 182–3
   Justin, 173–7
   Luke/Acts, 60–1
   Paul, 24–5
   see also supersession; Via Media
Torah observance, 42–3, 50–4,
      18–19, 14, 25, 28, 37, 38,
      45, 47, 83, 84, 90, 104, 132,
      144, 152, 153, 173, 177,
      178, 204, 212, 222
Trypho the Jew
   see Justin

Via Media, 161–2, 74, 133,
      152–4

Printed and bound in Great Britain by
CPI Antony Rowe, Chippenham and Eastbourne